WARRIORS IN FIRE BOOTS

A TRIBUTE TO THE VALOUR OF FIREFIGHTERS

ARTHUR LOCKYEAR

Published by Jeremy Mills Publishing Limited
www.jeremymillspublishing.co.uk

First published 2011

ISBN: 978-1-906600-54-9

Cover Image
Saved, Charles Vigor
Courtesy of the Fire Service College

ACKNOWLEDGEMENTS

This book is dedicated with great affection, respect and gratitude to my Dear Pat. She has supported and encouraged me throughout my career as a firefighter, and indeed during my work to organise and promote the Sunderland Remembrance Parade.

She is my dearest love, my rock, my wise counsel, and my best friend.

Without her, this book would not have been written.

The author wishes to acknowledge the following serving and retired firefighters who have encouraged and contributed to his development as a firefighter, or have supported his voluntary work to promote the City of Sunderland Remembrance Parade.

Eddy Fulton.	'Reg' Thompson.
'Dusty' Ashman.	'Jeff' Usher.
'Paddy' Moran.	'Kev' Hepple.
'Phil' Brookbanks.	Jim Bremner.
Iain Bathgate.	John Adamson.
John Cleary.	Jim Clark QFSM.
Paul Shrubb.	Pete O'Donnell.
Tye Robinson QFSM.	Brian Hesler QFSM.
'Fred' Elton, OBE, QFSM.	Charlie Collier.
Richard Bull CBE, QFSM.	
Sir Graham Meldrum CBE, OStJ, QFSM.	

I wish to thank the following people for their kind assistance in researching this tribute:

Michael Kernan QFSM, Honorary Historian, the Fire Service College

Mrs Linda Stratman, Mrs Denise Robertson MBE and General Sir Peter de la Billiere KCB, KBE, DSO, MC★, DL, for their good advice

Stewart Thain, Assistant Keeper (Research), Aberdeen City Council

Graeme Kirkwood Strathclyde Fire & Rescue for sharing his extensive research

Mark Frost, Assistant Curator, Dover Museum

Mike Harmer and John Abbot re: the fire on HMS Sandhurst

Ms Mary McGlynn and Ms Jo Sheringham, Clydebank Central Library

Mr Gary Haward

Mr Ron Henderson

Anthony Hindmarsh of Sunderland Library Service

Baroness Tessa Blackstone and Mr Tim Blackstone

Mrs Margaret Bancroft, daughter of DCFO William Tozer QFSM

Alan Forbes and Joe Tinney, Strathclyde Fire & Rescue

Mrs Evelyn Elmslie, widow of DCFO Bill Elmslie DSM

Fred Elton OBE, QFSM

Roy Bishop OBE, QFSM, formerly Deputy Commissioner of London Fire Brigade

Terry Jones of the London Fire Brigade photographic department

Mr James Dunlop, George Medal

Mrs Yvonne Nicholson, wife of Roderick McKenzie Nicolson, George Medal

Mr Mike George, Queen's Gallantry Medal

Former Chief Fire Offficer Neil Wallington, Queen's Commendation

Mr Brian McBride

The Public Records Office Northern Ireland

Mr Ron Simpson of the Coroners' Service for Northern Ireland

Chief Fire Officer Brian Hesler QFSM, Northumberland Fire and Rescue Service

The Liverpool Records Office

Deputy Chief Fire Officer Alan House QFSM, Hampshire Fire and Rescue Service

Mrs Stephanie Maltman of Firemen Remembered: World War II London Firemen and Firewomen's Remembrance Group

Jane Rugg of the London Fire Brigade Museum

John Agar, formerly of West Midlands Fire Service, for sharing his information on the Netchells incident

Maurice Johnson, formerly Chief Fire Officer of Oxfordshire

Ian McMurtrie MBE, Honorary Curator, Lothian & Borders Museum of Fire

Mike Pinchen, formerly of LFB, for sharing his information on Edward Morgan GM

Mr Dennis Young, son of Lawrence Barclay Young GM

Mr Roger Lombard, father of Fleur Lombard QGM

Mr Bob Bonner of Manchester Fire Service Museum

My much-valued Aikido students Kevin Creaghan and Richard Thompson, for their IT skills

Mr John Chipperfield, Archivist of the *Oxford Times*

The *Lennox Herald*

The *Scottish Daily Express*

The Newcastle *Journal*

Fire Magazine

The *Sunderland Echo*

The *Manchester Evening News*

Durham County Council Archive

The Chief Constable of Durham Constabulary

The Media Resources Unit of Tyne & Wear Fire & Rescue Service

Chief Fire Officer Iain Bathgate of Tyne and Wear Fire and Rescue Service

Commissioner Ron Dobson of London Fire Brigade

Chief Fire Officer Vij Randeniya of West Midlands Fire Service

Jo Jones, Photographic Assistant, West Midlands Fire Service

Mr Reg' Haley QFSM for his research on the Llanreath Oil fires

William Broadhurst and Henry Welsh for their kind assistance with incidents in Northern Ireland

CONTENTS

Having known Arthur Lockyear for more than thirty years, I can say with some degree of certainty that this book reflects not only his highly developed sense of tradition, and his unquestionable pride in having served as a firefighter, but his long and respected experience as an operational Officer, his indefatigable commitment to the ethos of Remembrance, and his penchant for putting pen to paper.

The majority of people must at some time have been fascinated by tales of heroism, and I have most certainly experienced such emotions when reading Arthur's manuscript. Although most of my professional life has been spent in the fire service, the narrative which unfolds on these pages graphically illustrates the tenacity and sacrifice of so many firefighters whose stories were, hitherto, unknown to me. It is to the author's credit, and to the best advantage of all who profess an interest in the history of firefighting, or the anatomy of courage, that he has written this book.

Although it would seem that courage, commitment and selflessness in adversity are axiomatic of the firefighter's calling, I personally have never been able to comprehend what it is that impels a person to commit to risking one's own life, with all the odds stacked against survival. Perhaps the reader will be equally perplexed by this concept! However, the broad vista of gallantry so lucidly presented in this book will, I feel sure, help the reader gain a deeper appreciation of that most esteemed of human virtues, and perhaps even engage with the heroes therein.

Much of this book refers to the role of firefighters during the Blitz. Arthur has most certainly presented a fresh and inspirational perspective on this aspect of the World War II.

Here described in vivid prose is a very readable, not to say spellbinding, account of the actions of individuals who are marked ineradicably as heroes and consequently are assured of their place in the pantheon of great firefighters. I hope the reader will enjoy this thought provoking, and stimulating tribute to valour, and that today's 'Warriors in Fire Boots' will take motivation from its pages.

T. F. Elton OBE, QFSM
Formerly Chief Fire Officer of Durham County Fire Brigade,
and latterly of Tyne & Wear Metropolitan Fire Brigade.

The inspiration for this book is owed not to one person, nor one experience, but to many influences, involving some-extraordinarily courageous people whom I have had the great fortune to have met in the course of organising the Sunderland Remembrance Parade. Those gallant luminaries include Dick Annand VC, John Bridge GC, GM & Bar, and former Auxiliary Fireman Harry Errington GC. This book is a sincere tribute to the latter of those heroes; and indeed to all firefighters who have given of their best in exacting and dangerous circumstances.

The history of firefighting in the UK can be traced from the 'Vigiles' of the Roman occupation, through the great fire of 1666, to the loss of Chief Officer James Braidwood in Tooley Street, South London in 1861; from the Blitz of the great cities and industrial areas of this country, to the disastrous loss of nineteen men at Cheapside Street, Glasgow in 1960, to more recent and no less tragic fatalities. In this book I seek to honour firefighters from the time of Queen Victoria to this twenty-first century, by outlining their stories of loss and courage, as a sincere mark of homage to colleagues who have served their country and their communities with great distinction as firefighters. This of course is without detriment to the courage displayed by members of the public, or of the other emergency services who have saved life from fire, and it is my honour to outline the gallant stories of Robert Little and Leonard Ford in this introduction.

On 26th February 1960 Leonard Ford was working in the premises of his employer, Associated British Window Cleaning Co, at Fulham Road/Radcliffe Gardens, Fulham, when he was told that people were trapped on the upper floors of a building which was on fire. He hurried to the building, where his work mates had brought a three section extension ladder to rescue a woman who was trapped on the top floor. Ford extended this ladder manually to its full extent by climbing up it, bouncing it against the face of the building and pushing up the extensions as he climbed. When he reached the head of the ladder, which was resting between two ornate cornices fronting the left hand windows on the third floor, he realised that he could not carry the woman down because the ladder was not long enough, despite the fact that it was in a nearly vertical position. The woman was in extreme difficulty, enveloped in smoke from the waist up and was on the point of collapse. With his right foot on the second rung of the ladder from the top, Ford placed his left foot on the cornice and held the woman against the face of the building. At this stage she partially collapsed on to him, causing him to lose his balance. With his free hand he grabbed at the top rung of the ladder, and regained his balance, at the same time supporting the dead weight of the woman across his shoulders. By this time the Fire Service arrived and a wheeled-escape ladder was pitched and extended to where Mr Ford was. With very great difficulty and danger to himself, Mr Ford managed to transfer the inert body of the woman to the firefighters who had reached the head of the escape. The unfortunate woman was then carried safely to the ground. For his great courage in executing this daring rescue Leonard Ford was awarded the George Medal.

Robert Little became a constable with Durham County Constabulary in May 1907, and having served nineteen years at locations such as West Hartlepool and Consett, he was posted in the rank of Sergeant to the coal-mining township of Seaham Harbour.

In the early hours of 14th December 1930, a fire broke out in a house in Vane Terrace, Seaham Harbour, occupied by eighty-three year-old Miss Mary Watson and her two nieces. Little was having his meal at the sub-divisional office in Tempest Road when the alarm was raised by Miss Dinah Watson, who ran to the police station; and a call was immediately put through to the fire brigade. Without pausing even to grab his helmet, Little ran the hundred or so yards to the scene of the fire, and entering the building went upstairs through the billowing clouds of choking smoke. He was followed by Miss Mary Watson, who had to retreat because of the heat and the irrespirable atmosphere created by the products of combustion. Little entered the lady's room, and nothing more was seen of the gallant officer, which caused great concern. Consequently a local miner, believed to be the next door neighbour, entered the house and tried to open the bedroom door, but was unable to gain access; he was after a few minutes forced to withdraw because of being almost overcome by the heat and smoke. As he reached the foot of the stairs he heard a resounding crash and saw an explosion of rubble, dust and flame as a bedroom floor collapsed into the kitchen. By this time the ceiling of the entrance was well alight, which would have rendered his route of egress impassable within seconds.

On the arrival of the fire brigade the door was broken down, and Sergeant Little was found with the elderly woman lying across his legs, and it was evident that he had made a brave attempt to drag her out of the inner-room, and as he collapsed due to the effects of smoke inhalation he had, most unfortunately, wedged a chair against the handle of the door, preventing any assistance reaching him. Both Sergeant Little and Miss Watson were suffocated by the smoke.

Chief Officer Arthur Proud of Seaham Urban District Council Fire Brigade commented to the Sunderland Echo after the incident:

> 'We received the call from the police station …(and) we got the engine out and arrived at the scene seven minutes later, and by three o'clock we had water playing on the flames. The back of the house was blazing furiously, and flames were shooting out of the top windows. As soon as I heard there were two people in the house I rushed up the stairs but was almost blinded by the smoke and flames. I was unable to burst the door of Miss Watson's room open, and called for one of the firemen, and with the aid of his axe knocked out a panel in the door. When I put my head through the hole I found that a chair was wedged against the door thus preventing it from opening. I pushed it away and succeeded in getting the door open. We found Sergeant Little with his head towards the door.'

Robert Little was accorded the honours of a full police service funeral, and his coffin was borne on the local fire engine to St. John's Church, Seaham Harbour, escorted through streets thronged with the people of Seaham, by an Honour Guard of firefighters of Seaham Urban District Council Fire Brigade and of his fellow Sergeants bearing wreathes.

The portrait of Robert Little, who was awarded the King's Police Medal for his gallantry, hung for many years in entrance of the old Seaham Harbour police station, and whenever the author visited that establishment as a boy, he was always awed by this gallant police officer's portrait.

Within a long and proud lineage of firefighting in the UK, stands one episode above all others: the Blitz, the firefighters' Golgotha. In 2001, Mayor Rudolf Giuliani of New York likened the horror of the Twin Towers attack to that maelstrom of choking, eye-gouging smoke; lacerating heat; shrapnel-showered streets, exploding bombs and collapsing buildings, which in the autumn of 1940 and throughout 1941 left UK firefighters dead, dying and maimed, and Fire Service widows and orphans by the hundred. I would respectfully submit that many of the men and women of Britain's wartime fire service were, during this period, as much in mortal combat, saving lives and extinguishing fires, as were our much respected veterans of Normandy, Monte Cassino, or Kohima. It is my honour to pay tribute to them.

In the course of relating these stories of gallantry I have taken the opportunity to mention the courage of men and women who served as fire watchers, fire guards and members of fire teams, and those of other services who proved their valour in the most trying of circumstances whilst working alongside the Fire Service. It is my intention to pen a more comprehensive tribute to the wartime service of members of those other services.

This book is, most obviously, not an exhaustive list of gallantry medallists or of deaths in service, but a broad and sincere mark of respect to fallen comrades. Some firefighter fatalities have been omitted because of a lack of information, and others for good reasons of sensitivity. However, their loss is not forgotten, and I salute their courage and service. The mention of some audacious stories are very brief indeed, as I have been unable to obtain detailed information on the firefighter in question or the circumstances of the award. Also some of the wartime British Empire Medal awards may well be incorrect in chronological terms, although I apologise on both counts, I do not feel that either caveat should preclude their inclusion.

This is an account of firefighters at the testing point, and my personal tribute to those Warriors in Fire Boots.

Arthur C. Lockyear MBE
Formerly Sub-Officer 1317 of Tyne & Wear Fire & Rescue Service.
Durham City, 21st May 2010.

'Courage is not simply *one* of the virtues, but the
form of every virtue at the testing point.'

C. S. Lewis

'A Fireman to be successful, must enter buildings;
He must get in below, above, on every side, from opposite houses,
over brick walls, over side walls, through panels of doors, through windows,
through loopholes cut by himself in the gates, the walls, the roof; he must
know how to reach the attic from the basement by ladders placed on
half burned stairs, and the basement from the attic by rope made fast
on a chimney; His whole success depends on his getting in and remaining
there, and he must always carry his appliances with him, as without
them he is of no use.'

Sir Eyre Massey Shaw
Second Chief Fire Officer of London

'Perfect courage consists in doing unobserved what
we could do in the eyes of the world.'

Le Duc De La Rochefoucauld
Maxims

THE LIFE AND DEATH OF
JAMES BRAIDWOOD

James Braidwood, the first Chief Fire Officer of London, was born on 3rd September 1800 in Edinburgh and received his education at the city's highly respected Royal High School until he reached the age of thirteen years, when he commenced training as a surveyor, later working in his father's building business.

On 28th April 1824, Edinburgh suffered a disastrous fire, which was followed by a second such event on the 24th June. In considering the scale of the loss suffered, some fifty houses having been destroyed and a number of lives lost, the City Fathers decided that the fragmented fire cover provided by various insurance companies, and the lack of a single person being in command, had contributed to the awful level of destruction caused by these fires. Consequently in 1823, Braidwood, with no training in firefighting whatsoever, was appointed to the position of Master of Engines for the Burgh of Edinburgh, the first Municipal Fire Brigade in the UK, and probably anywhere in the world. One of his first acts as Chief was to purchase three new large fire engines from London at a cost of £530 each. He formed his small corps of firefighters from carpenters, plumbers, smiths, masons, and tilers – the latter having the obvious and very appropriate advantage of being used to working at height – and formed them into a coherent and structured unit. His rationale in employing tradesmen was explained thus: 'They are more robust in body, and better able to endure the extremes of heat, cold, wet and fatigue, to which firemen are so frequently exposed.'

Braidwood's firefighters were permitted to continue in their trade, but were drilled on a regular basis, which provided a sense of method and proficiency in their firefighting skills. They were, the reader may be interested to note, drilled at four o'clock in the morning by Braidwood, as this would neither interfere with their normal work as tradesmen, nor attract unwanted crowds of spectators, and because 'Exercising in the dark has obvious advantages.' One of his favourite venues was the North Bridge, where he trained his men in the use of chains to descend the seventy-five feet to the street below. They also practised putting one another into a canvas bag and lowering it to the street below, on which manoeuvre Braidwood wrote: 'The men are very fond of this exercise, the bagging of each other seems to amuse them exceedingly.'

Braidwood personally took charge of these training exercises, and given that his force was divided into groups by colour of helmets, red, blue, grey and yellow, and that they trained separately at this unearthly hour, his sense of dedication went far beyond the normal call of duty. During his tenure he personally attended almost every fire to which the Brigade responded, carefully listing meticulous details of each fire in logbooks, and following each incident, whatever the time, day or night, he would conduct a debriefing with the men who had attended, to identify any useful lessons learned, and any techniques that could have been better applied. Under his direction their firefighting tactics developed from merely applying water in a reckless and unproductive manner, to one of searching for the seat of fire, and applying the extinguishing medium at close quarters.

Braidwood developed into a chief officer of flair and conscientious application, as is evidenced by his adroit structuring of the brigade, and the award of the silver medal of the London Society of the Arts in recognition of his invention of a fire-escape. This same august body invited him to author a guidance on the construction and use of fire appliances, the training of firefighters, provision of water supplies, the design of hydrants, and methods of firefighting; this was probably the first standard operating procedure ever penned. Even as late as the close of the nineteenth century, his book was widely considered an authoritative work, which speaks well for Braidwood's understanding of the science of firefighting, and the soundness of his ground-breaking views. This publication must surely have established him as a leading authority on firefighting, and given strong support to his application to head the newly formed London Fire-Engine Establishment.

He was a man ever mindful of the needs of his men and their safety, and would not allow any man to risk danger or death without good cause, even issuing each firefighter with an eighty foot length of rope to use as an emergency means of escape should his egress be cut-off whilst firefighting. He was himself a man of remarkable fortitude, and level head leadership in the face with danger. On one occasion when a fire was reported in a gunpowder store, he entered the building despite the likelihood of an explosion, and at great risk to his life carried a cask from the cellar, and then, re-entering, brought out another, thus preventing a calamitous explosion. At another incident on 12th August 1827, it is recorded that Braidwood virtually single-handed carried and dragged nine persons out of a burning building, undoubtedly saving their lives at no small risk to his own. The renown in which Braidwood was held is evidenced by the following extract from the report of the Edinburgh Fire-engine committee for 1826 which stated: 'Mr

Braidwood, the Master of engines ... upon all occasions of fire his steady coolness, self-possession, good judgement and intrepidity have been most marked, and deserving of approbation.'

By 1832 a number of London-based insurance companies, who each ran a private fire brigade, agreed to cooperate in forming a Fire Engine establishment, and Braidwood was appointed superintendent in overall command of the new joint force of some fourteen engine stations. Soon after his arrival in London, Braidwood became aware of the enormous potential for serious outbreaks of fire in the great warehouses on both banks of the Thames. Consequently he acquired a number of boats with pumps to be used as fire floats and introduced a uniform size of hose coupling. Showing a grasp of structural fire protection far in advance of his peers, Braidwood advocated the partitioning of warehouses from basement level to roof void, and the fitting of iron doors to prevent fire spread.

Braidwood was to command the London Fire Engine Establishment for some twenty-eight years, during which time a number of innovations in the art and science of firefighting were developed. However, his tenure was, regrettably, to end in tragedy.

At approximately half-past four in the afternoon of Saturday 22nd June 1861, parties of men were at work at Scovells' warehouse in Cotton's Wharf on the south bank of the Thames near to London Bridge. Foreman James England was on the second floor of the building when he saw smoke coming from below. Running down to the next level, he heard a cracking noise and discovered a quantity of jute (probably containing oil) smouldering, and giving the alarm, ran to obtain a bucket of water to deal with the outbreak. After discharging the contents of the bucket onto the blaze he consulted with Mr Doyle, the Wharf Superintendent, and a runner was sent to Tooley Street fire station to raise the alarm. Further attempts were made by England to subdue the flames with buckets of water; but the smoke became so thick that it overwhelmed them, and he and his men were compelled to retreat as the fire began to spread with alarming speed. Warehouse workers tried to attack the fire, using hose lines taken aloft via ladders pitched to the outside of the building, but again these measures proved futile.

The first engine from Tooley Street fire station arrived at 4.45 pm, led by Alfred Tozer, and news of the rapidly deteriorating incident reached Braidwood at Watling Street station. He and his crews, nicknamed 'Jimmy Braiders', responded with alacrity, Braidwood knowing from experience that given the time of day, the internal metal fire-doors were likely to be open, thus providing the fire with all the oxygen it might require to develop freely. The fact that the huge warehouses crowded together in the narrow streets were filled to overflowing with oil, tallow, tar, cotton, saltpetre, bales of silk and chests of tea, much of it stored in a dangerous fashion, gave Braidwood and his men serious concerns that a blaze of major proportions would very quickly develop. Despite their apprehension, the firefighters would little have thought that this fire would burn for a whole month, and cost their much respected chief his life.

Braidwood arrived with a number of hand-operated pumps capable of supplying ninety gallons of water per minute, which required two horses to draw them, and twenty-plus men to operate them. These pump crews were recruited from bystanders who were usually only too happy to assist, as not only did they receive a shilling for the first hour of labour, and sixpence for each subsequent hour, they were also supplied with copious quantities of ale. This first attendance also included two large floating-engines (early fire boats), and Braidwood's crews were soon attacking the fire with a number of water jets. Assessing this critical situation Braidwood saw that the first floor of the warehouse was well alight, with a dense body of smoke issuing from all windows and loop-hole doors, and that the fire was already spreading to adjacent buildings. It must have been obvious to him that the incident would soon be beyond his control. This overwhelming and life-threatening situation was further exacerbated by the receding tide and the general lack of effective water supplies. Braidwood therefore took the decision to order on almost all of the resources of the London Fire Engine Establishment to this incident. Soon crowds of excited people were crowded onto London Bridge to watch the firefighters at work, whilst others thronged the streets on both sides of the Thames, to get a view of the biggest fire London had witnessed since 1666. The public houses stayed open throughout the night, and the pickpockets had a most productive and enjoyable time; which is rather more than can be said of Braidwood's brave firefighters.

Meanwhile Braidwood ordered his two fire-floats which were lying off the wharf, to get two lines of hose ashore, and this proved to be a great asset to the firefighting operations. He then instructed Engineer Tozer to take a line of hose up to the roof of one of the warehouses. Shortly after having carried out this order Tozer heard and felt the reverberations of a loud explosion coming from the cellar of that building, and observed a great belch of white smoke, following by an intense tongue of flame which shot upward through the smoke to engulf the whole building in fire. Realising that his means of escape had been seriously compromised, possibly fatally so, Tozer reacted quickly and secured the branch of his hose with a length of rope, and was able to slide down the charged length of hose, which had by good fortune been hauled up the outside of the warehouse.

Interestingly, Alfred Tozer was the officer-in-charge of the fire engine sent to Scutari during the Crimean War to protect the hospitals and other base establishments, and became a friend of both Florence Nightingale and Major-General Charles Gordon, later known as Gordon of Khartoum. Tozer was also the first London fire officer to be awarded the Silver Medal of the Royal Society for the Protection of Life from Fire. He was appointed Superintendent of Manchester Fire Brigade in 1862, where he transformed the organisation into a full-time professional body, and most commendably cut fire losses in that city by some seventy-five percent. He later founded the National

Alfred Tozer, hero of Tooley Street

Fire Brigade Widows and Orphans Fund, and became a highly respected national authority on firefighting, as indeed his mentor Braidwood had been in his day.

By now the warehouses were burning furiously, and the intensity of the heat had become crushing; this, combined with the extreme physical exertion of the operations, brought the firefighters almost to their knees with exhaustion. At seven o'clock Braidwood received word that his fire floats had moved so close to the fire to obtain a better effect with their jets, that their woodwork was scorched, and the crews themselves were suffering greatly from heat. Clouds of choking smoke, made all the more irrespirable by the various merchandise involved, spread overhead, and despite the best efforts of Braidwood's men the ferocious conflagration continued to spread, jumping between buildings. Moored to the wharf were several schooners carrying barrels of oil, tallow and tar, and attempts were made to float them into the middle of the Thames with tugs, but these efforts were unfortunately in vain, as the tide was still very low. These schooners in their turn caught fire, and in a short space of time were lying burnt out at the water's edge; their blazing cargoes floating in a line along the banks of the river 100 yards deep and a quarter of mile long.

Several further explosions took place as Braidwood toured the fire-ground, encouraging his crews and bringing refreshments to them when he could. About half past seven he made his way through a passageway from Tooley Street towards an enclosed space near to the river bank where four of his men were working two jets of water. Having spoken with the men to encourage them in their endeavours, he paused to speak with fire brigade foreman Richard Henderson, who had been overcome with smoke inhalation, the intense heat and the extreme exertion of firefighting. The caring and compassionate Braidwood administered a drop of brandy to Henderson and ordered his removal to fresh air. As he moved on to visit other crews, a loud and menacing crack was heard above the cacophony of the fire, and it could be seen that a large section of wall was bulging alarmingly. Immediately all hands ran for their lives, but tragically their exit was not swift enough, and with a resounding crash, tons of masonry fell upon them.

At first it was believed that an explosion of saltpetre had brought the wall down. At the inquest held at St. Thomas' Hospital on Tuesday 25th June, evidence was given that no explosion had been heard, and that no saltpetre was stored in that area. It is likely that the structural collapse was as a result of the water used for firefighting swelling the compressed bales of cotton on the top floor of this building, forcing out the walls. This, coupled with the intense heat which caused the expansion and distortion of the cast-iron structural elements, brought the whole edifice crashing onto the unfortunate and gallant Braidwood.

Immediately firefighters working nearby ran to assist in the extrication of their Chief, as a second explosion rained a mass of burning material onto the remains of the wall; at this point further rescue attempts were seen as hopeless. The fire continued unabated, with flames sweeping through wharf after wharf, engulfing warehouses and ships; sending rivers of burning liquids discharging into the Thames, forming an enormous lake of fire. A growing multitude crowded the vicinity, thronging roof-tops and church steeples, whilst opportunistic boatmen risked all to salvage such goods as they might be able to find. At one stage the fire, in a prophetic vision of the first night of the Blitz, blazed for almost a quarter of a mile along the riverbank, turning the sky bright red, and bringing great warehouse walls crashing into the Thames, revealing an inferno raging where, but a few hours previously, goods had been stored.

In the path of the fire lay a quay in which two ships were stranded, the tide having been too low to permit of their evacuation. Fire crews were put to work in a crucial attempt to prevent the vessels becoming involved before the tide flowed high enough to permit their removal. At the first opportunity two tugs entered the dock, and once towing-ropes had been thrown aboard and secured, the vessels were brought out through the encroaching flames, setting fire to the rigging of one of the ships. Immediately the firefighters discharged a jet of water onto the burning ship, and promptly extinguished the flames, to the great acclaim of the huge crowds on both sides of the river.

By ten o'clock the fire seemed to be at its worst, as it was not until night fell that the tremendous spectacle could be fully seen in all its awesome and terrifying grandeur. The whole south bank of the Thames from London Bridge to below the Custom House appeared as one breathtaking, gushing torrent of flame, glowing with an intensity that made it painful to view, and which cast a minatory and ruddy glare on everything near and far. There was hardly a breath of wind, but what little there was came from the river, gently turning the blinding mass of smoke and flame across Tooley Street to the London Bridge railway station, lifting thousands of burning flakes and embers into the air. As the great flames leapt high over gaunt ruins, the roar of flames, and shouts of the excited thousands drowned even the incessant dull thumping of the fire engines as they pumped water. It really must have seemed that the inferno would eventually engulf the whole of the metropolis.

Half an hour later 600 bags of saltpetre, or potassium nitrate, exploded in a storehouse near to where Braidwood had met his death. From out of the waterside warehouses, tons of molten tallow were pouring into the river, which was by now crowded with boats; some which had been hired by sightseers. These rivers of burning tallow, and the intense radiated and convective heat did, however, keep these vessels on the north shore of the Thames. When the tide turned, enormous amounts of tallow were carried downstream, and as far away as Millwall watermen were collecting it by the boatload, and in many cases selling it for considerable sums. It is believed that a number of lives were lost that night by those attempting to salvage solidified mounds of this animal fat. In one instance, four young men were seen in a boat in front of the eastern part of Hay's Wharf, with enough tallow on board to fill the craft, when suddenly a great flood of boiling oil gushed out of one the burning buildings, and surrounded the boat, igniting its highly flammable contents. The men were seen to plunge into the water, but were never seen alive again. Tallow filled the streets and wharfs around the blaze, making life even more difficult for the firefighters, and one fire appliance, whist being repositioned, was lost into the dock due to the oleaginous surface underfoot.

Among the spectators was Queen Victoria, who watched the tragedy play-out from the roof of Buckingham Palace until nearly midnight. She later wrote: 'The whole scene was startling. Westminster's white towers were rising to the right of the conflagration, the moon shining beautifully. Sitting, watching and looking down upon the great town with the raging of this fearful fire was a very impressive, though sad sight. The messenger and police Inspector whom we had sent to enquire returned saying that the loss of property was fearful. A good deal of shipping had been destroyed, and that poor Mr Braidwood had been killed. It made me very sad.'

Soon after midnight the shell of the warehouse in which the fire began fell outwards with a horrendous crash. On the following day attempts were made to recover Braidwood's body, but a large cellar storing oil, adjacent to the mountain of masonry that had become the Chief's temporary headstone was well alight, and so precluded any recovery attempts. Also on that day the Prince of Wales (later His Majesty King Edward VII) visited the scene of ongoing devastation, and a message was carried by the Earl of Stamford from Queen Victoria to enquire as to whether Chief Officer Braidwood's body had been recovered.

Braidwood's charred and barely recognisable body was found on 24th June by Alfred Tozer, who cut the buttons and epaulettes from Braidwood's fire tunic which, with great solemnity, he distributed to each of the Establishment's foremen, so that each might retain a *memento mori* as a mark of respect for the departed merit and great valour of their now lifeless Chief.

James Braidwood was accorded the honour of a great public funeral, which was so very well attended by the people of London, that it was compared to that of the Duke of Wellington some nine years earlier. This imposing parade held on Saturday 29th June, stretched for a mile and a half, and was led by the Band, and a 700-strong detachment of the London Rifle Brigade (a volunteer unit and forebear of the Royal Green Jackets, now the Rifles) and included representatives of the London Fire Engine Establishment, other London based Fire Brigades, and detachments from the Lancashire and Yorkshire Fire Brigades, waterworks companies and the Metropolitan and City Police Forces.

James Braidwood was laid to rest in the grave of his son-in-law, who had been killed in similar circumstances at a fire in 1855. Throughout the day the bells of every city church, with the exception of the great bell of St. Paul's – which only tolls on the death of the Sovereign or the Lord Mayor of London – boomed out their unhurried tribute to a great 'warrior in fireboots' who had served the people of London with great commitment, and in doing so had forfeited his life.

James Braidwood, the Father of firefighting, has now been commemorated in the city of his birth with a seven-foot bronze statue crafted by Kenny Mackay, and unveiled by Professor Sir Timothy O'Shea the Principal of the University of Edinburgh. The campaign to erect this memorial was led by former Firemaster Frank Rushbrook CBE, and supported by Lothian and Borders Fire and Rescue Service, the City of Edinburgh Council, and the Surplus Fire Fund (set up from charitable donations after the Great Fire of Edinburgh in 1824).

FIREFIGHTERS IN NINETEENTH-CENTURY GLASGOW, LIVERPOOL & MANCHESTER

THE DEATH OF FIREMAN JOHN HARRISON

Between two and three o'clock on the morning of Friday 5th December 1856, a serious fire broke out in an extensive block of buildings situated between Queen Street and Buchanan Street in Glasgow, which was occupied by a number of firms involved in the manufacture and use of various fabrics. By the time the first fire engine arrived at the scene, the building was well alight, with flames issuing furiously from the windows at the west side. A messenger was immediately dispatched to the Central fire station, and they responding with all possible speed, were very soon on the spot with three engines, and the firefighters hard at work in an attempt to extinguish the flames.

Within a short period of time it was apparent that their efforts were proving unsuccessful, and as the roof fell in, there was an imminent danger of the fire spreading to the adjoining tenements. Consequently messengers were sent to the Southern, Western and Northern engines to request assistance. As they arrived some time after three o'clock the burning building was truly a spectacular sight, with flames reaching high into the night sky, illuminating the city for miles around, and throwing showers of sparks into the air. So serious was the situation, and so overstretched were the firefighters that a number of Army officers who had been enjoying themselves at a formal ball in the nearby Corporation halls arrived on the scene, still clad in their full dress uniforms, and worked with great diligence at the engines for over an hour.

About a quarter past three, firefighters Thomas Main, Allan Todd and John Harrison of the Central Brigade forced open a door on the first floor, leading to Messrs Black & Co.'s packing room, and were in the act of breaking open an inner door, when the floor suddenly gave way, throwing the men onto their backs. Before they could recover themselves, the flooring of the level above came down upon them with a tremendous crash. Despite the disastrous and extremely hazardous situation which faced the remaining firefighters, with debris covering the area, the irrespirable atmosphere caused by dust rising from the structural collapse mixing with the smoke from the fires, the instability of the building, and the distinct possibility of the flames reaching them, Main and Todd were almost immediately extricated by their comrades; but Harrison, having been first into the room, could not be reached, despite all efforts by the firefighters on the scene. His body was eventually recovered about eight o'clock the following morning, and it was deduced that he must have met with a quick death; his back having been fractured by a joist which had fallen from the upper floor. The deceased man, who was of excellent character, was regarded as one of the most capable and courageous firefighters in the brigade. Indeed, at a fire in Roslin Terrace, shortly before the incident which so cruelly ended his life, he had sustained burns to his foot, but continued with his duties and later had to have his boot cut off. When asked by his Superintendent why he did not go home at once after being injured, he replied, 'You would have thought me too thin skinned.' He was twenty-seven years of age and left a widow and two children. The other two men were taken to the Infirmary.

The fire during this period was raging in every corner of the building, and at four o'clock the east wall gave way, throwing a portion of the south gable through the roof, and into the showroom of adjacent premises. Five firefighters who were working on a wall opposite the east gable, narrowly escaped death or serious injury, as they had, fortunately, been withdrawn to a safe distance just minutes before the collapse, which brought down a portion of the wall on which they had been standing.

At the same time the internal partitions gave way, and forced open the iron doors in the adjacent premises of Messrs Stevenson's, which being filled with cotton copes, quickly took fire. However, the strenuous and committed exertions of the firefighters succeeded in keeping the flames under control, and prevented the loss of this tenement. By half past five the flames were dying down, leaving the building a complete ruin, with nothing left standing but the front wall, and various portions of the internal fittings, which continued to smoulder.

Shortly before seven o'clock in the evening of Tuesday 21st October, 1873 flames were seen issuing from the second floor of a large block of warehouses belonging to Messrs. D. & L. Hughes, in Forster Street, Liverpool, near to the Sandhills railway station. These extensive premises were of multi-occupation, and consequently used for the storage of various materials, including bales of cotton (on the floor involved in the fire) and grain on the two floors above the blaze. The fire was discovered in its early stages by warehousemen returning from their tea-break, and the alarm was raised. A patrolling police constable conveyed the relevant information available to Derby road fire station, and thanks to the 'state of the art' telegraphic communications system connecting the

Liverpool fire stations, the steam fire engine Livingstone and other appliances were soon mobile to the incident.

The first fire crew in attendance was from Derby Road, and they were joined very quickly by Superintendent Hancox who arrived with the Livingstone; however, by this juncture the fire had spread dramatically, and a serious fire situation now faced the firefighters. Because of the excellent water supplies available to the fire crews, no less than eleven jets of water were brought into use, which despite the problems brought by unwelcome high winds, the intensity of flames was eventually reduced by the great volume of water that was directed into the blazing structure. The fire crews eventually succeeded in reaching the uppermost storey of the building, despite the overwhelming volume of smoke, and the distinct possibility of the edifice becoming dangerously unstable; indeed, during this part of the operations the roof failed. By ten o'clock that evening the crews had surrounded and controlled the inferno to such a degree that the likelihood of spread to adjoining premises was greatly reduced.

It was in the latter stages of this occurrence that the body of twenty-five year-old police-fireman Henry Counce (named as Croume in the Daily Courier of 22nd October 1873) was discovered. He had apparently been overcome by the heat and smoke, and had suffocated; his body was severely burnt when found. A second firefighter was seriously injured when a falling bale of cotton, or perhaps part of the structure, fell on him, rendering him unconscious. His condition was exacerbated by the amount of smoke he had inhaled prior to being discovered by his colleagues. No cause of ignition was established.

On the early morning of 26th May 1874 a serious fire occurred in a four-storey building in Cherry Lane, Marybone, Liverpool, which had formerly been used as a flour and rice mill, and was now used as an oil cake and cotton store. It was reported that police Inspector Kerrin had passed the premises at approximately half-past one that morning, and there was no indication of fire. Ten minutes later a constable discovered flames issuing from the ground floor, and the alarm was raised. Fire engines from Hatton Gardens, and hose-reel appliances from Rose-Hill and Chisenhale Street were dispatched. They were soon in attendance, and swiftly to work with several hose-lines from the steam fire engines fed by plentiful water supplies. By two o'clock most of the interior of the building was well alight, and fifteen minutes later part of the roof fell in with a loud crash. At intervals other parts of the structure failed, creating a dangerous and very unstable environment for the firefighters. Around three o'clock that morning, at the height of the firefighting operations, police-fireman Thomas Boyd ascended a ladder pitched to a wall opposite the burning building to obtain a better position from which work his branch onto the fire through an open door. The jet-reaction caused by the force of the jet of water leaving the branch, and his precarious position on the ladder caused Boyd to fall backwards. The unfortunate firefighter landed on his head, inflicting a deep wound from which blood flowed across the road. He was at once conveyed to the Northern Hospital.

The fire was brought under control by four o'clock that morning, and operations continued for another two hours, when control of the incident was handed over to the Salvage Brigade. Boyd was reported later that day as having lost a great deal of blood, both from his head wound and his ears, was still unconscious, but showing signs of recovery. This was, regrettably, an over-optimistic prognosis and the unfortunate firefighter Boyd died on 8th June. This tragic loss occurred only three months after the death in similar circumstances of police-fireman Alexander Burgess at the sugar refining premises of Messrs H. Tate and Sons in Manesty Lane, Liverpool. During firefighting operations Burgess was working a branch from a ladder and was some thirty feet above the ground when the Chief Constable Major J. J. Greig, who was standing at the foot of the ladder saw one of the coping stones of the building fall and shouted a warning. The firefighters supporting the ladder were fortunately able to avoid the falling masonry, but the stone struck Burgess on the head and shoulders, he fell to the ground doubled–up, and the ladder fractured in two. On arrival at hospital of Burgess, who was a single man and had served as a constable for four years and specialised as a fireman only months previously, life was pronounced as being extinct.

In November 1885 a fire broke out in a large six-storey warehouse in Portland Street, Manchester. When the fire brigade arrived, the greater part of the three upper floors was well alight, and at one of the windows on the top storey a man could be seen through the miasma of smoke to be greatly distressed, and heard to be shouting for help, as his retreat down the staircase had been cut off by the spread of fire. The wheeled escape was immediately brought into use, and once in position firefighter George Wright quickly ascended the ladder, but on reaching its head found that it was several feet short of the window. By this time the flames were spreading to where the man was located, and a jet of water was directed at him to afford him protection from the heat. Meanwhile fire brigade Engineer John Hunt climbed the staircase of a neighbouring building and gained access to the roof of the burning warehouse, where he lowered his life line down to the unfortunate man, who, taking hold, was lowered to firefighter Wright who was on the escape ladder.

Unfortunately the stress of the situation proved too much for the casualty, and he fainted as he came within Wright's reach. Wright, not having time to secure him on to his shoulders in the manner of a fireman's lift, managed with great difficulty to hold him over one shoulder, and began his descent, with only one hand to hold them both to the ladder. The chances of a successful rescue being accomplished were not great as there was the likelihood of the man slipping from Wright's shoulder, or that the rescuer would be overpowered by the man's weight, and both would come crashing to the ground. Another firefighter, seeing the danger to which both men were exposed, quickly climbed to where his comrade was struggling to keep himself and the casualty on the ladder, and by taking some of the weight off Wright's shoulder, enabled him to bring the man down without further incident.

Within a few minutes the whole building was enveloped in flames, and several firefighters ascended an adjoining staircase with a line of hose. Unfortunately the fire spread was so rapid that flames shot through the windows of the staircase, making their situation untenable, and they were compelled to abandon their position without even having time to take their line of hose with them. Wright placed himself in the greatest danger of having his retreat cut off by waiting until he was sure that each of his crew had safely exited the now blazing building before leaving at the last moment. Strenuous firefighting efforts were made and despite the aggressive spread of the blaze the flames were eventually subdued.

A few months later a fire occurred in London Road, Manchester, and the flames spread rapidly through the building, trapping a man and his wife in a back room on the top floor. Before the arrival of the fire brigade, the man jumped from the window of the room to his death. One of the crew, firefighter Dudley, carried a ladder down a passageway to attempt to rescue the woman, but due to the position of the wall it would not reach the window. Dudley climbed onto the wall, and with the assistance of firefighter Bowen placed the foot of the ladder unsteadily on the wall with its head just reaching the window. The flames were coming from the window where the unfortunate woman was trapped as Bowen courageously climbed the ladder, which was kept steady by Dudley, and brought the woman to safety. As it was believed that someone else was inside the room Bowen re-entered, and having made a search in the most difficult of conditions assured himself that all persons were accounted for. Some indication of the fierceness of Bowen's ordeal whilst searching was indicated by the burns on his hands and face, and the singeing of his whiskers.

At eleven o'clock on the evening of Thursday 5th January 1893, a fire broke out in the six-storey cotton warehouse known as Mena's in Juniper Street, Liverpool. Despite the best efforts of the city's firefighters the flames spread to two adjoining warehouses storing the same commodity, which were soon well alight, involving more than 10,000 bales. The Liverpool firefighters were reported as tackling the blaze with great energy, but because of the dense and unventilated smoke from the fire in and around the building, and the immense quantities of combustible material, they were unable to locate the seat of the fire, until the roof of the first warehouse fell in with a resounding crash at about five o'clock the following morning. Up until this time a great volume of black smoke had issued from the burning buildings with tongues of flame showing occasionally, but when the collapse came the whole area was illuminated by the now unconstrained and rapidly developing conflagration. At the time of the structural collapse, five firefighters were working on the roof of the building, and it was feared that they had been lost when the roof failed. They had, however, with great and decisive presence of mind, managed to escape with their lives by jumping from the roof of that warehouse onto another, across an open space of more than four feet, six storeys above an open courtyard. This feat was made even more hazardous by the slippery condition of the roof owing to a heavy frost.

Shortly afterwards, the wall of the warehouse abutting on Costain Street fell out, and at a quarter-past ten that morning the wall in Juniper Street also collapsed with a terrible crash. Several firefighters were in the vicinity at the time, and shortly afterwards it was confirmed that two of them, Police-Firemen John Beere and John Watt, were missing. When it was seen that the wall was shaking a warning had been shouted and Beere and Watt with a third firefighter ran from the now swaying building. On reaching safety, the third man, who had suffered only a blow on the shoulder from a brick, turned to see if his comrades had also escaped the collapse, only to find that they had not, and had presumably been buried beneath hundreds of tons of debris. In response to this tragedy he was joined almost immediately by all Fire and Salvage Brigade personnel who set about removing the wreckage of the building with their bare hands, and trying desperately to locate the unfortunate firefighters with great energy and grim determination, despite having spent the whole of the previous night fighting the fires. Other firefighters quickly commandeered picks and shovels from various businesses in the locale, and after an hour of arduous work, they managed to locate the bodies of the two men, who were only identifiable by the Brigade numbers on their tunics; Watt having been decapitated, and Beere's body crushed beyond recognition. Watt when found had his arm reaching out as though in self-protection from the falling wall, whilst Beere was found body outstretched with his face to the ground.

When the huge wall crashed into the narrow street killing the two firefighters, others further away from the collapse were heard to exclaim: 'Poor Logan is gone.' Most fortunately, the aforesaid Inspector Logan had survived uninjured, as he had, shortly before the tragedy unfolded, moved the branch and hose line he was holding further inside the building to obtain a more effective position for directing his jet of water. Logan had just left the stairway and completed this relocation when he heard a tremendous rumble and roar as the outer wall and adjoining staircase crashed into the street. The Liverpool Courier of Saturday 7th January 1893 reported on this aspect of the incident thus:

> It was just after this ... that he heard his subordinates regret his supposed loss.
> He was, however, able to descend the staircase, and step over the debris, and
> thus reassure his men that he was uninjured. Brave and experienced as
> Inspector Logan is, the catastrophe beginning with his own perilous position,
> and the lamentable death of the two firemen gave him a very severe shake. Mr
> Logan states that shortly before the dreadful occurrence he had inspected the
> outside wall, and found that it showed not least signs of weakness or fracture.
> Indeed it is a most unusual thing for a front wall to collapse. It is about six
> years since a Liverpool fireman was killed in a similar manner.

The fire continued to rage with intense fury within the three warehouses throughout yesterday afternoon, but it fortunately did not extend its ravages to the adjoining warehouse, which also was stored with cotton. The wall forming the back of the warehouses, and separated from another block facing the Leeds and Liverpool canal by a passage about four feet in width, was still left standing; but it by no means appeared secure, and will doubtless also fall in. The heat from the fire was intense, and the smoke at times rose from the burning cotton in great volumes, almost overpowering the men who were battling the flames. There was a good supply of water, however, and by dint of well directed effort there was an appreciable diminution of the power of the devouring element at a late hour last evening. The task of playing with the hose was not without considerable danger to the men, as portions of the wall which in places were left standing were exceedingly unsafe and threatened to fall at any time. During last night a small body of the fire brigade was left to combat with the smouldering cotton; but, technically speaking, the fire had been got under in the afternoon, and the danger to its extending to the other warehouses had been obviated. Too high praise cannot be accorded to the firemen, who carried on their work the entire time under the most dangerous circumstances, and were well directed by Inspectors Logan and McCormick.

The inquest on the deaths of Police-Firemen Beere and Watt was opened on Saturday 7th January by the city Coroner Mr Sampson, and the jury as well as viewing the bodies of the 'Fallen' firefighters visited the scene of the fire. During the inquest, sympathy on the loss of the men was expressed by the foreman of the Jury and the Chairman of the Liverpool Watch Committee, Mr Hornby.

At about eight o'clock in the evening of 16th May 1894 a fire was found to have broken out in the large and comparatively new Nordinger's warehouse complex at the corner of Princes Street and Portland Street in the centre of Manchester near to the Town Hall. Within five minutes of the alarm being received by the Watch Room at Manchester Central Fire Station, crews of firefighters were at the scene. By this time the flames were spreading rapidly throughout the building, with the third and fourth floors being well alight, and a dense volume of smoke pouring out of the windows and other apertures throughout the building. No sooner had the fire brigade commenced firefighting operations, when it was reported that someone was trapped at the top of the rear staircase, and a number of firefighters were detailed to search for this person and bring him to safety.

On entering the building the firefighters were stopped in their tracks by the overpowering intensity of the heat and the almost impenetrable wall of smoke; but with jets of water being played on them to diminish the effects of the fire, they were able to force their way through the suffocating fumes and make their way up the stairs.

On reaching the top of the staircase they found that the missing man had managed to escape to the roof via a skylight, and as it was extremely difficult to reach him without the aid of ladders, the firefighters returned to the street to report the situation. Meanwhile a wheeled escape ladder had arrived at the incident and it was extended to its full working height of sixty-six feet, but this was still insufficient to reach the iron guttering on the roof where the casualty was. A messenger was therefore dispatched to fire brigade headquarters to order on the eighty feet escape, and on its arrival firefighters Lawrence and Clayton ascended the almost vertical escape ladder, despite seemingly impossible and desperately dangerous odds stacked against them.

On reaching the head of the ladder, Lawrence found that despite its very steep pitch, it had not extended as far as the roof. In order to reach the guttering Clayton climbed as far he could up the ladder and with one hand on the escape to keep his balance, he placed his hand firmly against the wall thus enabling Lawrence to gain additional footing by using his arm as a platform; by this means Lawrence was able to pull himself onto the roof. Here he found the casualty, William Schott, in a dazed condition, and so unstable that it was feared that he might at any moment fall through the skylight. Lawrence quickly seized hold of the man by the shoulder and lowered him over the edge of the projecting gutter to his colleague, firefighter Clayton, who had remained at the head of the ladder. Clayton, by great effort and dextrous handling of the semi-conscious man, managed to place his feet onto a round of the ladder, as Lawrence precariously held the spouting with one hand whilst keeping his grip on the shoulder of the casualty. Throughout this extremely hazardous aerial operation the great crowd of spectators in the streets below were kept silent by Superintendent Savage. Together Lawrence and Clayton, with great courage, brought their charge to the ground, to a resounding cheer. The fire was subdued within an hour of the rescue being effected.

The Manchester Watch Committee minutes of 24th May 1894 record that: 'Superintendent Savage reports that he does not recall 'a more striking case of courage and ability' than the rescue of a man from the roof of a burning building by Firemen Lawrence and Clayton. Resolved to award the medal for bravery.'

Early in the morning of 7th January 1898 a large fire raged in the centre of Glasgow, costing the city the lives of four of its firefighters.

About ten minutes to three that morning Mr Charles Kinloch, a clerk in the office of the District Superintendent of the North British Railway Company at Queen Street Station was passing near to the premises of Messrs W. & R. Hatrick & Co, a firm of wholesale and export chemists and druggists, when he observed smoke issuing from the basement underneath the shop of Messrs Bankier. Kinloch then ran towards the fire alarm at the corner of Bath Street, but on the way met police constable Troup, who, having been told of the outbreak, broke the glass and actuated the bell. At the same time PC Troup gave information at the Northern Police Office, which was close at hand.

The Glasgow Fire Service responded to the alarm call by dispatching horse-drawn steam pumps and handcarts, which raced to the scene from the Northern and Central Divisional Stations, under the direction of Chief Officer Paterson to the premises in Renfield Street. The stock held in the premises was extensive and consisted of drugs, oils, dry-salts, spices and various chemicals. The building, which was 120ft long by thirty feet high had an imposing frontage, including a small tower with a battlemented base at each end. These premises occupied the greater part of the block, which comprised shops with two flats above, and other apartments in the roof space, and extended from 152 to 170 Renfield Street.

When Captain Paterson arrived with the engines from the Central Station the flames were bursting from a small tower and smoke was issuing from most of the windows, and it could at once be seen that the fire would be an extremely difficult one to tackle, as not only were the contents of the building hazardous, but the northern portion of the property in which the fire originated adjoined a block of dwelling houses. Jets were immediately got to work on the burning woodwork from Cowcaddens Street through an entrance to a tenement, as well as from various points in Renfield Street.

The fire had apparently begun in the basement, and due to the interior design of the building, the wood cladding on the walls, and highly flammable nature of the materials stored therein, the spread of the fire was swift, travelling up through the building to the roof by means of hoist well, where it had taken hold. A large crowd of local people gathered, who were kept at a safe distance by a detachment of police under the command of Superintendent Sutherland, of the Northern Division.

Within an hour and a half of its discovery the fire seemed to be practically extinguished. James Hastie, the foreman of the Central Division, John Battersby, a first-class fireman in the same division, and David Smith, a second-class fireman in the Northern Division, were on the roof with a line of hose, and Charles Orr, a second-class fireman of the same division, was on the second floor. Other members of the brigade were in different parts of the building. Suddenly at about twenty minutes past four, there was a dull roar right in the centre of the building, and flames shot up high in the air; pieces of stone were thrown right across the street, and the crowd, fearing that the front of the building had given way, rushed down Renfield Street. At the time a considerable number of firemen were on top of the building endeavouring to get at the burning wood in the ceiling, and with the exception of those standing in the windows, the rest fell down among the burning debris. The air became thick with dust, and the street and pavements white with powdered lime. At first there was no indication that anybody had been injured. The north tower was still standing, and this was the point to which the firefighters had gone with the object of stripping the roof, exposing the rafters, and directing water onto the charred wood.

A few seconds after the crash a number of salvage men, who had been covering up goods in the premises to the extreme south of the block, came down a staircase and evacuated to the street. There is no doubt that if the explosion had occurred ten minutes earlier, the death toll would have been much greater, as not only were the men of the Salvage Corps in the shops and the upper flats, but some members of the fire brigade had gone down to the cellars. They had either accomplished their task there, or had come up for hose, for at the moment of the collapse they were on the street. Men were dispatched for ladders while others shouted to ascertain the whereabouts of any men who might be inside the wrecked building, and a search was made of every opening by which a man could possibly escape from the rubble. Those who had been looking at the scene from the windows on the opposite side of the street had kept their eyes fixed on the toppling mass of stone, and one man shouted, 'I saw three of them on the top floor just before the roof fell in. There! They are standing at the window.'

It was now certain that several firefighters were inside, and the men on the street continued to shout as loudly as possible, but no reply could be heard. At last a faint cry came from the centre of the burning mass, and in a few seconds a fireman emerged from the flames, and reached the street through the broken window of one of the shops. He was, needless to say, in a sad condition, his face pallid, and he was covered from head to foot with dust. As the other firefighters reached him he cried out in great distress: 'I saw them, I saw them – Hastie and the others. They're at the back. I was carried down. I couldn't help them. I could do nothing.'

The extremely serious nature of the fire was obvious to all, and an urgent search for the missing men commenced without delay. Men who had been outside the building went right in among the flames in their determination to rescue their comrades. Soon two men were rescued, and then a third.

It was with difficulty that the crowd were kept out of danger, and although they were at a distance, it soon became known that Orr was dead, and that his head had been crushed. The other two were carried on stretchers to the ambulance wagons which had been summoned, and were standing at the corner of Renfrew Street. The more severely injured of the two was John Watson, whose spine was fractured. He had been working a jet of water on the fire from the staircase, and ran up to the second landing to obtain a better vantage point. While he was there the building collapsed, and some object, probably a piece of masonry struck him on the back. He was found by a policeman lying beside Orr. Laurence Hamilton, who was injured internally, was conveyed to his home in College Street.

A mournful little group of firefighters took the bruised remains of Orr to the Buchanan Street Station Hotel where he was laid on the tiled floor of the corridor, with his battered helmet covering his face. The body was at once placed in a coffin and conveyed to his home in College Street. It is believed that he was in the back court when the explosion took place and he was killed by large stones falling upon him. The back wall of brick was almost entirely blown away, leaving a gap nearly thirty feet wide, and the yard was littered with stones and wood. Some of the debris extended a distance of over thirty feet, to dwelling houses which look into the yard, but not even a window of these houses was broken. The rest of the debris fell back into the interior of Messrs Hatrick's premises.

When it was discovered that some of the firefighters were missing, a messenger was dispatched to the Central Station in College Street for the roll of the brigade. There had been in all twenty-seven firefighters called out to the fire, seventeen of whom belonged to the Central division, and the remainder to the Northern. In addition, there were fifteen salvage men on duty. When the roll was called, it was found that three members of the brigade were missing: James Hastie, John Battersby, and David Smith.

James Hastie, foreman at the Central Fire Brigade Station; was a native of Edinburgh, and previously a member of the Leith Fire Brigade. He joined the Glasgow Fire brigade on 28th November 1891, and was at once appointed foreman at the Western Division Station, Cranstonhill. He was a widely read, genial, thoughtful man, attentive to his duties, liked by everybody, a teetotaller and a Quaker.

Thirty-seven years old, John Battersby, a first-class fireman at the Central Station, entered the service of the brigade on 9th December 1889 and was highly respected by his comrades. He left a widow and eight children, the youngest of whom was only three months old, the eldest being a girl about sixteen years of age. By trade he was a joiner, and was the son of Bailie Battersby, a member of what we would now know as the Fire Authority.

David Smith was forty-four year-old native of Govan, and a second-class fireman in the Northern Division, who had been a seaman prior to entering the brigade. He had been connected with the brigade for twenty-one years, having joined it on 20th November 1876. He left a widow and three young children.

Charles Orr, who was also a second-class fireman in the Northern Division, was a native of Paisley, and thirty-seven years of age. He joined the brigade on 30th October 1891 and left a widow and three children, two boys and a girl. By trade he was a tinsmith. Just after Orr had been called to the fire, his wife sent an urgent message to the fire station asking him to come home as his little girl was dying. However, before the message reached Renfield Street, Orr was dead.

The two men injured were thirty-three year-old John Watson, a native of Perth, who was hospitalised in the Royal Infirmary with a fractured spine, and Laurence Hamilton, who suffered internal injuries. The brother of Chief Officer Paterson had a narrow escape, having just stepped out of Messrs Bankier's shop when the explosion took place. Several other members of the brigade narrowly escaped injury. Nothing is known as to how the explosion occurred, although there was of course much conjecture. Messrs Hatrick's warehouse contained many inflammable liquids, including quantities of ether and any of these may have exploded in the fierce heat.

The arrangements for the funeral were of an elaborate character, with the helmets of the four men placed immediately above the name plates of their coffins, and their belts and hatches at the lower end. Outside the church many thousands of people had gathered soon after midday, and watched the early arrivals of those invited to take part in the service. The event assumed something of the proportions of a great public demonstration, and a large detachment representing the Glasgow Fire Brigade and other cities and burghs, including Edinburgh, Paisley, Govan, and Partick was present. They assembled at the Central Fire Station, in close proximity to the church, and came round in marching order, followed soon afterwards by a band and pipers leading a detachment of the Argyll and Sutherland Highlanders, and a similar number of cavalrymen of the Royal Scots Greys. The drums of the Highlanders' band were draped in black, and the soldiers were drawn up to the east of the church, their line extending as far as North Albion Street.

While the service was still in progress, four hose carriages from the Central Fire Station, each drawn by horses and in the charge of uniformed fire brigade drivers took up positions in the centre of the street opposite the church. Shortly before the close of the service a Royal Naval detachment arrived and joined the military, as did also a contingent from the Corps of Commissionaires. By 2.30 pm there were indications that the service was drawing to a close and preparations were made for the removal of the coffins to the vehicles; soon afterwards they were brought out from the side door, each carried upon the shoulders of six firefighters. The procession was now got quickly into position. With the exception of a few carriages for the accommodation of some of the immediate female relatives of the deceased, everybody attending the funeral walked to the Necropolis. About a quarter to three the signal was given for the procession to move off, and the band of the Highlanders played Beethoven's Funeral March No.1 with striking effect. To the impressive strains of the music the parade turned and processed slowly up North Albion Street led by the Band and Pipes and a detachment of the Argyll and Sutherland Highlanders, representatives of other Fire Brigades, Salvage Corps and Fire Insurance Offices.

The remains of the 'fallen' firefighters were borne on hose and ladder carriages, followed by relatives and friends of the deceased, and members of the Glasgow Fire Brigade and Police Force. Turning into College Street the cortege passed the Central Fire Station, where the blinds of the building were drawn, and the men on duty came to the front to pay a final tribute to their departed comrades. A few yards further along the cortege passed into High Street. Here, as indeed at every point of the route, the crowd was enormous and the progress of the procession was followed with profound respect.

THE EARLY PART OF
THE TWENTIETH CENTURY

EXPLOSION AT THE NATIONAL FILLING FACTORY, MORECOMBE

On the evening of Monday 1st October 1917, a disastrous explosion and fire occurred at the National Filling Factory (one of the government's principal munitions' works) on White Lund, Morecombe. The blast was so powerful that its impact was felt as far away as Burnley, some thirty-plus miles from the incident. Five-hundred and thirty-seven men and 813 women were employed there (one being the author's grandmother, Alice Lockyear *née* Lawton); fortunately most were on a meal break at the time, and no loss of life was incurred except amongst those fighting the fires. There were on the premises at that time some 20,000 shells wholly or partially filled, and about 300 tons of high explosives.

The works Fire Brigade made a heroic and determined attempt to extinguish the fire, but the flames spread with an alarming speed. Three violent explosions shook the place, killing or injuring several firemen and civilians assisting them. Throughout the next thirty-six hours explosions continued at frequent intervals, for as the shells became heated they detonated throwing masses of burning debris onto neighbouring buildings, so spreading the fires. It was impossible to save the factory, but there was valuable property nearby, including sheds where a million shells were stored. The work of isolating and subduing the fire was extremely dangerous, and the measure of success attained was largely due to the courage, resource and self-sacrifice of the many persons who took part, including members of various fire brigades who came from all parts of Lancashire and surrounding areas to fight the fires.

Fireman William Counsel had reported for duty as usual at the National Filling Factory at 5.30 pm on the evening of the explosion, and commenced routine work with Fireman Edward Hackett. At approximately 10.30 pm that night as they returned to their unit they saw the first signs of fire, which appeared to have broken out in the roof of number 6C unit, and they immediately ran to investigate. On their arrival they found two of their colleagues, firefighters Peck and Inglesent, directing a jet of water onto the fire. Counsel immediately assisted with this work until further hose arrived, and then commenced to run-out a second line of hose, and then quickly went to turn on the water supply to the branch. Meanwhile Hackett together with another man, firefighter Rapson, ran out a line of hose to a fireman Taylor. At this point the first explosion occurred. Hackett was thrown to the ground by the force of the blast, and he eventually managed to regain his feet, and made his way to the other side of the fire and gave assistance to Taylor who was still attacking the flames with his jet. Taking himself back to where his comrades were working their jet, Counsel found that there was no sign of any of the other firefighters and that hose was covered and obstructed by debris. He then joined Hackett and Taylor, and they decided to try and save the transit sheds, and attempted to get yet another line of hose to work from a hydrant. In his statement Edward Hackett wrote:

> Explosions were terrific at this time, and I said to Firemen Taylor and Counsel: 'Can we live in this'? Fireman Taylor encouraged Counsel and myself to go on, when another fearful explosion took place. We were blown over the runway. Counsel and I crawled … and took shelter behind a railway wagon. We then withdrew to a ditch …, and crawled to the military offices and there we found … soldiers and some girls. The girls were prostrate. This was about 3.30 am. The soldiers, Counsel and myself decided it was not safe to remain there, so we all removed to the Heysham Road behind the magazines. We took one girl on a stretcher; another girl the soldiers carried in their arms; the other girls walked. We then met the officer in charge of the soldiers, who was taking cover on Heysham road. I asked the military officer if he would give Counsel and myself permission to withdraw to safety with them. He said he could not take responsibility for us, and so we went to the entrance gates.

Fireman Thomas Tattershall was in Unit 6C of the factory when he first saw the fire. He immediately attacked the flames with a portable fire extinguisher, but unfortunately he made little or no impact on the blaze. This particular unit held a large amount of explosives in bags, half of which were burning, and the TNT was melting and flowing across the floor in flames. Tattershall ran down the stairs and alerted the fire station, and he together with firefighters Inglesent and Taylor worked together to fight the fire. Taylor took a branch and a line of hose up onto the runway when the first explosion occurred and he was blown several yards away, sustaining a head wound and a broken arm, as well as severe shock.

Works Constable William Seery was on duty that night and saw a flash of light come from the number 6 Stemming House, and then saw flames coming from the roof. He immediately sounded his whistle to give the alarm, and tried to actuate the sprinkler system. Whilst searching the area to ensure that all employees had been evacuated, he went to the door of the number 12 Change House, when the first explosion took place, and the building collapsed around him, pinning him under wreckage. After eventually extricating himself, and receiving first aid treatment, Seery gave assistance to a number of soldiers in trying to get a jet to work on the flames.

Thomas Coppard of the Works Police reported that at 10.30 pm he saw the roof of the number 6 C Stemming House on fire. He advised a number of women workers in the vicinity to keep calm, and to leave the factory as soon as possible. He proceeded to the telephone exchange to ensure that orders as regards a fire situation were carried out. A number of firefighters passed him as they hurried to the blaze, and at this point the first explosion took place. Coppard guided some of the women staff to a shelter in the fire station, and afterwards escorted them from the premises. Proceeding to the telephone exchange he was informed by PC Chapman, the operator, that he could not obtain a reply from Lancaster Fire Brigade. A motor car was then dispatched to Lancaster Fire Station to raise the alarm with them; by this time there were further explosions and the fire was spreading rapidly, despite the strenuous efforts being made by members of the Works Fire Brigade in tackling the blaze. As the situation became more critical, arrangements were made for locomotives to be brought from Lancaster to remove rolling stock containing live shells. In his statement Coppard wrote:

> I returned to the danger zone and advised all I saw to leave the factory at once. The fire by this time had obtained a strong hold and was increasing and I could see that the factory was doomed, explosions continually taking place. I returned to the main gate where I saw Mr Stokes, General Manager, and reported to him that everything was being done to try and keep the fire under, and that workers had left the factory ... I remained at the main gate with several constables until it was unsafe to remain any longer. I advised all to shelter under the railway bridge, the general offices were then all on fire, but nothing could be done to save them; the motor garage also being alight. I went to the railway bridge, where I remained for a time and afterwards visited the police office. While (I was) there a loud explosion took place blowing in the windows. The ambulance room appeared to be on fire. I proceeded there and saw two stretchers alight ..., I dragged them out, the floor also being on fire. I then got some water and extinguished the fire. I ... returned to the main gate for the purpose of obtaining a motor-car to proceed to the railway officials at Lancaster to remove ... railway wagons containing live shells, some of the wagons being on fire, and the shells exploding.

However, this task was undertaken by Chief Officer Wheeler of the Works Fire Brigade, but unfortunately the engines sent from Lancaster were unable to remove the wagons, and two locomotives from the factory were eventually able to take them to a safer location.

The following are extracts from reports on the incident by witnesses who were present at the filling Factory:

Traffic Regulator Edward Abbott:

At the time of the outbreak I was in the Shunter's Cabin. I ran to 12 change House, and it was on fire, the girls were coming out ... and they asked me which way to go. All went except one who was very distracted. The first explosion took place and I pulled her down beside me. I was making away when three firemen were blown out of the runway. I had seen them playing [their jets of water] on the fire before ... I think one of them was a man called Topping. I picked the first man up I came to, whilst picking him up foreman Dudson came along and we led the injured men to where we thought it was safe. Dudson went for a stretcher and I went back with two or three other men to the injured man and we got him to one side. Topping, if that was his name, appeared to have big gash in his side and was covered with blood.

Constable Thomas Boustead, Works Police:

At 5.45 on the first instant, I went on duty and was stationed at the Number 6 magazine. About 10.05 pm I was patrolling near the magazine when I met a fireman. As we passed we exchanged words, and on looking round I saw a flame ... shoot up from the roof of number 6 Steaming House. The fireman at once ran towards the outbreak, and I ... followed him. I ran down the railway line and ... met a number of girls. I escorted them to the military gate ... and told them to get away from the factory as quickly as possible. I then returned to the fire ... I remained near to the Number 6 Transit Shed and saw the firemen playing [their jets of water] on the flames, with apparently good results, as the flames appeared to get less. Shortly afterwards there were several small explosions, followed by two loud explosions. I was knocked to the ground and after recovering myself, I got up and made for the military camp.

Fireman Richard Taylor of the Works Fire Brigade:

As soon as I got to my post I saw firemen Inglesent and we compared watches ... [he] then went to his supper. In about one minute he came running back, and told me there was a fire. I saw the fire was in the direction of 6 unit, it had the appearance of a ball of fire on the top of the building, ... similar to the sun setting red. I immediately instructed him to send a telephone message to the fire station … I do not remember seeing him alive again. I ran three lengths of hose out from the nearest box … and I played (the jet) on the fire myself for a few minutes. Then Fireman Counsel came to me. I left him there whilst I went to the hydrant … I found that Firemen Rapson, Hackett and Webster had ran three lengths out. They handed the branch to me on the runway. I called for another length and they handed it to me. I ran it out and coupled it and played on the fire over the safety wall….

The first explosion took place at this time. It blew me over and debris was all about. I took shelter under the wall of 5 unit. After a few minutes I got onto the runway again. I then found Searcher W. Topping, he was calling for help and bleeding from the mouth. He was helpless, but conscious. I carried him … and left him in [the] charge of two soldiers. I returned [and] ran three lengths [of hose] out with the assistance of firemen Hackett and Counsel onto the runway to stop the fire spreading to the transit sheds. The fire then got too hot and we had to retreat. I lost sight of firemen Hackett and Counsel at this time, and went to another hydrant at the back of number 3 explosive house, and ran two lengths out there, and played on the number 3 exploder house to try and save it … Fireman Scott [came to me] and we retreated … as we thought that it was well saturated, and I considered that there was more danger of the box room getting on fire, which was very near to the number 2 magazine. So Scott and I … then went on to the number 1 and number 2 magazines to flood them. Whilst doing this …. We found Firth Dole [the fitter's labourer] lying on his back … badly injured. Fireman Scott, Albert Shaw … Edwin Howarth [both Over-lookers] and fireman Wilson carried him to the entrance gates.

The following report was submitted by Inspectors W. A. Wearing and F. Johnson to the Chief Constable of Lancaster Borough Police:

Sir,

We beg to report for your information that at 10.40 pm on Monday the last instant, we heard a loud explosion, followed by a flare of light in the direction of White Lund. The first explosion was followed by two more in quick succession, and we concluded that the filling factory at White Lund was on fire. Mr Superintendent Scott, County Police Station, Skerton, was communicated with by telephone, the filling factory being within his district and he confirmed our belief that the above works were on fire, and he requested that we turn out at once with the fire brigade. The alarm was given, also instructions for the ambulance to be got ready, and proceed to White

Lund. Also, for all doctors to be notified, as well as the Royal Infirmary. Inspector Thompson was left in charge here, and we proceeded to White Lund with the motor fire engine and seven firemen.

On arrival at White Lund [we] along with Mr Superintendent Scott walked towards the Filling Factory, but found that it was almost impossible to get near, owing to flying debris and bursting shells. A message came from the works for everyone in the vicinity to clear away at once, … as no good could be done for some considerable time. Explosions kept taking place every few minutes throughout the night, and Mr Stokes, the manager … agreed that it was not safe to go near the works until daylight … and so far as the authorities could ascertain all the women employed there had been got off the premises quite safe.

Early on Tuesday in company of Mr Stokes, we proceeded to the factory … and examined the locality of the magazines and desired that if possible we should make an effort to prevent the fire reaching them. We decided to try and soak the contents of the magazine and adjoining buildings as requested. Mr Superintendent Savage of the Preston Fire Brigade had by this time joined us with … several firemen. The two brigades worked conjointly and water was obtained from a pond at a farm about half a mile away. The contents were well saturated and it was considered fairly safe to leave that part of the works for the present, but a watch was kept for fear of any burning debris falling near and setting alight any of these buildings. Whilst working here the firemen of both brigades [Preston and Lancaster] ran very great risks, owing to the explosions taking place frequently and pieces of shell and debris falling all around them. They all showed the greatest courage and devotion to duty, working as smoothly and unconcerned as though they were in no danger at all. The men of both brigades are, in our opinion, deserving of the highest praise.

We next turned our attention to extinguishing the fire at and about several hay stacks and the remains of a grain stack, which were in close proximity to several other stacks within the precincts of the factory, pumping water with our motor-engines from a ditch which runs along the White Lund road side. At about 3.00 pm all these fires were extinguished, and we then proceeded to the main entrance of the factory with a view to ascertaining whether it was possible to find a suitable place inside the works where water could be pumped from, on to the burning wagons, etc, near to the centre of the works, as soon as it was considered safe to enter. On arrival [we] found several brigades there, and some of them were arranging to proceed just inside the works to a well, where there was a plentiful supply of water.

About 2.00 pm Wednesday, when the explosions had become less frequent, and it was decided to enter the factory, a meeting between officers in charge of the various brigades was held, and Mr Pringle, the Chief Constable of Blackpool, being the senior officer present, it was mutually arranged that he should take charge.

On entering the factory our brigade accompanied by Bolton brigade, penetrated to a considerable distance along a road leading to ... where the fire originated. A dam was set up from which both engines pumped, this dam being supplied by ... the Liverpool, Manchester and Salford brigades from a well not far from the main entrance. The Blackpool engine was stationed on the road outside the works, and pumped water from a ditch to augment the supply from the other engines. All fires were extinguished, and all debris in the danger zone was well saturated by 8.00 am.

Some of the brigades left on Wednesday, and the remainder went away on Thursday morning, but on request of Mr Stokes, our engine and men remained standing by until noon on Friday, by which time the works pumping machinery had been put in working order. The work for all members of the brigade was exceedingly dangerous, owing to the flying debris, but we are glad to be able to report that no injury was sustained by any member.

Signed
W. A. Wearing, Insp.
F. Johnson, Insp.

Statement of Superintendent Alonza Scott of Preston Fire Brigade:
With one motor-fire engine and seven men Preston Fire Brigade reported to Morecombe police office at 6:30 on Tuesday morning, and were immediately dispatched to the White Lund Filling Factory. On arrival shells and other missiles and debris were flying through the air, and they we were ordered to take cover behind a block of buildings along with Lancaster Fire Brigade, and a number of ambulances and doctor's cars. They remained there for twenty minutes, after which we went to the west wing of the building which was now on fire. As the water mains were out of commission due to the explosions, water was pumped from a pit half a mile away, and Savage was in

charge of this operation. Preston Fire Brigade then directed their jets onto TNT magazines and explosives' houses, [and continued] throughout the day and night, and stood-by at the site until 8:00am the following day.

Superintendent C. E. Scott of Lancashire Constabulary was on duty at Skerton police office, on the evening of 1st October, when at about 10.40 pm he heard the first explosion, and, thinking it to be an air raid, went immediately to the communications office, but found that no warning had been received. Scott then ordered one of his constables to make telephone contact with the White Lund factory to ascertain if the explosion had come from there; ominously no reply was received. Shortly afterwards a member of the public called into the police office, and reported a fire and explosion at the Morecombe Filling Factory. Superintendent Scott at once directed information to be sent to Lancashire Constabulary headquarters and to nearby police sections, so as to get all the available police officers to White Lund at once. He also telephoned Lancaster Borough Police to request the attendance of their fire brigade.

Scott arrived at about 11.00 pm and found the whole area in disarray, with roads congested with people fleeing the district owing to the explosions which were now occurring regularly. Possessions were discarded, and premises left open and abandoned. Local police by this time began to arrive and they took charge of the management of the main roads and surrounding properties, securing the transport infrastructure leading to the factory. In his report to the Chief Constable of Lancashire, Superintendent Scott wrote:

> I beg to report for the information of the Chief Constable that Lancaster Fire Brigade was first to arrive … soon after 11.00 pm, and as the explosions were severe, they went onto Morecombe police station, and remained until it was safer to enter the works. Preston Fire Brigade followed at about 6.00 am on 2nd October, 1917, and these brigades were playing [their jets of water] on the flames when other brigades arrived.

> Works police man Coppard was last to leave the factory, taking shelter with others under the railway bridge close to the factory. About 2.00 am Coppard again visited the factory, and extinguished a fire which had got hold of two stretchers near the ambulance room. At 5.30 am he was again at the entrance gates, and at 7.00 am he visited the magazines and bonded stores and found them safe from fire. I and other police [officers] got as far as the railway bridge just outside the factory, and remained there for some time. But owing to the severity of the explosions, and the fire spreading, I considered it too dangerous to remain, and moved all who were there to the end of the road leading to the factory.

I remained on duty regulating traffic on the roads for 33 hours until 9.00 pm 2nd October, until relieved by Superintendent Jackson. I should like to add that all ranks were near at hand all night, and would have rendered good service had they been needed, although the air at times was filled with pieces of shell and shrapnel.

In a memorandum dated 5th October 1917 regarding this major incident, Second Officer Sloan of Manchester Fire Brigade reported:

At 11.44 am on the 2nd instant, a message was received … from Messrs Vickers Works, Barrow-in-Furness, saying that there was a serious fire at the National Shell Filling Factory, Morecombe. The Chief Officer spoke to Messrs Vickers, and then got in touch with the Chairman of the Fire Brigade Sub-Committee, Alderman Fildes, and as a result ordered the 2nd Officer and eight men to proceed to the fire at Morecombe. At 12.26 pm the Second Officer and eight men left with No. 9 motor pump. While on the road and outside Preston towards Lancaster a detachment of Liverpool Fire Brigade, a motor pump and lorry loaded with hose was passed.

Lancaster was reached at 2.10 pm and on all sides was seen the effects of the explosion, here a representative of Messrs Vickers boarded the Blackpool engine and went to the fire. The Works Fire Superintendent Mr Whelen said there was no water except what was in the small dykes in the works and adjacent land; the fire mains were also broken. No. 9 pump was taken inside the works and two jets got to work on railway wagons loaded with filled shells, also on a range of buildings stocked with Tri-Nitro-Toluol. The shells … were bursting frequently and the men were instructed to take cover when the explosions occurred. The Liverpool engines and men arrived about 3.15 pm and got to work from the roadway, so did Blackpool, No. 9 motor and men being the first of the fourteen brigades who attended to enter the works. When this portion of the works fire had been extinguished the Liverpool and Manchester engines were moved to a tributary of the river Lune about two miles along a road skirting the works, here the stream was dammed and lines of hose attached, and with the fittings being interchangeable, the work went well and enabled the fire to be stopped travelling towards the Paint Stores, … and magazines.

At 4.00 am the third Salford Engine arrived having had an accident en route to the fire. This engine got to work from the dyke and pumped to No. 9 motor as the Liverpool engine was getting a poor supply. Whilst work was proceeding a shell burst, knocking several men down with shock, then all the men were withdrawn till daylight. The fire was reduced to smouldering heaps over a wide area, and the local brigade of Lancaster assisted by the Barrow Ship Yard and Barrow Corporation could well have dealt with what remained.

Colonel Milson attended about 10.00 am and asked for the officers in charge of the fire engines from Manchester, and Liverpool, also the other towns. He thanked the officers and men on behalf of the Minister of Munitions, Mr Churchill, for the splendid work done. During the afternoon of the 3rd instant, four works firemen were brought from the ruins, one man having a branch pipe in his hand, later three workmen and one women, eight in all. The cause of the fire, up to the time of leaving, was unknown.

The MBE was awarded to Major Sharpe the Factory Danger Officer, and Mr E. T. Wheeler the factory's Chief Fire Officer. The Kings Police Medal was awarded to the following firefighters:

Superintendent Fred Brocklehurst of Bolton Fire Brigade
Superintendent William Bramwell Hodgson of Morecombe Fire Brigade
Superintendent D'Arcy Benson Moffat of Barrow (Vickers Armstrong) Fire Brigade
Superintendent Richard Newsham of Barrow Corporation Fire Brigade
Chief Inspector George Albert Oakes of Liverpool Fire Brigade
Superintendent Alonzo Savage of Preston Fire Brigade
Second Officer Daniel Devine Sloan of Manchester Fire Brigade
Inspector William Andrew Wearing of Lancaster Fire Brigade

Mr W. J. Pringle, the Chief Constable of Blackpool, is cited in the list of recipients of the Kings Police Medal held at the National Archive Kew, but there is no record of his having received the award.

The Edward Medal in silver was awarded to the following workers at the National Filling Factory: Inspector Thomas Coppard of the Works Police, Fireman Thomas Tattersall, and to Engine Driver Thomas Kew and Shunter Abraham Clarke who together uncoupled forty-nine ammunition trucks holding 250,000 live shells from trucks already on fire with their contents exploding, and shunted them out of the danger zone to prevent further explosions. Later that morning, Kew, in company with Foreman Charles Taylor (who was awarded the British Empire Medal) repaired the water tower situated to the rear of the fire station, whilst shells were exploding in the area. In all twenty-five awards of the British Empire Medal were made including that to Telephonist Mary Agnes Wilkinson who was blown off her bicycle twice as she was called to duty at the exchange in Cable Street, where she stayed at her post for 24 hours; the award recognised her devotion to duty.

A local newspaper, *The Morecombe Visitor*, made the following report in its edition of 10th October 1917: 'The neighbouring fire brigades rendered much courageous and valuable assistance, and the Minister of Munitions has telegrammed his appreciation and thanks to each of them.'

FIRE AT MESSRS J. H. BRANTON & CO, ALBERT EMBANKMENT, LONDON

During the early morning of Wednesday 30th January 1918, one of the most serious catastrophes to be visited on the London Fire Brigade occurred when a fire call was received at 03.55 hours to a three-storey brick building used for the storage of cattle food occupied by Messrs J. H. Branton & Co on the Albert Embankment.

On their arrival the fire brigade, after a belated call by a passer-by, found visibility very poor owing to a thick fog, and billowing heavy smoke from the burning linseed cake, linseed oil, and spices, and consequently had to don smoke helmets. Entry into the building to commence firefighting operations was badly hampered by the collapse of part of the roof and top floor, the debris from which blocked the stairways and rooms. An escape ladder was pitched against the building, to facilitate hose lines being taken on to the roof and other advantageous points so that water jets could be brought to bear on the fire. Because this building was relatively small, and stood alone, as neighbouring premises had been demolished for development, the fire was easily surrounded by the crews.

By the time of Superintendent Barrows' arrival the fire was almost extinguished, and whilst surveying the incident he heard a loud cracking noise from the building and ordered all personnel to evacuate, and gave directions for the escape ladder to be moved. Three firefighters were on the wheeled-escape, and two on another ladder pitched nearby, one on the top and one on the foot to steady it, the remainder of the crew being on the ground; altogether some twelve men were in the immediate area. Suddenly Sub Officer Cornforth of Clapham Old Town Station shouted a warning, and there was a tremendous crash; and although those on the ground were able to run towards the river side of the Embankment, they could not escape the two outer walls, which bulged and fell outwards onto the escape and the ladder, collapsing onto the fleeing firefighters. Only five of the crew escaped serious injury, with six men being buried in the debris. Sub Officer Cornforth who called the warning of collapse was hit by a huge block of stone and killed outright, as were another five other firefighters: Firemen A. A. Page, J. W. Johnson, (both from Vauxhall), E. J. Fairbrother, W. E. Nash, and J. E. Fay (all three from Kennington). Sub Officer W. W. Hall died on the way to hospital, and Superintendent Barrows and Station Officer Partner were injured.

No time was lost in commencing work to effect the rescue of the men buried beneath the debris, but the injuries received by the firefighters trapped beneath the fallen masonry must have been almost immediately fatal. The collapse of the top floor evidently weakened the supporting walls, so causing a subsidence in the integrity of the first floor, and consequently bringing about a total collapse of the structure.

Although not a particularly old building the dampness from the nearby marshes had disintegrated the mortar to the point of it being granular, which would certainly have been a contributory factor in the collapse. The principal use of the premises was the manufacture of a lactose substitute for rearing calves; however, none of the chemicals used in the process would have been liable to spontaneous combustion. All electrical wiring was encased in metal tubes, but a short circuit had occurred sometime previously, and it was presumed that it had been caused by rats on the premises gnawing through the insulation on the electrical flexes. Based on this circumstantial evidence it was considered that this was the only feasible cause of the fire, with the possibility of shrapnel splinters from an earlier air raid causing a smouldering outbreak in stock being considered the secondary causation. The possibility of material soaked in linseed oil, a liquid which oxidises easily, spontaneously combusting seems not to have been mentioned.

In his report on the incident later that day to the Divisional Officer in charge of the 'E' District of London Fire Brigade's Southern Division, Superintendent J Barrows stated:

> I submit that at 3.44 am of this date a call was received from a stranger to a private house alight at Albert Embankment, S.E., to which the Motor Escape, Motor Pump and 10 men from No.94. Station Vauxhall and Motor Pump and 6 men from No.87. station Kennington responded.

> At 3.55 am, a 'home call' message was received, viz:- It is a building of three floors about 40 x 40 ft. used as Pepper Mills alight, one hydrant in use. No.3. Westminster Motor Pump and 6 men were ordered and I attended with No.80. Motor Car and 2 men. On my arrival I found the upper floors of a building of three floors about 45 x 30 ft. [used as cattle food manufacturers] well alight, and part of roof and upper floor had fallen in. The fire was practically extinguished by the use of two hydrants and one Motor Pump and the stop [message] sent back [to the watch room] accordingly.

> At 5.34 am, owing to a considerable amount of turning over to be done, a message was dispatched to the effect that appliances would be detained for a time and a few minutes later another message asking for a Sub-officer and four men to be sent on with a view to the appliances and myself returning home.

At about 5.45 am, I was on the ground floor and in consequence of hearing a cracking noise, cleared everyone out of the building. Owing to the ground mist and smoke, the front of the building was hardly discernible, a hydrant was still being used up the Escape, I went to the front of the building with the men with a view of making up and removing the Escape, when suddenly I heard Sub-officer Cornford call out 'Look out Sir' and saw the building collapsing. I called out 'drop everything and run', but was knocked down by the falling debris and part of the Escape, being subsequently extricated by our men from amongst the debris. On making enquiry, I found that a message to the effect that the building had collapsed and that several of our men were buried and ambulances were required had been sent back. I gave instructions for the debris to be searched for the bodies of our men, then saw the Divisional Officer South who, on hearing of the nature of my injuries ordered me home.

The funeral took place in Saint Mark's Church, Kennington, which was overflowing with almost 200 firefighters of all ranks from London and many provincial Brigades, led by Chief Fire Officer Lieutenant-Commander Sampson Sladen, as well the Chairman of the London County Council the Marquis of Crewe, the Chairmen of the Local Government Board and the LCC Fire Brigade Committee, the Commissioner of the Metropolitan Police, Sir Edward Henry, and former Chief Fire Officer Rear-Admiral de Courcy Hamilton. As all eight coffins covered with the Union Flag and bearing the helmet, belt and axe of the deceased were borne into the church, the congregation rose to their feet and bowed heads in reverence. The Bishop of Southwark, Dr Hubert Murray Burge, in a brief address to the congregation spoke of the uncertainty of life, especially amongst those called to exiguous duty, and of the 'greatness' of such men whom that day they mourned, saying:

'We are gathered not so much in sorrow as in reverence to the example of duty, done unflinchingly without any thought of self, which these men have left behind.'

The funeral cortege to the cemetery at Highgate where six of the deceased were to be laid to rest in the 'Firemen's Corner', was about a quarter of a mile in length, and included six motor pumps bedecked with wreaths. At Lambeth Bridge where the disaster had occurred, the procession momentarily halted. As it moved off, the ranks of silver, brass and black helmeted men opened and lined the route, saluting the hearses as they passed.

So great an impact did this tragic loss of eight London firefighters in so short a space of time have on a society well used to the carnage of the Western Front and Gallipoli, that the following message of sympathy was sent to Chief Fire Officer Sampson Sladen on behalf of His Majesty King George V:

'It was with deep regret that the King heard of the deaths of your officers and men who lost their lives on Wednesday, January 30th. The dauntless courage with which they faced their perilous duties was truly characteristic of that splendid spirit which animates all ranks of the London Fire Brigade, and I am commanded to request you to convey to the relatives of the sufferers an expression of His Majesty's heartfelt sympathy in their bereavement.'

The Marquis of Crewe, Chairman of the London County Council also wrote offering his sympathy and added:

'It is the same sympathy which I should offer to the family of a man who gives his life in the war. The call of duty is the same and the sacrifice is the same.'

THE NETCHELLS GAS WORKS INCIDENT, BIRMINGHAM

Wednesday 26th February 1919 dawned on a Birmingham Fire Brigade still suffering the acute manpower shortages caused by the Great War; it was a day that would see two workmen dead, and two firefighters killed in an attempt to rescue them.

Birmingham Fire Brigade had been under the command of Alfred Tozer since 1906, and had a rank structure which graded firemen on a scale which reflected their responsibilities. The first actual executive rank was that of Station Officer, followed by that of District Officer in charge of District Stations in more urban areas of high population, industry and commerce; it was on these stations that Breathing Apparatus was held. These early BA sets comprised a cylinder of oxygen which fed a constant supply via a breathing bag into a 'coverall' helmet with a leather skirt; inside the helmet was a face seal to prevent the intrusion of fumes and smoke. A chemical absorbent removed the exhaled carbon dioxide from the wearer; the helmet was placed over the head of the firefighter, with the fire-tunic buttoned over the leather skirt, the intention being to isolate the wearer from the atmosphere.

The Corporation Gas Works, situated in the Netchells area, about two miles north-east of the city centre, manufactured town gas, which contained carbon monoxide, which is unstable, toxic and highly flammable. Once town gas had been manufactured it was stored in holders with the flow to the distributive system being controlled by valves in the basement of the Governor House. For some weeks prior to this incident the valve supplying the Birmingham area had been leaking, and had been temporarily sealed with clay whilst a new valve was made. The new valve was so heavy that it was necessary to break through the floor to lower it into position. It was decided to carry out the work in the afternoon as the pressure in the gas main would be lightest. Work commenced at 2.30 pm under the supervision of the Assistant Works Engineer; with one man wearing a smoke helmet and two others ready to assist. Immediately the cover had been removed there was a serious and continuous escape of gas which soon overwhelmed those without protection. The alarm was sounded and fellow workers at the plant made attempts to rescue their colleagues, which resulted in them being reduced to a state of collapse. All the windows in the Governor House were broken in an attempt to ventilate the premises, and at 3.18 pm a call was made to the fire brigade.

On receipt of the call Chief Fire Officer Tozer was informed, and he ordered all breathing apparatus sets to be despatched to the incident without delay. The first fire appliance on the scene was from Lingard Street, just a few hundred yards away, and the officer in charge, Acting Station Officer Alfred Moon, found a chaotic situation, with a very serious escape of gas, two workmen trapped in the basement, and a number of other employees, including the site engineer, incapacitated. Station Officer Moon quickly donned the 'Proto' breathing apparatus, tied a line around his waist, and descended into the basement and quickly reached the casualties. Moon signalled for more line to be paid out, but this was misconstrued as distress on his part, and he was quickly hauled out. Moon again entered the basement only to be overcome by the fumes and collapse as dead weight on the line; his linesman was also overcome.

Chief Officer Tozer arrived in time to see Fireman Herbert Dyche of Moseley Road fire station, donning breathing apparatus, and cautioned him against proceeding any further than the mouth of the aperture if he felt any effects of the gas. Dyche entered the basement and almost immediately collapsed. On seeing their comrade 'go down', two other firefighters immediately tried to haul him out of the basement, and had almost managed to pull him clear when they also collapsed. In this now critical situation, firefighters had to be forcibly restrained from attempting the rescue of their colleagues, and it was only on the advice of a doctor that nothing further could be done were rescue attempts abandoned. A hole was eventually knocked in the wall so that hose could be used to pump water into the main in an effort to reduce the flow of gas. It was only on the arrival of an engineer from another site that it was confirmed that it was impossible to close down the main, as the continued escape of gas was due to back pressure. The main was finally sealed by the insertion of bladders which on inflation sealed the pipe and stopped the leak. It was not until 6.00 pm that the bodies were recovered from the basement. Four other firefighters had to be hospitalised, as well as three site workers. There were also a number of other firefighters who had collapsed but were treated on site.

Following the funerals, serious questions were raised in both Council Chambers and by the local press, many of them directed at Chief Officer Alfred Tozer. At the inquest, the chief was only able to say that the equipment was only tested 'periodically', and was uncertain of its age. The equipment was examined by the highly respected Professor of Mining Sir John Cadman of Birmingham University, who as Assistant Manager at Silverdale Colliery and HM Inspector of Mines had worked to reduce loss of life in mining, gaining the North Staffordshire Mines Rescue Brigade's medal with five clasps. Professor Cadman found defects in both breathing apparatus sets due to dirt and wear and tear. One tear was found in a breathing bag which, it was suggested, had been done when the set was being cleaned following the incident; there was also a wide variation in the supply of oxygen to all of the sets in use by the Brigade. It is believed that the inherent weakness of the equipment was in the skirt attached to the helmet, which was placed and secured under the fire tunic. With carbon monoxide being lighter than air, and escaping at high pressure from the hole through which the firemen would have to enter the basement, the gas seeped under the tunic and skirt into the helmet, and once in the breathing circuit could not be purged.

The recorded verdict of the Coroner was one of accidental death in each case, but he took the opportunity to comment on the bravery of both firemen involved. He also recommended that a rescue section be formed within the Fire Brigade and trained to deal with such incidents. As a result finance was made available to form what was almost certainly the first Fire Service specialist rescue team in the UK. It was very much influenced by the experiences of the Mines Rescue Service, and trained by the University's Mining Department. The members of the team were selected as to their suitability and temperament, and required to undergo regular medical examination. New 'Proto' BA sets and resuscitation equipment were purchased, and basic entry control procedures formulated. Eventually a dedicated rescue tender was acquired, staffed by up to eight men, and located at the Chief Station.

Alfred Moon and Herbert Dyche were awarded a certificate from the Royal Humane Society, and the Meritorious Medal of the Professional Fire Brigade's Association – erroneously described in the press as the 'Fireman's VC'! Their gallant actions were recorded on the Roll of Honour at Birmingham Central Fire Station.

FIRE AT CROSS HOUSE, JUNCTION WESTGATE ROAD & FENKLE STREET, NEWCASTLE-UPON-TYNE

On 23rd December 1919 a fire broke out in large stocks of celluloid film in the basement premises of the Famous Laskey Film Services, in Cross House, a seven-storey office block, located at the junction of Westgate Road and Fenkle Street, Newcastle-upon-Tyne. The fire took hold very quickly and shot up the lift shaft, thus spreading the fire to the upper floors and trapping many office workers. Many were saved thanks to the heroic efforts of the fire brigade, but sadly eleven people died. The heroism of sixteen firemen, police officers, and civilians was recognised with bravery awards; most notable was the award of the Albert Medal to Fireman Thomas Brown, who was also promoted to the rank of Station Officer, and had his name added to the Roll of Heroes of the Carnegie Trust Fund in recognition of a daring rescue carried out with a hook ladder. (Hook ladders were narrow, very portable ladders thirteen feet and four inches in length, weighing some twenty-nine pounds, and having a two feet two inches long hook at its head by which means the ladder could be 'secured' to window frames, parapets, etc. for the purpose of scaling a building.)

Fireman Thomas Brown Albert Medal,
Newcastle-upon-Tyne Police Fire Brigade.
Courtesy of Tyne and Wear Fire and Rescue Service.

The following is an eyewitness account of the rescue efforts from the *Newcastle Journal* of 24th December 1919:

> I was attracted to the scene, with many hundreds of gay Christmas shoppers, by the clouds of thick, throat-irritating smoke, which rolled down into Grainger Street. It was pungent and smelt of celluloid. Overhead were faint cries, such as birds of passage make sometimes when winging their way through the night; but as Westgate Road was neared the cries developed into high-pitched screams of distress and terror. They were the screams of girls with faces blanched. Westgate Road seethed with excited people whose faces were upturned towards the heights of the 'flat-iron' shaped building. I pushed my way forward as far as I possibly could.
>
> The Fire Brigade had just arrived and men and women were commencing to moan and sob. Two typists had jumped from high storeys onto the pavement, one being killed instantly and the other succumbing shortly afterwards; and now the firemen's escape ladder thrust upwards against the Fenkle Street side of the building was yards short of the top floor, where were many girls and men. At almost every window of the upper storeys there were men, girls and youths crying for help and the situation looked desperate. Some of the horrified spectators lost their heads and cried 'Jump, jump!' and others made megaphones of their hands and yelled 'Sit still!' and 'Stay there!'.
>
> Two women beside me fainted; a man somewhere was moaning like a stricken beast; there were screams of terror and cries of rage from men nearby. One at my elbow kept saying thickly 'Oh! God, Oh! God!'. It was the only prayer he could think of and yet another swore hysterically. Away up yonder, 80 feet from the pavement they said it was, the cluster of girls and men looked as though they were standing on the rim of a giant torch. We prayed that they would have patience; that they would not fling themselves headlong to the pavement rather than be consumed by the devouring flames which were now within a few yards of them. 'The firemen are getting sheets', someone shouted near the base of the building and we all cheered; yet how long it seemed before there were significant movements on the parapet. Suddenly a man shot earth-wards towards the extended sheet manned by firemen, police and volunteers. There was a dull 'whup' as his body struck the sheet and the crowd cheered and small boys put their fingers to their mouths and whistled shrilly. Hats and handkerchiefs were waved to encourage the girls and when one boldly took the plunge the cheering was intense.

Again, encouraging words and whistles, yet there was hesitation up there on the parapet. A girl whose blouse gleamed dully seemed to be in terror and she came whirling down. She seemed to turn three somersaults in the air, but another dull 'whup' indicated she had been well caught. She was a slight little thing, wearing her hair down, and in the course of her flight she damaged her back.

Four persons were rescued by means of 'jumping-sheets', one man fell away from the sheet, losing his life, and no less than nineteen people were brought to safety by means of hook-ladders and escapes. Brown personally assisted thirteen people from the fourth floor, and a further three from the parapet to safety via his hook-ladder onto the wheeled-escape below. It was during these rescues that people began to jump. To attain the roof from the fourth floor window sill, Brown managed to reach the hook of his ladder on to the top-floor cornice, but this could not provide any kind stability as the teeth of the hook could not effectively grip this stone moulding, which projected only some eighteen inches. Consequently Brown ascended the hook-ladder, a precarious and fear-provoking piece of equipment at the best of times, as it swung by its unsecured hook, and without the heel of the ladder being stabilised against the building. Reaching the head of the ladder, Brown climbed up and over the projecting cornice, an extremely difficult and dangerous manoeuvre, as the ladder would tend to swing in to the building. At this juncture, a sixty foot horse-drawn escape arrived, was pitched and a firefighter quickly ascended, and was able to steady the bottom-most round of the hook-ladder, as Brown held onto the hook, to allow the trapped persons to mount and climb down the ladder onto the escape.

On the arrival of this second escape ladder, a section of the crowd rushed forward to assist the firefighters in extending it, however they only succeeded in jamming the locking pins, which had to be dislodged by means of an axe. The *Newcastle Journal* continued its narrative:

> The last girl and a man were brought down by ladder, thanks to the heroism of a fireman named Brown. Whilst inmates of the burning building were jumping from side windows into blankets, Brown ascended the escape with a hook ladder. He entered an office window which resembled a furnace door and, amid the cheers of the crowds emerged shortly afterwards upon the parapet. The flames were about him when he ran along the parapet, hooked the ladder onto the edge and went in pursuit of the man and girl who had scrambled to the Westgate Road side of the building. He brought them back and was so successful in reassuring the girl that she bravely swung off the parapet onto the ladder and commenced to descend. From below a fireman on the escape grasped the bottom of the ladder, which had been swinging in the wind, and guided the girl and man to safety.

The delight of the crowd knew no bounds and rousing cheers were given the firemen who now devoted their energies to quelling the fire. Rescue work was carried out under superhuman conditions. With all possible speed the fire brigade commenced to get the fire escapes and the firemen, cheered frantically by the dense crowds, gradually got their ladders fixed up on the balcony. Here again their efforts were thwarted as the ladders burnt through and dropped to the ground.

Another eyewitness wrote to the newspaper: 'Never have I seen a fire attended with so many thrilling scenes, memorable in character and associated with the display of so much resource, daring and courage on the part of the firemen. Brown was an inspiration to his comrades in the rescue work. How he managed to 'stick-it' perched on the dizzy heights of the burning structure, in the face of a veritable furnace and at times enveloped in volumes of smoke, was a marvel and his bravery fairly roused the crowd's enthusiasm.'

As a consequence of the loss of life at this incident, and the resultant public criticism, the strength of the city of Newcastle Police Fire Brigade was doubled, and the Celluloid and Cinematograph Film Act was passed through Parliament to control how and where this extremely dangerous material was stored and used.

Brown's great courage and determination in pursuing this almost suicidal rescue attempt is a humbling, but shining example of all that is best in the firefighter. He was truly a Warrior in Fire Boots.

★ ★ ★

Three serious outbreaks of fire, one causing the deaths of two firefighters, took place in Glasgow on Saturday 2nd July 1921. The first occurred in the morning in Castle Street where damage estimated at £8,000 was done in the premises of the Glasgow Waste and Sponge Cloth Manufacturing Company. The second and most destructive broke out in the early evening in a large block of buildings at the east corner of Miller Street and Argyle Street, which, was completely gutted, and caused £200,000 worth of damage. The third, which was apparently due to a spark from the Argyle Street fire, took place in a block of buildings at 127 and 133 Trongate, where the premises and stock of several firms were involved to the extent of a loss of £12,000.

The corner block involved in that Saturday night's destruction was an ornate structure of four floors and a basement, measuring eighty feet by sixty feet, with the three top floors occupied by Messrs Wallace and Weir, mantle makers, clothiers and wholesale warehouse, and the street portion was occupied by Bowman's Economic Stores, drapers and house furnishers. It was in a section of these stores that the fire was first noticed, and the alarm was raised shortly before seven o'clock in the evening.

At that time Messrs Bowman's shop was still thronged with customers, who despite the panic which ensued were, fortunately, able to get clear of the premises before the situation became dangerous. Because of the inflammable materials stored on the various floors, the building was soon entirely involved in the outbreak. The flames had secured a firm hold and spread rapidly, and when the first fire crews arrived from the Central Brigade station it was apparent that further assistance would be required.

Reinforcements were summoned from the Central, South, East, West, Springburn, and North Divisions, all of whom arrived within a few minutes. In an incredibly brief time Argyle Street and the adjacent thoroughfares were filled with a network of hose lines, which poured great volumes of water on the flames, now burning brilliantly in the calm summer evening air.

Under the direction of Mr Gillan, the Deputy Chief Officer, who was in charge in the absence on holiday of Mr Waddell, the Firemaster, the firefighters made great efforts to prevent the fire from spreading to neighbouring blocks. Notwithstanding the enormous volume of water that was being used, the flames continued to eat their way upwards.

Several of the firefighters were engaged on the ground floors of the buildings fronting Miller Street when the interior collapsed, burying many of them in the wreckage. Three of the men were soon rescued by their comrades, and as it was seen that they had sustained injuries, St Andrew's Association ambulances were summoned, and they were conveyed to the Royal Infirmary. The injured men were Neil M'Donald of Western fire station, who was injured about the arms; David Beveridge of Partick fire station, who received slight leg injuries, and William Prentice from Central fire station, whose hands were badly cut. At the Infirmary they received medical attention, and were removed to their homes. Meanwhile it was discovered that Frederick True and James Farquharson, both of the Western fire station, were missing.

Their colleagues made every effort to rescue them, working desperately to get through the barrage of smoke and flame to search among the ruins, despite the constant risk of upper floors giving way and the intensity of the fire. When it was seen that there was no hope of getting the men out, the firefighters were visibly affected, but did not slacken in their work of extinguishing the fire. Throughout that evening there was still the sound of heavy crashing as floors gave way and tumbled downwards, carrying with them the clinging fragments of previous falls and causing the flagging fires on ground level to blaze up into momentary fierceness and to send up fresh clouds of smoke.

The large crowds which witnessed the fire in Argyle Street, were painfully aware that two of the firemen involved in the operations to extinguish the blaze had been buried by falling wreckage, and that hope of their rescue had been abandoned. By eleven o'clock the great block of buildings seemed entirely gutted. The masonry stood gaunt and stark in the darkening gloom, as the flames died down the searching jets of water reached them, and smoke belched through the windows. Still there seemed sufficient wreckage left to cause a resounding crash as it was released by water or by the burning away of its last support. The crowds of sightseers, drawn from all parts of the city by the glare to join the usual Saturday night throng in that busy thoroughfare, watched with fascinated interest the fireman's fight with the flames. However, their curiosity was a source of inconvenience, and it required the services of a large staff of policemen, who were present under the direction of Assistant Chief Constable Smith, to keep them at a safe distance and give the firefighters room to work.

The scene looking eastwards from a point near the burning block was striking as the gloaming deepened, with a great many members of the public waiting, anxious to learn whether there was any hope for the missing men. All through the long summer night the firefighters worked, removing the wreckage in the search for their comrades, and it was not till seven o'clock on Sunday morning that the bodies of the men were found. By the appearance of the corpses it was believed, at the time, that death must have been instantaneous when the heavy masses of wood and iron fell on them.

On the night of Saturday 24th December 1927 firefighters James Conn, David Jeffrey, Harry M'Kellar, and Morrison Dunbar of Glasgow Fire Brigade lost their lives while on duty at a fire in the east end of the city.

The scene of the fire was a six-storey warehouse in Graham Square, and owing to the threatening circumstances many tenants of adjoining dwellings were advised to evacuate. A poignant feature of the fire tragedy is that the men of the Eastern Division were enjoying Christmas festivities with their families in the Fire Station when the call was received which was to bring death to some of their colleagues.

The incident occurred in Graham Square, a cul-de-sac on the north side of Gallowgate, which led to an entrance to the Corporation Cattle Market. The east side of the square consisted of a modern tenement, and of a brick building of six storeys. This building, which was totally destroyed, along with corrugated iron sheds, and a warehouse at the rear, contained business premises, workshops, and a hotel. These premises included a firm of engineers, an auctioneers, wholesale grocers, seed merchants, and a firm of cabinetmakers.

The alarm was raised about 8.00 pm when two constables on duty in Graham Square observed that fire had broken out in part of the premises. Later examination revealed that the outbreak had originated in a hoist at 34 Graham Square, which was used by several of the firms in the block. The constables smashed the fire alarm and turned out several detachments of the Fire Brigade. By this time the fire was extending to other parts of the building. On the arrival of the first two detachments of the Fire Brigade from Central Station the great volumes of smoke pouring from the building indicated that the flames had taken a firm hold, and further reinforcements were summoned. Firemaster Waddell took charge of the operations.

Immediately, the fire was attacked both from the interior of the building and from the street. The intense heat, the density of the smoke, and the general threat to the structure, made it obvious at an early stage of the operations that it would have been highly dangerous for the fire crews to remain for long periods inside the building. Therefore, adopting what methods they could, the firemen continued the main attack on the fire from the roadway in Graham Square, from the roofs of buildings to the east and south of the premises involved, and from the top of the fire escape. It soon became apparent that the entire structure was in danger of collapse, and that any measures adopted by the Fire Brigade would be futile except to restrict the area of devastation. At this point the flames were being strongly fanned by a north easterly breeze, and pungent smoke hung in dense clouds over the streets bringing showers of sparks. Clouds of toxic smoke drifted towards the Gallowgate area, where large crowds of spectators had gathered, including local people who had been Christmas shopping when the fire occurred, many of whom were unable to reach their homes, and experienced grave anxiety as the flames darted ominously higher.

The tenement building which adjoined the ruined warehouses was considered at this time to be within the danger zone, and the tenants were advised to leave their homes. There were apparently nine families in the tenement, and the alarm was raised when most of the children had hung up their stockings and retired early to bed in eager expectation of Christmas morning. Some of the tenants elected to leave, and these assembled in the street to watch the fire crews battle with the flames, but others stayed in their homes during the entire course of the fire.

A thrill ran through the watching crowd when the roof of the burning building collapsed and sent up an awesome pyrotechnic display of flame and sparks, to be followed a few minutes later by the thunderous crash as large portions of the walls collapsed into the interior of the structure, causing dust and smoke to rise in great suffocating clouds. With this fresh development, the spread of the fire was checked, and within half an hour the outbreak was under control, and the occupiers of the tenement were allowed to return to their homes. About ten o'clock the fire was judged sufficiently under control that several detachments of the Fire Brigade were ordered to prepare to return to their stations. As the fire appliances were about to depart it was discovered that four firemen from the Central Division were missing. Exhaustive inquiries were made and a search at once begun, but it was feared that the men had been trapped in the building when the walls and flooring had collapsed. So far as can be ascertained, the four missing men, along with others, were on the third floor at the south end of the building when the flames were first attacked. At that time the fire was confined largely to the northern end of the building, and it is assumed that the crews working inside had courageously pressed on through the smoke some distance into the building to make a more effective attack on the seat of the fire. It is believed that as the firefighters moved deeper into the burning building, the north end of the structure, towards which the men had gone, had fallen inwards, bringing with it several floors in a downward rush of destruction. Several of the firefighters who were inside managed to get clear, and at that time it was thought that all had emerged safely.

When the first collapse occurred one of the fire officers had at once dashed into the building and up the stairways right to the top flat to warn the crews. He met one fireman who was under the impression that he was the last to leave. Fireman David Jeffrey had been last seen when he called for more hose, and it is one theory that, having collected an extra length of delivery hose, he and his colleagues had courageously penetrated towards the seat of the fire, unknown to their comrades, who were all at work at various points throughout the building. There seems no doubt that they were caught in the devastating fall of beams and brickwork, and buried in the immense heap of debris. It was believed that their deaths must have been practically instantaneous.

As portions of the remaining walls were in an extremely dangerous condition, it was recognised, reluctantly, that it would be unwise to risk the lives of other crew members in an immediate endeavour to extricate the missing men from among the still smoking wreckage during the darkness of the night. Several firefighters were posted on duty, and immediately daylight broke on Christmas morning a well equipped rescue party of firemen were dispatched to take up the tragic task of attempting to recover the bodies of their unfortunate comrades.

A preliminary search found that it was impossible to interfere to any great extent with the debris until the unstable and smoke-blackened walls which marked the site had been taken down. Throughout Christmas Day teams of firemen, working in relays, continued their tragic work, endeavouring to locate the bodies of their unfortunate comrades. They dug amongst the broken masonry with picks and shovels until darkness descended, but no trace of the bodies could then be found. Flare lamps were obtained in order that the work of the rescue might not be interrupted.

Portions of shafting and heavy machinery had become so intertwined when the floors collapsed that it was extremely difficult to separate and remove the twisted metal from the debris. A number of skilled operators armed with oxyacetylene burners were obtained from the Corporation Tramway Department, and many pieces of metal were cut through, and the task of removal was thus made marginally less difficult. As the broken masonry, charred timber, and twisted machinery were taken from the building, these were removed to the street by a large number of workmen. Throughout the night firefighters laboured heroically, but their efforts to reach the entombed men were still unsuccessful when daylight broke on Boxing Day.

Another crew of firefighters took up the search, and were engaged all day in removing the tons of debris which separated them from their now lifeless comrades. By the afternoon they had succeeded in penetrating to a considerable depth in the centre of the ruined building. For two and a half days the search was carried on without success until three of the bodies were eventually found close to each other. The bodies, which were badly mutilated, were identified principally by means of their clothing and various articles found in the pockets.

After a service had been held in St David's (Ramshorn) Church, the funeral procession passed along Ingram Street to proceed to the Necropolis with the coffins mounted on four fire engines, and as the first of these hearses slowly passed the fire station, in front of which a guard of uniformed firemen was posted, the fire alarm sounded. The ringing of the signal was heard by the large crowd of spectators, many of whom assumed it to be a pre-arranged part of the programme, something of a Fire Brigade equivalent for the sounding of the Last Post! The guard of firemen waited until the fourth of the coffin bearing carriages had passed them, but, with that concession to the proprieties of the occasion, they instantly rushed inside the building to man a couple of engines. The sliding doors of the station were pushed open, and the two motors, fully manned, emerged at speed, and driven through the thronged street, travelling in an opposite direction to that taken by the funeral procession. A considerable length of the extensive concourse had still to pass when the engines were driven out, and the carriages had to draw aside slightly to allow the fire appliances to pass. The public quickly realised that the ringing of the fire bell was a genuine alarm, and not a concerted tribute to fallen comrades.

THE SECOND WORLD WAR

'The whole fury and might of the enemy must be turned upon us.'
Winston Leonard Spencer Churchill

THE PRELUDE TO THE BLITZ

Operation Dynamo, the evacuation of more than 330,000 French and British troops from the coast of Northern France in May and June 1940, although the result of a devastating defeat is, without question, one of the most renowned events in British military history; and an inspirational example of what can be achieved by courage, indefatigable determination and organisational excellence.

Only eighteen days before the start of the evacuation the combined British and French armies had been viewed as being at least the equal of the Germans, with 125 British infantry battalions under General Gort's command, and the allies having a strong numerical advantage over the enemy in terms of artillery and armour. On 10th May the 'Phoney War' came to an abrupt end with a sudden German attack into Belgium and France, and saw His Majesty King George VI ask Mr Winston Churchill to form a coalition government. After only ten days German tanks of the Panzer Group von Kleist reached the Channel, and consequently the British Expeditionary Force and three French Armies were trapped around the channel ports.

The possibility of an evacuation from Calais, Boulogne and Dunkirk was first raised by the Commander-in-Chief of the British Expeditionary Force, General Lord Gort VC. As a result, Vice-Admiral Bertram Ramsey, the Flag Officer Commanding Dover, who was a very experienced Naval staff officer, was appointed to organise this great, and perhaps over-optimistic cross-channel exodus. A number of very serious problems faced Ramsey from the outset, principally the shallow waters around Dunkirk which precluded the use of destroyers and the fleet of passenger ferries he had at his disposal.

Deputy Chief Fire Officer William Tilley Elmslie Distinguished Service
Medal of Newcastle and Gateshead Combined Fire Service.
Courtesy of Tyne and Wear Fire and Rescue Service.

What Ramsey lacked was sufficient small boats of shallow draft to transport men from the beaches to the ships waiting offshore.

Captain W. G. Tennant, the Naval Officer appointed by Ramsey to take charge of the naval shore embarkation parties in Dunkirk, requested that a flotilla of small craft, not designed for war, be brought together from the rivers and coastal waters of England. They included river launches, lifeboats, yachts, pleasure steamers, fishing boats, working sailing barges, and the London fireboat Massey Shaw. This vessel, the pride of London Fire Brigade, was built by J. Samuel White of Cowes, Isle of Wight at a cost of £17,000, and was commissioned in July 1935. She was stationed at Blackfriars Pier, and attended her first major fire at Colonial Wharf, Wapping in September 1935.

On the morning of 28th May 1940 Captain Tennant asked for ships to be sent in to the mole at Dunkirk, which had been found to be a practical substitute for the harbour quays. A number of destroyers came alongside the mole and embarked large numbers of waiting troops, while others lifted men from the beaches. However, there were still not enough small craft to ferry soldiers from the shore, and not enough skilled personnel to control their handling in the swell, which led to the swamping of many boats in the hands of soldiers not experienced in nautical matters.

It was in these catastrophic circumstances that twenty-five year-old Able-Seaman William Tilley Elmslie of HM Minesweeper Dundalk was ordered to take a boat to the shore to bring some of the waiting soldiers on board. Elmslie, along with other members of the ship's company, set out with machine-gun fire peppering the sea, and bombs bursting around them, rocking the boat and enveloping them with spray. So violent did the sea become that at one point the boat overturned, and the other sailors swam back to the ship, believing the extremely hazardous and rapidly deteriorating situation to be nothing less than hopeless. But Elmslie, a small but physically very strong man of an indomitable disposition, somehow, and with great determination, righted the boat, and defying the bombers brought a number of soldiers back to the Dundalk alone. Mr Elmslie is reported to have said of the action that day:

'I glanced back at the beach and saw a German fighter streaking across the sands, his machine guns cutting through those columns of soldiers like a reaper slicing through corn. Our own guns were hammering away furiously. One dive-bomber came hurtling straight at us and we were convinced he was going to hit us, but at the last moment he swerved and went wide.'

For his fortitude and commitment in aiding the withdrawal from the beaches of Dunkirk, Bill Elmslie was awarded the Distinguished Service Medal, and was in 1942 mentioned-in-despatches for fighting a fire on board the ship on which he was serving. Mr Elmslie joined the National Fire Service in 1947, becoming a firefighter with Newcastle and Gateshead Joint Fire Service the following year, on the return of the Fire Service to local authority control, and was appointed Deputy Chief Fire Officer of his brigade in 1967. He was, without doubt, one of Tyneside's most respected and renowned fire officers, and remained a very hands-on, practical firefighter at heart throughout his most distinguished career.

With her once-gleaming brasswork camouflaged with grey paint, and a compass bought from a local ships' chandlers, the Massey Shaw under the command of Sub Officer A. J. May, cast off from Blackfriars ready for her first crossing of the English Channel on Friday 31st May to attend the biggest 'persons reported' call ever! As well as Sub Officer May the crew (both regular and auxiliary firefighters) consisted of H. Youngman, S. Inge, W. J. C. Brown, W. J. R. Gillard, C. G. Wilson, T. J. Gibbs, W. H. A. Ray, N. P. Morris, G. A. Briancourt, A. E. Beaumont, D. R. D. Gale, F. Low, R. J. W. Heyler, F. G. Codd, G. S. McGregor, E. G. Wright and R. Haybrook.

On the first night of her journey she berthed at Holehaven on Canvey Island, and the following morning set-off for Southend, where Commander Aylmer Firebrace, the Chief Fire Officer of London, met the boat to wish them God-speed. As she approached Ramsgate, Massey Shaw became part of a great armada whose gallant crews faced the prospect of many journeys, and multiple rescues amid dive-bombing and strafing by the Luftwaffe. An additional problem for all the little ships was that they were unable to understand, or respond to naval signals at night, and because of a lack of light the likelihood of being sunk by their own side was a very real possibility.

While still an hour out from Dunkirk her crew saw the first ominous signs of the carnage that lay ahead, with debris covering a thankfully calm sea, and the sky sinister with the billowing clouds of black smoke from huge oil fires. The noise of both the conflagration, and the enemy barrage became louder by the minute as they approached the besieged and battered town. At first sight the shore of Bray Dunes (a township in the Nord department of northern France, located on the Belgian border) seemed to have a number of broad break-waters extending far into the sea; they were in fact lines of troops waiting to be collected, some 15,000 of them. Under the direction of a Royal Navy officer the Massey Shaw, now under constant attack, was guided closer to the shore through a minefield. Once in position she dispatched a light skiff, capable of carrying perhaps half-a-dozen men, towards one column of waiting soldiers, and it very soon became submerged as the troops attempted to board. They were then persuaded to wade further out and were able, with difficulty, to reach the Massey Shaw, and were hauled aboard by the London firefighters.

The feasibility of bringing the fire boat further into the shore was discussed, but rejected as being likely to damage the vessel as the propellers would in all probability 'take ground' and render it useless. A stranded RAF speedboat was then located in shallow water and it was decided to try and make use of it. The Sub Lieutenant and one of the firefighters then swam ashore with one end of a rocket line, and once ashore they hauled a grass-line (a floating rope designed for such purposes) and made it fast to the speed-boat's stern, as the bow was facing the shore. The crew of the Massey Shaw began to haul on the line, and the speedboat slowly began to move into slightly deeper water. Unfortunately once the waiting troops saw what was happening, about fifty of them quickly jumped into the boat and others onto its cabin roof. As it was obvious to the firefighters that the speed boat would soon capsize, an attempt was made to secure the line to its bow; unfortunately this course of action failed, and was abandoned.

About eleven o'clock that night, another attempt was made to commence rescue efforts, and the Royal Navy officer together with two of the firefighters rowed ashore, in darkness through the sunken vehicles and other dangerous obstacles revealed by the tide. The grass line was made fast between the Massey Shaw and an abandoned lorry on the beach, and the boat used to ferry six men at a time from the shore along the line to the fire-boat. This brought a further forty men (of the Royal Engineers) on board. Once the fire-boat was fully loaded with casualties, she then made for England. However, sandbars just off the French coast meant that she, like all other rescue vessels, would have to travel along the coast for some distance to reach a channel into deeper water. The western route from Dunkirk to Kent was shortest, at thirty-nine nautical miles, but would bring vessels within range of the French gun emplacements at Calais, which had been captured intact by the Germans; a less hazardous route of fifty-five sea miles was eventually created by clearing an opening in the minefields. Some sixty-five evacuees on the fire-boat were delivered safely to Ramsgate by seven o'clock the following morning, despite the most determined efforts of a German bomber, which dropped a bomb that only just missed the craft.

Twelve hours later with changes to her crew, and a Lewis gun mounted on her deck the Massey Shaw again left for Dunkirk, only to find the situation even more critical. Her crew worked continuously for hours on end bringing men, many of them wounded, from the shore to a waiting troop ship. Major problems were encountered in transferring stretcher bound casualties from shore to the Massey Shaw, and again from the fire-float to a waiting paddle-steamer, as both vessels were very much at the mercy of the swell of water. When finally ordered to return home, she brought another forty troops out of the hell of Dunkirk to England, fortunately this time without the attention of the Luftwaffe.

Even though the little ships and the more fortunate members of the British Expeditionary Force were back in England, their problems were not at an end. Quite apart from the continued aerial attacks by the Luftwaffe, there were vast and serious logistical problems to be addressed. Once the exhausted and hungry troops had disembarked, many needed to be clothed, directed to feeding centres, and any medical needs attended to. An immense and complex network of rail transport was organised to move men from the coast to barracks, or ad-hoc camps which had been hastily set up to accommodate them. A great many of the ships involved in the rescue had to be made sea-worthy as quickly as possible by teams of hundreds of sea-going engineers brought to the Kent ports, mainly from London for this purpose.

The Massey Shaw made three crossings to Dunkirk, ferried 500 men from the beach to larger ships off-shore, and brought back a further 106 men to England. She also rescued from the oily, corpse-strewn waters crew members of the French auxiliary vessel Emil de Champ, which had struck a mine and sunk off North Foreland, on the Kent coast where the English Channel becomes the North Sea. The Massey Shaw received two quite singular honours in recognition of her service during Operation Dynamo, she was the only civilian crewed ship to be mentioned by Vice-Admiral Ramsey in his dispatches to the Lord Commissioners of the Admiralty, and Sub Officer Aubrey John May was awarded the Distinguished Service Medal; and crew members Henry Albert Wray and Edmond Gordon Wright, both Auxiliary Firemen, were awarded oak leaves to indicate their mention-in-dispatches.

The Massey Shaw which gave sterling service during the Blitz was retired from service in 1970, and has been restored by volunteers from the London Fire Brigade with the support of the National Lottery. A plaque on her bulkhead commemorates her part in the story of heroism in the face of overwhelming adversity that embodied the 'Dunkirk Spirit'.

The Summer 1980 edition of the *London Fireman* magazine carried the recollections of Station Officer R.W.J. Helyer who was a member of the crew of the Massey Shaw during the rescue mission to Dunkirk. I am grateful to the Commissioner of the London Fire Brigade for his permission to quote from that article.

> We knew that things were not good in France. Sub-Officer May called a
> group of us together and said, 'We're in trouble. The British Army is stranded
> on the beach not far from Dunkirk. Will you volunteer to go over there?'

> We agreed readily and scampered around getting the things we'd need. There
> was a bit of a delay while we got a certified river pilot because they wouldn't
> let the Massey Shaw out of the Thames without one, but we eventually got
> one, and shoved off at about four o'clock. We anchored for the night at Hole
> Haven, on the corner of Canvey Island, had a breakfast at the 'Lobster Smack'
> the following morning and then moved on to Ramsgate, arriving at about
> eleven. Our crew came from the LFB and the AFS and most of us on the
> Massey Shaw were stationed at Blackfriars.

> At Ramsgate we tried to get some metal sheeting for the engine covers, but as
> I recall we weren't successful. From this point we had a naval officer in charge
> of us, and flew the White Ensign. There were dozens and dozens of boats of all
> shapes and sizes moving out to cross the Channel, while Spitfires and ...
> Blenheims cruised around overhead. Left to my thoughts in the engine room I
> wondered what I had let myself in for. Many of the crew had been in the First
> World War, but I was the youngest ... at twenty-two. We had a look out of the

hatch occasionally and when Dunkirk appeared on the horizon there was
a thick pall of smoke going right across the seafront. We steamed in towards
Dunkirk and then turned along the coast towards De Panne. There were
bombers overhead, but I was down below and could only hear things rather
than see them, which was as much as I wanted at the time. When I did poke
my head out of the hatch I could see a French destroyer, completely burnt
out. It was a dead calm sea and there were wrecks everywhere. You could see
masts sticking up and out of the water from boats that had received direct hits
from enemy bombers.

We were unable to get right into the beach because of our propellers, but
smaller boats were picking up soldiers. There was a lot of machine-gunning
and bombing going on. Eventually we got some soldiers on board from one
of the other boats, and after a while we could hardly move. Coming up on
deck for fresh air you could see the troops on the beaches. The sky was thick
with aircraft while out to sea there were four or five destroyers lobbing some
stuff in land. At one stage we wanted to get a line to a launch with our rocket
system, but it fell short. I put on a life jacket, pulled in the rocket line and
swam ashore with it. The bombs and shells were coming down all the time
and it really was frightening. Anyway I swam to this RAF launch which was
crowded with soldiers. They said that they were stuck until the tide came in,
but somebody gave me a hand and we tied a bowline to the towing bollard on
the launch. Behind the craft was a naval officer who said we'd never be able to
tow the launch out with that crowd on her. I told them on the launch, but it
was useless, they wouldn't get off. Someone on board unhooked the line and
threw it off, so I had to swim back to the Massey Shaw.

We had about 70 soldiers on board and nearly all of them were drying off in
the engine room. A few sat on the upper deck where they could find room.
We were on the go all the time putting the engines into ahead, astern, stop,
ahead, etc. Eventually we got away at about three o'clock in the morning.
There was a red glow all over Dunkirk and the oil fuel tanks at the entrance
were well alight. We got back to Ramsgate without being machine-gunned.
We had some tea and digestive biscuits, but I remember we were still very
hungry and absolutely exhausted.

Speaking of a subsequent journey aboard the Massey Shaw during Operation
'Dynamo', Station Officer Helyer said:

When we moved out again we were warned about mines, which was
particularly worrying for us as we had no protection against magnetic mines.

We were nearly opposite Margate and I was in the engine room when I heard a tremendous crash. I nipped up the hatch to look and saw a plume of smoke not very far away. It was the Emile de Champs, a French auxiliary vessel, that had struck a mine. She sank within two minutes. She had something like 350 people on board and nearly all of them were lost. We picked up 30 survivors, all of them badly injured.

The first survivor we picked up saw the monitor on the Massey Shaw, thought we were the enemy and tried to swim away rather than be rescued. It was a real mess we felt so sorry for these poor devils. One man was split like a kipper, from his hip to his heel. We put them everywhere, all of them seriously injured, covered in blood and with broken legs and arms. To make matters worse just as we were about to move off we got a line round one of our screws and had to put one of the engines off the run. We signalled to HMS Albury, a minesweeper loaded with French troops, to ask if they could take the injured, but she replied that she had no doctors aboard. We were about to head back to Ramsgate with one engine when HMS Albury signalled again to say they'd found some French doctors on board, so we went alongside and transferred the injured before making our way back to Ramsgate.

As we came off the Massey Shaw we were told that someone was needed to make a broadcast to Canada. There were no volunteers so, being the youngest, I was chosen. Whether or not it was ever broadcast I don't know because, believe me, I was so tired all I wanted to do was sleep.

Over 200,000 men arrived in Dover in only nine days, and with enemy shells and bombs causing 3,059 alerts, killing 216 civilians, and damaging 10,056 premises, Dover became the front line of this new and not so phoney war; a symbol of Britain's wartime courage and tenacity, and the core of Kent's 'Hellfire Corner'. The Dover Patrol flotilla, anchored in Dover Harbour, provided an early target for German bombing raids, and on 27th July 1940, HMS Codrington, a Flotilla leader for A-Class Destroyers built on the river Tyne by Swan Hunters, was sunk at the Camber by Stukas, and the neighbouring vessel HMS Sandhurst, (F.92) an ex-merchant ship built by Harland and Wolf of Belfast, the supply and repair ship for the Dover patrol, was damaged. Codrington had been in the thick of action at the Dunkirk evacuations where in the course of eight trips she had brought back over 5,000 soldiers to the UK, including Major-General Bernard Law Montgomery, Commander of the British Expeditionary Force's 3rd Division, and was one of the few destroyers to have escaped major damage. From 3rd June Codrington was deployed at Dover carrying out patrols in the Channel, and covering the evacuations from the French Channel ports. On 12th June she was deployed as the base of the Senior Naval Officer (Afloat) during Operation Cycle, the troop evacuation from Le Havre.

The harbour was attacked again at 7.45 am on the 29th, by thirty Stukas protected by fifty Messerschmitts, and fires were started in ships and oil stores. One of the enemy's bombs fell alongside Codrington, and the subsequent explosion broke her back and she sank. Fortunately only three of her crew were wounded. The raids continued throughout the day. The Royal Air Force report of air activity for 29th July 1940 reported that:

> At 0718 hours, preceded by one sortie over Dover at 24,000 feet, four raids assembled in the Calais-Boulogne-St Omer area and at 0734 hours were consolidated as one raid of 80+ aircraft which flew from just east of Cap Gris Nez to attack Dover. Reports received indicate that the damage was comparatively light with few casualties. One merchant vessel (already damaged) and one small yacht were sunk and one naval unit was damaged. The actual number of bomber aircraft engaged in the attack is estimated at 40 Ju87s, and these approached in two waves of 20 aircraft each, covered by approximately the same number of Me109s. Four fighter squadrons were sent up and shot down eight Ju87s (confirmed) and seven Me109s (confirmed), and also five Ju87s and two Me109s (unconfirmed). AA accounted for two Ju87s. Our losses were two Spitfires and one Hurricane.

Incendiary bombs quickly started a fire on HMS Sandhurst, which was carrying torpedo warheads and munitions, and was moored alongside the Eastern Arm (the site of the present ferry terminal), and posed particular problems which were not helped by the onset of a further air attack and being surrounded by burning oil. However, the most serious problem was the breaking of nearby pipes from the oil depot on the cliffs, which caused a fire of such seriousness that it threatened to engulf the entire ship. Dover Borough firefighters aided by the Auxiliary Fire Service rushed to the scene and commenced firefighting operations. When the air raid warning sounded again, all firefighting crews were ordered to abandon ship, and the fire began to spread rapidly, turning the deck plates white-hot, and threatening to involve the torpedoes, ammunition and fuel on board. With a massive explosion likely at any moment, a number of the firefighters volunteered to remain on board and continue fighting the fire despite the on-going air raid, and with great fortitude and courage they succeeded in bringing it under control after a long and extremely hazardous twelve hour struggle. Executive Chief Officer E. H. Harmer, Second Officer Brown and Section Officer Campbell, together with other firefighters, volunteered to return to the blazing ship and, despite the continuing air attack succeeded in subduing the fires, after a means of access was cut into the ship using oxyacetylene equipment. HMS Sandhurst was, amazingly, still seaworthy and sailed to the Thames a few days later for repairs, partly manned by the Dover firefighters who continuously pumped water from her hull.

George Medallists Ernest Herbert Harmer, Cyril William Arthur Brown, and
Alexander Edmund Campbell after their investiture at Buckingham Palace.
Courtesy of Mike Harmer.

Chief Fire Officer Harmer of Blackpool County Borough Fire Brigade.
Courtesy of Mike Harmer.

The George Medal was awarded to Ernest Herbert Harmer, Cyril William Arthur Brown, and Alexander Edmund Campbell and six firefighters: Station officer Harold Thomas Hookings, Fireman Ernest Alfred Foord, and Fireman Edward Jesse Gore of the Dover Fire Brigade, and Auxiliary Firemen Arthur Thomas Cunnington, Lionel Rupert Hudsmith, and John McDermott received the King's Commendation for Brave Conduct. The citation, on page 5768 of the Supplement to the *London Gazette* of 30th September 1940, reads:

'In a recent large scale attack by enemy bombers on Dover Harbour, fires were started in ships and oil stores. Air raids continued throughout the day. During the attacks all members of the Dover Fire Brigade and Auxiliary Fire Service engaged at the fires did excellent work in difficult and dangerous circumstances, and the fires were eventually extinguished. The individuals named above volunteered to return to a blazing ship containing explosives, in which they fought the fires while enemy aircraft were still in the neighbourhood'.

The minutes of the meeting of Dover Council of 29th October 1940 made reference to the award of three George Medals at one incident thus:

A letter was submitted from the Secretary of State, Home Office, Fire Brigade Division, stating that His Majesty the King had been graciously pleased to award the George Medal to Executive Chief Officer E. H. Harmer, Second Officer C. W. A. Brown, both of Dover Fire Brigade. And Section Officer A. E. Campbell, of the Dover Auxiliary Fire Service in recognition of their gallantry on the occasion of a fire, caused by enemy action, in Dover Harbour, and in vessels lying there in July, last. In a recent large scale attack by enemy bombers in Dover Harbour fires were started on ships and oil stores. Air raids continued throughout the day. During the attacks all members of the Fire Brigade and the A.F.S. engaged at the fires did excellent work in difficult and dangerous circumstances and fires were extinguished. The individuals named above volunteered to return to a blazing ship containing explosives, in which they fought fires while enemy aircraft were still in the neighbourhood'.

Tug Master Frederick John Hopgood was also awarded the George Medal for his bravery that day. During the air attack on HMS Sandhurst, Hopgood's Tug was one of a number of vessels moored alongside a jetty. When the bombing ceased Hopgood went onboard a craft lying alongside to assist in tending a wounded man. By this time the three vessels which lay abreast alongside the jetty, were in imminent danger of taking fire from burning oil. The outermost of the three vessels could not be moved under her own steam, her engines being disabled, and Hopgood, aided by his engineer and members of his own crew and those of other craft, managed after considerable difficulty to tow all three vessels clear of the danger area. His display of courage and seamanship at a time of danger and confusion, were instrumental in saving the three vessels which would most probably have been lost.

On the day that HMS Sandhurst was attacked, twenty-seven year-old Mr Benjamin Abbott who was employed by Mears Bros, a construction company, was working in Dover harbour. Mr Abbott's son has penned the following taken from his father's recollections of that day:

> Saturday 27th of July, 1940 was the end of the working week. It should have been easy. It was a lovely day, and dad would have left our home in the village of Shepherdswell which was about nine miles north-west of Dover about seven am to begin work by eight. But this was no ordinary day. In a very short time Dad fell into the human equivalent of a wasps nest. A Royal Navy supply ship, HMS Sandhurst, had been attacked and hit in the English Channel, and had managed to reach the shelter of Dover's eastern docks, where she came under further continuous attack. The Germans must have thought that they had hit the jack-pot, for here tied up close to the submarine pens was not only a supply ship loaded with a cargo of oil, shells, torpedoes and other ammunition, but also the destroyer HMS Codrington, and a number of motor-torpedo boats, and other small craft nearby.
>
> According to Dad there was an all out, and very heavy attack in which the Codrington sustained a broken back and was sunk; whilst the Sandhurst was hit several times, but remained afloat. The determination with which the Germans concentrated their attack on HMS Sandhurst, suggested that they must have realised what they were on to.
>
> The Naval authorities, aware of the catastrophe that occurred when an ammunition ship blew up in harbour in Nova Scotia, Canada, destroying half the town and killing thousands, immediately called for help to remove the ammunition. What was required with the utmost urgency were civilians who were not only prepared to put their lives on the line by helping off-load the ammunition, and so potentially save many lives, but who could also drive a dump-truck fully laden with ammunition along the Admiralty Pier, and off-load at the nearby storage caves.
>
> No-one would go near the ship until my father jumped onto the only dumper truck big enough to do the job. He was immediately ordered to get off the truck by his foreman, and to leave company property alone, or face the sack. Dad needless to say ignored the order and drove out along the breakwater's Eastern Arm to where the burning Sandhurst was anchored. There, with the help of a mate called Mr Harle, and members of the

Sandhurst's crew, he succeeded in unloading all the ammunition, making a great many perilous trips and off-loading the ammunition in caves at the foot of the East Cliff.

If you think that driving a load of potentially high explosive ammunition is dangerous in itself, you'd be right. But when Dad did it there was a heavy and sustained air attack going on, and he was driving his hazardous load along a narrow pier through great palls of thick black, choking smoke caused by the fracture of oil pipes which were discharging into the sea. The pipes carrying oil being pumped from the Sandhurst had been hit and fractured by bullets, and the oil had leaked over the pier wall into the sea reaching several small boats. Incendiaries had set these craft alight and the blaze had quickly spread to the Sandhurst. All of this was going on in a relatively confined area on the top of a stone pier awash with water and oil, as the local fire brigade struggled to bring the fires under control.

A great many people felt that dad should have received one of the George Medals that were awarded, indeed there was some petitioning of the authorities on his behalf. But I don't think dad was too bothered. He was though awarded the King's Commendation for Brave Conduct, and we as a family are very proud indeed of his courage and dedication.

George Medals were also awarded to Chief Fire Officer Edward Parsons Twyman and Fireman Frederick Walter Watson Margate Fire Brigade.

At the height of the Battle of Britain, serious fires were caused when a series of bombing and machine-gun attacks took place at the airfield at RAF Manston near to the Kent coast. Both the regular Fire Brigade and the Auxiliary Fire Service were mobilised to this location, and worked under the most dangerous of conditions, saving much valuable equipment, and extinguishing the fires before night fall. Two firefighters were detailed to enter a burning building at the airfield wearing breathing apparatus, and Chief Officer Twyman led another team (not so equipped) by crawling into the structure under the descending smoke layer and formed a 'chain' whereby material was passed out and the whole of the stock saved from the fire. On another occasion oil stores were set alight and the only available water supply was an underground tank which was situated within five feet of where a delayed action bomb had fallen. It is said that Chief Officer Twyman spoke to Fireman Watson asking, 'Well Fred, there's an unexploded bomb five feet away. What are you going to do?'

Watson replied stoically, 'If you're sticking it Chief, so am I.' So this source of water was utilized, and for five hours Fireman Fred Watson, although fully recognising the danger carried out his duties as pump operator standing close to the bomb, which later exploded leaving a tremendous crater, whilst the fire was tackled.

During the firefighting operations a further air raid took place, and a high explosive bomb exploded within twenty feet of where the firefighters had taken cover. Despite being shocked the firefighters resumed their work and continued with it during a later machine-gun attack. Chief Officer Twyman showed great qualities of leadership, setting a fine example to his firefighters who had fulfilled their important and dangerous task in a most professional manner. Fireman Watson by his courage and devotion to duty enabled the only water supply to be utilised, and later commented:

'I had my duty to do, and never had time to think about the bomb; but I did laugh when a RAF chap placed a piece of wood over the hole (crater), probably, I suppose, to stop me falling down it!'

The outstanding acts of courage which earned Fireman Jack Owens, Leading Fireman Clifford Turner, and Messrs George Howe, George Sewell, and William Sigsworth the award of the George Medal, took place in the aftermath of an air raid on the Salt End Oil installation, Hedon, near Kingston upon Hull on 1st July 1940.

Enemy action had seriously damaged several petrol tanks, and an extremely serious fire situation was ensuing, which if allowed to spread would have destroyed enormous quantities of spirit that were invaluable to the war effort. Mr George Howe, Manager of Shell-Mex and B.P. Ltd., displayed outstanding leadership and organisation in directing the firefighting operations, and was conspicuously brave in entering a tank compound which contained burning spirit to open the valves so that stock could be transferred, so taking fuel from the fire. He was ably and gallantly assisted by Mr William Sigsworth, Manager of the Anglo-American Oil Company Ltd., who also entered the compound and was untiring in his efforts to extinguish the flames. Mr George Sewell, the Shell-Mex Maintenance Engineer, led a party of men into the tank compound, and was continually on the tank roof whilst the gas inside was burning, and endeavoured to extinguish the flames by 'playing' a foam jet over the tank top and placing sand bags over the roof curve.

At this major incident Fireman Jack Owens volunteered to work a foam jet from the top of an almost red-hot tank, as this was one of the few places that the foam could be usefully applied. He could only reach this dangerous vantage point after wading through petrol and water to a depth of four feet. His clothing was thus soaked with petrol and water, and so might have been ignited at any moment causing his inevitable death. Leading Fireman Clifford Turner of the Kingston upon Hull AFS carried out a similar courageous set of actions in assisting Mr Howe in fixing a hose on a tank top surrounded by flames.

Jack Owens was presented with the George Medal by His Majesty King George VI on 27th May 1941 at Buckingham Palace, and went on to join the Royal Navy on 8th December 1942. Jack was posted missing believed dead on 22nd May 1944, and is buried in the public cemetery, Houlgate, Calvedos, Normandy. Mr George Sewell was awarded a Bar to his George Medal for his actions during another air raid on the Salt End Oil installation on the night of 8–9th May 1941. On this same night another George medal was won in Kingston-upon-Hull by Auxiliary Fireman John Coletta, who volunteered to position himself with a jet in a narrow back street to the rear of the Wilberforce Museum, when this very old building had been set on fire as a result of enemy action, and a collapse of said building was almost inevitable. Coletta stayed at his post until the fire had been extinguished.

The above were not, of course, the only gallantry awards received by firefighters in this part of the UK; during the following twelve months of air raids the British Empire Medal for gallantry was awarded to the following firefighters and fire watchers in east Yorkshire for their courage and commitment to duty:

Firefighters Arthur Bucknall, Tom Davison and George Edward Blades were engaged in fighting an oil fire, and although enemy aircraft were using this fire as a target indicator for their bombing runs, they worked continuously to subdue the flames, and prevent further spread. During operations one of the tanks ruptured and torrents of blazing oil ran down the nearby streets and affected many houses, in one of which a woman and her five children were trapped. Without hesitation or any consideration for themselves, and regardless of the obvious and very serious danger, the three firefighters rushed into the house, and although the heat was almost unbearable, succeeded in removing the woman and children to a place of safety.

During a particular air raid high explosive bombs demolished a number of houses in Grimsby and consequently people were trapped in the ruins of their homes. Cries could be heard coming from one house and Fireman Edward William Sanderson of Grimsby Auxiliary Fire Service climbed on top of the debris and began removing bricks until the bedroom ceiling was reached. This was lifted and Sanderson lowered himself into the space and brought out two casualties, he then started tunnelling through the highly unstable wreckage where he remained for three hours despite the likelihood of the structure collapsing at any moment. Sanderson was eventually able to locate and rescue a further three casualties.

John Henry Slater and James Snitch, members of a Works Fire Service, in Kingston-upon-Hull, were on duty during an air raid when bombs were dropped on the works causing a number of serious fires, and inflicting damage to the water mains. In order to make use of an emergency water supply it was necessary to open a valve which was under a building which had partially collapsed, and was burning fiercely. Snitch attempted to reach the valve but was compelled to withdraw because of dense smoke and falling debris. Mr Slater, the officer in charge, joined him and after clearing away a quantity of rubble, both firefighters succeeded despite the intense heat and smoke in reaching and opening the valve, thus providing a plentiful supply of water for firefighting operations. Also in Hull a number of incendiaries were dropped on a building, and one lodged on the roof immediately above a tank of varnish. In order to deal with the bomb Edward Saunders, a Fire Watcher, stood on the tank and, using an axe, made his way through to the roof, and on reaching the bomb knocked it to the ground outside. Saunders acted with great presence of mind and by his prompt and brave action prevented a serious fire. On or about the same night Mr Henry Lamb, a Firewatcher at the Ministry of Labour, Hull, was on duty when a neighbouring building was burnt out and a hall used for the women's department of the employment exchange caught fire. He helped the AFS personnel to operate a hose on the interior of the hall and at great personal risk subsequently entered the premises and extinguished the fire. His brave action most certainly saved the exchange building from destruction.

Between August 1940, and January 1942, almost 4,000 people were killed and 3,500 seriously injured in the Merseyside area as the result of German air raids. Liverpool was the most important provincial port in Britain during the Second World War, and it was a vital route for military equipment and supplies to the country, and so, in recognition of this, the Headquarters of the Royal Navy Western Approaches Command was transferred from Plymouth to Merseyside in February 1941.

The Liverpool docks were also home to important munitions factories, and Royal Navy 'U-boat hunters' were stationed at Bootle. As heavy bombing had immobilised London's port facilities, the Mersey became even more important to the war effort. The first German bombs landed on Merseyside on 9th August 1940 at Prenton, Birkenhead. In the following sixteen months, German bombs killed 2,716 people in Liverpool, 442 people in Birkenhead, 409 people in Bootle and 332 people in Wallasey. The worst periods of bombing were the 'Christmas Raids' of December 1940, and the 'May Blitz' of 1941. It was against this background that Section Leader Robert Francis Carson of Liverpool Auxiliary Fire Service, and Sergeant Harold Alexander Wright of Liverpool Police Fire Brigade were awarded the George Medal for their gallantry at two separate incidents.

Following an enemy attack at 0041 hours on 18th August, 1940 when four high explosive bombs caused considerable damage to the areas of Yeoward's Coburg Shed, East Brunswick Avenue railway siding, and to Queen's Road No 1 Graving Dock, East Brunswick Granary Liverpool, fire broke out in the skeleton framework of a pneumatic elevator in the latter industrial area. It was impossible to place a wheeled escape against the elevator on account of the debris which had fallen from the badly damaged roof. The outbreak of fire took place high up in the framework and it was clear that the fire could not be tackled by hand held jets at ground level. The only solution was that some-one should make the dangerous climb up the elevator girder work. Torn steel sheets, broken timbers and displaced iron work projected at many places, and slates and debris were still falling, but without hesitation Section Leader Robert Francis Carson placed a line of hose and a branch over his shoulder and successfully made the climb. Holding onto the branch and directing the jet of water despite being precariously perched high above the ground, and fighting the jet reaction of the hose, he extinguished the fire in about ten minutes. On another occasion when the area covered by his Division was attacked by succeeding waves of enemy aircraft causing a great many fires, Section Officer Carson, in the face of the intense heat, mounted a stairway onto the blazing upper floor of a shed which contained goods of a hazardous nature, and by his courageous firefighting actions he prevented the spread of this fire. He then went to where buildings on both sides of the dock yard were blazing furiously. Regardless of the dangers involved he made his way through the narrow entrance and so made possible the use of suction hose to draw water from the dock to supply the firefighting pumping appliances.

For these outstanding acts of bravery, coolness and disregard of personal safety whilst laying out lines of hose, and so saving much valuable property whilst under enemy attack, which contributed greatly to the morale of his colleagues, Section Officer Carson was awarded the George Medal.

On 31st August 1940 the Customs House, Canning Place, Central Liverpool was struck by high explosive and incendiary bombs causing structural damage and a very serious fire resulted. Enemy aircraft soon retuned, dropping more high explosive bombs all round the scene of the incident and spraying the building with machine gun fire, including the area where the firefighters were working. Sergeant Harold Alexander Wright of the Liverpool Police Fire Brigade was given command of a fire crew working on the roof of the building, and in spite of the very dangerous circumstances of the ongoing air attack, his crew, encouraged by his example and resource, remained on the roof. They were successful in limiting the fire, which at one time appeared likely to involve the whole of the Customs House, to a section of the top floor of the building. Sergeant Wright carried out his duties in charge of a squad of firefighters in a manner which displayed his complete disregard of his own personal safety. He and his men were operating on the flat roof of the building, and the example and leadership shown by him were an inspiration to all. For his gallantry and leadership at this incident Sergeant Wright was awarded the George Medal.

During 1940 and 1941 a great many awards of the British Empire Medal were made to firefighters in Liverpool, and indeed throughout the north-west of England, the following paragraphs present an outline of some of those gallant stories, many of which, regrettably, I have been unable to put a date to, but they non-the-less deserve to be included in this tribute.

In the early part of 1941 Sergeant Arthur Diamond Boyd a member of the Liverpool Fire Brigade for twenty-one years, had already been involved in several serious incidents during the heavy bombing raids that were visited upon the city, and was in charge of a crew of firefighters at a serious fire caused by enemy action. During firefighting operations he climbed to the apex of a tall adjoining roof to obtain a better view of the fire, and so make a more thorough assessment of the situation, and from here he calmly directed operations. In spite of his precarious position, and the very obvious danger of the naptha tanks which were in the immediate vicinity exploding, Boyd remained on the roof until the fire had been brought under control, and the building and its contents saved. On two other occasions Boyd by his courage and promptitude was responsible for preventing serious fires during ongoing enemy air attacks.

A serious fire due to enemy action had broken out in storehouses in Liverpool, and in spite of the fact that continuous dust explosions were taking place, and that the fire appeared to have a hold of the building that was impossible to subdue, Sergeant Alfred William Humble of the Liverpool Fire Brigade courageously and with a great sense of command took control of a serious and rapidly deteriorating situation, and by prodigious efforts prevented the fire from travelling across a gantry, thereby saving the adjoining building. During the operations there was an ever present danger of explosion from time delayed bombs which had landed nearby, and had it not been for the gallant action of Sergeant Humble, and his great initiative and leadership, the fire might well have been far more serious than it eventually was.

During an air raid, firefighter Charles Bigland of Salford Fire Brigade was sent to a gas works where an incendiary bomb had penetrated the top of a gasometer, causing a great tongue of flame which acted as a beacon to enemy aircraft. Bigland fearlessly climbed the steel ladder sixty or so feet to the top of a nearby gas holder carrying a line of hose, and once in position lay flat on his stomach directing the powerful jet of water onto the flames, remaining in that position until he had succeeded in subduing the fire. Gas works employees then sealed the hold with a steel plate and clay.

Acting Sergeant Thomas Callaghan of Wigan Borough Fire Brigade displayed great courage and resource when fighting fires caused by enemy action, when a fire spread to a dynamo room at a particular incident, and the on-site engineers were unable to switch off the electrical current. Callaghan was fully aware of the possibility of being subjected to a fatal electrical shock, but insisted on taking over the hose and extinguished the fire. He showed great qualities of leadership, and while he took risks himself, he was constantly mindful for the safety of the firefighters around him.

Auxiliary Fireman Arthur Stoakes of Manchester AFS acted as a motorcycle messenger over four days of air attacks with only three hours rest. During this period, amongst other duties, he carried messages when the telephone system failed, and extinguished a number of incendiary bombs. He distributed petrol by means of a rope sling, carrying one container of fuel on his chest and one on his back, being fully aware of the possible, if not probable, dangers of ignition in an ongoing air raid. His actions in delivering this petrol kept units working until other means of transport were available. Stoakes' conduct at all times was courageous and efficient.

During an air raid over Liverpool Mr Ernest Sidney Leatham, a Ministry of Health Fire Watcher, was taking shelter with some colleagues in a basement when the building above was hit by high explosive bombs and set alight. Leatham managed to release himself from the debris, and went for help. Finding a fire crew, he brought them to the now blazing ruins, and assisted and directed their operations, so that the trapped men would not be drowned by the water from the fire hose. Constable William Hunter of Liverpool City Police who was also on the scene, dug away through the debris and located one of the men pinned down by beams. Despite the limited space the Constable removed rubble, sawed through the timber, and released the casualty. While Hunter was working Mr Leatham began burrowing through the debris to the other victim, but was unable, owing to heavy obstruction, to reach him unaided. Whilst waiting for help Leatham salvaged valuable documents, and at intervals crawled down the tunnel to the trapped man to re-assure him. He was eventually released after seven hours. Hunter and Leatham worked in considerable danger from both the fire which was raging overhead, and from falling masonry.

Auxiliary firemen Alexander Conway and Edward Hayes received the British Empire Medal for releasing five women and a child from a wrecked house, after it and surrounding buildings had been demolished by a high explosive bomb. Conway and Hayes clambered into the wreckage, and whilst one firefighter supported a collapsed floor on his back, the other used a saw to cut away timber to make a way through the compacted debris and masonry. Conway crawled through this highly unstable and dangerous passageway, and having located casualties was instrumental in rescuing five women, and a child. One of the women, who was embedded up to her neck in debris, was sitting in an arm chair and was hysterical. Conway and Heyes had to cut their way through a floor that had been turned on end, to reach the unfortunate woman, and Conway carefully removed sufficient debris from the women to enable him to cut away the arms of the chair and so release her. These operations were hampered throughout by the escape of gas from a fractured main, dust clouds and the constant shifting of the wreckage caused by the presence of enemy aircraft overhead who inflicted substantial damage to a neighbouring street with high explosive bombs.

Later in the summer of that year a high explosive bomb dropped in the yard of the Oil and Grease Company's premises in Norfolk Street, Toxteth, Liverpool, causing a large number of drums of grease, and a vat of tar to break open with the force of the explosion and take fire. Within the space of a minute a serious fire situation had developed with a wave of blazing tar and grease flowing down the street, and into alley ways, capped by a wall of flame which threatened to spread to the high adjoining warehouses.

Patrol Officer Alister McWilliam Ross of the Liverpool Auxiliary Fire Service responded to this call as officer in charge of pumping appliance, and on arrival was faced with an urgent and extremely hazardous incident. Ross immediately ordered sand to be put down to dam the flow of the burning tar.

Above the noise of the fire and the ongoing bombing, loud screams were heard coming from a school next to the burning premises, and Ross, taking a heavy axe and covered by a protective screen of water from one of the hose lines, worked his way up the street through the burning river in an action thought suicidal by his comrades to the school door; knowing full well that a loss of water to the cooling jet, and one slip on his part would inevitably mean a dreadful and painful death. Breaking open the door he found two women, who were by this time hysterical as they clearly saw the burning river of tar flowing insidiously past their door, and Ross had forcibly to haul them from the building, through the flames to relative safety, where again his own life was put in great peril by the struggling, panic-stricken women This accomplished, he returned to the school to search for any further casualties, and having assured himself that all persons were accounted for rejoined his crew and resumed firefighting operations. For his gallant and decisive actions Patrol Officer Alister McWilliam Ross was awarded the George Medal.

THE OIL TANK FIRES AT LLANREATH.

The first major firefighting incident of the war was one that would test the strategic integrity, and the organisational responsiveness of the Fire Service almost to breaking point. It was not the anticipated armada of bombers delivering Guernica-style air attacks, but a relatively small raid on the Admiralty Oil Depot, Llanreath. The Air Ministry report for 19th August 1940 stated:

'At 1345 hours, a Ju88 was intercepted and destroyed near Taunton; at 1500 hours, 1 Ju88 was destroyed near Southampton and at 1715 hours, 1 Ju88 was destroyed near the Isle of Wight. Oil tanks at Llanreath (Pembroke); aerodromes at Harwell, Little Rissington and Shrivenham, and targets near Oxford, Swindon, Wroughton and Burley were attacked'.

At 3.15 pm on Monday 19th August, a twin-engined Junkers 88 bomber escorted by two fighter aircraft mounted an almost leisurely attack on the Admiralty Oil installation at Pembroke dock, without any interference from anti-aircraft fire, starting fires that burned for almost three weeks. The bomber was seen to dive and drop a 'stick' of bombs. So began an incident which would stretch to the limit all those concerned.

The construction of this storage facility, of seventeen tanks, each one hundred or so feet in diameter, had been commenced in 1925, and with the alarming prospect of a second war with Germany looming, someone with great presence of mind ordered a moat 1,500 feet long, 400 feet wide, and forty feet deep to be dug as a bund to hold the serious spillage which would, inevitably, occur should the installation be attacked and the tanks ruptured.

The normal peacetime fire brigades in this vicinity were at that time small organisations comprised mainly of part-time members, and were, as the hope of peace haemorrhaged away for the second time in a quarter of a century, reinforced by the newly formed Auxiliary Fire Service in order to deal with wartime fires. Arrangements had also been made through emergency defence legislation for fire brigades to assist each other, and this is what happened immediately at Pembroke dock when the extent of the fire, and its potential loss were assessed. Further appliances were sent from other areas of Wales including the relatively large fire brigades of Cardiff and Swansea.

Throughout the first full day of operations the firefighters of South Wales worked with great courage and determination to hold back this most awesome fire, and prevent its spread. These crews were frightened, dirty, overwhelmed, hungry, and in the furnace-like heat of the fire-ground, exhausted and constantly parched. Within twenty-four hours of the attack three tanks were on fire, three others were in imminent danger of becoming involved, and the bund was gradually filling with burning oil. The smoke plume stretched 1,000 feet into the sky, and was some 400 or so feet across, which caused severe problems for the oncoming fire appliances as in certain locations visibility was nil, and the constant roar of the burning tanks prevented appliance drivers from hearing other traffic approaching. As the fires spread to more tanks, despite the determined efforts of the firefighters in attendance, it became necessary to call for further assistance from the nearest available resources outside of Wales. The surrounding regions (the country having been compartmentalised into administrative regions each headed by a government-appointed Commissioner) were eventually to send crews and appliances from the Bristol and Cheltenham areas, and the city of Birmingham was able to contribute a contingent 100 firefighters-strong from its well established professional fire brigade. One of the Birmingham contingent, firefighter Bob Knight, volunteered for what was to be an exceptional feat of bravery, scaling a ladder placed against a burning oil tank in conditions of appalling danger to plug a hole from which scalding oil was gushing, which would have become huge tongues of flame had the fire reached it.

For the firefighters on the ground it was a long hard slog fraught with great danger as fresh tanks succumbed to the shrivelling heat and collapsed, spilling their contents to add to the conflagration. Nevertheless cooling jets were brought to bear from the extremely hazardous locations of bund walls and the tops of surrounding tanks by intrepid firefighters. This was, though, merely a prelude to the main battle, as foam-making branch pipes needed to be brought into operation to quell the fires within the tanks, and smother the fires running loose on the surface. Those directing foam jets into the blazing tanks often found their task rendered more difficult by the alignment of the steel roof plates, distorted by heat into cylindrical form and effectively shielding the blazing surface from the foam streams.

When the Regional Commissioner for Wales had been appraised of the enormity of the situation, the need for many hundreds of firefighters, and the fire's probable consequences on the war effort, he sought the advice of the Home Office on who to appoint to command this potentially catastrophic major incident. It was decided to assign the Deputy Chief Inspector of Fire Brigades at the Home Office, Mr Tom Breaks, who was a former Chief Fire Officer of Sheffield, and whose firefighting experience was second to none. As a result of his outstanding service on the Western Front during the First World War dealing with a number of very serious fires started by enemy artillery in fuel installations and supply dumps, the French government awarded him the coveted Croix de Guerre. However, on his arrival from London even he was astounded at the magnitude of this incident, and whilst making an initial assessment of the situation, a German aircraft swept low over the site firing its machine guns at the crews, which must have focused his mind on the perils of the job in hand!

Breaks continued the tactics instituted by Mr Arthur Morris, the first Chief in command at the commencement of the incident, by keeping the burning tanks isolated with powerful water curtains. Although the oil installation was near to the shore-line, and there were two large tanks filled with water, maintaining the large and constant supply of water which was necessary for cooling the unaffected tanks was a major problem, especially when the tide went out. There were also problems with the use of fire boats as some were unable to make the journey because of gale force winds, whilst others in attendance had a draught too deep to allow prolonged operation. These challenges were, however, as nothing compared to the disastrous events of the evening of the fourth day. Breaks, whilst touring the fire ground, was approaching a group of five firefighters who were cooling a burning tank, when a great tongue of flame erupted from the tank without warning, and enveloped the men. The five who died that day were: Frederick George Davis, Clifford Miles, John Kilby, Trevor Charles Morgan and John Frederick Thomas, all from Cardiff. The *Fire* magazine of October 1940 reported the inquest on the firefighters who had been killed as follows:

> Amongst those engaged in fighting a fire in an oil installation ... were five of a contingent of AFS from Cardiff. Near them was Mr Tom Breaks ... a Home Office Inspector of fire brigades, engaged in making a report on the outbreak. Suddenly Mr Breaks saw a sheet of flame leap from one of the oil tanks. He was the last person to see the quintet alive. All perished by flame, and perhaps suffocation.

> At the inquest Mr Breaks said that he was present at the fire for the purpose of making a report on it for the Ministry of Home Security. Fire extinction was proceeding more or less satisfactorily. At about 1315 he was on a mound between two oil tanks, and about 20 feet in advance of him were five AFS

men, wearing oil-skin clothing, with a branch at work on one of the tanks. Atmospheric temperature was very high, although there was a wind almost approaching gale force.

[Mr Breaks said in evidence] 'Suddenly a huge burst of flame seemed to leap from one of the tanks, and to envelope the five men. I shouted to them 'Run for it' and hearing their shouts in response, I started to run to a safer spot. I felt the heat of the sheet of flame, but I was able to get away because I have become accustomed to that sort of thing, and also I had a start of about 20 feet compared with these five men. The last I saw of them was when they were running away from the flames. The rupture or bursting of the tank was entirely unsuspected and it was now assumed that intense heat reduced the metal of the tank to the molten stage, and the oil, under terrific pressure, burst outwards in a sheet of flame. There was, however, no undue risk in firemen working so close to the tank, and while I have no desire to evade any responsibility, the men had been placed there by one of their officers, and they may have been visited by that officer several times while at work'.

Later Mr Breaks stated that with fires of that type there were always contingencies of extreme danger to firefighting personnel, and it was never known when such a contingency might present itself. The Coroner said it was evident that such an accident could occur unexpectedly and inexplicably. The nation owed a debt of gratitude to 'the five brave men'. Mr A. J. Wilson, director of the Cardiff Fire Brigade, speaking on behalf of the Cardiff Corporation, said that the five men had nobly served the nation, and had met death while performing duties of equal value to those performed in front line trenches. Mr Wilson added:

'The risks undertaken by firemen are immense and, in my view the courage with which firemen perform their duties is not fully appreciated by the general public. All I can do is express the sympathy of the Cardiff corporation with all those bereft and to thank the people of this town for the great kindness they have shown to the Cardiff firemen'.'

The next day most of the Welsh firefighters, who were by now weary after days of firefighting, were relieved by crews from Bristol and Birmingham, who would have been able to see the malevolent throb of the tank fires from many miles distant as they travelled through the night. One can only imagine their trepidation. On their arrival the air was thick with the products of combustion, three tanks were alight and a further two had collapsed. Local people saw firefighters from towns that were many miles from them, proceeding to Pembroke docks on gleaming appliances, dressed smartly in their fire kit and having a look that reflected both their very understandable sense of trepidation and their enthusiasm to tackle a great fire. They also saw firefighters returning from Pembroke Dock with their blackened, scorched faces drawn and pinched, their heads bowed with fatigue, eyes reflecting the terrors they had endured, their clothing soaked in oil looking like a collection of rags, as they staggered along almost shell-shocked, some being helped by comrades; whilst others with bandages over their damaged and unseeing eyes, looked for all the world like the line of gas-blinded 'Tommys' on the Western Front, in John Singer Sargent's famous and emotive painting, come to life.

One of the strongest contributions was given by Cardiff Fire Brigade, whose contingent included many professional and very experienced firefighters, which was most certainly a munificent gesture, as most brigades would have kept their most skilled men in readiness for an enemy attack on their own area of responsibility.

Throughout that week a total of 650 firefighters from twenty-two fire brigades were engaged in firefighting operations, using fifty-three pumping appliances, and nine miles of hose. Apart from the five who were killed, thirty-eight firefighters were admitted to hospital with serious injuries, 241 'minor' cases, mainly involving eye injuries, and 241 admitted with burns.

No less than thirteen George Medals were awarded to firefighters for their efforts at this major fire. The recipients were:

> Robert John Knight, Birmingham AFS
> William Victor Philpott, Bristol Fire Brigade
> Ernest Smith, Bristol Fire Brigade
> Bertram Charles Ernest Arkell, Bristol Fire Brigade
> Walter Bryant, Bristol Fire Brigade
> Albert Victor Thomas, Bristol Fire Brigade
> Maurice Charles Day, Bristol AFS
> Frederick Charles Revelle, Bristol AFS
> Lewis Jack Watts, Bristol AFS
> Daniel James Collins, Cardiff Fire Brigade
> William Brown, Cardiff AFS
> Norman Groom, Cardiff AFS
> Mathew Acornley, Milford Haven Fire Brigade

The British Empire Medal was awarded to Maurice Sadler Bristol of AFS, and Alfred Richard Bridgely Hart of Newport AFS.

Mr Breaks was later awarded an OBE for his services at the incident. A handful of other firefighters were awarded the King's Commendation for Brave Conduct including Chief Fire Officer Arthur Morris of Pembroke Fire Brigade, who had assumed command of this major incident prior to the arrival of Breaks, and whose preliminary measures were largely responsible for the fire being contained within the precincts of the plant. The omission of Chief Officer Morris from the medal list caused a great deal of consternation, as many felt that Morris, a very well respected and courageous officer who had remained at or near to the incident for seventeen days, was deserving of higher recognition.

Chief Officer Arthur Morris, a man of dignity and integrity, would never comment on the question of awards for this fire, and died in 1970 having earned much more than a medal, for he had the approbation and esteem of his brother firefighters, and indeed the people of Pembroke.

SUPERINTENDENT THOMAS BRUCE OF SUNDERLAND FIRE BRIGADE

The George Medal was awarded to Superintendent Thomas Bruce of Sunderland Fire Brigade in recognition of his gallant conduct when a German bomber crashed in Suffolk Street, in the Hendon area of the town destroying a shop and dwellings on the night of 5–6th September 1940.

This is perhaps the best-known and well remembered air raid on Sunderland as the aircraft, a Heinkel He 111, was brought down relatively close to the centre of the town. The aircraft, flying from Soesteberg in Holland, crossed the coast of Sunderland at 11.15 pm, and was immediately caught in the crossed cones of the anti-aircraft search-light beams, facilitating a quick response from the gunners. Accounts by eyewitnesses described a shell from the town's 'ack-ack' bursting near to the Heinkel's tail, causing dense smoke to issue from the aircraft prior to its crash in Suffolk Street, seriously damaging the dwelling of John and Rachel Stormont and their fifteen year-old daughter Jean, who were sheltering from the air raid.

On receipt of the call to this incident fire control dispatched Superintendent Bruce along with two tenders, additional foam and foam making equipment, and three auxiliary pumping appliances. Tom Bruce, an experienced and well respected fire officer, was confronted with a scene of total devastation. A shop and house had been destroyed by the impact of the aeroplane, two dwellings were well alight, and the Stormont family were trapped in their now blazing air raid shelter, which was covered in debris from both the Heinkel and the damaged buildings. The official account of his actions stated:

> When an enemy bomber aeroplane crashed, destroying a shop and dwelling houses, and badly destroying other properties, petrol and oil from the bomber were scattered over a wide area, setting fire to the buildings. Three persons were also trapped in a wrecked surface air-raid shelter which was covered in debris from the demolished houses. The shelter itself was on fire, and rescue operations were greatly hampered by the flames and heat given off by the

burning petrol. In addition, concentrations of petrol vapour were exploding continuously. Superintendent Bruce at once called for volunteers to assist himself and Fire Sergeant Robert Patterson in attempting the rescue of the persons trapped in the shelter. Chief Inspector Middlemist, Detectives Cook [later Assistant Chief Constable of Durham Constabulary] and Buddles, and PC Simpson all immediately volunteered and rendered valuable assistance in removing heavy concrete slabs and other debris from the shelter. Superintendent Bruce led the operations to dig under the debris, during which his clothing was badly burned. Their efforts resulting in the rescue of three people from the wreckage. During the rescue operations it was found necessary to play a jet of water on the feet of the trapped persons and the officers engaged in the work, as their clothing was being burnt by blazing petrol. The officers concerned displayed exceptional courage and showed disregard of the possibility that further bombs may have been in the fallen plane and might have exploded at any time during the operations.

On the completion of this arduous and courageous rescue John Stormont was brought out injured, his daughter Jean had sustained leg injuries and later had both hands amputated, and Mrs Rachel Stormont was found to be dead. All of the Luftwaffe aircrew were killed, and were afforded a military funeral by the personnel of nearby Royal Air Force Usworth (now the site of the Nissan motor-car plant).

On 1st April 1948 Thomas Bruce GM was appointed the first Chief Fire Officer of the Borough of Sunderland, after having become a fireman in 1925, then serving as the Superintendent of the Borough Police Fire Brigade from 1939 to 1941, and as Assistant Fire Force Commander for No. 1 Region of the National Fire Service. He was awarded the King's Police & Fire Service Medal in 1952 for his outstanding service, and took up an appointment in Egypt in 1955 as Deputy Chief Fire Officer of Ismalia, where, during the Suez Crisis of 1956, he was imprisoned for fifty two days.

THE THAMESHAVEN OIL FIRES.

On 5th September 1940 serious fires were caused by enemy action on oil depots, wharves and factories in Purfleet and Thameshaven on the north bank of the Thames estuary, which led to a long, drawn-out and extremely serious situation for the Fire Service and war effort.

Because of the extensive and calamitous fire situation caused by this air raid London Fire Brigade was asked to supply fifty pumping appliances to support the efforts of the local firefighters. The officer-in-charge of this column of fire appliances was instructed that, in accordance with the Fire Brigades' Act 1938, he was not under any circumstances to assume control of this incident; but was to place himself and his crews at the disposal of the local senior fire officer.

As the line of LFB appliances snaked through the night-time blackness of the Essex countryside, the crews would have been only too aware of the hazardous nature of their mission as they heard the drone of the Luftwaffe overhead, and saw the intimidating, pulsating glare of the oil tank fires in the distance. As they arrived at what must have seemed like Armageddon, five large tanks were well alight and roaring their anger, with seven others in imminent danger of becoming involved. This was an extremely serious and major incident, which would very obviously require the total, immediate and protracted commitment of all fifty of London's fire crews. It was then something of a surprise when the officer-in-charge of the column was informed by the fire-ground commander that the situation could be managed without the use of London's contingent, and directed that all but five of the LFB pumps be returned. Needless to say the fire was far from being under control, and to exacerbate this critical and life-threatening incident to absurd and surreal proportions, the local chief informed the London officer that, as he was a part-time firefighter and had a business to open in the morning, he was now going home! As there was no local representative to take command, the London officer went to a telephone box and called the London Fire Brigade control, appraised them of the gravity of this farcical situation, and asked for his pumps to be returned. He was again advised in unequivocal terms that he had no authority to order appliances to an incident outside the LCC area, and must find the senior local fireman and take orders from him. However, he was informed that Lieutenant-Commander John Fordham, one of London Fire Brigade's most experienced principal officers was to be dispatched to Thameshaven.

On his arrival the somewhat irascible Fordham found that the situation was even worse than he had envisaged, with a further tank now alight. He therefore contacted London Fire Brigade and demanded the immediate attendance of fifty pumps and three fire-boats; only to be told that even he could not assume command or request assistance. He was, however, informed that the Regional Commissioner for Essex and East Anglia, Sir Will Spens, was being contacted, and that he would designate someone to assume control of the incident; incautiously adding that Sir Will's staff were disinclined to awaken him at such a late hour! Fordham, renowned as a direct and no-nonsense officer, advised them in coruscating terms that if nothing were done to provide the firefighting resources necessary, he would have no compunction in telephoning the Home Secretary. Sir Will Spens was a sixty-two year-old administrator and theological academic who had worked with some distinction in the Foreign Office during the First World War, and was the highly respected Master of Corpus Christi College, Cambridge. However, he was no adept of crisis management or strategic firefighting. Neither, it has to be said, was the young man from Cambridge Borough Surveyor's Department who was delegated to take charge of this extensive oil fire.

On the arrival of Sir Will's man, Lieutenant-Commander Fordham advised him in strong terms that he must, without delay, order on fifty pumps and three fire-boats, delegate operational command to him, and then take a back seat. The reinforcements were soon dispatched, and the arduous and extremely dangerous work of fighting the fires was at last underway, with firefighters often having to wade chest deep through hot oil, to bring their foam jets within range of the fires. As the incident developed, firefighters were mobilized from brigades throughout the south of England.

Later during this protracted and major incident, following a further enemy engagement on 8th September, a number of petroleum storage tanks at the Pufleet Oil Depot took fire and blazed furiously. When one of the tanks exploded in the form of a boil-over, Patrol Officer Arthur Leslie Swansborough of Southend-on-Sea Fire Brigade immediately gave orders for the firefighters to abandon their equipment and run. One unfortunate firefighter, in scrambling over oil pipes, fell into a large hole containing oil and water and, owing to the slippery nature of the sides of the crater, it was impossible for him to get out unaided. Swansborough, despite the extreme danger of further explosions and fire spread, immediately turned back and rescued the man from the crater which a few seconds later became a mass of flames from the burning petrol; the heat from which was so great that both men received burns on the neck and hands. Patrol Officer Swansborough's courageous action undoubtedly saved the life of that firefighter, and he was awarded the George Medal.

During a serious fire resulting from an enemy air attack (believed to be the above incident) the valve of a tank holding 6,000 tons of benzene was alight at its lower extremity and burning fiercely. To attempt to extinguish this blaze it was necessary to employ an extremely dangerous tactic, and upon calling for volunteers, some members of the Ilford and Chelmsford Auxiliary Fire Service immediately came forward. A thirty-foot extension ladder was pitched against the side of one of the tanks, and Patrol Officer George Ralph Holliday Payne of Ilford, and Sub-Officer Joseph Henry Warren of Chelmsford made the precarious climb to the top of the tank. Once there they removed the cover of an inspection hatch, releasing dangerous and highly flammable gases, and inserted a swan-neck branch to enable water to be poured into the tank without a firefighter having to remain at the manhole. Once this was accomplished, Leading Fireman Frederick George Keen, also of Chelmsford AFS, mounted the ladder, and on reaching the inspection hatch commenced packing wet sacking around the manhole to prevent fumes from escaping. When a second swan-neck branch was inserted it was found that gases were again escaping, and Leading Fireman Keen again ascended the ladder and packed yet more wet sacking around hatch. At the time of these operations the tank was in a very dangerous condition, leaning over to one side, and in the likely event of the contents overflowing, they would have poured down the side of the tank on to the burning valve, thus igniting the whole tank and gravely endangering the lives of those dealing with the fire. All three firefighters were awarded the British Empire Medal for their courage in tackling this fire.

Leading Fireman Charles Walter Saitch and Patrol Officer Cecil Hearn with other members of Brentwood AFS were in an area where pipelines were alight, with petrol ankle deep, and the flames spreading rapidly, and it became necessary to drive a piece of wood into a larger shrapnel hole in a tank from which petrol was pouring. To achieve this, Saitch mounted a ladder to reach the hole, but was saturated with petrol. Patrol Officer Hearn went to his assistance with a second piece of wood and supported Saitch while he drove it home with an axe. The remainder of the crew fought the fire to prevent it reaching their comrades and by their united efforts saved this and several other tanks. Both men were awarded the British Empire Medal.

Twenty-six year-old Auxiliary Elizabeth Anne Emery of Station 7 Carmelite Street, EC 4, was driver to one the London Fire Brigade Superintendents, and in that capacity attended a great many serious fires, very often being subject to great danger. Her professional behaviour was noted as follows:

'Her conduct throughout has been remarkable for her unchanging composure and coolness in all circumstances, and the entire absence of any fear, even during heavy bombing attacks. She has invariably carried all duties assigned to her without the slightest hesitation, and in addition to her driving she has many times during severe raids acted as a runner to her Superintendent, and conveyed important messages'.

During the raids on Thameshaven on 6–7th September, Auxiliary Emery showed a brave and highly developed sense of duty: when bombs were being dropped near to oil tanks and all personnel were heavily engaged in firefighting operations, she proved her initiative and readiness to help by taking portable fire extinguishers from the appliances, and climbing over fences and rough ground proceeded to deal with small incendiaries which had fallen near to oil tanks in an adjoining compound. She carried out this work undaunted by the high explosive bombs which dropped during this time in the area. Her actions most probably prevented one or more unaffected tanks from becoming involved. For the next five nights Auxiliary Emery was on duty, sometimes for as much as fourteen hours at a stretch, and throughout the autumn of 1940 she attended a great many major fires. In supporting a recommendation for the award of the George Medal her senior officer wrote:

'I have noted this driver on numerous raid occurrences and have been struck by her very cool and courageous bearing. Particularly at times when heavy explosive bombs have been dropped in the vicinity. When at fires she has not been content to perform her driving duties only, but has set herself out to be of utility in whatever capacity possible to her Superintendent. On several occasions she has performed messenger service between Mr Welch and myself, and has carried out work in a very competent manner. I strongly recommend that her service be recognised'. Auxiliary Elizabeth Anne Emery was awarded the British Empire Medal to acknowledge her outstanding service.

On 9th September during operations at Purfleet Oil Depot, it became necessary to stop a serious leak of oil from a hole that had appeared in the top of a tank which had been on fire. The flames had been extinguished but the oil pouring out of the tank was very likely to catch fire again. Fireman Henry Bernard Neale of Leicestershire Auxiliary Fire Service was a member of a support column sent to this major incident. Enlisting the aid of two firefighters from another unit, he secured a thirty-foot extension ladder and a wooden plank. He then climbed the iron ladder which was secured to the side of the tank and with help hauled the extension ladder to the top. Neale was joined by a Senior Officer and the Depot Engineer, and with the ladder now fully extended he was dropped over the other side of the tank, where he opened a lid on the top of the tank to ascertain the depth of oil, which was found to be roughly eight feet from the top. The senior officer then descended the ladder and with some difficulty plugged the hole in the tank with soft wood. This whole of this operation from start to finish was an extremely hazardous undertaking. Apart from fires in the vicinity and the likelihood of certain gases being given off in the tank, one slip on the top would, without doubt, have proved fatal.

Neale also played a major part in saving another tank which had been holed about four feet above the base, from which burning oil was pouring. The crews played two very powerful jets at the leak, driving the flames away, and two further jets were brought into action to divert the flow of oil at the base of the structure, creating a passage between the tank and the fire. Neale and another firefighter bridged the gap between the tank and the bank with a ladder, and proceeded to plug the hole with wood. While this operation was in progress, two more jets were directed above the heads of the two men, creating both a protective water curtain and providing some degree of cooling to the tank. If at any time the two cross jets had failed to beat back the burning oil, both men would most certainly have been seriously injured by the flames, possibly fatally so.

Also on that terrible night at the Purfleet oil depot, Auxiliary Fireman Cyril Alfred Reeves entered a retort house (a structure erected for the processing of shale, to extract oil through heating) where petrol was flooded on the floor, when a flash-over occurred, igniting the petrol vapour. Another auxiliary fireman became entangled in a chain and was in imminent danger of being burnt to death. Reeves, despite the extreme heat and the very obvious prospect of becoming fatally trapped by the surrounding flames, displayed outstanding bravery in remaining to assist in the release of his comrade. For their gallantry and devotion to duty during these difficult and extremely hazardous operations Henry Bernard Neale and Cyril Alfred Reeves were awarded the George Medal.

The British Empire Medal for gallantry was also awarded to forty-eight year-old District Officer John Richard Unwin (although the recommendation was for an award of the George Medal), for his work at the Thameshaven incident and other major fires.

Unwin, a fire officer of some twenty-eight years service worked at the London Fire Brigade Headquarters on Albert Embankment, and was regularly dispatched to attend various major incidents to provide specialist advice especially where there were particular difficulties with rescue work or in the use of firefighting equipment. He carried out this technical work with conspicuous gallantry and a complete disregard of danger and fatigue. In his supporting statement for an award to District Officer Unwin, Superintendent W. E. Norwood stated:

'DO Unwin is recommended for gallantry on carrying out routine work of an exceptionally hazardous nature, often under bombing and blackout conditions. His devotion to duty has been mainly responsible for the saving of lives, and appliances endangered by as a result of enemy action. Incidents worthy of special note included salvaging of Home Office and LFB appliances bogged at the Thameshaven oil fire, removal of about 40 appliances in dangerous positions owing to spread of fire caused by further bombing (Surrey Commercial Dock), releasing people trapped under vehicles during black-out, and 5 AFS men pinned under vehicles, adjacent to a bomb crater with a gas main alight'.

One of the critical elements of the firefighting operation at this oil storage facility, and indeed at all such incidents, was the protection of those tanks not on fire with large cooling jets. At Pufleet in the early part of December 1940, one such tank sprang a leak, allowing a large quantity of oil to escape, which formed a pool of oil and water around the tank about eighteen inches deep. Another tank which was blazing furiously burst near the top and poured out blazing oil. The only way to check this rush of fire was to turn a drencher branch-pipe into the blazing pool, and consequently the officer in charge gave orders for a this piece of equipment to be got to work. Section Officer Sydney Arthur Wright of Southend-on-Sea Auxiliary Fire Service immediately dashed forward to get a branch free from the holder to which it was securely tied, and turn it into the pond forming around the tank, and so drove the fire back. Although the fire was raging within two feet of him, he was not deterred from persisting in his efforts. If this had not been successfully carried out, some five additional oil tanks, of a capacity of some 20,000 tons of oil, would have become involved. In carrying out these duties he displayed conspicuous bravery and leadership which inspired the greatest confidence in all the officers and men present. His actions at more than one point definitely prevented the fires from involving other premises and he handled the various serious situations excellently throughout a very long and strenuous time. Section Officer Wright was consequently awarded the George Medal.

THE FIRST DAY OF
LONDON'S BLITZ

In the Summer 1986 edition of *London Firefighter* magazine, Mr G. A. Haselup spoke of his recollections of 7th September 1940.

> I was a Sub Officer stationed at 48E district in Peckham. I recall that sunny Saturday afternoon, 7th September 1940, when at approximately 4 pm the air raid siren sounded to herald the beginning of the Blitz upon London which lasted nearly two months. As dusk fell and turned into night so the skies became illuminated like an evening sunset, by the fires started by enemy action. The main target of attack was concentrated within the London dock areas where thousands of incendiary bombs fell, causing fires which soon became conflagrations, requiring the attendance of ten and twenty pumps. The whole of the Brigade's resources were mobilised and reinforcements were ordered in from other brigades.

> Warehouses and wharfs throughout each dock area contained tons of various types of merchandise which burned fiercely. Crews firefighting within these areas were some times surrounded by fires. Others faced walls of flame such as the situation at Rum Quay within the London dock where thousands of gallons of spirit were stored. This area was completely destroyed by fire. Buildings within Woolwich Arsenal containing unknown stores of war material gave grave problems to our crew. The great timber fire at Surrey Commercial docks resulted in great stocks of resinous timber from all parts of the world being completely destroyed by fire. Some crews had to swim to the opposite quay to save their lives. There were gas works, power stations and the

Thames Haven oil storage plant in which London crews were praised for their efforts; each of these situations presented many difficulties to the firefighting crews. The courage of the officers and men was remarkable, each man not knowing what unforeseen dangers they faced such as the collapse of the building in which they were engaged or becoming trapped under masonry or being caught within the blast of an HE bomb which could mean death or injury. Casualties among personnel increased. It was within the early stages of the blitz that our fire-ground in Peckham received its baptism of fire. A heavy fall of incendiaries caused numerous fires, one of which was at a paper warehouse on the bank of the Surrey Canal.

During the course of firefighting a high explosive bomb fell into the building killing Hutton and his crew, whose bodies were never recovered.
The trailer pump was blown into the adjacent canal. The towing vehicle was blown some distance away, finishing up on the roof of a private house. This incident was followed by another tragedy when thirteen firemen attached to our 'Z' sub-station in Grove Lane, Camberwell, lost their lives due to the station being damaged by enemy action. Local crews, including mine, took part in the rescue operation.

Another memorable night was Sunday 29th December, 1940, the raid that almost destroyed the City of London. It commenced at 6.00pm and within one hour six sections of the city, Moorgate and Aldersgate Street were destroyed by fire. Two fire stations situated within this area had to be evacuated, the stations being numbers 33 Redcross Street and 35 Canon Street. Great damage was done to historical buildings. Every crew engaged fought hard to overcome the situation, but we were handicapped due to the shortage of water. The river service was unable to give full support in relaying water to the area because the Thames was at low tide, and fire boats had to moor in mid-stream. The 'all-clear' was sounded at 10 pm after four hours of constant raiding. According to the records kept, fires within the City and central London during the night of 29th December, 1940 totalled 1,500 and 2,000 appliances were used to tackle the whole situation. Despite the intensity of the raids all fires were reported under control by 4.30 am on 30th December.

It was on 13th June, 1944 that the pattern of aerial warfare changed. The flying bomb replaced the German bomber force. The first of these weapons launched against London fell within the Bethnal Green area of East London. Our work changed and the personnel were seconded to the rescue services.

The scenes that all crews faced upon arrival at each incident were mainly of widespread disruption within the residential areas of London. Rows of dwellings, sometimes a block of flats, were laid flat with victims trapped beneath masonry and other forms of debris from which cries for help could be heard. Great care had to be observed during rescue operations in avoiding further falls of debris which could hinder the progress of rescue. There were also many unpleasant scenes, witnessed by each of our crew, of civilians who were caught within the blast of a bomb and were laying in roadways, etc., some dead, others badly injured and awaiting attention.

Records state that from 13th June, 1944 until 18th March, 1945 a total of 2,380 flying bombs landed within the south east districts of London. I am proud to have served with officers and men whose courage never failed in peace and war in facing the dangers and hazards met while firefighting.

Saturday 7th September 1940 saw the direction of Reich Marshal Goering's strategy change, from attacking the Royal Air Force, to destroying London and her people.

The Blitz apparently began by accident, as Goering had given specific orders to his crews to avoid civilian targets, but on 24th August 1940, German bombers apparently searching for the oil tank farms at Purfleet and Thameshaven had drifted off target and attacked the centre of London instead of their intended targets. Angered by this attack on London's civil population, and believing the raid had been intentional, Winston Churchill ordered bombing raids to be carried out on Berlin for the next three nights. The Germans, especially Hitler, were incensed, since they had arrogantly believed that Berlin could not be reached. Demanding revenge, Hitler ordered Goering to turn his attentions on London and other major British cities. There followed fifty-seven continuous nights of bombing by the Luftwaffe.

This first attack took place in the middle of an afternoon of sunshine and blue skies, and outwardly the social ambience of the capital was redolent of the late summer peacefulness of other happier, less violent times; although in the minds of many there were misgivings. In the previous week enemy raids had approached close to the capital; but up to that hour very few would have predicted the scale of the horror and pandemonium that were soon to be visited on London.

The wail of air raid sirens heralded a portentous overture to the first attack which began at 1635 hours. It came in two waves, totalling some 348 Luftwaffe bombers escorted by over 600 fighter aircraft in a formation twenty miles wide, and forty miles long which spread over Kent, making for the Thames Estuary, East London and the aerodromes situated to the north and south of the capital. By 1814 hours all enemy raiders were homing on their target areas. During engagements the Hurricanes and Spitfires of Royal Air Force Fighter Command destroyed seventy-four enemy aircraft (plus thirty-four 'probables' and thirty-three damaged), taking casualties amounting to twenty seven aircraft and fourteen pilots killed or missing. Soon incendiary devices and high explosive bombs, many of them strapped to oil drums to aid the potential conflagration, were raining down on the docks, and commercial and residential areas of East and South London, and the result was an inferno in the docks that blazed from end to end for a whole week. An enormous plume of black smoke obscured the sun, and brought the darkness of night to what should have been a bright and lazy late summer's day for the people of London.

At Greenwich a gasometer was hit and fortunately did not explode but produced a magnificent and colossal blue flame that lasted but seconds, whilst at Purfleet the oil storage tanks were ablaze with their contents pouring out fearsome rivers of fire, and great billows of lurid black smoke. With bombs now falling from the second wave of aircraft, fire crews throughout London were responding to an overwhelming crisis situation. For some 80% of the AFS volunteers this was to be their first experience of real firefighting. The oft-voiced phrase 'A Baptism of Fire' can never have been more appropriately used. So severe was the situation in the area covered by West Ham Fire Brigade that its control room requested the London Regional Fire Control based at Lambeth Headquarters to mobilise a further 500 pumps!

In the London Fire Brigade's area the Acting Chief Fire Officer, Major F.W. Jackson, had his own pressing and overwhelming problems and was compelled to deploy a further 500 pumping appliances between St. Katherine's and the West India Docks, and commit an additional 200 pumps to the Surrey Docks, Rotherhithe.

The Surrey Commercial Docks on the south bank of the Thames had a river frontage of one and a half miles, and extended a mile or so inland towards Bermondsey, where it was surrounded by Rotherhithe Street and Redriff Road. Along these dock basins, or under cover of open-sided sheds stood one and half million tons of timber, which soon became overwhelmed by the incendiary attacks. Deck cargoes on the vessels in the basins, wood chippings around the wood stacks, and even the wood and tar road blocks were blazing furiously. Such was the maelstrom in this area that many fire crews found themselves cut off by the flames, and like those on South Wharf were eventually taken off by a fire-float which nosed its way into the dock; some even had to escape by jumping from one barge to another.

Pageant's Wharf fire station operated as a focal point for the desperate firefighting operations in Surrey Commercial Docks throughout the raids, even though it had been hit and set on fire. Members of the Women's AFS stayed on duty throughout this holocaust, and tendered to the injuries of those firefighters brought in suffering from burns and blindness brought on by the sparks and smoke. As the night wore on, so many injured firefighters needed help that other stations had to act as first-aid posts.

Incendiary bombs had started fires not only in the stacks of timber piled high at Surrey Docks, but in the cargoes of ships waiting to be unloaded. The blaze spread throughout the 250 acres with great rapidity, jumping from stack to stack as the wood resin liquefied and reached its ignition temperature. Scorching wind currents created by the severity of the fire drew embers up into the night sky to be deposited on other combustible material, to start new fires for the now desperately over-stretched firefighters to deal with. The author has, in conversation with Londoners who can recall that terrible night, been told that the atmosphere in the Bermondsey area was heavy not just from the black choking smoke, but with the smell of burning spices, tea, rubber, and other commodities from the blazing warehouses. Amongst the most vivid recollections were the spaghetti-like lines of delivery hose, heat crumpled dock-side cranes, the incessant roar of the fires, and what seemed to be the whole of the sky illuminated blood-red with the flames.

So seriously did the newly formed Churchill Government view this concerted and intensive air attack on the capital that the code word 'Cromwell' (indicating either invasion imminent or invasion begun, depending on interpretation) was signalled to all Home Forces. One can only imagine the great sense of dismay and dreadful foreboding in all who received the code word, as the concept of the 'bomber always getting through', had instilled in the wider populace a sense of fatalism, and a fear of the ultimate weapons of that era, which was exacerbated by the (then) recent overwhelming and brutal successes of the German forces in France and Low countries. Indeed, it must surely have been more especially felt by those who could remember at first hand the slaughter of an earlier war with Germany, little more than two decades before.

The incessant raids of the following week cost the lives of 2,000 Londoners, and more than 10,000 were either injured or entombed in the wreckage of bomb damaged buildings.

The air raid warning which sounded over the South Wharf area of Rotherhithe, South London that 7th September, was followed by considerable enemy air activity, with heavy concentrations of high explosive and incendiary bombs falling, which consequently caused serious fires in a number of industrial buildings, including wax-paper mills, and sparks from this inferno were carried to the nearby nurses' home setting it alight. A number of staff worked in a courageous and concerted attempt to subdue the fires and prevent its almost inevitable spread, until the water supply failed. By this time even more incendiaries had been dropped in the area of the wharf and as a result the pier was alight in several places, as were a number of barges and barge moorings. Consequently fires were blazing inside the wharf, and all around. The fire brigade had meanwhile begun operations to remove residents from the hospital to a boat moored near to a pontoon, and had, eventually, to order all staff to evacuate the premises because the worsening fire situation. All female members of staff, with the exception of Sister Hope, ran down the now-burning 264 foot-long pier, to the boat alongside the pontoon. Most unfortunately, an incendiary bomb fell onto the pier, causing its collapse before Sister Hope was able to join her colleagues. At this point the staff and casualties were taken from the now blazing pontoon by a skiff commanded by Senior Fireman Barrett across the river to Millwall, where local people, despite their own extreme difficulties and fearful concerns, gave them shelter, and much-needed cups of tea (truly the spirit of the Blitz), before they were moved to a public air raid shelter.

Sister Hope, now stranded on the pier, took shelter in the hospital with another member of staff, Stoker Hobbs, until they were rescued by two firefighters, Sub Officer Timothy Muir and Auxiliary Firemen Samuel Melvin, who, despite the terrible inferno raging all around them, and being fully aware that their chances of surviving a further rescue attempt were not great, made a re-entry to the hospital and brought Sister Hope and Stoker Hobbs to relative safety. Muir and Melvin escorted both people between fiercely burning wards out of the hospital building, and towards the road through burning trees, and placed Sister Hope in a fire appliance, which provided her with some small relief from the extreme pain brought by the radiated and convective heat. Bombs continued to fall, and eventually the decision was made to withdraw all personnel from the area of the blazing hospital, because of the presence of an unexploded bomb. During the evacuation they moved cautiously along the debris-strewn roads, through choking and blinding billows of smoke until the fire appliance carrying Sister Hope careered into a water filled bomb crater, and she had again to be rescued by Fire Service personnel. She was taken to Cherry Garden Fire Station where she was kept until the 'all clear' sounded next morning. She afterwards stated that she would not have attempted an escape through such overwhelmingly dangerous conditions without the support of the firefighters, to whom she was particularly grateful. For their courageous actions that first dreadful night of the London Blitz, Sub Officer Timothy Muir and Auxiliary Firemen Samuel Melvin were both awarded the George Medal.

Also recommended for the George Medal, but awarded a British Empire Medal, for his brave actions in the area of Surrey Commercial Dock was Acting Sub-Officer Richard Henry Ashton who had served some seventeen years as a London firefighter. On this first night of the London Blitz about fifty persons were cut off by fire at South Wharf, Rotherhithe, and were in imminent danger of being driven into the river by the advancing flames. Ashton, who was in charge of a fire-boat, was able to move this mass of stranded people who were taking refuge on a dumb-barge (a freight vessel designed to be towed on inland waterways, without its own means of mechanical propulsion). This rescue was executed with great difficulty, and whilst the air raid was still at its height. Ashton towed the unfortunate people along the river which was congested with other barges, many of which were well alight, and eventually disembarked them in relative safety at Nelson's Dry Dock, Rotherhithe. In his report on this incident, and the courageous actions Sub-Officer R. H. Ashton's, and Section

A fire-boat crew manoeuvre their vessel in training.
Courtesy of London Fire Brigade.

Officer James Bowtell who was the Coxwain, in saving so many lives, Company Officer G. Spurrett stated:

'Cut off by fire fifty Auxiliaries and civilians were forced to seek shelter in a barge. Sub-Officer Ashton who was in charge of a fire-boat gave instructions for the taking in tow of a barge, and this was successfully accomplished under his guidance. His Coxswain, Section Officer Bowtell, had the extremely difficult job of navigating the fire-boat with the barge in tow. It is worthy of mention that the line used for the towage was a Home Office two and a half inch line, which in view of the weight to be towed, called for the utmost care. Sub-Officer Ashton and Section Officer Bowtell showed coolness and skill under extreme conditions'.

A major incident occurred at 1800 hours that evening when the gas works in Old Kent road was hit, damaging an acre of buildings and setting three million cubic feet of gas alight; requiring the attention of eighteen pumps. So great was the strain now being brought to bear on London Fire Brigade that an almost ruthless system of prioritisation had to be adhered to. Consequently when at 1807 hours it was reported that fifty houses on the Deptford/New Cross border were in danger, only one trailer pump could be sent. However, when four minutes later a fire was reported at the premises of 'Seibe-Gorman', a heavy unit and eight trailer pumps were dispatched, as the factory was manufacturing breathing apparatus for the use of submariners.

Company Officer Mrs Beatrice Maud Plimmer of London Women's Auxiliary Fire Service and Samuel Stillwell, an Auxiliary Messenger, were both based at the Pageant's Wharf fire station Rotherhithe Street, in the Surrey Commercial Docks, and although within reach of a number of other fire stations such as Dock Head and Deptford, it was effectively on an island due to the swing bridges, and consequently it could take some considerable time for appliances to make their way to fires in the area of that station. On the nights of 7th, 8th and 9th September 1940, during ferocious and constant enemy action on the London Docks, Mrs Plimmer showed great courage and coolness whilst in charge of the Women Auxiliaries when large fires and intensive enemy bombing were persisting in the London dock area. In addition to maintaining effective communications, she organised a casualty reception post, provided refreshments for duty personnel, and saw to the comfort of her injured colleagues. In recommending her for an award of the British Empire Medal, Station Officer A. E. Dear wrote in his report:

'In addition to maintaining communications, Company Officer Plimmer organised a first aid post and emergency canteen at 50 Station. Injuries were dressed and tired and hungry men given rest and refreshment. Mrs Plimmer's leadership and example inspired all the women under her command, who all displayed courage under very trying conditions'.

At the great fire of Surrey Docks on 7th September, Auxiliary Messenger Stillwell was discovered holding a previously unattended branch of a hose line until eventually relieved by firefighters. To hold a high pressure jet fed by large diameter delivery hose without assistance for some considerable time with no means of controlling or stopping the flow of water requires enormous reserves of physical strength and determination. Indeed, to let go of such a branch would, because of jet-reaction, most likely seriously injure or even kill the 'Branch-holder'. Stillwell, once he was relieved of this arduous task continued to deliver messages and bring drinking water to officers and men who were unable to leave their positions throughout that night of air raids. Although Stillwell was at this major incident on the first day and night for over fourteen hours, and on the five succeeding nights, he carried out his duties at fires in the same area with great courage. He was quite indifferent to the danger he was in, and although ordered to take shelter from the falling bombs, he turned up on a number of occasions later in the night and the next morning bringing drinking water to men on the hoses. The officer in charge of London Fire Brigade's 'F' Division and the river area, Chief Superintendent G. J. Adams, wrote in support of this messenger being officially recognised for his work:

'The boy was indifferent to the danger he was in when I saw him at the docks on the night of 7th September, 1940, and although ordered to shelter, he turned up again and again later in the night, and the next morning carrying drinking water in an old can to the men on the branches. I was ready enough to accept a drink from him myself, and his continued cheerfulness was very encouraging'.

Percy William Harris, a forty-four year-old insurance agent, was a part time Company Officer, and had just reported for duty on that afternoon at Plumstead fire station, when the air raid warning was sounded. Shortly before five o'clock the station received a call to the Royal Arsenal at Woolwich, and consequently Harris was a member of one of the first fire crews to arrive at this incident.

The 120-acre site of Woolwich Arsenal, five and a half miles to the east of Surrey Docks, stored large quantities of highly volatile nitroglycerine, acid and explosives, as well as great piles of more stable, but no less dangerous, small arms ammunition and large calibre shells. On arrival, several locations within the arsenal were well alight, and because of a lack of firefighters in the early stages, some of the 'medium' sized fires had to be tackled by crews without the direction of an officer. Harris was directed to tour these fires to give guidance, and in doing so he displayed great qualities of initiative and leadership, inspiring the crews, who were under bombardment for the first time, by his cool and commanding presence. It was when these initial fires were being brought under control that the enemy commenced a second wave of attacks, subjecting the arsenal to an even heavier assault with high explosive and incendiary bombs, causing many large fires, demolishing buildings, and registering a direct hit on a crowded brick-built shelter, close to where Harris and his comrades were dealing with a shop which was blazing fiercely. On seeing the explosion Harris ran to the shelter and managed to extricate five casualties, although it was later ascertained that three were already dead.

This second attack by the Luftwaffe had serious consequences on the firefighting operations in the area of Woolwich Arsenal, as a great many major fires were started, and considerable damage done to the water mains, and hydrants were thereby rendered useless. Harris, although not a full-time firefighter, had conscientiously studied the principles of water-relay operations (this is where a base pump would draw water via suction hose from a river or other source, and relay it via lines of delivery hose to a second pump, and the water would then be impelled to subsequent pumping appliances, and thence to a final pump and directed onto the fire. The distance between pumping appliances would depend on a number of factors including the performance of the pump, and the gradient between each appliance of the relay. The effectiveness of a water relay is very much dependent on the ability of each pump operator), and was acquainted with the topography and layout of the area, and in particular the nearest potential water supplies in and around the Arsenal. Company Officer Harris directed on-coming appliances to ditches and other emergency water sources, and his knowledge, his energy and great inventiveness, were invaluable in the task of surrounding the fire, which had involved some fourteen large buildings.

By three o'clock the following morning, another wave of German bombers had commenced their attack, and a range of buildings, and a number of loaded railway trucks, became involved, causing further serious concerns for the officer in charge. However, Company Officer Harris continued to work with undiminished energy, and was soon able to report that several pumps had been brought into position, and were tackling the fresh outbreaks of fire, and that adequate water supplies were available to them. The report recommending Harris for the George Medal went on to say:

'This man throughout the night of the 7th and 8th September was an outstanding example of unselfish voluntary service, never sparing himself in the slightest degree, and rendering by his initiative, courage, and endurance, valuable assistance at a time of extreme danger and discomfort. It can be recorded that Harris on the occasion in question worked almost continuously from the time he reported for duty on the 7th until late afternoon on the 8th September, a total of 22 hours. He then, after a brief rest, reported for duty again for the whole of the night of 8th September. Since that date he has regularly reported for part-time duty, and has been present at nearly every large fire in the Plumstead area.'

Also at the Royal Arsenal that night, twenty-seven year-old Reg Cooper from Station 56 Eltham was noted as displaying great initiative and devotion to duty when a fresh wave of air attacks caused an even larger fire in the early morning of the 8th, which necessitated the urgent redeployment of pumping appliances. This severely affected the stamina and morale of the crews, who had endured hours of intense, taxing, and exceptionally dangerous firefighting. Cooper, at this critical stage realised the importance of more hose being available to tackle this conflagration, and by his great

Heroes with grimy faces.
Courtesy of London Fire Brigade.

initiative he produced from relatively great distances sufficient equipment to achieve a successful outcome. Superintendent F. Dann wrote of his efforts:

'Cooper during a period when all ranks were making strenuous efforts to tackle a serious outbreak, stood out as a striking example of devotion to duty; his untiring efforts contributed in no small degree to the quick extinction of the fire.'

For his work that night Auxiliary Fireman Reginald Charles Cooper was awarded the British Empire Medal.

At 7.00pm that evening, Temporary Sub-Officer George John Tagg, who was attached to No 80 fire station in Clapham, was sent out of his district with his crew, where he had already been fighting fires for the past hour and a half, to deal with a number of very serious incidents in the Woolwich area. On their arrival the sight which greeted Tagg and his comrades was one of enormous confusion, and there were already a great many casualties in the area, as the second raid of the day had just commenced and heavy bombing was well underway. It was a scene from Hell, with the burning wharfs, jetties and warehouses forming a backdrop to blazing barges and other craft drifting everywhere, some sinking, so creating the impression of a vast and unstoppable river of flame; with the ubiquitous, heavy pulsating sound of the enemy bombers above, punctuated by the screams of their bombs accelerating through the air. This seemingly cataclysmic situation was exacerbated by the failure of water supplies, the incessant noise of the explosions and crashing buildings, the choking, blinding smoke, and the presence of a fresh wind which, most unhelpfully, fed the intensity of the flames. Warehouses on both banks of the Thames stocked with all manner of flammable and combustible goods took fire, sending torrents of molten liquid pouring onto quaysides where crews were desperately fighting the flames.

During peacetime major fires attended by many appliances and their crews would certainly attract all the operational talent and experience a fire brigade might possess, and certainly involve the Chief Officer or his deputy directing operations. However, owing to the many large and extremely dangerous fires burning in the area of Woolwich arsenal at that time, at which all local fire officers were fully engaged, Tagg, in spite of his junior rank, was put in charge of a series of great fires which were raging in the Royal Dock Yard, and around Commonwealth Buildings. These included six large blocks which were well alight. Besides these, several other buildings were beginning to take fire, including two timber sheds, vehicles, rolling stock with contents, and various combustible materials stored in the open.

Sub-Officer Tagg, in assuming command of this overwhelming and potentially catastrophic situation remained composed, displaying great courage and outstanding qualities of leadership in tackling this formidable task. His first assistance message was to 'Make pumps twenty', which in peacetime would have been considered quite an audacious decision for a junior officer. In this instance, however it was a measured and very conservative response to a serious and deteriorating situation, which took into account the already major demands being put on the assets of the Fire Service. Despite the meagre resources available, Tagg managed to restrict the spread of fire, and even saved some buildings whose roofs and top floors were alight. Tagg's excellent qualities of leadership, his encouragement and courageous endeavour proved an example to those under his command and rallied them; particularly those who had not previously been under bombardment, or indeed attended a major fire.

Due to the failure of the water mains because of enemy action, Tagg ordered his pumping appliances to draw water from the river; unfortunately on the turn of the tide their suction hose was left 'high and dry', so bringing another failure of water supplies, which would thwart the best efforts of the firefighters. Sub Officer Tagg immediately set about locating an alternative supply, and found two large swimming pools, which were not scheduled as emergency water supplies, and did not appear on the local water maps. This was an excellent example of professionalism and initiative on the part of this junior officer who was carrying a very heavy load of responsibility, on unfamiliar ground, in the most trying of circumstances.

As the incident developed, a block containing a large store of sulphuric acid became involved in the fire, and being a highly exothermic substance, brought the added danger of reacting with the firefighting water by boiling and spitting dangerously, and producing dense and pungent fumes. As no breathing apparatus was available, Tagg entered the buildings without protection, emerging half-blinded and in great pain. Once his eyes were dressed, he carried on with his work without resting. On handing over control of the fire on the arrival of DO Handley, the situation, although still serious, was on the way to being under some degree of control, and Tagg gave this senior officer all assistance necessary until the fires were surrounded and subdued at 7.00 am the following morning. During the time that Tagg was in command of firefighting operations he gave exemplary leadership and direction to the operations. But for his great inventiveness and courage, there is little doubt that the fires would have reached conflagration proportions. In recognition of his service, Tagg was awarded the British Empire Medal. On 29th December 1940, he was seriously injured when the appliance he was in charge of sustained a near miss from a high explosive bomb.

During that night intense enemy action extending over many hours caused widespread damage to a considerable area of London. Possibly the most seriously affected area was Silvertown, which was described as a raging inferno, and a complete evacuation became necessary. Major damage was inflicted on Southwark, Battersea, Bermondsey, East and West Ham, Poplar, Plaistow, Barking, Hackney, Stepney and Rotherhithe.

It was in Rotherhithe that Annie Matilda Wilkins and Bessie Constance Wulbern of the London Women's Auxiliary Fire Service were posted to sub-fire station No. 41 'V', at Midway Place School, Bush Road. These women were alone in a sub-station while the immediate neighbourhood was being subjected to the most concentrated

Tired, wet, and dirty, but with good humour, the survivors
of another night's firefighting make their way home.
Courtesy of the Fire Service College.

bombing. Throughout this raid they continued to receive and broadcast all messages accurately and calmly, and reporting crews were ordered to their correct fires with precision and speed. At one stage of the raid the building was rocked by the blast of bombs falling on the nearby tarred rope factory, which unsurprisingly was well alight almost immediately; then a high explosive bomb hit the school itself, putting the lights and phones out of use.

Auxiliary Wulbern at first thought that she had been hit as she could feel what she thought was blood running down her face, and dripping onto the floor. However, by the light of the burning factory, and the now blazing school they found that the blood was in fact coffee essence coming through the ceiling from the canteen above! When the station was struck by incendiary bombs and set on fire they reported this occurrence by telephone to the local station, and very courageously remained at their posts until ordered to leave by the officer in charge. As they could now do nothing and there being no shelter, the women stood in the roadway outside until a car came and took them to Stn 41 Deptford, where they attended to the many injured who were laid out on the appliance room floor.

On this hellish night, the British cargo steamer SS Zouave was berthed in Surrey Commercial Dock, Rotherhithe, when heavy attacks with incendiary and high explosive bombs were made on the area. Ship's fireman Edward McLean was detailed to patrol by the timber sheds alongside his ship, and during the course of his duties he picked up and threw a number of German incendiaries into the water. Throughout this period of heavy aerial bombardment, McLean showed great courage, determination and commitment, refusing shelter from the bombing, and continued to risk his life by disposing of unexploded bombs, and extinguishing fires before they developed, especially those that fell amongst the nearby wood stacks. Through his bravery and fine example his ship was on several occasions saved from damage, and the danger of a serious fire in the timber sheds averted. Fireman McLean was awarded the George Medal in recognition of his gallant service that night. Most regrettably, the SS Zouave was sunk by two torpedoes from U-305 on the night of 17th March 1943, when it was a part of convoy SC-122 in the north Atlantic, south east of Cape Farewell.

THE FIRST NIGHT OF THE BLITZ FOR THE OTHER SERVICES

The extent of the horrors of 7th September 1940 and how they impacted on the people of London cannot be overstated. Armageddon replaced the 'Phoney war' in a matter of earth-shattering minutes, with devastating fires sweeping parts of the capital, and widespread death and destruction being visited upon this great city. It can only have been viewed as the prelude to invasion, and the 'slamming' of a figurative 'cell door' on the people of the 'Sceptred Isle', which would incarcerate them in a regime of brutal subjugation. Given the enormity of this human disaster, and the involvement of so many of London's emergency and essential organisations it would, in the writer's view, be totally inappropriate to view this event only in terms of Fire Service gallantry. Here in tribute is a summation of the commitment, selfless humanity, and valour of those who worked alongside the firefighters on that cataclysmic night.

On that first night of the London Blitz, firefighters numbered among the rescued as well the rescuers. In one incident six London firefighters were seriously injured and trapped in the ruins of dock buildings in Redriff Road, Bermondsey; an area which had been burning for three hours. The local Air Raid Precautions Incident Officer John Arthur Blake was informed that a firefighter was lying injured somewhere in the area of Redriff Road, and would require transportation to hospital. At great personal risk Blake drove to where he believed the firefighter to be, whilst on either side of him property was ablaze and burning debris was falling continually onto the roadway. During this perilous journey a bomb exploded in front of his car, wrecking it completely. Despite this setback and the inevitable shock he was now suffering, Blake then continued on foot and, climbing a space in a burning fence, gained access into the inner dock buildings. As the area had been evacuated, no assistance would have been forthcoming had he sustained injuries.

After searching through what remained of the buildings, Blake found six firefighters lying amongst blazing debris, all seriously injured. Faced with this critical situation Blake had no option but to leave the casualties, and make his way back to the road. Here he found a telephone undamaged by the air raid, and contacting his control room ordered an ambulance. While receiving this call the Deputy Controller heard two heavy detonations through the telephone. It transpired that two bombs had blown Blake away from the telephone. After recovering from the shock, he returned to the phone and re-established communications with the control centre.

The wounded firefighters were removed to hospital, where three of them eventually recovered. There can be little doubt that, were it not for Blake's courageous actions, none of the men would have survived. On the same day Blake was informed that persons were trapped in an Anderson shelter in Ambrose Road, Bermondsey, which was completely surrounded by fire, thus preventing any attempt at rescue. Blake, without hesitation, went through the flames and succeeded in extricating three people, all of whom were suffering from shock. For his courageous and determined rescues of all nine people Blake was awarded the George Medal.

Also that first night a high explosive bomb blew an Auxiliary Fire Service tender into the front garden of a Port of London police station, pinning two of its crew members underneath, fatally injuring them. The explosion also fractured and ignited a gas main, setting nearby trees and hedges on fire, and the trailer pump attached to the appliance was blown some distance away, killing the other three members of the crew. PLA police officers Acting Inspector Alfred Boniface, Sergeant Alfred James Tulett and Constables Henry William Edwards, William Innes Manson and Thomas William White, were quickly on the scene, and made frantic efforts to free the trapped firefighters. Unfortunately their endeavours were to no avail, as it was impossible to move the tender, which eventually had to be lifted by a crane. Enemy aircraft were overhead and bombs were falling, and shrapnel flying throughout the immediate area during the rescue operation, which was not abandoned until it had been established that the trapped firefighters were dead. Inspector Boniface also volunteered during an intense air raid to assist firefighters to recover the body of an AFS man from under a large amount of burning debris, when the area was illuminated by a number of large fires, which presented a very visible target for enemy aircraft overhead. Port of London police officers Boniface, Tulett, Edwards, Manson and White were all awarded the British Empire Medal for their courageous part in assisting the Fire Service that night.

Many acts of gallantry were performed on this terrible night by people from all walks of life, for instance the George Medal was awarded to Miss Grace Rattenbury of the Women's Voluntary Service & Invalid Children's Aid Society, who volunteered to help evacuate children from the dockland area of Sunderland Wharf during an ongoing and very severe air attack in the area of Keeton's Road, Rotherhithe.

With her WVS vehicle she commenced a shuttle run to a first line rest and feeding centre, through smoke-engulfed and rubble strewn streets, some of which were almost archways of flame, to the sound of bombs bursting and anti-aircraft ordnance exploding, and the hellish illumination of parachute flares. With great determination and courage she endured this fearsome backdrop and continued driving back and forth until the last woman and child had been evacuated from the danger area, whilst overhead enemy aircraft continued to drop bombs. The severity of the fire was such that it threatened the one single span bridge left open, so cutting people off from the 'mainland' of South London. The road itself was in an extremely dangerous condition owing to the worsening fire situation, bomb craters and a delayed action bomb which had fallen nearby, yet Miss Rattenbury continued her spirited work in a calm and confident manner, and displayed a great example to all by her selfless and unhesitating actions. On more than one occasion, whilst assisting the ARP Wardens, she had to throw herself to the ground to escape the blast from bombs which were again falling in the vicinity, and her car was badly blistered by the encroaching flames.

Also on that night, twenty-four year-old Mrs Joan Creed, a widow of Donnybrook Road, Streatham, who was employed as a Clerical Assistant in the Social Services' office in Tooley Street, South London, was working in the Rest Centre at Keaton's Road School, Bermondsey. During the first attack of the night, the Rotherhithe area was badly damaged, and as dusk approached a second wave of bombers was heard overhead, the enemy using the glow of the great dockside fires to assist in locating their objectives. This second raid was particularly intense, and lasted until dawn. The Keaton's Road Rest Centre was in a strategically very dangerous location, being very close to Southwark Park, where a number of anti-aircraft gun emplacements were located, and the Surrey Commercial Docks which was ablaze from end to end; the whole area was continuously being strafed by the Luftwaffe.

During the evening and well into the night the centre was called upon to accommodate many hundreds of people who came streaming from the inferno which was the dockland area, through clouds and dust, dirt and smoke, and over rubble, bodies and serpentine lengths of fire brigade hose, looking in a very poor condition, being dirty, dishevelled, understandably frightened, and hurrying to reach some form of safety. These refugees in their own city huddled together in the darkness of the rest centre's ground floor air raid shelter, hoping to be spared, and looking for their friends and neighbours who had also escaped the first of the night's horrors. Amid this scene of savage pandemonium, the rest centre staff marshalled the new arrivals throughout the night and attended to their needs. Near to midnight two bombs fell on the centre exploding and bringing great havoc and causing many casualties, including members of staff, one of whom was killed, with others suffering shrapnel wounds, including Mrs Creed.

Regaining her feet after the first explosion, Mrs Creed immediately went among the ruins of the school, and searching in the debris helped a number of the refugees, one of whom, a boy of about four years of age, was found to be dead when she picked him up. Laying the boy carefully down by the other fatal casualties, she then assisted with the rescue work by acting with a soldier as a stretcher bearer. She was so engaged when the second bomb fell, throwing her to the ground, with the soldier on top of her. Both rescuers, with great fortitude, simply got up and got on with the job in hand. Throughout the night she acted as an ambulance attendant, and escorted casualties on a number of journeys, eventually, about four o'clock in the morning, it was noticed by her colleagues that she was bleeding profusely from wounds in her lower leg and thigh, and she was persuaded to rest and receive treatment at a first aid post. Having been patched-up, Mrs Creed, with bandaged legs, reported for duty at the local Social Services office, making little of her injuries or her stressful experiences.

For her courage and outstanding devotion to duty on the first night of the London Blitz, Mrs Joan Creed was awarded the King's Commendation for Brave Conduct.

George Medals were awarded to George Goshawk and Bertram Mathewman of the London Auxiliary Ambulance Service who were both posted to Auxiliary Ambulance station 126 at Invicta Road School, SE 3, for their courage and devotion to duty on that night. During the ongoing air raid both men staffed an ambulance vehicle, and set off to collect casualties from premises at Hyde Buildings, Rotherhithe Street, South London, where a serious fire situation was ongoing. On arrival they found that the road leading to the building was seemingly impassable as a sheet of flame was raging across the street. Without hesitation they drove the ambulance through the fire, and with the help of a police officer loaded the vehicle with casualties.

Whilst they were carrying out the rescue of the casualties, the heat from the blaze became so overwhelming that not only were they in great and mortal danger from collapsing under its furious onslaught, but the stretchers they were using became almost too hot to handle. After a short while, the building became so structurally weakened that the danger of being killed or trapped under tons of burning debris escalated from being a distinct possibility, to almost a certainty. However, undeterred Goshawk and Mathewman courageously stayed with their work until warned by the police to evacuate immediately, as the building was in imminent danger of collapse; which, in fact, is what happened immediately the ambulance had left the area. Both men delivered their patients safely to hospital and reported back to their station for duty. By their steadfast actions under the most trying and dangerous of circumstances, they acted in the finest traditions of the Ambulance Service, and brought great credit on that organisation.

Forty-seven year-old midwife Mrs Maude Smith was instrumental in saving the lives of a number of people who were in great and imminent danger from the raging Dockland fires that night. Mrs Smith on a number of occasions went to the assistance of her patients, and other women and children, during the interminable air attacks of that night, completely ignoring her own safety, even when her dress caught fire. She collected a party of women and children, and took them to a relatively safe place outside of the docks. Her courageous dedication to her duty both, before, during and after this first night of the London Blitz was described in the following terms:

'Her whole conduct … was of the highest order of self-sacrifice and devotion to the welfare of her patients, whom she sheltered and delivered in her own home, and cared for in every possible way'. Unfortunately the very brave and indefatigable Mrs Maude Smith, already a widow, lost her two sons in a naval action the following month.

During that raid an Anderson shelter in Denas Street, Poplar was seriously damaged by the burst of a high explosive bomb, which greatly distorted its structure, twisting it in the ground and closing up the entrance. Inside the occupants were dead, dying or injured, and those still alive were unable to move. A fire was raging from a broken gas main very close to the shelter, whilst a mere 250 yards away a timber yard was blazing furiously. Mr E. J. Hunt, the officer in charge of the Poplar Rescue party who were in attendance, with great difficulty crawled through the wreckage into the shelter, and succeeded in cutting a hole in the steel wall with oxyacetylene apparatus, through which he was able to bring the casualties out. Unfortunately only four were alive. This rescue was carried out under air raid conditions, and whilst there was little chance of the fires spreading to the scene of the rescue, the blaze showed a very visible light to the enemy overhead, and indeed a number of high explosive bombs were dropped in the immediate vicinity during the rescue operation. The other members of the crew were: W. Flodin, T. K. Samways, J. F. G. Hurley, and J. W. Cruise, who all contributed to the rescue of three women, and a girl from this serious situation by their gallant and efficient work, under the most hazardous of conditions.

Fifty-three year-old Mr William Austin of Dockhead, was a skilled member of a rescue team led by Incident Officer Mr J. A. Blake, and were returning to their Town Hall headquarters in Bermondsey from an incident in Redriff Road in a Rescue Party lorry, when the scream of falling bombs was heard as they approached the junction of Southwark Park Road and Ambrose Street. The driver pulled the vehicle to a sudden stop and all passengers immediately took cover under the lorry. One bomb fell only some ten yards in front of them, and they were covered in debris, and another had fallen on an unoccupied cinema, and although the crew searched the ruins of the building, no casualties were located. As they left the cinema, screams were heard coming from the direction of Ambrose Street, and on running to the scene found that an oil bomb had dropped directly onto an Anderson shelter, with the resulting serious blaze taking hold of the adjoining house. Although the heat from this dreadful device was tremendous, and it seemed that no one could survive such an inferno, Austin ran through the corridor of flames into the shelter, and successfully brought out the five occupants. As a result of his exertions and extremes of heat and smoke to which he had been exposed Austin collapsed, and had to be carried from the area.

William Austin for this most courageous and daring rescue was awarded the George Medal.

One of the primary targets for the Luftwaffe was Beckton Gas Works on the north bank of the Thames, west of Barking Creek at Galleon's Reach. This plant operated by the Gas, Light and Coke Company, was one of the biggest sites of its kind in Europe, covering 550 acres, and holding nine large gasometers; and had two deep water piers in the Thames, enabling direct unloading from steam colliers bringing coal from collieries in the north-east of England.

On this first night of the London Blitz Beckton Gas Works was subjected to a very heavy raid, and high explosive and incendiary bombs caused many fires within this potentially highly explosive site. As a result of these explosions, high-pressure steam was escaping and dense clouds of sulphurous fumes blinded and choked the on-site staff dealing with an increasingly desperate situation. During operations the Superintendent of the works Mr Wiliam Gordon Adam and his works officer Mr Llewellyn Treleaven Rinder entered an area which was well alight to make a risk assessment of the situation. They were then joined by the Assistant Valve-man Frederick James Winchester, and all three men entered a retort house to close down the valve to a broken main. Whilst carrying out this task a bomb fell close by and Rinder was blown through a doorway. Despite this, Adam, Rinder and Winchester eventually located the valve and brought the flames from the damaged main under control. As the raid continued throughout the night these men entered burning retort houses on at least

As turntable ladders tower over London's burning warehouses,
firefighters bring more hose to complete the job.
Courtesy of London Fire Brigade.

three occasions to shut off valves, showing enormous courage and coolness in the face of great danger.

The Chief Valve-man on site, Mr Frederick John Redman – already a holder of the Military Medal from a previous conflict – was responsible for saving some of the gas holders by turning off the valves, which was a protracted and arduous process. To carry out this task he worked between blazing sheds and pumping stations, with bombs falling all around him, with the added danger of exploding mains and gas fumes. Redman displayed great courage and endurance throughout the night. An assistant Valve-man, George Cornelius Bond remained at his post throughout the night and directed the operations necessary to save the complicated plant in his charge. His bravery and persistent devotion to duty were an inspiration to all working with him.

Mr Leslie Cyril Godwood and Mr Andrew Thomas McGuire, both employed as ambulance drivers, performed rescue work in the open during the heavy bombing of this plant, and showed great gallantry in collecting casualties and conveying them to hospital.

In recognition of their outstanding and gallant efforts Adam, Rinder and Redman were awarded George Medals, and Winchester, Bond, Godward and McGuire were awarded the British Empire Medal.

The wrath of Hitler's Luftwaffe was visited with particular ferocity on the riverside areas covered by the Port of London Authority. The inferno at the docks eventually spread to cover some 250 acres, and a great many employees of the Port of London Authority demonstrated enormous courage and dedication to duty in the face of extreme and overwhelming danger on that first day of the Blitz.

The supplement to the *London Gazette* of 24th January 1941 cites many acts of gallantry relating the early days of the London Blitz in September 1940, including two separate incidents which earned members of the Port of London Authority the George Medal viz:

> William John Allum (Master), and Henry Edward Allen (Deckhand) of a PLA Tug:
> During a heavy air attack on the Docks the tug was putting out fires on barges and towing other out of danger. The tug Master was hailed from a life boat by members of the crew of a motor vessel and informed that their vessel had been bombed and set on fire. Allum and Deckhand Allen boarded her and having put out several fires commenced to play a hose on the stern of the ship which was threatened by fire from the dock-side. Allum decided that the vessel must be shifted. He accordingly called for and obtained volunteers from another vessel to go on board and assist in the removal of the burning ship. Both tugs then proceeded to move her to a safe berth, Deckhand Allen going aboard and acting as dock pilot and directing the volunteer crew aboard. Allen

was a member of the first crew of the tug who had remained on duty with the night shift.

The conduct of the tug Masters and their Crews under circumstances of great danger is worthy of the highest praise and in particular tug Master W. Allum displayed great initiative, resource and leadership. Deckhand H. E. Allen showed devotion to duty as well as coolness and courage'.

Captain John Penfiled Epps (Dockmaster), Ernest John Pridmore (Master of Tug) and Henry William Oliver (Master of Tug):
Captain Epps personally organised members of the staff under his control into parties of firefighters to extinguish outbreaks caused by a very large number of incendiary bombs which were dropped on London Docks. He carried on through the whole of the night when many severe fires threatened, and under his direction, tugs and craft, including some oil barges which were in danger of catching fire from the burning sheds and debris, were removed to a place of safety. Those which had caught fire were taken in tow and the fires extinguished. His devotion to duty under very serious conditions on this and subsequent occasions undoubtedly checked the progress of serious fires and saved much valuable property.

E. J. Pridmore, Mater of Tug, led the first crew of his tug in extinguishing fires caused by incendiary bombs and assisted in preventing serious fires at wharves. He helped to remove laden barges and craft in the docks which were in danger of fire. Throughout the period of heavy raids on the docks Pridmore has shown conspicuous ability, initiative and devotion to duty in circumstances of extreme danger. H. W. Oliver, Master of Tug, was in charge of the second crew of the Tug which, in addition to removing ships and barges to safety, landed and gave assistance to victims on an air raid shelter which had received a direct hit from a HE bomb.

Both crews showed remarkable devotion to duty throughout and rendered valuable assistance.

Shortly after 2230 hours, Monson Road sub-fire station was shaken by the blast from a number of high explosives which had fallen in nearby Hunsdon Road. Many windows in the station were blown in, and slates from the roof came crashing down. A crew with a trailer pump were dispatched to the scene. When they arrived they found Monson Buildings had been hit, with some loss of life. A couple of hundred yards away in Avonley Road, the crew of a heavy unit which had been dealing with fractured gas and water mains, heard the heart-stopping whistle of falling bombs, and saw them come down on the South Eastern Hospital, known as the Fever Hospital.

The George Cross was posthumously awarded to Albert George Dolphin of Bromley in Kent, who had worked as a porter at the South Eastern Hospital, New Cross, South London.

One of the high explosive bombs fell on the kitchens of Ward Block One, killing four nurses who were in the ground floor kitchen, and injuring the night Sister and patients in the adjoining ward. Nurse Sole, who was in the ward kitchen on the first floor, was thrown through the collapsing floor into the passage below. Together with others, porter Albert George Dolphin rushed to the site and found her pinioned by a block of masonry across her legs. While they were working desperately to try and free the nurse, the wall next to them was heard to crack and it subsequently collapsed. The rescuers had ample time to jump clear before the masonry fell, but Dolphin remained where he was and his body was subsequently found lying face downwards across the nurse with his head towards the wall, which had collapsed on top of him. When the wreckage was cleared, Dolphin was dead, but the nurse who was eventually extricated, was still alive, although severely injured. There is no doubt that Dolphin, although well aware that the wall was about to collapse, deliberately remained where he was, and threw himself across the nurse's body in an endeavour to protect her. This he succeeded in doing at the cost of his own life.

Dolphin, who had worked at the hospital for twenty years since his discharge from the Royal Fusiliers after serving on the Western Front during the First World War, was awarded a posthumous George Cross in recognition of his great and selfless gallantry.

After a night rendered sleepless by gut-dissolving fear, and a seemingly endless cacophony of exploding bombs, roaring anti-aircraft artillery, and collapsing buildings, the fortitude, pragmatism and good humour shown by Londoners on the morning after the first great and terrible raid became the genesis of that oft-used phrase 'The Blitz Spirit'. With whole streets of houses laid waste in the many areas of the Metropolis, particularly the East End and South London, hundreds of families collected what few belongings they now had, heaped them into barrows or perambulators, or onto horse-drawn carts (as was the case with the author's mother-in-law on the occasion that she was bombed out), and with young children gathered up in their arms, travelled to find sanctuary with friends or relatives, or began the search for another house to call home. Of course many would, understandably, be shocked and downhearted, but generally the spirit of the Londoners was surprisingly determined and unshaken, as they left behind wrecked homes, shattered memories, and in some cases even their dead.

The 150,000 men and women of London's vast Civil Defence network, many of whom had been derided and defamed as skivers, a waste of money, and Army dodgers during the 'Phoney War', proved their inestimable worth that night beyond all doubt, with hundreds if not thousands of acts of courage, commitment and humanitarian devotion to duty. A night of staring death squarely in the face did not deter or intimidate the firefighters, police officers, ambulance crews or other rescue workers, who spent hours battling to hold lines of high pressure hose as they fought against the scorching heat of raging fires, rendered first aid whilst masonry and debris crashed about them, drove casualties between blazing buildings, or entered structures on the brink of collapse to search for casualties.

All worked hour upon hour throughout that night, enduring the overwhelming dangers with little thought for their own welfare, comfort or safety; well maybe with an occasional curse or grumble! The gallant tales of brave and self-sacrificing acts performed by ordinary Londoners in the most extraordinary of circumstances are legion, and most go unrecorded, but to those who were there, those memories will be ineradicably printed on their memory and in their spirit. To those of us who were not there, we can only salute their outstanding dedication and bravery. On the first night of the Blitz, 430 civilians were killed and 1,600 seriously wounded.

THE REMAINDER OF
SEPTEMBER 1940

On the night of 8th September 1940, a great stream of bombers came out of the Cherbourg and Somme areas at about 2000 hours, crossing the coast between Isle of Wight and Dungeness, and proceeding to London.

Major damage was done at Acton, Leyton and Poplar, and rail lines were blocked at Broad Street and St Pancras Stations. Serious fires occurred at Chiltern Court and Madame Tussauds in Baker Street, while at Southgate the Metal Box Company's factory, and the Lindley Aircraft Company's Works were damaged, subsequently affecting the war effort, and a paint works at Homerton was hit. A very dangerous fire was caused at the British Oil and Cake Mills at Sun Wharf, Lime House, and there were severe fires resulting in extensive damage to property near the Bank of England and Mansion House, and major fires in Great Arthur and King William Streets. At this latter location a large fire involved a number of buildings, and owing to the wider ongoing situation, the arrival of turntable ladders to attack the blaze with high level monitors was delayed.

Fifty-one year-old senior fireman Alfred North of number 63 fire station Canon Street led a team of firefighters via debris-strewn and smoke-filled stairwells to the upper floors of two eight-storey buildings where a fire had assumed serious proportions, and was threatening to spread to other properties; the blaze was also showing significant light to enemy aircraft overhead. By his considerable initiative and leadership in leading the attack on the fires, and bringing a number of his colleagues with their heavy equipment including many lengths of hose, through these buildings, the fire was confined to the two original structures.

At the same incident, Section Officer William Benjamin Mendham, also attached to station 63, worked unceasingly for over eight hours leading crews into various buildings which were considered as being highly unstable due to the effects of high explosive bombs. Where the fire had gained a hold and was spreading, he vigorously participated in and directed the firefighting tactics. Earlier in the evening he had attended a major fire in Watling Street which was burning fiercely, and escorted two crews, each bringing with them a line of hose, with one branch being got to work on the ground floor and another on the first. Later in the operations the crews were withdrawn, and shortly after the whole structure collapsed. Mendham ordered that these jets be directed onto the buildings opposite, which saved them from major damage from radiated heat. Mendham, despite the pressures of his supervisory responsibilities under the most demanding of circumstances, took his turn on the branch, and provided a great example to his firefighters.

Both North and Mendham were awarded the British Empire Medal for their gallant and dedicated work that night.

On 10th September 1940, Auxiliary Fireman William Charles Skillern was in charge of the first fire appliance attending a call to a building on fire in Mecklenburg Square, Holborn. On arrival it was found that a major portion of the building had collapsed, part of the basement and the upper portion of the premises were on fire, and persons were reported as trapped in the basement. Skillern immediately took command of firefighting operations, and at great personal risk crawled through the debris into the basement where the casualties were entombed. From this position he directed and encouraged the activities of the crew in their efforts to release the unfortunate people. As a result of his fine leadership, and the courageous example to his men, twenty people were successfully rescued. Skillern was awarded the George Medal for his part in this incident.

On the same night Station Officer James Harris of the London Fire Brigade displayed outstanding initiative and courage at many large fires, and was awarded the George Medal. His almost reckless courage in the face of very grave danger was conspicuous when a fire occurred in buildings at the Royal Arsenal, Woolwich. His success in stopping the fire at a particularly vulnerable spot saved a number of buildings and magazines. As a result of their courageous work under extremely hazardous circumstances in saving four buildings containing high explosives at the same incident, Fireman James Storer and Auxiliary Fireman Stephen Kinlan were also awarded the George medal. They remained at their post in the face of flying debris and exploding shells of various calibres and, by their action set an example of courage to their comrades.

Also on 10th September 1940, during an aerial bombardment a bomb fell causing a large crater on a kerbside, demolishing the lower part of the ground floor and basement of the Star public house at the junction of City Road and Old Street, fracturing gas services and a large water main. Several persons suffering from shock and abrasions were sheltering in the basement of this public house, which was rapidly filling with water. A trailer pump attended from station number 37 Z, Old Street and immediately on arrival Auxiliary Fireman Aylmer Maurice Young, with the assistance of Auxiliary Fireman Richard Smith, without hesitation, and at great personal risk, entered the basement, which by this time had filled to a depth of about five feet with water, and in complete darkness succeeded in rescuing six people. Young continued to search the cellar and located a seventh person, who was pinned beneath the water by a fallen girder. Notwithstanding the difficulties and dangers posed by the rising water, Young, displaying great courage and determination, managed to extricate the man and facilitate his removal to the street. Whilst Smith at great personal risk remained at the demolished opening, standing in about five feet of water, and assisted Young in passing the rescued people to the street. In their reports regarding the multiple rescues at this incident, Sub Officer A. S. Ost and District Officer C. S. Tobias wrote as follows:

Sub Officer A. S. Ost:
I was officer in charge of the Sub-Station and shortly after the trailer pump had responded to a call I proceeded to the scene of the occurrence. When I arrived Young was already in the basement of the house with rising water up to his chin, and was guiding the inmates to the opening to the street. In my opinion it was entirely due to his great promptitude and initiative on arrival of the appliance that only one person was drowned and even this might have been obviated had that person not been trapped by the girder. When I arrived at the scene of the occurrence Smith was in the basement which was almost full of water and was passing inmates to safety.

District Officer C. S. Tobias:
I attended this occurrence, arriving at the moment when Young was extricating the deceased person. I am of the opinion that he carried out a dangerous and difficult task with great courage. Smith was in the position stated above, and I consider that his action in entering and assisting the first man was worthy of some recognition.

Young was awarded the George Medal.

In the early hours of the following morning during the ongoing air attack, forty-two year-old Sub Officer Leonard Ewart Fox, a professional firefighter of twelve years service and stationed at Battersea, was in charge of an escape carrying appliance proceeding to a fire in Fownes Street, Wandsworth, when a delayed action bomb exploded, demolishing several houses, burying the appliance under debris and causing injury to the crew. Despite injuries to both thighs, Fox's first thoughts were to have another fire appliance mobilised to the original incident in Fownes Street, and to have assistance brought to his now-incapacitated crew. With great effort on his part, Fox managed to cover the 200 yards to the fire station on foot to request that the necessary assistance be mobilised, after which he lost consciousness and had to be removed for treatment. District Officer W. J. Neal describes this incident in his report thus:

'At about 0216 hours on 14th September 1940 a violent explosion was felt at this station, a few moments later Fox entered the station in a dazed condition and stated that ambulances were required at Fownes Street, then he collapsed. Had it not been for this effort … undoubtedly some time would have elapsed before assistance could have been sent to the scene of the occurrence.' In recognition of his courage, and determined sense of duty, Sub Officer Fox was awarded the oak leaf insignia of the King's Commendation for Brave Conduct.

A number of awards were made to individuals to recognise not one brave deed, but in some cases continuous exemplary service in the most arduous conditions. One such case was District Officer Harold Hydes, a professional firefighter for some twenty years, who worked from fire station 28 at Commercial Road, Whitechapel, who was recommended for the George Medal, only to receive the lesser award of the British Empire Medal. In his recommendation, Major Jackson, the acting Chief of London Fire Brigade stated:

> Hydes had been in charge of a station which has been subjected to severe bombing. He has displayed exceptional leadership, courage and initiative and set an exceptional example under the most trying of and dangerous circumstances at fires due to enemy action. During this period of time he was in sole charge of fires at: Carlisle Avenue on 8th September, 1940; Goodman's yard on 9th September; and St. Clare Street on 17th September. He also attended St. Katherine's Dock on 10th September; Buckle Street on 8th September, and carried out his duties in a most efficient and satisfactory manner until relieved by a senior officer.

Chief Superintendent A. R. May of London Fire Brigade stated in corroboration of the above officer's continual good work: 'Mr Hydes has on a number of occasions been in sole command of large and serious fires due to intensive enemy bombing in this area, all of which he has handled with great resource, courage and fine leadership. At the St. Katherine's Dock conflagration, he carried out his most responsible work under the most long and arduous conditions in a manner which calls for the highest praise and recognition.'

Superintendent S. W. Barnes added in his report: 'During the progress of the fire at Goodman's yard, I visited a nearby fire and noted the efficient manner in which Mr Hydes was dealing with the situation, showing the greatest possible resource and

After the onslaught fire crews 'damp down' the remains
of burnt out building with ground monitors.
Courtesy of Tyne and Wear Fire and Rescue Service.

leadership. With the utmost confidence I left him in charge of that area, and I commend his conduct for recognition.'

The most decorated firefighter of the Second World War, Edward William Robert Morgan, was born in Ramsgate, Kent on 21st March 1907 and after leaving St George's Commercial School in 1922, he joined the Merchant Navy, serving until 1932. Morgan then served with the Royal Naval Reserve, whilst living in Poplar. On 1st December 1932 he joined the London Fire Brigade, attending the training school at Southwark, and on completion of his initial training on 29th March 1933, he served at Kingsland Road, Burdett Road and Homerton fire stations. In June 1938 he was promoted to Sub Officer, serving briefly at Whitechapel before transferring to Euston fire station on the 19th October that year.

With the expansion of the Fire Service in London due to the declaration of war, Morgan was made Acting Station Officer in early September 1940, and his own Station Officer, Joseph Tobias, was appointed as Acting District Officer. Consequently the firefighting establishment of some 120 'Red Engines' of the London Fire Brigade was supplemented by almost 2,000 AFS motorised and trailer pumps, which were crewed by 23,000 auxiliary firefighters.

During the night of 16th–17th September 1940, hostile activity was of a greater intensity than on previous nights, and was in two distinct phases. At 1940 hours raiders were plotted coming out of Cherbourg and Le Havre, followed by a steady stream of enemy aircraft from Dieppe. From 2350 hours raids were concentrated on London, East Anglia and the South-eastern counties, and at 0020 hours, fresh raids originating from the Dutch Islands approached East Anglia and the Thames Estuary, some penetrating as far as London. The second phase commenced at 0330 hours, aircraft being plotted out of the Dieppe area towards London; this second phase continued until 0530 hours.

During this series of air raids, a large six-storey warehouse in Great Portland Street received direct hits from incendiary bombs. When the Fire Brigade arrived, the two upper floors were well alight, and fire was rapidly spreading to other parts of the building. A turntable ladder, hose lines and jets of water were got to work in a concerted attempt to stem the rate of fire spread. As the incident progressed the fire was attended, and commanded by, District Officer Tobias. Whilst these operations were in progress, the crews were subjected to a further air barrage, with one bomb severely damaging the Turntable Ladder, killing two Euston firefighters, Thomas Curson and Albert Evans, and mortally injuring District Officer Joseph Tobias, who died the following day. Other personnel were severely injured; water mains were fractured and gas mains set alight. The blast from the bomb caused severe damage to surrounding properties, and the task of rescuing the injured, and retrieving the dead was made even more hazardous by falling masonry. It was at this stage that Morgan assumed command. It was due to his calm manner, courage and leadership in dealing with the situation that enabled the injured to be rescued and removed to hospital, the water supply to be reinstated, and the fires fought and prevented from developing into a conflagration.

An extract from the official Brigade report states: 'Station Officer Morgan showed initiative and set an excellent example to the men under his command in taking charge and extinguishing a fire in Great Portland St on 16th September 1940, after renewed bombing of the fire had wrecked a 100 ft turntable ladder and killed and injured a number of the crews and the officer-in-charge of the fire. Recommended for George Medal'. This recommendation for the George Medal was down-rated to the British Empire Medal, which was awarded on 28th March 1941.

With reference to the bomb-damaged turntable ladder at this incident, a remarkable, and, as it turned out, fortuitous series of events quickly overtook the firefighter on the head of the fully extended TL. As the firefighter in question was about to secure himself to the head of the ladder with a safety harness, the bomb that was to kill his colleagues fell past him, exploding in the street below, blowing the chassis of the turntable ladder sideways into the front of the building, and the rear wheel, axle and turntable itself, weighing some four or more tons, was thrown over the frontage and came crashing to rest on a nearby rooftop. The upper extension of the ladder on which this firefighter was working caught on a structural projection, and revolved so that it was hanging in front of the still blazing building, throwing him into the street, where he was buried by falling debris. After a search he was found alive, though seriously injured, and managed to survive the war.

Recommended for the British Empire Medal as a result of his bravery that night was Section Officer George William Whiteland of Station No 74, Camden Town, who whilst attending an incident at the St. Pancras Hospital, carried out his work with marked efficiency, coolness and devotion to his duty, being well aware of the presence of an unexploded bomb, which was lying in the psychiatric ward where he was assisting in the evacuation of some fifty patients from that area. Unfortunately Whiteland was to receive no official recognition of his good work that night.

The air attacks over this eight-week period lasted from dusk to dawn, an eight-hour stretch in September which gradually extended to twelve hours as the winter nights lengthened. But firefighting seldom stopped with the dawn, and it was quite usual for the men to work from ten to fifteen hours at a stretch, with long hours spent in clothes heavy with water, with hearts heavy with fear and apprehension. As this first major Blitz on the Capital progressed, the nights grew colder, and the hardships of working in full and constant exposure to personal danger became more and more wearying. But throughout, fires were fought in the open when bombs were falling, and night after night heavy explosives and incendiaries rained down on the unfaltering firefighters, who were also in mortal danger from fire-damaged buildings, and the constant risk of being hit by flying glass and shrapnel from both German bombs and our own anti-aircraft artillery. The reputation of the Fire Service was greatly enhanced at this time and during a famous speech by Winston Churchill he dubbed the firefighters, 'Heroes with grimy faces'.

Eyewitness accounts of London during the Blitz have proved to be both tragic and awe-inspiring. In one event from October 13th 1940, a group of people hearing the air raid sirens took to a public shelter in the basement of a five story block of flats, only for a bomb to strike a direct hit on the building. They were trapped by the wreckage, and as the water and sewage pipes had ruptured the entombed people drowned as rescue teams struggled to reach them. Eleven days later, 154 bodies were recovered. Tragic accounts such as that were common during the Blitz, with bombs falling on a daily basis, to the point where they almost became a routine inconvenience. When people heard the air raid sirens, they would head for the Tube stations, public shelters, or even the Anderson shelters that many people had in their backyards, which were essentially corrugated tin boxes that would never have survived a direct hit. In many instances, people would just hide under their kitchen tables, wait until the planes had passed, and then get on with whatever it was they had being doing before they had been so rudely interrupted!

HARRY ERRINGTON GEORGE CROSS

The first direct Fire Service recipient of the George Cross was Auxiliary Fireman Harry Errington of the London Auxiliary Fire Service. Harry was born in London in August 1910, to Polish parents, Soloman and Bella Ehregott, who had arrived from the city of Lublin in eastern Poland in 1908, and anglicised the family name to Errington when Harry was born; when by coincidence the family lived in Poland Street, Westminster. Harry was educated at the Westminster Free School, and won a trade scholarship to train as an engraver, though later he became a cutter under the direction of his uncle who was an established 'out-door tailor' with several contracts in Saville Row. Harry remained in the business until retirement.

In 1939 with the impending outbreak of a second European war, London Fire Brigade expanded to take in some 23,000 auxiliary firemen and women; amongst them was Harry, who was at the time of his gallant act posted to No. 72 fire station Shaftsbury Avenue.

On 17th September 1940, the day that the German High Command postponed the planned invasion of Great Britain, and when a bomb hit Marble Arch Underground station killing seventeen people, fireman Harry Errington was in a basement used as a private air raid shelter for the Auxiliary Fire Service, in Rathbone Street Sub-Fire Station, just off Oxford Street. This shelter was situated below a large three-storey garage. It was here, on a concrete floor, that Harry and his comrades 'bedded-down' on their blankets, after having worked fighting the flames of the Blitz, almost continuously for more than a week. Shortly before midnight the garage received a

Harry Errington George Cross.
Courtesy of the Fire Service College.

direct hit which caused all floors to collapse, bringing debris and cars crashing down from upper levels, killing some twenty people including seven firefighters. The force of the blast blew Harry across the room, and when he regained consciousness he found that he was standing amid a fierce fire which was spreading quickly across the basement. Dazed and injured, Harry was making his way to the exit when he heard screams above the terrible dissonance of the ongoing air raid, and realised that it was shrieks of pain. As a response Harry picked up a blanket which was lying on the rubble, and used it to shield his head and shoulders from the intense and almost lacerating heat, and made his way back through the now thick, black choking smoke to search for a casualty. Harry eventually located one of his comrades, fireman Hollingshead, pinned under a mass of debris, and lying face down and buried to his waist in rubble, with his bare back exposed to the searing heat. Not having tools to hand, Harry commenced to clear away the rubble with his bare hands. The intensifying fire situation made the operation both extremely painful and difficult, and Harry had to continue to protect himself from the blast of the radiated heat with the blanket held in one hand whilst removing the red-hot debris with the other. On freeing his injured colleague and carrying him out of the building, Harry found a second firefighter, John Terry, trapped under a heavy radiator. Having brought the first man to safety Harry returned, and despite the weight of the debris pinning the man, the extreme pain in his already burnt hands, the exhaustion he must have been suffering from the exertions of the first rescue, and the desperately worsening conditions Harry, with extraordinary gallantry, continued to work until he had effected the rescue of the second casualty. Fireman Terry was in such a debilitated state that Harry had almost to carry him via a narrow staircase out of the blazing basement to the relative safety of the outside courtyard, and thence through an adjoining building into the street. Both rescues were carried out despite the probability of the building being engulfed in fire and collapsing during the ongoing air raid. Although severely burned, both men survived and supported the recommendation of Harry for an award.

The following are extracts from statements which supported the nomination of Harry Errington for a gallantry award:

> At 2350 hours on 17th September, 1940 No, 72 Z annexe (Jackson & Alum's Garage, Rathbone Street, W1) was struck and almost demolished by a high-explosive bomb. Three auxiliary firemen (Errington, Hollingshead and Terry) were in the basement of the building and as a result of the explosion and collapse, the two last-named, were pinned under the debris and unable to extricate themselves. Errington was blown across the basement and although injured and slightly dazed, he was still capable of movement. A fierce fire broke out and Hollingshead and Terry were in imminent danger of being burned to death. Errington instead of making good his own escape, immediately went to the assistance of the other Auxiliaries, in spite of the fact

that it was necessary for him to shield himself from the heat by means of a blanket. He succeeded in rescuing Hollingshead and Terry, and after dragging them away from the immediate danger of the fire carried them separately up a rear staircase, through an adjoining building and so to the street. Without doubt Errington's action saved the other two Auxiliary's lives and I have no hesitation in stating that this rescue was carried out under difficult and extremely dangerous conditions …

H. R. Lucas, District Officer:
The statement above is inadequate to describe the bravery displayed by Auxiliary Errington, as my life was saved only by his efforts and endurance. His calmness, bravery, and quick thinking in a highly dangerous situation were beyond praise.

J. Hollingshead:
I entirely agree with the above statements. It was solely due to Auxiliary Errington's action that my life was saved. The fact that a serious fire had already broken out and debris was still falling bears witness to his bravery in remaining to effect two difficult rescues, when he did not even know whether the single remaining means of egress from the basement was still passable. As on all occasions when I have worked with him at fires, he took no thought of his own life.

J. E. Terry.

Major Jackson in his statement of recommendation for the award of the George Cross to Auxiliary Fireman Errington said of Harry and this incident:
    … No. 72 Z station annexe … received direct hits by high explosive and incendiary bombs. The three-storied building was almost demolished and a serious fire broke out which necessitated the attendance of twenty pumps for extinguishment. Seven auxiliaries were killed, several injured, and some pinned or trapped beneath debris. After working with his bare hands for some five or six minutes, he managed to release first one, and then the other of his comrades dragging them in turn from the imminent vicinity of the fire and burning debris. While he was so engaged burning debris was falling into the basement and there was considerable danger of a further major collapse of the building.

A town in north-east England recovers from the previous night's attack.
Courtesy of Tyne and Wear Fire and Rescue Service.

He then carried them out one at a time up a narrow stone staircase, partially
choked with debris into a court yard, also covered in debris. From there he
made his way through an adjoining building and thence into the street.
Hollingshead and Terry in addition to other injuries, were burned on the
shoulders and back, and were certified to be suffering from severe burns
(third degree), a fact that illustrates the conditions at the time of the rescue,
and the extreme courage and endurance of the rescuer. There can be no
doubt that this rescue … was carried out under appalling conditions at very
considerable risk to himself and obviously without any thought for self
preservation. By his act he displayed exceptional bravery and endurance.

For his extreme courage and outstanding endurance under the most appalling
conditions, Harry Errington was awarded the newly instituted George Cross. This
recognition of gallantry was soured by the disgraceful treatment meted out to Harry
under the Civil Injuries Act. This particular piece of legislation applied to the Fire
Service, and ruled that firemen injured in war service could only be kept on full pay
for thirteen weeks. As Harry's burns had still not healed he was compulsorily discharged
from the Service.

Harry Errington GC was the first guest to be invited to the City of Sunderland
Remembrance Parade by the Parade Steering Group in November of 2000, and he
died on 15th December 2004, aged 94 years old. Harry's medal group, which also
included the Defence Medal, the Queen's Coronation Medal, the Queen's Silver
Jubilee Medal and the Queen's Golden Jubilee Medal, is held by the Museum of the
Association of Jewish ex-Service men and women; although Harry did not serve in
the armed forces. The writer is indeed proud to have known Harry Errington GC as
a friend, and as a brother firefighter and Freemason.

On 18–19th September Section Officer Cyril Leopold Meyrick Rogers of Croydon
AFS at great personal risk made an attempt to enter a house in Langland Gardens,
Shirley, Croydon which had been hit by a bomb and demolished, but had to withdraw
because of the heat and dense almost impenetrable plumes of choking smoke. Rogers
then instructed one of the firefighters to direct a jet of water at and around him, as he
made a second attempt to enter the wrecked dwelling despite the escape of gas which
was now making the operation extremely difficult. Ignoring the difficulties brought
about by an almost irrespirable atmosphere, and the extreme danger of further structural
collapse, Section Officer Rogers showed great courage and perseverance in digging
his way through the debris. Working in an extremely confined space, and at times
actually holding the weight of the wreckage on his back, he managed to effect the
rescue of a man and two women. For his gallant and determined actions that night
Section Officer Cyril Leopold Meyrick Rogers was also awarded the George Medal.

On that same night, thirty-six year-old Louise Rainbow of Number 2 fire station Manchester Square was in charge of the watch room at John Lewis's premises in Oxford Street, when a number of bombs landed in the vicinity as the fire appliances were turning-out to a fire. One of the bombs started a fire in the store itself, and with great presence of mind Section Officer Rainbow remained in communication with the local fire station, informing them of the occurrence and asking for assistance; she then proceeded to extinguish an incendiary bomb and materially assisted in preventing fire spread. Section Officer Rainbow although recommended for the George Medal, was awarded the King's Commendation for Brave Conduct.

On the day war broke out, nineteen year-old Miss Gillian Klaune Tanner drove from her home near Cirencester, to London to volunteer her services to the war effort. On arrival the Women's Voluntary Service directed her to the Auxiliary Fire Service where she became a driver. This young woman raised in comparative rural comfort, whose main activity had been horse riding, was at first distressed to learn she was being posted to Dock Head, in south-east London, which she thought of as 'the slums'. She was, however, to gain the respect of her colleagues, and the public by her great courage and unruffled dedication to her duty.

On the night of 20th September 1940, Firewoman Gillian (known to all as Bobbie) Tanner was instructed to load her thirty cwt lorry with 150 gallons of petrol in two-gallon containers, to proceed to where six serious fires were blazing to replenish the pumps. She set off from Dockhead fire station across London Bridge and through streets lined with blazing buildings, with all the noise and menace of an air raid in full blast. Shrapnel from anti-aircraft guns rattled on the pavements but, undeterred, Bobbie drove on through the dock gates towards the inferno that was her destination.

It was an awe-inspiring sight, as the great warehouses along the dockside blazed whilst small groups of firefighters wrestled with powerful jets of water that seemed to make no impression on the flames. Clouds of sparks rose high into the sky, carried aloft by the terrific heat up-draught as enemy bombers cruised threateningly over-head. Bobby reported to a control officer and was instructed to deliver her fuel to a section of pumps working on the quayside. Each can weighed about seventeen pounds, and Bobbie carried her petrol from pump to pump topping up the tanks, exercising great care since the glowing hot exhaust manifold lay only inches from the tank filler cap. Such an operation calls for a steady hand and a cool nerve at the best of times, and more so with the distraction of being under attack by enemy bombers. One careless move or a blast from a nearby explosion would have splashed petrol over the manifold with disastrous results. After a period of considerable physical exertion and nerve-wracking effort, all the fuel was distributed, whereupon she collected up the empty cans and returned them to her station.

The outstanding act of courage and commitment to duty on the part of this young woman, earned Bobby Tanner the only George Medal to be awarded to a female member of the fire Service during the war.

That night Auxiliary firemen Jack Johnson, aged thirty-one years, and Dennis McCarthy, forty-seven years of age, both well regarded as highly motivated and very effective firefighters and working out of station No 43 at Lindsell Street, Greenwich, were on a branch fighting a serious fire at Scott's Sufference Wharf, Tooley Street. The explosion of a nearby bomb caused a wall adjacent to where they were working to collapse, throwing them both to the ground and partially burying them in the debris. Although badly bruised and shocked they immediately recommenced their efforts in subduing the flames, which not only prevented the fire spreading, but prevented a light being shown to the enemy bombers who were still overhead. In a statement made after this incident, District Officer J. W. Pullin wrote in recommendation for both men to be awarded the British Empire Medal:

'Auxiliary firemen Johnson has attended numerous fires under my direction since the commencement of the bombing of London, and has always shown a readiness to carry out the orders given by his officers no matter how hazardous the duty. Auxiliary fireman McCarthy since his attachment to Greenwich fire station has shown on every occasion when attending fires an utter disregard for his personal safety and a great readiness to carry out orders given to him by his officers and thus shown an example to the remainder of the appliance crews with him.'

During an air raid on 24th September 1940, a high explosive bomb hit the factory of pharmaceutical chemists May & Baker Ltd, of Rainham Road, Dagenham, striking a hangar where highly flammable material was stored and starting a fire. William Thomas Beeson as officer in charge of the Works Fire Brigade got his crews to work immediately, and on making an assessment of the situation it was obvious to him that the principal danger lay in the involvement of a stock of metallic sodium – a highly reactive element, which is a soft, bright, silvery metal which floats on water, and is likely to decompose in such circumstances leading to spontaneous ignition. The metallic sodium was burning fiercely and Beeson recognised that the use of water as a firefighting medium would only exacerbate an already very serious situation, one further complicated by streams of burning flammable liquids flowing through the area where his crews were working and clouds of toxic fumes given off by over a ton of assorted chemicals scattered by the bomb. Moreover the explosion had thrown two large 500 lbs cylinders of compressed ammonia into the seat of the fire.

One of the cylinders did in fact explode, flinging burning sodium metal in all directions, as well as producing the conditions of a gas attack. Beeson was burnt about the face, but was saved from further serious injury by the prompt and energetic intervention of Fireman Lewis Fisher, who rendered him invaluable assistance. Without counting the risk to his own safety, Fisher was foremost among the crew members tackling this serious and potentially catastrophic fire under Beeson's direction. When the ammonia cylinder exploded, Fisher found that several of the crew were injured.

He then got them all to the relative safety of the nearest underground shelter, whilst a first aid party was summoned. Fisher returned immediately to his firefighting duties, and made a valuable contribution to bringing the blaze under control. His fearlessness, cheerfulness and devotion to duty were beyond praise.

Both William Thomas Beeson and Lewis Phillip Fisher were awarded the George Medal for their actions that night.

The May & Baker factory, designated as a high risk by the Fire Service, was again hit by enemy action in early 1944, and ten pumping appliances were dispatched as an immediate response. So potentially serious was this fire, that the incident was soon escalated to fifty pumps; the principal concern being for the protection of the plant manufacturing Mepacrin, an anti-malaria drug, which was supplied in great bulk to General 'Bill' Slim's 14th Army. Loss of this production would have slowed, if not halted the 14th Army's rout of the Japanese Forces from Burma. The incident, commanded by Divisional Officer Cyril de Marne, was executed with great professionalism and initiative, thereby averting a possible catastrophic reversal of fortunes in the Far East campaign.

On the night of 25–26th September, 1940, serious bombing again took place over south London, and a number of fires were started in the Brixton area. A fire call was received to Loughborough junction on the Southern Railway system, and at 0035 a pump was dispatched from Brixton fire station with Station Officer Lawrence Coombs in charge. Whilst attending to this fire, which was quickly extinguished, Coombs noticed another fire a short distance away, which was showing sufficient light as to easily be detected by enemy aircraft. On investigation it was found to be a range of factory buildings covering an acre of ground, and used in connection with the storage and packing of grain; part of the factory was well alight, and Coombs immediately sent back an assistance message requesting both additional pumping appliances, and senior officers to establish an effective command and control infrastructure. Two lines of hose were got to work from Coombs's appliance which was situated on a narrow drive on the eastern side of the blaze, and where the railway line was seriously threatened by the spread of the fire. Coomb's firefighters were in a difficult and dangerous situation, but it was not possible to provide assistance to them at that time, as the decision had been made that protection was urgently required on the north side of the incident, where another large building was in imminent danger of becoming involved. When the reinforcing appliances arrived, he therefore sent them to the north side, and it was only through his determined leadership that the men were able to prevent the fire from spreading to the railway lines on the eastern side of the fire-ground.

As other large fires were begun in the neighbourhood by a further attack of incendiaries, the senior officers in attendance were designated to take command of those incidents, and consequently Coombs was left in sole charge of the original fire. More high explosive and incendiary bombs were dropped on the factory building and the fire became much more intense, and as the water mains in the area were seriously damaged by the bombing, the situation was further exacerbated by a lack of extinguishing media. This was the critical state of affairs which confronted this Station Officer at the first major fire he had commanded since being promoted, but fortunately Coombs had made a study of the emergency water supplies available in that locale, and after an extensive search of the area, made under the most difficult conditions, an unaffected source was located about half a mile from the fire.

When further assistance arrived, he was able to direct those pumps to that location, and organise and direct a water relay. He was then able to mount a concerted attack on the blaze from the west side where a timber yard and other buildings were seriously threatened by the potential fire spread. By this stage of the incident he was badly in need of more resources, and it was only by his initiative and prudent use of the seven pumping appliances and their crews which were under his command, that the fire was held in check. Even with the fresh water supplies, the nature of the contents of the building, and the fresh wind that was blowing still made this fire a grave risk to the surrounding properties, and it would not have been unreasonable for Coombs to request further appliances. However, being fully aware of the great demands being put upon the resources of the Brigade, he carried on throughout the night and into the morning without further assistance, refreshments or relief. Most of the firefighters under Coomb's command were inexperienced but, by his inspiring example and unfailing energy, he was able to impart confidence to them. He was awarded the British Empire Medal to recognise his resourcefulness and clear, cool judgement under the most exacting and dangerous of conditions which contributed materially to preventing what undoubtedly could have been a major conflagration.

On the night of 28–29th September 1940, as a result of enemy action three houses in Cavendish Place, Eastbourne were completely demolished, and seven persons were trapped under the wreckage. The efforts of the fire brigade were a great contributory factor in the ultimate release of five of the persons trapped. Chief Fire Officer Sydney Albert Phillips, in particular, acted with much energy and resource, making many excursions under the wreckage in an attempt to locate and rescue the casualties, directing the rescue operations and generally encouraging his men. During the operations to locate and extricate the remainder of the casualties it was discovered that an unexploded high-explosive bomb was lying some 200 feet away from the scene of operations. Because of the imminent and extreme danger this presented, volunteers were called for to continue operations. Alfred Ernest Blackmer, Edwin Humphrey May, Francis Charles Stevens and Ernest Lawson Turney of the Eastbourne ARP rescue party were amongst the first men to volunteer, and the lion's share of credit for these courageous rescues must go to these gallant volunteers.

Blackmer, Stevens and Turney were involved in work to penetrate the wall of a cellar, through a matchboard refrigerator lined with cork and then through another

William Mosedale George Cross of Birmingham Fire Brigade.
Courtesy of West Midlands Fire Service.

twelve-inch concrete wall. This work was carried out in extremely hazardous conditions, in a very confined space with the ever-present prospect of heavy debris falling on them. Through their untiring and dauntless efforts three of the trapped persons were rescued. Edwin May laboured unceasingly throughout the night in a most gallant manner, whilst Blackmer and Turney, overcome by cold and the effects of escaping gas and water in the cellar, had to be removed from the scene of operations. Once they had recovered, both men returned to work and continued to give strenuous assistance to the task of releasing a young girl who was pinned down by timber and debris, the weight of which had failed to be moved even by the combined efforts of six jacks! Eventually after strenuous and heavy toil the timber was at last lifted.

The whole of these courageous actions were carried out in the most appalling conditions. In their efforts, which greatly contributed to the ultimate rescue of five of seven the persons, these men laboured in an atmosphere rendered foul by escaping gas, in a cellar filled with water. Further they worked for much of the time with the knowledge that they were well within the explosive range of a delayed-action bomb. The Chief Fire Officer of the Eastbourne Fire Brigade, Sydney Albert Phillips, attended the scene of this structural collapse with his fire crews and directed initial operations, making a number of excursions under the wreckage (despite it being no part of his duties), and gave an outstanding example of leadership through his great energy and resourcefulness which gave encouragement to his firefighters, and contributed to the eventual release of five of the casualties. Blackmer, May, Stevens and Turney were all awarded the George Medal for their gallantry.

Also on that night a house in Kensington Gardens Square, Bayswater, London was severely damaged by a high-explosive bomb, and a woman was trapped by a heavy amount of debris on a bed, which was in a very precarious position on the partly demolished third floor. At great personal risk, Auxiliary Fireman Herbert Charles Barker crawled across the floor of this ruined house which was hanging at an angle, and secured a line around the casualty. He was then able, with some assistance, to pull her from the bed to safety. For his courageous rescue Auxiliary Fireman Barker was awarded the George Medal.

THE LATE AUTUMN
OF 1940

As the autumn of 1940 wore on, the air raid warnings sounded earlier with each passing week as the sun began to set a little sooner every day, and the prospect of a winter's war of attrition on the home front became a dreadful and realistic prospect. The full moons of September and October became an enormous asset to the bomber crews of the Luftwaffe, as London was revealed to them almost as clearly as in day time, and the river Thames became a shimmering silvery ribbon that acted as a marker for their bloody attacks. These 'Bombers' Moons' brought with them the phenomena of spring tides, that is when a particularly low tide occurred during the night, at the height of the air raid, causing immense problems with respect to water supplies, and the movement of fire boats.

Given the catastrophic events of the previous few weeks, the men and women of the fire and ambulance services, and of all the other emergency and essential services, when leaving home to report for duty each evening, must have felt very much like a condemned man talking an early walk to the scaffold so as not to be late! Making their way through crater-pocked streets, littered with broken slates, woodwork, glass and bricks, they must have wondered what that night's attack would bring, and whether they would see another day break. However, once at work with the enemy bomber force overhead, any thoughts of fear, sorrow, foreboding or weakness were put to one side, and the work of rescue and firefighting was carried out to the very best of their abilities.

The enemy's night-time air activity on Tuesday 15th October 1940 began at 1830 hours when fleets of aircraft were plotted leaving Luftwaffe airfields in Holland and the Dutch islands, the Somme/Fecamp area, Le Havre and Cherbourg. The principal target for this particularly heavy night of bombing was London, but a steady stream of bombers was tracked heading for Birmingham.

In London as a result of these air attacks, high-explosive bombs damaged the Southern Railway power station at Wimbledon, the Metropolitan Underground Railway at Whitechapel High Street and the South Metropolitan Gas Works at Greenwich, damaging a gas holder. Waterloo Station was attacked twice during the day at 0916 hours and at 2010 hours. Serious track damage resulted from the first attack, platforms 3 and 4 were hit, and a train was wrecked. A large crater on the line was made, into which an express train from Euston had overturned. In the West Ham area alone a forty pump fire took place at Silvertown Lubricants, and a twenty-five pump fire at Pinchin Johnson Ltd. At 1940 hours high-explosive bombs fell on Morley College, Westminster Bridge Road, which was used as a rest centre. Some 185 people were rescued in the early stages of the incident, and operations commenced to extricate a further ninety persons who were trapped in the debris.

During this carnage a high-explosive bomb fell on BBC Broadcasting House, a large building in Portland Place, St. Marylebone, causing a fire and trapping a number of people under the wreckage. At 2105 hours a call was received at Number 2 fire station, Manchester Square, to report a fire at these premises, with persons reported as being trapped in the wreckage. A trailer pump from Manchester Square was dispatched and a despatch rider sent to inform District Officer Allan Frank Locke, a professional firefighter of fifteen years service with the LFB.

On arrival, the first crew found that a small fire was in progress on the fifth floor of the building, caused by the explosion of a delayed action bomb, and this was extinguished by means of first aid firefighting equipment. But given the extensive structural damage, the number of persons unaccounted for, and the possibility of fire spread from the dozen or so surrounding buildings which were well alight, Station Officer Arthur Bacon sent an assistance message requesting ten pumps to deal with the situation. A search was then made for a former London firefighter, Mr G. Robilliard, who was working for the BBC, who had been last seen on that floor prior to the explosion. Robilliard was eventually located, seriously injured and badly burned, and his life was certified as being extinct by a doctor who was on hand. On the arrival of District Officer Locke pumps were made to thirty and two turntable ladders requested, as the situation had deteriorated.

By this time the Chief Superintendent of London Fire Brigade's A Division, Mr C. P. McDuel, was in attendance, and it was brought to his attention that two more persons were trapped on the fifth floor. He delegated District Officer Locke to take charge of the rescue operations on this level, and proceeded to the rear part of the third floor, which had taken the full impact of the explosion, where several other people were buried under debris, and made an assessment of this very serious situation. Studio three, a room of about twenty-four feet by twelve feet, had collapsed under the weight of the destabilised floors above, entombing a number of persons, three of whom were believed to be still alive. The Chief Superintendent then called all fire brigade personnel who were not still involved in work to the third floor, and the next phase of the rescue commenced.

During the firefighting and rescue operations a number of small fires broke out on the roof of the remains of the BBC Broadcasting House, and neighbouring buildings, and consequently the turntable ladders were in constant use attacking these outbreaks. At one stage in the incident the wind changed, causing the branch-man on one of the turntable ladders to become engulfed in flames.

To release the first person from the ruins of the studio, it was necessary to tunnel a distance of eight feet under the debris, and as masonry and a ventilation shaft were obstructing the excavation, it was necessary to have them raised; the attendance of an emergency tender and a breakdown lorry were therefore requested for jacking equipment. The work of tunnelling was carried out by District Officer Locke using a saw and his bare hands, and the woman who was pinned deep within the wreckage of Broadcasting House, in a doubled-up position between a door and some wooden partitioning, was eventually released after two hours of intensive and dangerous work in very cramped and almost irrespirable conditions. To reach the second person it was necessary to tunnel a further six feet and cut away a millboard partition, and after another hour's work that person was extricated.

Station Officer Arthur Bacon who had been assisting Locke then took over, and with the help and support of Sub-Officer George Weston tunnelled a further three feet into the wreckage and reached a man who had been seriously injured, and was pinned in a very difficult position under the wreckage; this man was eventually extracted after a further two hours of work. In his report of 18th October 1940 concerning this series of rescues at Broadcasting House, Chief Superintendent McDuel wrote, 'Mr Locke and Station Officer Bacon, I consider, carried out the work of rescue under extremely difficult and dangerous conditions, and in connection with this, I would like to call attention to the very fine work carried out by Acting Sub-Officer Weston in assisting Station Officer Bacon.'

The Director-General of the BBC, Sir Frederick Wolff Ogilvie, wrote in a letter dated 29th October 1940 to Commander A. N. G. Firebrace, who by this time was not in command of London Fire Brigade but Regional Fire Officer for London:

> I am writing to ask, on behalf of the Corporation, if you will be so good as to express to the members of the London Fire Brigade who were here on the night of 15/16th , our very warm appreciation of the skill and courage they showed both in putting out the fire, and in extricating the injured from one of our studios.

All who saw their work, and I happened to be among that number myself, speak of it in the highest terms. And I should like, if I may, particularly to mention Divisional Officer Locke who tunnelled under the wreckage to extricate the injured, spending two and a half hours at a single stretch, at great danger to himself, and refusing to be relieved. He was wholly exhausted by his work when he came out.

May I submit that his name should be considered as a candidate for the George Medal.

District Officer Allan Frank Locke was awarded the George Medal for his part in the operations at the BBC that night; Station Officer Arthur Bacon although also recommended for the George Medal was awarded the British Empire Medal, and Sub-Officer George Weston the King's Commendation for Brave Conduct.

After handing control of the BBC incident to a more junior rank, District Officer Locke returned to his district control room at Manchester Square, and was informed that a sub-station in Chelsea had received a direct hit. Locke immediately proceeded to this location despite the ongoing air raid, and by great luck he and his dispatch rider were uninjured when a stick of three bombs exploded near to them in the Hyde Park area. On arrival at the Chelsea sub-station Locke found that a large bomb had caused severe damage to the station. One firefighter was killed, several were wounded and receiving treatment, and that one man was unaccounted for. Locke joined in the search for their missing comrade, and he eventually found a steel helmet some twenty yards away, and the now-dead firefighter lying face down in the gutter.

Later in the evening Locke was dispatched to a fire at Sutherland Street, Pimlico where he found a landscape of total devastation, with fire appliances, ambulances and other vehicles damaged and on fire. The cause of this extensive destruction was a high explosive bomb which had fallen earlier in the evening and a landmine which had floated from the skies ten minutes before Locke's arrival. Despite the appalling situation facing all firefighters in and around Sutherland Street, Locke's attention was caught by the extraordinary and surreal sight of an auxiliary firefighter in shirt sleeves, minus fire tunic, sitting at the edge of the bomb crater with his feet dangling in the water. It was not that the man had taken leave of his senses, or was suffering some form of shell shock, but merely that he, a pump operator, was calmly cleaning the strainers of two trailer pumps, oblivious to the fires blazing around him, the explosions, gunfire, the scream of falling bombs, and frantic firefighting activity!

After controlling operations at a number of major fires in the west-end, Locke was taking a much-needed cup of tea in Westminster fire station when he was informed that Brompton fire station had received a direct hit from a parachute mine, and that a number of persons were missing. Responding to this information, he walked through the appliance room to his car, just as bombs falling nearby blew the appliance room doors open. On reaching the area of Brompton fire station, Locke found all approaches to the station choked with debris, and accordingly he had to proceed on foot. This was a ten-pump incident with eight firefighters missing. In due course three men were brought from the wreckage; regrettably none were to survive. From this incident District Officer Locke proceeded to an incident in Westminster where a bomb had struck an extended turntable ladder killing one firefighter and seriously injuring several others, this was followed by an oil bomb which had hit that particular appliance, setting it alight. The officer in charge of this fire informed Locke that the firefighter who had been positioned at the head of the turntable ladder had had a remarkable escape when the bomb struck the upper extension where he was positioned, crashing it into a blazing church roof, rendering the firefighter, not surprisingly, unconscious. Fortunately the man soon came to and was able to unhook himself from the ladder, and managed to make his way to ground level relatively unharmed.

The following night Wandsworth fire station was demolished in an air raid, and six of its firefighters were killed.

On 20th October 1940, Leading Auxiliary Fireman Frederick Edward Christopher Meaks was the officer in charge of the crew of a fire appliance at Commercial Pier Wharf when the ongoing and extremely serious fire situation compelled them to commandeer a barge which was alongside them to effect an escape. Meaks, hearing that a number of nurses had been driven by the fire onto another dumb barge at South Wharf, put-off alone in a small boat in an endeavour to rescue them. Owing to the severity of the fire the mooring lines of a great many barges had been burnt through, and consequently some fifty vessels were adrift, half of them alight. As a result Meaks had to steer his craft through this hellish scene, with the very real possibility of being burnt to death or drowned. He was, however, carried downstream by the tide, and eventually picked up by the fire-boat James Braidwood. Although unsuccessful in his rescue attempt, he displayed great courage in this extremely hazardous endeavour. Meaks resumed firefighting until the next morning when he again took charge of his crew at Odessa Wharf, and he continued to fight the fires throughout the following day – 'His cheerfulness and indifference to danger were inspiring'.

District Officer Plimmer wrote in support of an award of the British Empire Medal for Meaks: 'As officer in charge of 50 Pageant's Wharf, I can certify that Leading Auxiliary Fireman Meaks was in charge of his crew at Commercial Pier Wharf on 7th/9th September, 1940, and at Odessa Wharf on 8th September, 1940. His leadership warrants commendation.'

The OBE was awarded to London Fire Brigade Chief Superintendent Trevor Frank Watkin, in recognition of his cool courage, excellent example, and complete grasp of difficult situations, and his exceptional ability in dealing with many of the large fires which occurred in the south east area of London during the intensive air raids of

September and October 1941. Watkins attended 123 fires, twenty-five of which were major incidents, including the oil tanks at Thameshaven, the Royal Arsenal Woolwich on three occasions, Siemens Woolwich, and the fire stations at Churchdown School and Invicta Road which received direct hits. Throughout this period Watkins displayed the greatest qualities of leadership, initiative and bravery, and was never overawed by the great responsibility which was placed upon his shoulders in commanding so many major and extremely dangerous fires, under air raid conditions.

His hands-on qualities of leadership were shown when he attended a serious fire in the 'Danger Buildings' of the Royal Arsenal, and was the first firefighter to enter the smoke-logged and extremely hazardous area to commence ventilation of the products of combustion to ease the workload of the fire crews who were then entering with lines of hose. During air raids where there were no fires in his district, Watkins continually travelled around his area of responsibility to visit his fire-crews, and despite the long hours, stressful operations, night work and fatigue, his administrative work was carried on ably during the day.

On the night of 8th November 1940 there was a heavy raid in the neighbourhood of fire station 3 'W' situated at the Millbank School, Erasmus Street, Westminster. At 2240 hours a high-explosive bomb fell on an adjoining building, and the blast caused serious damage to the school. After the explosion the three women auxiliaries left on the premises set about restoring the blackout, and recommenced their watch-room duties. Twenty minutes after the explosion a stick of incendiaries fell around the school, and as all fire crews were off-station dealing with other fires, two of the women, Ivy Winifred Spears and Mary Weaver, commenced to deal with offending pieces of ordnance, and between them they extinguished nine of the incendiary bombs in the schoolyard which were illuminating the area to the obvious advantage of the Luftwaffe. Once they had accomplished this task it became obvious that three fires had broken out on the roof. Taking a stirrup pump and bucket of water they made their way through the school, and out onto a flat first-floor roof, and by the precarious use of a chair they managed to gain access to a higher level between two gable ends. Auxiliaries Spears and Weaver then made a brave attempt at extinguishing these fires, but given the inadequate firefighting equipment at their disposal, their courageous efforts were unsuccessful. They were, fortunately, able to make contact with a crew working near to the Erasmus Street fire station, and assisted these firefighters to get a jet of water to work on the roof, and they remained there fighting the fire until such time as it was certain that the outbreaks had been completely extinguished, so releasing the fire crew to proceed to other incidents. Shortly after midnight more incendiary bombs were dropped onto the building, setting fire to another area which was being used as a rest centre. Spears and Weaver again tackled the fires and succeeded in keeping them in check until a pump could be got to work.

During the whole of the period in which the foregoing incident took place, a heavy raid was in progress with shell splinters falling, and two other high-explosive bombs and numerous incendiaries fell in the vicinity. In a recommendation to have these two Women Auxiliaries awarded the Oak Leaf insignia of the King's Commendation for Brave Conduct, Deputy Chief Officer Major F. W. Jackson wrote on 19th May 1941, 'It was under these very hazardous and trying conditions that Women Auxiliaries Spears and Weaver displayed courage, coolness and initiative, and without a doubt did much towards saving the building from more serious damage.'

On 11th November 1940 a high-explosive bomb struck the edge of a gas holder in the Gas Works at Walsall, making a hole in the crown of the structure and igniting the gas. On the arrival of the Fire Service, jets of water were brought to play on the gas holder in an attempt to keep it cool, but flames were still to be seen coming from the aperture. Throughout the proceedings Mr Fred Thickett, the works foreman, Section Officer Thomas Pearson of the Walsall Auxiliary Fire Service and Superintendent Richard Noel Hateley of the Corporation Gas Department were on the edge of the structure, never more than three feet from the fire. Efforts were made to 'stop-up' the opening by means of corrugated sheets. This was only partially effective, as flames continued to shoot through the hole. Section Officer Pearson and foreman Thickett then endeavoured to cover the opening with a tarpaulin, and with Superintendent Hateley they stepped onto the holder and pulled the sheets over the gaps that remained. During this time the three men were near to the centre of the crown of the holder and in very grave danger, as the holder had sunk near to the ground and there was a serious risk of explosion. Showing complete disregard for their own safety, Thickett, Pearson and Hateley succeeded in their efforts and extinguished the fire. Superintendent Richard Noel Hateley was awarded the George Medal, and Mr Fred Thickett and Section Officer Thomas Pearson the British Empire Medal.

At 10.00 pm on 16th November 1940 a high-explosive bomb fell into the yard of Fleet Central School, in Mansfield Road, London NW 3, where fire station 75 Z was located. Extensive damage was caused to the school, a number of fire appliances were destroyed and set alight, four Auxiliary firefighters were killed, and twenty-two injured. On duty in the watch-room when the explosion took place were Auxiliary Daisy Irene Swingler who had served for eighteen months, and Section Officer Dorothy May Bunting who had herself only been with the Fire Service for two years. Both women, although suffering badly from the effects of the blast and partially buried in debris, managed to extricate themselves. With as much composure as they could muster, Swingler and Bunting set to work in a most professional manner in the darkness, and the now dust-laden atmosphere of the wrecked watch room, to re-establish telephone communications, and send an assistance message to Kentish town fire station. Both of these Auxiliaries remained at their posts, calmly sending and receiving messages and maintaining the all important communications links in spite of the deaths and injuries visited upon their colleagues, and the devastation all around them, until the station had to be abandoned.

In the report which recommended Auxiliary Swingler and Section Officer Bunting for the King's Commendation for Brave Conduct, Major F.W. Jackson, Deputy Chief Commanding the London Fire Brigade wrote: 'Both these members of the Women's Auxiliary Fire Service did invaluable work in collecting records and tracing the next of kin of casualties, and assisting at the subsequent roll call at the Sub-District Station, and their behaviour throughout was an outstanding example of calm courage and devotion to duty, which was an Inspiration to all who came into contact with them.'

Although Birmingham had been subjected to air attacks throughout 1940, the first significant raid occurred on 25–26th August, resulting in twenty-five deaths. The following night saw a severe raid on the area of Snow Hill which caused severe damage, and no less than an astounding 224 jets of water had to be used to bring the subsequent blaze under control, some of which were fed by a fire float pumping from a branch of the canal. On 25th October the Luftwaffe made concerted efforts to destroy the centre of the city, and at 1906 hours that evening fire control received the 'red warning'. The first emergency call was received ten minutes later for the Holloway Head area of central Birmingham, which held thousands of 'back to back' residential properties. It was not until 0300 hours the following morning that all fires were under control, by which time 276 fire calls had been received, and 548 pumping appliances put to use, including 111 from other brigades.

At the end of October, Deputy Chief Inspector of Fire Brigades at the Home Office, Mr Tom Breaks (mentioned earlier for his involvement in operations at the oil tank fires at Llanreath) was dispatched to Birmingham at the behest of the Regional Commissioner to make an examination of the organisation and operational competence of the Birmingham Fire Brigade. On his arrival Breaks called an immediate meeting of the Brigade's officers, who had been fighting fires with little rest for ten days, and by his vituperative comments, which strongly implied inefficiency on their part, he caused great damage to the morale of this very professional Brigade at a time when their self-esteem as firefighters was all important. He also upset the Councillors on the Fire Committee, and consequently was recalled to the Home Office, and replaced by Captain B.A. Westbrook, Chief of the Fire Brigade Division of the Home Office.

During the night of 19th November 1940 a large and concerted attack by some 350 bombers took place. The alert sounded at 1851 hours and the raid lasted almost ten hours, during which time some 425 fire-calls were received by the Fire Brigade, and 641 fire appliances (including 109 from other brigades) were in use. The raid was intensive and developed quickly, spreading over a large area of the city. District Officer Calypso Clarence Gammon of the City of Birmingham Fire Brigade was in charge of a large fire that night at Messrs Partridge and Lawrence Ltd, 25 Tenby Street North,

Birmingham, the premises of which were severely damaged by high-explosive and incendiary bombs and were ablaze from end to end.

The only means of accessing the seat of the fire was via two covered passage ways on either side of the factory. It was in one of these passages that Auxiliary Fireman Wilson was rendered unconscious, and buried in the debris when one wall of the building collapsed, having apparently ventured too deep whilst engaged in firefighting operations. Leading Fireman James Hogan, under whose direction Wilson was acting, heard the fall of debris and immediately proceeded to the scene. When he arrived, all that he could see was a length of partially buried hose. He immediately went for assistance and DO Gammon went back with him, and both men commenced to search for Wilson, whom they found in a sitting position and surrounded by burning debris, with his legs pinned under a large concrete girder. The flames from the burning building were rapidly sweeping towards him. With the assistance of Acting Officer John Evans and Leading Fireman Hogan, DO Gammon set about removing the red-hot brick work with his hands, and despite the fact that other parts of the wall were continually falling on and about them they succeeded in reaching Wilson. By this time the fire had almost reached him, but despite the intense heat and great risk which he knew he was running, DO Gammon succeeded in lifting the concrete girder from the trapped man's legs and extracted him. Wilson was conveyed to hospital where it was found that he had a broken collar bone, a lacerated wound to the scalp and severe bruising.

The three officers concerned in the rescue all say that had not DO Gammon been able to free Wilson immediately they would have had to leave him as the heat was so intense, and walls were continually falling. These officers and particularly DO Gammon, who directed the rescue, displayed great courage and a complete disregard for their own safety. Gammon received burns to the neck and hands but continued to direct fire operations after the rescue without stopping to receive treatment. During the time the rescue was being effected, the surrounding district was subjected to an intense bombardment, including the dropping of land mines, and the whole of the area was reduced to ruins. Gammon, known as 'Clip', was born in Whitstable, Kent and came from seafaring family, hence his unusual name. He was commended in 1911 and 1913 for his work with the Fire Brigade, and in the Great War he served with the Royal Engineers. The award of the George Medal was made to District Officer Gammon, and that of the King's Commendation for Brave Conduct to LFm James Hogan and Acting Officer John Evans for their part in the rescue of Wilson.

One of the major incidents of that night was at the BSA Small Heath works, and although there is no record of firefighters losing their lives at that fire, and no gallantry awards were made, it was a major incident for the fire brigade and the other services, and most certainly merits a mention in these pages. At 9.25 pm a low flying aircraft dropped two bombs on the Small Heath works, which was one of the principal targets for the Luftwaffe, and marked on every German navigator's map of the area. The factory's strategic importance to the war effort was its massive production of weaponry, including some 1,250,000 rifles, more than 468,000 Browning machine guns, and over 42,000 Hispano 20mm Cannons for Spitfires and Hurricanes.

On receiving the fire call rescuers rushed to the scene, including the BSA's own fire brigade who pumped the Birmingham and Warwick canal dry that evening in their attempts to control the fire; sixty fire crews also attended the scene. The explosion when it came caused the concrete floors to collapse, trapping the dead and many of the survivors. Fifty-three workers were killed and eighty-nine were injured. One of the last survivors to be rescued had been entombed for nine hours. It was six weeks before the last of the bodies could be removed.

There were many medals awarded for bravery in the rescue that night – the number awarded indicates the scale of the disaster – including Alfred F. Stevens, BSA Electrician, Private Albert Bailey, Home Guard and John Hadley of the ARP who were all awarded the George Medal. Five men were awarded the British Empire Medal, four the King's Commendation for Brave Conduct, and an MBE was awarded to the Nursing Matron of BSA Small Heath, Miss Ada Mary Deeming.

Bailey, after having assisted with a number of more easily effected rescues, crawled under the debris to search for further casualties until his path was blocked by concrete, through which he could hear voices. By knocking a small hole through the concrete he was able to ascertain that four men and a girl were trapped, but could make little progress due to the metal girder running through the concrete. Bailey was joined by Stevens who brought oxyacetylene cutting gear, and as they worked other rescuers played water on them, as the fires raging above the debris were making conditions intolerable and their clothes were smouldering. Eventually a hole was made which would allow the young woman to be rescued, but further work was required to effect the rescue of the four men, during which Bailey and Stevens were scalded by firefighting water percolating through the rubble. On completing the rescues, Bailey collapsed near to the entrance of the tunnel and was evacuated by ambulance. Stevens was able to continue in the search and extrication work and was part of a group of rescuers who tunnelled under the collapsed four-storey building, where they worked for three hours using oxyacetylene cutting equipment. They eventually located two people pinned under a heavy wooden bench which was pulled clear to allow them to be freed. Throughout this operation the building, which was completely demolished and still burning, was in an extremely hazardous condition, and on a number of occasions Stevens had to work with the oxyacetylene equipment upside down held by his ankles. Several times the order was given to evacuate as enemy air craft were circling overhead, but such warnings were ignored.

Two nights later and also in Birmingham, Walter Heath, the Captain of a works Fire Brigade situated in a high-risk target area of the city, near to the Grand Union Canal and the London to Birmingham main railway line, was on duty during a heavy air raid with Fireman W. Green, when incendiary bombs fell onto the works for which they were responsible. Heath and Green tackled and extinguished a number of these incendiaries, but one which had pierced the roof of a small storeroom proved less accessible. A line of hose was run up the winding staircase in the darkness, and it was an hour before the fire was under control.

Shortly afterwards an oil bomb fell and exploded, setting fire to a pile of timber in an adjoining yard, which quickly spread to the premises. Heath and Green immediately got two jets of water to work from opposite sides of the blaze, but this proved to be ineffective. To gain a better vantage point from which to direct his jet of water into the heart of the fire and onto the roofs of the single-storey buildings, Heath climbed onto a flat roof, taking his hose line with him, and stood for over seven hours fighting the fire. Through his determined and courageous efforts the flames did not reach the vital workshops. During this operation high-explosive bombs continued to fall. One actually dropped on the spot in the yard where Heath had previously been standing, demolishing the building and injuring both firefighters. For the first hour of his ordeal Heath was alone, as assistance could not immediately be spared. In all he was on duty continuously for fifteen hours, refusing to rest until the fire was under control, and the danger had passed. For his courage and steadfast commitment to his duty Walter Heath was awarded the British Empire Medal.

Also on Saturday 19th October 1940 a fire broke out aboard the S.S. Gandia, a Belgian-owned vessel built in 1906 for the frozen meat trade, berthed in the James Watt dry dock, Greenock. Ship fires are a phenomenon feared by all firefighters, and this particular one led to the deaths of two of them: Samuel Loveman and Daniel Gallacher. Whilst on board the vessel, Leading Fireman Gallacher, a man a little over thirty years of age and part of a team of firefighters attempting to locate the seat of a fire, fell thirty feet from the middle deck to the bottom of the No.2 hold, which was on fire. As he lost his balance, Loveman attempted to save him, and the two men were seen to fall together as if locked in each other's arms. Smoke was pouring from the hold, and the Brigade was faced with a critical and extremely dangerous task in mounting the rescue of the two men.

Firemaster Pratten who was in attendance at the incident immediately donned a smoke helmet and descended into the heavily smoke-logged hold. The heat was fierce, and it was impossible for him to see a hand in front of his face, but he remained below searching until he located Gallacher, who was seriously injured. With difficulty he tied a rope around Gallacher, who was hauled to the deck. Pratten was almost overcome by the heat and smoke by this time and he had the choice of returning to the deck or becoming the third casualty. It was with great difficulty that he climbed the iron ladder and reached safety. Fireman Hamilton then went down into the hold to search for Loveman, making a valiant attempt to locate him but, despite his smoke helmet, he had to leave before finding him. Another firefighter, Third Officer Robert M'Lellan, without hesitation made the perilous descent into the hold, and was fortunate to find Loveman's body, which was hauled with a rope. He had apparently been killed outright in falling. Gallacher, fully conscious and in considerable pain, was rushed to the Infirmary, whilst Loveman's body was taken to the mortuary. Witnesses of the rescue, who described the hold as a 'veritable death trap', stated that Firemaster Pratten and firefighters M'Lennan and Hamilton displayed great courage, and were deserving the highest praise for their action. The fire was extinguished within three hours. Loveman should have been off duty that day, but changed his leave.

As a large port city on the south-coast, Southampton was a major strategic target for the Luftwaffe and consequently endured large-scale air attacks during World War Two. There were fifty-seven attacks in all, over 470 tonnes of high explosives, and some 30,000 incendiary devices were dropped on the city, damaging or destroying 45,000 buildings. It was said that the glow of Southampton burning could be seen as far away as Cherbourg on the Northern coast of France. Nazi propaganda declared that the city had been left a smoking ruin.

Of those fifty-seven air raids, by far the most destructive were on 23rd and 30th November, and 1st December, and these attacks are generally referred to as Southampton's Blitz. There were reports of German aircraft strafing the streets with machine gun fire, and although the docks were an important strategic target, inevitably it was civilians who bore the brunt of the pain and suffering. The war over Southampton eventually left 630 civilians dead and 898 seriously injured.

During one of these major air raids on 23rd November 1940, a high-explosive bomb fell on the Central Railway Station, where Fireman George Tyrrel Robinson and his crew were working, killing three firefighters and seriously injuring a further four crew members. Robinson immediately rallied the remainder of his crew to deal with the situation, and rendered first-aid treatment to the injured men. He then drove two of the casualties to hospital, returned to the incident and took charge of operations until the incident was concluded. During the whole time he was working under very dangerous conditions. His coolness and gallantry in rallying and directing the crew after his mates had been killed, saved the fire from spreading, and his promptitude in dealing with the seriously injured undoubtedly saved their lives.

Also on 23rd November 1940, Fireman Roy Clifford Day was a member of an Auxiliary Fire Service crew which had no previous experience of sustained and widespread incendiary attacks. After continually fighting fires during heavy bombing, their fire appliance was damaged by the explosion of two high-explosive bombs immediately in front of them. It was eventually necessary for all the crew, except Day, to be removed to hospital. A further fire call was received, and Day, who was strongly advised to rest and recover, insisted on taking the pumping appliance to the scene of the incident by himself, through conditions even more difficult than those of his earlier journeys. He succeeded in reaching his destination and continued working most efficiently throughout the night. Day displayed sustained courage of a high order in difficult and dangerous circumstances which were quite new to him. Both Robison and Day were awarded the George Medal for the gallantry.

Six firefighters lost their lives during the raids of 23rd November, three from Southampton Fire Brigade and three from Winchester City Fire Brigade; a further thirty-six were injured.

Mr Kenneth George Giblett was the officer in charge of the Post Office Fire Brigade unit at the Telephone Exchange Building, Bristol, during an air raid on 24th November 1940, which started with pathfinder flares lighting up the city at 6.50 pm, bringing an overwhelming level of destruction to it. The area around Wine and Castle Streets was reduced to a mass of rubble, with bombs falling on College Green, Park Street, Queen's Road, Redcliffe Street, Thomas Street and Victoria Street. Many historic buildings were lost forever, along with 10,000 houses.

When a paint store adjacent to the Telephone Exchange Building was reported as being ablaze, the Post Office Fire Brigade immediately ran out a line of hose to tackle the fire, and sent information to the local authority Fire Service, and to the owners of the store. Mr Giblett secured a number of volunteers and broke into the store and commenced to attack the fire from within. Owing to a lack of firefighting equipment, and the nature of the contents of the store, the volunteers were unable to save the building, but it was not until the roof showed critical signs of failing that the firefighting party withdrew from the premises. Giblett and his team continued their efforts with buckets of water, despite the appalling conditions due to the ongoing air raid and the continual fall of high-explosive and incendiary bombs. He carried on throughout the night, directing the work of the Post Office Fire Brigade with courage and initiative. He set a fine example which others were proud to follow, and was primarily instrumental in saving the building from destruction.

Despite the constant threat of danger from bombs and fire, Mr Samuel Frank Pople, although not a part of the Post Office Fire Brigade, returned to the building, which had been evacuated, and succeeded in restoring communications with London. He then ascended to the roof of the Exchange with others to map out a plan of action in the event of the roof catching fire, but owing to the heat and insufficient water pressure, the plan had to be abandoned, and Pole organised a bucket chain team. The flames from the store were by now almost thirty feet high and blowing towards the roof; however, Pople and his men showed no sign of fear, and undoubtedly played a principal part in saving the telephone equipment from destruction.

Mr Austin Raymond Ashley, a member of the Post Office Fire Brigade, participated in an attempt to control the outbreak, but when reports were received that certain power supplies had failed, he returned to the building and restored the supply. He then continued essential maintenance duties, taking steps to mitigate water damage to equipment and assisted in organising a bucket chain to fight the fire. Ashley as a member of the Post Office Fire Brigade displayed courage and initiative, and with no thought of his personal safety, helped maintain essential services.

The George Medal was awarded to Kenneth George Giblett, and Samuel Frank Pople, and the British Empire Medal to Austin Raymond Ashley in recognition of their courageous, determined and dutiful work during this air raid.

STATION OFFICER WILLIAM MOSEDALE GEORGE CROSS

The second Fire Service George Cross recipient of World War II, William Radenhurst Mosedale, was born in March of 1894, in Hope Street, Birmingham. At the age of fourteen years Bill enlisted in the 5th Battalion the Royal Warwickshire Regiment, part of the newly formed Territorial Army, and in 1910 joined the regular army, serving with 5th Royal Irish Lancers – now the Queen's Royal Lancers. He became a keen boxer, winning regimental and command championships, and studied to gain education certificates during his time with the Army. In 1911 he had the honour of being a member of the detachment from his regiment that attended the Coronation of His Majesty King George V. Shortly after this great occasion his parents died, and he had to leave the service to look after his widowed grandmother and younger siblings. To support his family he worked briefly as a coal miner, but having experienced and survived a colliery accident he became a railway porter at New Street Station. Mosedale appeared before the Chief Fire Officer of Birmingham to be interviewed for a post as a full-time fireman, and commenced his distinguished career in August of 1914. He first served at Lingard Street as a probationary fireman, and later transferred to Handsworth, Aston and then the Central fire station. Given that most, if not all, fire appliances were horse-drawn at that time, his cavalry experience must have marked him out as a useful hand at an early stage. In 1919 he, with other colleagues, was gassed at the Netchells Gas Works Incident (mentioned earlier). Bill was to specialise in breathing apparatus rescue work, and later passed the examination for Graduate of the Institution of Fire Engineers with distinction, and was promoted to Station Officer in 1930. He was also awarded the Fire Brigade 'first star of merit' for his work with Birmingham University's Department of Mining in the science and practice of breathing apparatus; standing him in good stead for his wartime experiences.

On the night of 23rd November, 1940 Birmingham was pounded relentlessly by the might of the Luftwaffe for thirteen hours, and consequently Station Officer Mosedale was ordered to proceed with breathing apparatus to a house in Yardley Wood Road, which had collapsed, trapping three persons in the debris. As he left the fire station in the rescue tender the bombing intensified. One bomb fell in Showell Green Lane and then a second exploded twenty yards ahead of the appliance, leaving a crater thirty feet wide and twenty feet deep. Despite the best efforts of the driver, the fire appliance came to a stop leaning precariously over the void. Mosedale managed to extricate himself from the wrecked appliance, which was in imminent danger of falling into the twenty-foot-deep hole, and made his way to the nearest fire station at Sparkhill to report the situation. As quickly as possible he proceeded to the incident on a second breathing apparatus vehicle and carried out the rescue of two people from the ruined house. Mosedale then crawled back into what remained of the now demolished building, working his way through a mass of rubble which moved dangerously, as each Luftwaffe bomb exploded, and eventually located a third casualty unconscious under a pile of debris. Clearing a way through the debris Bill administered oxygen to the casualty, and with the assistance of the ARP workers extricated him.

On 12th December that year, Mosedale and his emergency tender crew responded to a report of the auxiliary fire station in Grantham Road, Sparkbrook having received a direct hit, with fourteen persons reported as being buried. The information was: 'Nothing left of it ... and the house next door down as well.'

When Mosedale arrived, the scene that greeted him was one of total destruction. Rescue teams were desperately trying to reach the entombed civilians in the house, guided by the screams of the occupants, whilst at the same time smoke was beginning to rise from the tons of rubble that but a short time before had been the continuously manned control room. His assessment was that rescue operations at the house were well underway and so he immediately started tunnelling operations to reach the area of the control room. A small rescue team quickly assembled to assist him, and very carefully he laboriously filled the rubble baskets by hand, passing them back and propping as necessary as he advanced. The whole operation was hampered by escaping gas and coal dust, and pressure waves from bombs falling in the vicinity caused the rubble to collapse. Consequently this first tunnelling operation had to be abandoned, and a second tunnel begun, this time using wooden props to stabilise the excavation, as they worked towards the casualties entombed in the control room, until their progress was obstructed by a large girder. A further rescue attempt was commenced, and the constant threat of collapse made the digging of this third tunnel a much slower operation, but eventually their efforts were rewarded when Bill's torchlight fell upon a huddle of men, one of whom had already succumbed to the oxygen-starved atmosphere. He immediately administered oxygen to the survivors before, one by one, they were led along the tunnel to safety. This operation, carried out in an almost irrespirable atmosphere, had lasted twelve hours under intense bombardment.

When Mosedale returned to the daylight of Grantham road he was aware of the concerns of the team struggling to rescue the occupants of the house next door. Many hours had passed and the crews had found the cellar entrance door almost hopelessly blocked. Making his way to the head of the tunnel, he commenced directing operations, aware that the seven people trapped within the cellar now had little chance of survival. Although the cellar had collapsed in on itself, Mosedale continued to remove rubble as he was convinced that he could hear a weak breathing noise. He set about his task with a renewed energy, quickly finding a tiny chamber created by the cellar collapse where four of the occupants of the house lay together with the bodies of their relatives. Bill again administered oxygen and managed to bring the four survivors out of the ruins.

Back in the street Mosedale learned that the firefighter he had earlier rescued had provided reliable information as to the location of several more of their colleagues who had taken refuge in the cellar of the fire station at the commencement of the air raid. Without hesitation, he once again donned his breathing apparatus and commenced yet another tunnelling operation. This time however, he was beginning to feel the effects of hours of working in a half lying, half kneeling position, the constant to and fro of rubble and props in such cramped conditions which demanded tireless concentration. Thanks largely to the accurate information given by the earlier survivors, Mosedale was able to drive his way straight to the cellar where, although severely injured, he found four men alive. At the completion of the operation to recover the bodies of the two men who had died in the cellar, the remains of the Fire Station shifted alarmingly and the tunnel collapsed.

The only report maintained at the Birmingham Central Fire Station of the incident at Grantham Road states: 'The AFS Station, 5/4 Sparkbrook, suffered a direct hit from High Explosives and fourteen men were buried. Three were found dead and four are still in hospital, the remainder have only comparatively slight injuries. The machine house was only slightly affected'.

Throughout that night Station Officer Bill Mosedale had been given the most valuable assistance by a number of individuals, including Doctor Mary Barrow and Firemen Alfred White, Charles Wilford and George Metcalfe, all of whom were awarded the King's Commendation for Brave Conduct. Doctor Barrow had exhibited great courage and resource, and entered the tunnel on a number of occasions to administer morphine to the injured, showing outstanding dedication and a disregard for her personal safety.

The *London Gazette* of 28th March 1941 lists his award of the George Cross and closes with the following words: 'These operations which lasted more than 12 hours, were carried out under intense bombardment. Twelve lives were saved by Station Officer Mosedale who showed outstanding gallantry and resource. In effecting the rescues he repeatedly risked his own life.' Although the citation refers only to the incident of 12th December, it has been generally held that the award also recognised the rescues carried out on 23rd November.

The gallant William Radenhurst Mosedale GC retired from the Fire Service in September 1944, and established a fire prevention consultancy in Birmingham which he operated from 1946 until 1965; he died on 27th March 1971.

Superintendent Sidney William Barnes of the London Fire Brigade displayed outstanding ability, leadership and tenacity in organising and supervising firefighting operations in the area of his command during ongoing air raids. His conspicuous bravery and devotion to duty throughout the whole period of heavy bombing, particularly at the West Warehouse, London dock, Wapping on 23rd September, Number 9 Warehouse, London Dock, Wapping on 20th October, 1940, and Warehouses in Wapping High street on 29th December, 1940, were an inspiring example to his men and as a result many serious fires were prevented from spreading. A warehouse containing tons of spices and essential oils was set alight by incendiary bombs. Below the warehouse was a vault covering several acres and housing over a thousand tons of rubber. Superintendent Barnes collected a party of AFS men and led them up a blazing staircase and directed the firefighting from the top floor until he was nearly overcome by the dense smoke and rising fumes. Although the building was gutted the vault and rubber were saved.

On another occasion a bomb set fire to a warehouse which supported on its fourth floor a large iron bridge weighing many tons. Superintendent Barnes took charge and conducted firefighting operations from one of the upper floors. Whilst he was so engaged the iron bridge, together with a partitioning wall, suddenly collapsed within a few yards of where he was standing. This however, did not deter him and although heavy bombing continued, he remained at his post until the fire was under control. He was awarded the George Medal, and later appointed to the post of Deputy Fire Force Commander for London in the National Fire Service.

In December of 1940 during enemy air activity high-explosive bombs demolished two houses in Liverpool, trapping a number of people. On arrival, Auxiliary Firemen Alexander Conway and Edward Heyes of the Liverpool AFS without hesitation clambered into the remains of the dwelling, and while Heyes supported the collapsed floor with his back, Conway commenced to saw away timber. Having created a passageway into the wreckage they crawled through this opening and released five women and a child. One woman who had been embedded up to her neck in debris was sitting in an armchair and was hysterical. Conway attempted to calm and reassure the woman and removed sufficient debris from around the casualty to enable him to use a saw. To reach her the rescuers had to cut their way through a floor which had been turned on end, and through the arms of the chair. The work was hampered throughout by an escape of gas from a fractured main. Bombs were dropped in adjoining streets, the district was subjected to machine gun fire, and the whole area was lit by the many fires occurring in the neighbourhood, so making rescue workers a more obvious target for the Luftwaffe. Conway and Heyes showed great courage and resource in effecting these rescues whilst under enemy attack, and were awarded the British Empire Medal.

SUNDAY 29TH DECEMBER 1940

The night of Sunday 29th December 1940 saw one of the most savage and intense incendiary attacks of the air war over the city of London, and Station Officer Edward Morgan of the London Fire Brigade, who had already been awarded the British Empire Medal for his gallantry, was again in action.

A force of over 100 He 111H Bombers of Generalfeldmarschall Hugo Sperrle's Kampf Gruppe 100 (known as 'the fire raisers') under the direction of Hauptman Kurt Aschenbrenner, opened that terrible night's raid with a systematic early evening attack. Their Blitz Kreig lit up the 'Square Mile' providing a glowing and very visible target for the oncoming bombers of Kampfgeschwader, twenty-seven, fifty-one and fifty-three flying from northern France with high explosive bombs. This attack was reputedly on the direct orders of Adolf Hitler, as a response to a humiliatingly heavy raid carried out on Berlin on 20th December by the Royal Air Force. It is, perhaps, interesting to note that Sperrle, who rose to fame as the commander of the infamous Condor Legion during the Spanish Civil War, actually spoke out against Goering's decision to change tactics from bombing Fighter Command airfields to the cities. This was not, it has to be said, out of any humanitarian concerns, but the solid pragmatic rationale that the Royal Air Force had not been destroyed, and that Fighter Command would be able to rebuild in strength if given the opportunity. Goering ignored Sperrle and remained adamant that the bombing campaign on British cities would break the will of the people.

The severity of this air raid on the city of London was not due so much to the size of the attacking force, but to the concentration of the attack, and the proximity of so many old buildings of wooden construction to one another, which facilitated a hellish 'domino effect' in terms of rapid fire spread. The situation was further exacerbated by a lamentable lack of fire watchers that night in this old commercial area, the predicted low tide for the river Thames, thus depriving London Fire Brigade of the medium of extinction, and the practice of owners of locking their commercial premises, so preventing easy access for the firefighters. The resulting fire spread was swift, terrible and all-consuming.

To add to the rapidly escalating problems visited upon the staff of Lambeth's fire control room regarding the situation in the city, the fires caused by ill-aimed incendiaries on the south bank were raging out of control. Buildings opposite Guy's Hospital began to burn, and then the hospital itself caught alight, and a desperate search for water was commenced. Fortunately a fire brigade officer found an underground rain water tank in the hospital which could only be reached from one of the basement corridors. To access this supply a trailer pump from Dulwich fire station was unshipped from its appliance, and wheeled and 'manhandled' with great difficulty by crews who were well aware of the urgency of this critical situation, through corridors, and eased down stairways with ropes and much effort, until it was close enough to the tank for its suction hose to be immersed, and the water delivered to another pump and thence to the branches. This supply was used to good effect, the fire extinguished, and so this great hospital was saved.

Fifteen minutes into the start of the raid with enemy aircraft still steadily coming in on their bombing runs, the fires north of St. Paul's were already out of control, and what were considered to be peripheral fires elsewhere in the city, and south of the river at Dockhead had by then reached major proportions. By 7.00 pm there was another conflagration at Golden Lane, and the regional scheme for reinforcements was put into action by the Home Office control staff.

London Fire Brigade's central control point for the city was in an underground room at Redcross Street fire station, where phone lines from nine reporting stations converged. The fires raging above the control room soon heated up the air, making breathing difficult for the operators and moving around the room became more uncomfortable by the minute. One by one the telephone lines went dead as cables melted or were broken by bombs or falling buildings. It was not long before a high-explosive bomb severed the main electricity supply, and those phone lines still working had to be operated by the light of hand lamps. Eventually the station had to be evacuated to Canon Street, and later in the evening to Whitefriars as the situation surpassed critical.

In Whitecross Street just around the corner from Station 68 Canon Street, fifteen fire appliances were lined up with their crews fighting a fierce blaze which had by now completely surrounded them, and leapt from building to building. Finally the crews had no option but to retreat when both ends of the street became blocked. The heat was so intense that one crew even had to turn their hoses onto an appliance which had caught alight from the radiated heat. These firefighters managed to escape by jumping onto tracks of the Metropolitan Railway, which fortunately were in an open cutting at that point. The tracks then went underground and the men walked to the relative safety of Smithfield goods yard under the mass of flames.

By 8.00 pm there were 300 pumps at work in the city, but by then the fires at Queen Victoria Street, Martins Le Grand, the Minories, and Gresham Street had been added to the list of those out of control.

The incendiaries dropped that night caused over 1,400 fires, including six which were classed as conflagrations, one of which covered half a square mile. The Guildhall was damaged, leaving only its walls standing; eight Wren churches were devastated, as well as a number of guild company halls. One of the Luftwaffe's major objectives that night was the destruction of the General Post Office on King Edward Street, with its all-important telephone and telegraphic communication systems; this was achieved less than an hour after the attack was commenced. Paternoster Row, famous for its book shops and publishers, was reduced to a burning wreck, sending hundreds of thousands of burning sheets of papers high into the sky, ready to spread the inferno further afield; it is estimated that some six million volumes were destroyed that night. Also damaged were five mainline railway stations, nine hospitals, and sixteen Underground stations.

Prime Minister Churchill viewed the survival of St. Paul's Cathedral as being imperative to the morale of the nation in general, and Londoners in particular; giving the instruction that at all costs, St Paul's must be saved. Unfortunately, the cathedral wasn't completely untouched; the High Altar was destroyed, and the crypt and some of the stained-glass windows suffered damage. However, St Paul's became the great beacon of a people's hope. One of the most evocative reports of BBC journalist Robin Duff describes of the cathedral surviving the Blitz: 'All around the flames were leaping up into the sky. There the cathedral stood, magnificently firm, untouched in the centre of all this destruction'.

Herbert Mason's iconic photograph taken that night captured the silhouette of the dome surrounded by the smoke of the City of London ablaze. The photograph was published in the Daily Mail, with the caption, 'It symbolises the steadiness of London's stand against the enemy: the firmness of Right against Wrong'.

On that hellish night Station Officer Edward Morgan and his crews were attending a large fire at 51–53 City Road, part of a larger fire which had spread to both sides of the road and was threatening to engulf the whole street. During the course of the fire, bombs were continuing to fall and the walls of several buildings collapsed into the roadway. It was at this time that a dark figure was seen to half walk, half stumble along the pavement, close to the building, stooping low beneath the heat of the flames as they flared out of the ground floor windows. The figure turned out to be an elderly woman wearing her gas mask. On removal of the mask she informed the firemen, who had run to her assistance, that her husband was following her from the cellars of the burning building, but two women who had been sheltering with them would not follow. Morgan, along with several others, immediately rushed to the building to carry out a rescue.

An extract from the official report details the actions:

> During the intense bombardment of the City of London on the night of 29/30th December, information was received that two persons were still in the basement of No 51 City Road. At that time the building was well alight from ground to top floor and the basement had also become involved. Stn O Morgan, accompanied by Sub O Hill, entered the building by the ground floor passage but were unable to advance owing to the terrific heat. The stallboard light and grille at the front of the shop leading to the basement were broken open and by this means entry was effected.
>
> Although the heat and smoke in the basement were intense the two trapped persons were finally located in a back room by Stn O Morgan, who, with

assistance from Hill, brought them to a position in the front part of the basement from which they were hauled up to the street. Sub Officer Hill was then helped out and finally Morgan, who was considerably affected by the smoke and, in a very exhausted condition was assisted up to the ground level by means of a line. During the latter part of the time the rescue was being effected the rear part of the building collapsed. Both Morgan and Hill showed utter disregard of personal risk …

Recommended for George Cross.

Signed – F. W. Jackson. Deputy Chief Officer Commanding London Fire Brigade.

This recommendation was subsequently down-rated to the George Medal. Sub Officer Charles William Hill of Hendon Fire Brigade was also awarded a George Medal for his part in this incident. The following letter in support of an award for Morgan's outstanding and courageous work was received more than two months later:

> 1 Cavendish Mansions,
> Portland Place,
> London. W 1.
>
> 8th March, 1941.

Dear Sir,

Thank you for letter of 3rd March, regarding the conduct of Station Officer E W R Morgan of the London Fire Brigade at a fire at 51 and 53, City Road on the night of 29/30th December, 1940. Although I cannot confirm his actual identity, I saw most of the incident and will give you as full a description as possible in the hope of being of assistance.

On my arrival, the whole of the building of Messrs. Johnson & Watts was burning, and flames from it were across the street and had actually set numbers 51 and 53 alight on the opposite side. Two trailer pumps had been abandoned temporarily, I imagine owing to the possible collapse of the wall. Later efforts, which eventually proved successful, were made to save (one) trailer pump …, involving considerable risk and courage from all men concerned. Actually, while this was being accomplished, three-quarters of the wall … collapsed into the (nearby) graveyard. The men then attempted to save the second trailer pump, the tyres of which were burning, and by this time all floors of numbers 51 and 53 were well alight. Two or three branches were being worked from the centre of the road, where the heat between the two buildings was considerable.

About this time, a woman wearing a civilian gasmask appeared through the smoke from beyond the point at which the men were working. I saw her questioned and led past me to receive medical attention. Apparently she indicated that there were people inside the building, because there was a shout for volunteers, and one of many men rushed forward immediately.

The remainder of this account is based on my own observation and on information given me from time to time. During this period I was … approximately 16 yards from [one of the trailer pumps]. The men broke into the building at pavement level and Station Officer Morgan went through the opening into the basement. The building now looked to me as though it would collapse inside at any time; if this had happened I do not think there was any doubt that the ground floor would have given way and the burning contents would have fallen into the basement on top of him. Also, there was a considerable risk of the wall collapsing on to the street blocking up the entrance made. In spite of these risks he made contact with two women trapped inside and passed them out to a man lying waiting at the entrance hole. If these two women are still alive it is undoubtedly due to the Station Officer's work. I consider it an action of very great courage, which should receive official recognition, and I am very glad to have the opportunity of submitting this report.

I spent some six hours in various parts of the city on the night in question and having had a short experience in the AFS can realise some of the difficulties which confronted the Brigade. I would like to express my admiration of the work done by all concerned,

Yours faithfully,

Walton Anderson.

It is interesting, not to say breathtaking, to note that in and around the area of the City of London and Southwark there were some 1,700 pumping appliances at work by 10.00 pm that night. Indeed the Home Office Fire Control organisation was asked to mobilise a further 300 pumps from outside the Capital, so serious was the situation.

Of 1,500 fires recorded in the London area on the night of 29–30th December, all but twenty-eight were in the square mile of the City of London. During that night's firefighting operations fourteen firefighters were killed, over 250 men and women of the LFB and AFS were seriously injured.

Seventeen gallantry awards were earned, including George Medals to Station Officer Arthur Ronald Thorn, a thirty-nine year-old professional fireman of more than thirteen years' service, and forty-four year-old Sub-Officer John Cornford who had twenty years of firefighting experience. At about 2030 hours on that terrible night, both of these fire officers were in attendance at an incident involving a number of fifty-foot-high warehouses on both sides of Southwark Street, South London which were well-alight, with flames sweeping across the sixty-foot-wide street, when a man was seen to stagger out of one of the burning buildings and collapse. Thorn and Cornford immediately ran about fifty yards through the heat, flames and smoke with debris falling around them, and brought the man clear of the area. Had either of these men tripped, or fallen, there can be little doubt that they would have forfeited their lives. Although fortunately neither Thorn nor Cornford were injured during this courageous rescue, the casualty, Mr Emery, later died in King's College Hospital of his severe burns.

At 8.30 pm that evening Station Officer Tom Nicholas Wilcock, who had served for eleven years with the London Fire Brigade, was in charge of a breathing apparatus appliance from sub-fire station number 80 at Clapham, and was proceeding along Peckham Road en-route to a fire at Anchor and Hope Lane, Greenwich, when a number of high explosive bombs fell in the vicinity of their appliance. The blast threw a great quantity of shrapnel and debris through the front of the appliance disabling the vehicle, severely injuring one crew member and incapacitating two other of the firefighters. Several trams and charabancs on the road were wrecked, and two gas mains, one on each side of the street, were fractured and set on fire; and the blaze consequently spread to involve some of the damaged vehicles. Station Officer Wilcock, although suffering great pain from glass splinters which were embedded in his skin, and shock from the effect of the blast itself, displayed great initiative and courage, by retaining his sense of command and taking control of a very serious situation which was getting worse by the moment. Wilcock gave orders for firefighting hose to be coupled to the street fire hydrants to deal with the outbreaks of fire, sent assistance and informative messages to his control room, and detailed his appliance driver to assist the crew member who had been seriously injured to a first aid dressing station.

Whilst assisting in the removal of casualties from the immediate area of the ignited gas mains Wilcock heard faint cries for help coming from the burning wreckage of the tram car. On investigation he found a badly injured tram conductor pinned under the wreckage of his vehicle. Calling on Sub Officer Frederick Walker for assistance he forced his way into the blazing vehicle, and although hampered by the smoke and heat managed, with some difficulty, to extricate the man, and with Walker removed him to a place of safety using a tram seat as an improvised stretcher. After completing this rescue Wilcock rendered whatever assistance he could until the arrival of reinforcing fire, ambulance and rescue crews. After his wounds had been dressed he returned to his fire station and calmly and quietly resumed his duties.

In the report on the incident, which included a recommendation for an award of the British Empire Medal to both Station Officer Wilcock, and Sub Officer Walker, District Officer H. C. Denyer wrote in his statement:

> I was in attendance about ten minutes after the occurrence, and the road was strewn with debris, and a number of casualties were still being attended to by the ambulance squads.
>
> When I spoke to the crew it was obvious that they had had a harassing time, and they were showing signs of distress. Those of the crew who had received injuries had had their wounds dressed, but refused to stand-off in view of the large number of fires that were raging at the time, and bombing was still in progress.
>
> On their return to the station they obtained another appliance which was put on the run with Station Officer Wilcock in charge.

In support of this statement, Chief Superintendent E. H. Davies added:

> I spoke to Station Officer Wilcock on his return to the station and in view of his condition suggested that he lay in for the remainder of the night, or alternatively, he could go home and see his doctor in the morning. Station Officer Wilcock declined this, stating he would redress his wounds and would prefer to remain on duty and carry on with his job because of the stress on the brigade at the time. He did this and has not gone sick.

Crew members firefighters Harry Blunden, James Calvert and Reg' Little were awarded the King's Commendation for Brave Conduct.

Section Officer Alicia Perris and Auxiliary Ellen Sophia Nightingale were on duty in the watch room of No. 68 Z fire station at Baltic Street School, EC1 on the night of 29–30th December 1940. During that night considerable and very intensive enemy activity took place, and the immediate area was subjected to the most intense fires. At about 2100 hours the school itself took fire and the situation became so critical that shortly afterwards the order was given to evacuate the station. Notwithstanding the seriousness of this extremely dangerous situation, Section Officer Perris, with the assistance of Auxiliary Nightingale, had the great presence of mind to remove a number of important documents and records to the relative safety of Redcross fire station. Some indication of the dreadful conditions which pertained that night, and of the extent of the fire spread, was that the asphalt covering the school playground caught alight.

On their arrival at Redcross fire station Perris took over the watch room duties until about 2359 hours, by which time the whole of the roof of this station was alight, and the surrounding buildings were ablaze. In order to avoid becoming trapped, these premises were also evacuated, and both women moved to Central Street fire station where they provided invaluable assistance in mobilisation and communications duties. Throughout the trauma of this night, Mrs Perris maintained her composure and courage; Auxiliary Nightingale also remained unruffled and continued to work efficiently throughout the incessant bombing.

At about 0700 hours, the fire at their own station in Baltic Street having been dealt with, Section Officer Perris resumed her duties there, and both she and Auxiliary Nightingale helped to prepare hot meals for the weary fire crews returning from firefighting operations. Chief Superintendent J H Ansell wrote of Section Officer Perris: 'This station was just within the large fire area, and became involved as the fire spread. The conditions resulting were undoubtedly of a terrifying nature. Section Officer Perris set an excellent example to her subordinates and others by the calm and courageous way in which she maintained her post under very trying conditions. She showed initiative and devotion to duty.'

On that night thirty-six year-old Station Officer Albert Ernest Bills of Number 5 Knightsbridge fire station, a professional firefighter of eight and half years service, was in charge of firefighting operations in the city of London. The large fires in this area were so intense that Bills brought all available appliances to work in his area of responsibility, and with lines of hose and branches formed a water barrage to both attack the blaze and attempt to halt its spread; this work was made all the more difficult and dangerous by the ferocious heat from the fires, the prospect of buildings collapsing onto them, and the constant fall of debris. Despite the enormous challenges Station Officer Bills maintained communications with his fire control, and organised water supplies. As the night wore on and the fires continued to rage, half of Bills' firefighters were practically blind through the smoke, and as a consequence of the worsening situation, and the very real prospect of being surrounded by this rapidly growing conflagration, Bills made the difficult decision to withdraw all fire appliances and evacuate his personnel to a place of relative safety. Before the area was eventually cleared of his firefighters and their equipment, Bills himself, with great courage and displaying a highly developed sense of duty, made an extensive search of all the surrounding streets to ensure that everyone had left the area, and was the last one to reach safety.

The London County Council report recommending Bills for an award of the British Empire Medal spoke of this firefighter as follows: 'Station Officer Bills set a splendid example to the men by his coolness, energy and initiative and performed his duties under great difficulties in an extremely efficient manner, shouldering heavy responsibilities with remarkable confidence and courage; the escape of the crews and the rescue of appliances from this sector was due to in no small measure to this officer.'

Superintendent G Bennison wrote in support of this recommendation: 'This officer by his energetic action and organising ability under extremely difficult and hazardous conditions contributed in no small degree to the saving of Redcross Street fire station from destruction. At a critical stage of the fire he set a splendid example by his complete disregard of danger in a successful effort to evacuate the men under his charge.'

Also on that night, District Officer David Reading, an experienced firefighter of eighteen years service, was in command of a large fire from 8.00 pm until 9.30 am the following morning. In the face of unparalleled and seemingly impossible difficulties due to the ongoing air raid, and the continuous eruption of structural wreckage caused by the explosions in the area, he made his way from street to street, from crew to crew directing operations to prevent the spread of fire, and trying as best he might to safeguard the welfare and safety of his firefighters, and withdrawing appliances when the situation became critical.

When the fires were at their height it was reported to him that two employees from an electrical supply company were still at their posts, despite the building where they worked being perilously close to becoming involved. With great difficulty Mr Reading succeeded in reaching both men, and after having appraised them of the gravity of the situation, assisted them to make their way out of the premises, which was by now heavily smoke-logged and with most of the exits cut off by the flames. By this time Reading was suffering acutely owing to the painful condition of his eyes due to the intense heat and smoke he had been subjected to throughout the night. In spite of his pain, he was able and willing to continue directing work in connection with the utilization of emergency water supplies which, at a time when the water pressure from the street hydrants was low, enabled the crews to save a large number of buildings from total destruction.

Superintendent G. H. Robinson wrote of Reading's work that night: 'District Officer Reading's work throughout the night of 29th December 1940, was carried out under exceedingly difficult circumstances and he showed excellent qualities in carrying it out. This is typical of his action at fires since September last. His physical condition after this night was such that a man of less determination might have given in. He was in my opinion largely responsible for two men from the Electricity Supply Company being taken to a place of safety, and for the saving of a number of horses from Whitbread Brewery.'

On the night of the 29th, Watch Room attendant Reginald William La Fosse was at No. 37 Sub-Station at 140 Tabernacle Street, London when, just after 6.00 pm, a number of high-explosive and incendiary bombs were dropped in the area of the station, and information was received that a number of landmines had also fallen. Landmines, unlike high-explosive bombs, did not give any warning whistle as they floated to earth, and the mayhem and destruction they brought would have been inconceivable only weeks before; with whole streets and their residents obliterated, and the surrounding district suffering greatly from the blast. As a result of enemy activity fire appliances were dealing with more than 130 fires, four of them of serious proportions, and the roads in that area became almost impassable due to fallen debris and bomb craters. During operations to deal with these outbreaks messages were received in the Watch Room requesting additional fuel for the appliances. La Fosse, acting entirely on his own initiative and with commendable promptitude, obtained a staff car, loaded it with cans of petrol from the fire station fuel stock, and proceeded to drive around the district, refuelling the appliances at various incidents. He also retrieved empty fuel cans, which if anything had even more explosive potential given that the air raid was still in progress, and the ongoing fire situation throughout the vicinity. He continued this work until all appliances were replenished.

In his recommendation for the award of the British Empire Medal, Deputy Chief Fire Officer Jackson wrote: 'Without La Fosse's initiative and disregard for his own safety many of the appliances would have ceased to operate, with the distinct possibility of the fires getting out of control.'

The following supporting statements were made:

On the night of 29th December, 1940 I was officer in charge of No. 37 Sub-District Station Shoreditch, and in the normal course of my duty took charge of various fires in the locality. After some time it became apparent that petrol would be urgently needed, and I returned to the local station and gave the necessary instructions. La Fosse who had been on duty from 1100 to 1700 hours during the day and was resting, volunteered to see that these instructions were carried out. From then until approximately 0315 the next morning he toured the ground supplying pumps that were short of petrol and oil, regardless of personal danger … His prompt action, initiative and devotion to duty were most exemplary.

Station Officer G. A. T. Farley:

On the night in question several serious fires were in progress in Tabernacle Street, Paul Street, Scrutton Street, Epworth Street, City Road, and Finsbury Market … and appliances were running low on petrol. A message was sent back to that effect, and shortly afterwards La Fosse reported to me that he had supplied certain pumps, and enquired as to the location of others that were in need of petrol. I found on visiting one fire after another that he had done his work well, and that all appliances had been replenished where necessary.

I consider his actions highly commendable, he having carried on without regard to personal danger.

C. G. Tobias District Officer

Auxiliary Joan Winifred Hobson was off-duty that night, but had arranged to sleep over at 62 Y Station, King's College, Strand, WC 2, where she worked as telephonist and watch-room worker. When a call was received for a fire at 20 Devereux Court, all appliances were deployed at incidents, due to the very heavy bombing. Of her own volition Miss Hobson, with two Auxiliary firefighters, collected five lengths of delivery hose, a branch, a hydrant key and bar, and a short ladder, and commandeered a car and proceeded to the incident. They fought the fire from a roof opposite the burning building for three and a half hours, and succeeded in checking the outbreak and saved the lower floor and surrounding buildings from fire spread. During this time Auxiliary Hobson calmly and cheerfully ran out hose from the hydrant to the third floor of the building, delivered messages, and actually took her turn on the branch to fight the fire, whilst intensive bombing was ongoing place.

In the report which recommended her for the award of the British Empire Medal her Station Officer wrote: 'When the facts of Hobson's firefighting efforts were brought to my notice, I visited the scene and verified the statements of the witness. It was apparent that the situation must have been one of extreme danger. The state of the top floors and the staircase are ample witness to the courage she must have displayed in helping to attack the fire from inside this building. I have no hesitation whatsoever, in recommending her for her gallant conduct under such dangerous conditions.'

On the night of Sunday 29th December 1940, the air raid warning went at 1807 hours, and within fifteen minutes a high-explosive bomb had fallen in the area of the fire station 37 W which was housed at Virginia Road LCC School, Shoreditch, causing the electrical power to fail; and consequently the watch-room staff brought out hurricane lamps to provide emergency lighting. By 1856 that evening all of the station's firefighters, with the exception of the member of staff detailed to guard the gate, were at incidents: there were fifteen known fires in the locality at that time. This left three Women Auxiliaries, Winifred Brock, Ivy Angel Trood and Ivy Louise Ashwell, as the sole occupants of the premises, and they dealt over many hours with a highly pressurised and critical workload, receiving, acknowledging and processing hundreds of messages, maintaining communications with other control rooms, keeping the mobilising board up to date, and entering and checking all information received in the log; during this period 130 fires were reported.

At 1900 hours a complete basket of incendiary bombs fell on the roof of the school and in the yard. No sooner had Auxiliary Brock extinguished these incendiaries then it was discovered that the roof of the school was alight. By this time the firefighter on the gate had been called away to deal with a fire at a nearby hospital, and so the three auxiliaries were left to deal with a very serious and highly dangerous situation. In spite of the fact that the roof was now well alight, and there was a serious risk of fire spread, Trood and Ashwell remained at their telephones, and dealt calmly and efficiently with the great number of fire calls, whilst Brock patrolled the building to keep a check on the fire situation. It was not until some three hours later that a pumping appliance could be spared to fight this fire. Once firefighting operations were commenced, water cascaded down the stairways and into the watch-room, making the working conditions particularly difficult. Throughout this time Ashwell, Trood and Brock continued with their watch-room work, taking time to brush the water from their office, and build a dam of sand bags to arrest the rush of water; and during this time, pressure of mobilising work permitting, helped the crews to salvage bedding, clothing and equipment from the water and fire damaged rooms.

Later in the evening it was reported that an unexploded landmine had landed and was hanging by its parachute in Arnold Circus, some 150 yards from the fire station. This resulted in over 300 people being evacuated from flats and other buildings near to the mine. Even throughout this final trauma of the night they remained at their post, displaying exceptional devotion to duty, courage and cool efficiency with an entire absence of any sign of fear. Women Auxiliaries Winifred Brock, Ivy Angel Trood and Ivy Louise Ashwell, although originally recommended for the British Empire Medal were awarded the King's Commendation for Brave Conduct in recognition of their work that night.

It is believed that the Luftwaffe dropped somewhere in the region of 100,000 incendiary bombs that night over the City of London.

THE RAIDS OF 1941

During an air attack on 10–11th January 1941 a number of houses in Reginald Road, Portsmouth were demolished by a high explosive bomb, and fires broke out. Two people were trapped beneath the mass of debris in which a gas main was burning fiercely. Leading Fireman Andrew Nures Nabarro of Portsmouth Auxiliary Fire Service took charge of operations, and despite great danger from collapsing buildings, the people were rescued and the fires eventually brought under control. It was entirely due to Nabarro's courageous efforts that the lives of these persons were saved. He then went to other fires at the Curtis Furniture Depository and at the electricity supply depot in Portsmouth, where he displayed great initiative in locating and organising water supplies. This resulted in the saving of much valuable property. Nabarro was awarded the George Medal for his gallantry.

Also in Portsmouth over the 10th, 11th, & 12th of January 1941 during air raids on the city, Michael Hogan of Vosper's Works Fire Brigade was working as part of a fire crew, and was twice blown from the quayside into the water by the blast effects of high-explosive bombs, and on both occasion climbed out and continued his work. As the raid increased in intensity, fire threatened to sweep towards and engulf a large air raid shelter occupied by women and children. A request was made for volunteers to remove the occupants to a place of relative safety, and although high-explosive bombs continued to be dropped in large number, Hogan made many journeys to conduct them to a safe area. Whilst thus engaged an incendiary bomb lodged on the windscreen of the van he was driving. He promptly extinguished it and continued with the evacuation. Hogan showed great bravery and continued to be engaged in firefighting operations throughout the next couple of days, and was subsequently awarded the George Medal. Mr John Godfrey Adrian Way-Hope, the Works ARP Control Officer was responsible for co-ordinating all the civil defence plans for Vosper's which were brought into operation during the period of these air raids. The award of the British Empire Medal recognised his devotion to duty and contribution to operations.

Also on the night of 11th January, 1941, Sub-Officer Robert Reginald Mathews, a thirty-three year-old professional firefighter who had served with London Fire Brigade for two and a half years was engaged with his crew from No. 34 fire station, Cable Street, Stepney, in firefighting at London Docks, Wapping. Whilst carrying out these operations a high-explosive bomb fell close to where Mathews' crew were working, killing one man outright and seriously injuring others, including Mathews. At the same time a number of employees of the Port of London Authority were also injured. Mathews although suffering considerably from lacerations to his right arm, severe contusions to the body, and a head injury, continued, while enemy aircraft were still overhead, to supervise firefighting operations, and succeeded in getting all the men to hospital. In the recommendation for a gallantry award Deputy Chief Fire Officer Jackson wrote: 'He displayed great fortitude and unselfishness in his repeated requests that others should receive hospital treatment before himself. With the extent of his injuries he was taken to the London Hospital, where he still lies. His general attitude was one of great regret that he had been injured and was unable to carry on with his work and his courageous conduct throughout was most praiseworthy.'

In support of the recommendation for Mathews to be recognised by an award of the George Medal, Mr A. E. Studd, the First Aid Officer for the London Dock Control wrote: 'I was in charge of the first aid post on Saturday 11th instant, and whilst selecting cases for priority of treatment this man (R. R. Mathews) requested on several occasions that I should attend to others first, and only upon subsequent examination of his injuries could I realise his courage and thought for his colleagues'.

In corroboration Station Officer H. G. Brown added in his statement: 'I ... can testify that Sub-Officer Mathews displayed great courage and fortitude in endeavouring to attend to his injured men under very dangerous conditions, regardless of his own injuries.'

On 13th January 1941 a petrol tank at the Royal Navy Fuel Depot, Catterdown, Plymouth was set alight during an intense enemy air raid. The roof of this tank was seriously damaged, and it was necessary to use a steel stairway on the outside of the tank, and then descend a ladder, which had become red-hot, to a depth of thirty–two feet to reach the roof. The fuel was well alight around the sealing rim of the roof and the tank wall; consequently the chances of an explosion known as a boil over became more and more probable. Patrol Officer George Henry Wright of Plymouth Auxiliary Fire Service without hesitation descended the internal ladder to the roof, and commenced his foam attack on the fire. Cyril George Lidstone, also of Plymouth AFS, seeing that Wright was experiencing great difficulties in extinguishing the blaze came down to assist him, fortunately reaching his colleague who was on the point of collapse, and prevented him falling into the raging inferno below. Lidstone then hauled hose and foam making equipment up the ladder, and together they brought the blaze under control. Both men displayed great gallantry, as they were fully aware of that an explosion of the burning oil would have cost them their lives; they were both awarded the George Medal.

Numerous potential targets in the south-west of England were in easy range of the Luftwaffe operating out of northern France, and consequently a great many devastating air raids took place in this region during the early part of the war, and a number of firefighters and other emergency workers were awarded British Empire awards in that region. The following paragraphs present an outline of those gallant stories.

Harry Reginald Horne, the Chief Engineer of Okehampton Fire Brigade, was on duty in Plymouth during an enemy air attack, when the tower of a high building near to where he was working caught alight, with a great danger of it spreading to other structures. As the water mains in the area were seriously damaged, Horne positioned his pump at the edge of the bomb crater in front of the building, drew water from this hole, and ran a line of hose up the internal staircase to the top floor. He entered the roof space below the tower, and using a ladder he gained access to the blaze, and with some difficulty extinguished the fire. During this operation, Horne was fully aware that there was a very real danger of the fire spreading to the lower part of the premises, which would have cut off any escape route. Horne was instrumental in saving the building, and by his initiative, devotion to duty and disregard of the dangers set a fine example to the men under his control.

Leslie Edmund Proctor Stephens, a messenger with Plymouth Auxiliary Fire Service was attached to a crew which was sent to deal with a large fire, during an air attack on Plymouth, when incendiary and high explosive bombs caused a great many fires. A high explosive bomb fell nearby, and Stephens sustained injuries and suffered from the effects of blast. In spite of this he continued with his duties, carrying messages and helping to fight the fires. Stephens, a boy of sixteen years, displayed great courage and high sense of duty throughout the period of raids.

Chief Fire Officer Richard George Andrews of Tavistock Fire Brigade was sent to Plymouth with his firefighters to assist in firefighting operations. Andrews and his crews were directed to deal with fires in a number of large retail premises, where he had lines of hose directing their water jets onto the roofs of adjacent properties to halt the fire spread. Despite the intense heat Andrews continued to reconnoitre the area of the fire to continually assess the situation, and lead his crews to more advantageous positions. Andrews and his crew remained at this incident for some nine hours in conditions of extreme danger. The Chief Fire Officer showed great determination, and perseverance, showing a fine example to his firefighters through his cheerful demeanour and disregard for his personal safety. He succeeded in preventing the spread of the flames and remained at his post until the fire was extinguished.

Also in Plymouth, fires were started as a result of a serious air raid, and spread rapidly to the narrow thoroughfare connecting two streets. Mains were damaged and water had to be taken from a large bomb crater nearby. The heat was intense and there was great danger from falling debris. Chief Fire Officer Cecil Browning Lyne directed the laying of hose to relay water supplies, despite the continual fall of incendiary and high explosive bombs, and was eventually able to extinguish the blaze. Except for a short rest, this officer remained on the fire ground for thirty-six hours during intensive air attacks. He showed courage and endurance of a high order, and under his energetic leadership much valuable property was saved.

Buildings adjoining an AFS station in Portsmouth were on fire and the office equipment in the watch room was brought down by a bomb blast. In these extreme circumstances the AFS telephonists Patricia Baxter, Hazel Taylor and May Georgina Witcher, continued to carry out their duties in a calm and efficient manner, until a direct hit was received by the fire station in which they were working, and they were buried under the resulting debris. Matters were made worse by the escape of gas, but although injured and suffering from the effects of the blast, Miss Baxter managed with great difficulty to crawl to the gas tap and turn it off, thus saving her colleagues who were injured and trapped under the wreckage from being asphyxiated. She then went to the assistance of Miss Witcher, who was pinned down under falling timber, and was suffering a head injury. Despite the roof of the building being alight by this time Telephonists Baxter, Taylor and Witcher ignored their own safety and helped salvage two vehicles and a mobile dam which would have been destroyed had they not been moved. They then helped bring down the sand-bagged buttress which protected the fire station, and used the sand to extinguish incendiary bombs which had fallen in the area. Refusing to rest, the three girls then went to headquarters and worked throughout the night in the canteen.

Bombs caused a number of blazes at a bus depot, where Fire Inspector Arthur William Larson of Plymouth Police Fire Brigade was in charge of firefighting operations, which were rendered extremely difficult and dangerous by exploding petrol tanks and burning oil. Larson, along with firefighters John Francis Cresswell Peace and William Albert Edgecombe, took up a most dangerous position from which to fight the fire, and remained there for more than three hours until the flames had been subdued. During the whole of this period high-explosive and incendiary bombs were being dropped, and the three men suffered considerably from the effects of blast and flying debris but refused to give up. They set a very fine example of courageous firefighting in circumstances where there was great risk of death or injury.

Incendiary bombs penetrated the glass roof of a factory in Portsmouth and started fires in various parts of the premises, and works Fireman Ernest Cuthbert Wilson immediately commenced directing firefighting operations. At the same time fires were started in an adjoining shed, nearby houses and on a derelict barge. A crew under Mr

Wilson's supervision immediately began tackling the fires, and to reach the now-blazing barge they had to wade through deep and glutinous mud with their equipment, while all around bombs continued to fall. Mr Wilson displayed great courage, resource and efficiency in extremely dangerous and difficult conditions.

On Friday 17th January 1941 extensive damage was inflicted as 178 high-explosive bombs and some 7,000 incendiaries landed on a snow-covered Swansea during the heaviest raid it had endured so far in the war; fifty-five deaths and ninety-seven non-fatal casualties were reported.

As soon as darkness fell a sustained attack on the docks and industrial area which would last several hours began, causing massive damage to the surrounding residential areas as many German bombs missed their primary targets, damaging dwellings, retail and commercial premises. One of the principal targets of the Luftwaffe was the ICI complex at Landore which was heavily involved in war production, with some twenty incendiary and high explosive bombs causing damage to roofs, leaving the plant itself undamaged.

Bombs fell on the Panamanian oil tanker M S Norvik which was berthed in Swansea Docks, and fires were started in a tank and on the deck. All of the ship's tanks were partially empty and therefore in a potentially extremely explosive condition. Fireman John James Jones, the senior refinery firefighter, together with a volunteer party assisted by members of the jetty staff and some of the ship's personnel, boarded the ship and commenced the extremely hazardous operation of extinguishing the fire in the tank; whilst others lashed hoses to the jibs of cranes in order to position the jets of water more effectively. However, there still remained a fire involving rope on the fo'c'sle head which was not readily accessible, and given the gaseous condition of the tanks, could have resulted in a major explosion. Fireman Jones made a hazardous climb up the damaged structure, without ladders, onto this deck and extinguished the fire by means of water passed up in buckets from the sea. It was an extremely dangerous climb in the dark with bombs falling, the ever-present danger of explosion, and a heavy barrage continuing overhead. Fireman Jones, by his dedication, displayed great courage and saved the tanker from destruction, and was subsequently awarded the George Medal.

On the night of 3rd–4th March 1941, Station Officer Edward Morgan of London Fire Brigade and crews from Euston were called to a fire in Ampthill Square, near Mornington Terrace. On arrival it was reported that four persons were involved including a woman and her child. An eyewitness statement by the local ARP Warden described what happened:

> Having witnessed the rescue of a Mrs Winifred Upton and her baby son
> Patrick from a fire in Ampthill Square on the night of Monday 3/4th March,
> I am glad to be able to record the heroism of the fire officer who effected the
> rescue. I was at the scene of the fire soon after the outbreak and saw the fire

escape raised. Two women were taken from the sill of the second floor right hand window and brought down. Station Officer Morgan was then seen to go up the escape to the third floor and reaching over to the left hand window take the child from the mother and bring the child down to safety.

All this time the mother was screaming and acting in a very hysterical manner. Whilst Station Officer Morgan was bringing down the child other firemen were trying to move the ladder over from the right to the left hand window, but, owing to the uneven road surface the ladder could only be brought to within about five feet of the window. The officer then again climbed the escape to rescue the woman. By this time volumes of smoke and flames were pouring from the ground, first and second floor windows, through which he had to pass. Upon reaching the third floor he attempted to reach the screaming, panic stricken woman, but found that it was not possible to get to her from his position on the ladder. Swaying the escape over towards the window he stepped onto the ornamental frieze beneath the window, and, keeping hold of the ladder with one hand, stretched out the other, grasped the woman's hands and dragged her bodily through the window. Before he could step back onto the swaying ladder, the woman, seeming to realise that she was hanging in mid air, commenced to kick and struggle. I fully expected to see the officer torn from his precarious hold and hurtle together with her to the ground, but, somehow with what seemed to be super human strength, he managed to get back onto the escape and swing the struggling woman to his shoulder. The ladder was now aflame, and the flames leaping from the window, had set the woman's clothing alight. Station Officer Morgan held her, whilst a colleague who had climbed up behind him put out the burning clothing. They then together brought her down, thus bringing to a close a rescue, which in my opinion, was the most heroic act, carried out with coolness and disregard to danger, which it has been my privilege ever to witness, during which I understand, the gallant officer received severe burns.

On the 7th May 1941 the Clerk of the Council received a recommendation for an award from the Deputy Chief Officer Commanding the LFB; which read: 'With reference to the attached recommendation for an award in respect of Station Officer Morgan, I desire to direct attention to the fact that, in addition to the award of the B.E. Medal for good work on the night of 16th September 1940, and to the present recommendation, Station Officer Morgan rescued a woman and child from a fire (not due to enemy activity), at 34, Ampthill Square, N.W.1, on 4th March 1941. Consideration is now being given to the question of considering him for the King's Police and Fire Service in respect of this latest exploit. These successive acts of bravery show that Station Officer Morgan is a brilliant example of a man of daring, fearless and exceptional courage.'

Morgan was subsequently awarded the Kings Police & Fire Service Medal for Gallantry. On the 29th May 1941 Morgan was promoted to Temporary District Officer B District and following the formation of the National Fire Service, (NFS), in September of that year, was posted with the rank of Column Officer, initially to B Division, then the A Division of 34 Fire Force. So came to an end Edward Morgan's busy and illustrious association with the famous Euston Fire Station. When the war ended, the NFS started to wind itself down for a peacetime service and reversion to local authority control. On 31st March 1948 Morgan relinquished his wartime rank, reverting to his substantive rank on 1st April, and taking up the position of Station Officer at A7 Fulham. However he was not done with his 'daring do' just yet. On 12th February 1954 he was called to Niton St, Fulham where he made safe and removed a bomb that had been placed in a pillar-box! Later that year he transferred to A8 Brompton during which time he again made the newspapers following his part in the rescue of a six month-old child from a flat in Danvers St, Chelsea.

Edward Morgan GM, BEM (G), KP&FSM, a most remarkable, renowned and courageous man, the most decorated firefighter of the Second World War, retired on 1st March 1961, and lived and worked in Ramsgate until his untimely death at the age of sixty-two; his body no doubt succumbing to the punishment it had received over many arduous years when serving the people of London with great distinction.

THE CLYDEBANK BLITZ

At 9.00 pm on Thursday the 13th March 1941, the wail of air raid sirens reverberated throughout a frosty, moonlit Clyde valley, as 3,000 metres above, Heinkels of the Luftwaffe's KGr 100 Bomber Group prepared to attack this most important of industrial areas. Their aim was to set Clydebank alight, and so create a beacon for the main bomber force, already en route from bases in France, Holland, Denmark and Germany loaded with high-explosive bombs. It is estimated that on that night the Luftwaffe dropped more than 100,000 1 kg incendiary bombs, which to be effective had to fall on combustible material. When they fell on industrial sites, largely composed of brick and metal, they had little effect. However, when they hit the Yoker Distillery to the east of the town, the forty acres of the Singer Sewing Machine factory's timber yard, which was stocked full, and the Auchentoshan Distillery, huge fires developed, and from the ensuing conflagration, whisky poured into a nearby stream creating a chain of fire which extended to the Clyde.

Schools and churches in the area were amongst the first victims of the incendiaries, and three oil tanks were bombed and one set on fire at Dalnotter, close to Auchentoshan. In every street a fire had taken hold, including the 'Holy City'– so called because its flat-roofed dwellings bore a resemblance to Jerusalem from afar – which was ablaze from end to end. At the factory premises of the Singer Manufacturing Company, part of the building had been taken over for the production of munitions, and the enemy action caused serious and extensive outbreaks of fire in that part of the plant. Firemaster Alexander Heron of the Works Fire Brigade personally extinguished a large number of the incendiary bombs, handling them on many occasions with his bare hands. Despite choking smoke, extremely high temperatures, and the very real prospect of being trapped beneath burning timbers, Heron led his firefighters into the burning wood yard, while others constantly directed their jets of water on them to prevent serious injuries from the crushing heat. Afterwards Heron attacked the fire in the building and made every possible effort to extinguish the flames. Firemaster Heron, a man of sixty-seven years, was on continuous duty without rest for 100 hours, and was subsequently awarded the George Medal for his outstanding commitment, leadership and gallantry. The Singer factory was able to return to pre-Blitz war production levels within a few weeks. The following firefighters were awarded the King's Commendation for Brave Conduct: John M'Lean, James Meicklejohn, John Morrison and James Webb.

Such was the intensity of this raid that, even with the outstanding degree of cooperation established between the local fire brigades, the emergency services were completely overwhelmed. Altogether 250 pumping appliances were in operation at fires, their crews were totally overstretched by the scale of events; five fire stations were hit during this raid, and fire service communications were seriously impaired by a direct hit on the mobilizing control centre. Oncoming appliances responding to assistance calls from neighbouring fire brigades were delayed by the bomb craters, and the wreckage of collapsed buildings which blocked the roads of Clydebank. The area of Second Avenue suffered eighty deaths, when a parachute mine demolished the frontage of 150 yards of terraced housing. Whole families were slaughtered as blocks of flats were reduced to piles of rubble in seconds, trapping and crushing some occupants who had sought shelter in lower floors. For nine hours, wave after wave of bombers repeatedly bombed Clydebank, which was still burning when the bombers returned the next evening to complete their task. When the All Clear finally sounded, 528 lay dead and over 617 had been seriously injured; 4,000 houses were completely destroyed, and a further 4,500 severely damaged.

Against this background of destruction, Fire Service Boy Messenger Neil Leitch, a part-time volunteer, immediately reported for duty on his bicycle on the receipt of the alert. He dashed from his home without wishing his family goodbye and reported to Partick Fire Station. Shortly afterwards, he volunteered to accompany a senior Fire Service officer to the Hyndland district, and was sent back to fire control at Partick Fire Station with a message for assistance. Messenger Leitch, who was only sixteen years of age, was thrown from his bicycle on more than one occasion by explosions, whilst endeavouring to deliver his message. On one occasion, he was so badly injured that he was carried into a first aid dressing station, and after the minimum of attention, he insisted upon proceeding with his message, contrary to the advice of the ambulance officers. He informed them that he must get through with this message, as it was very important, and in spite of his injuries, continued on his way to Partick Fire Station. Just before he reached the Station, it was hit by a high explosive oil bomb, and he received further injuries. Despite this, he very courageously carried on and finally delivered the message. Leitch subsequently succumbed to his injuries.

During this period awards of the British Empire Medal for gallantry were made to the following members of the Fire Service in this area of Scotland, being gazetted in the Supplement to the *London Gazette* of 12th September 1941:

It was reported that Patrol Officer Harry Smith of the Greenock Auxiliary Fire Service conducted himself with great coolness and disregard for his own safety when his sub-station was set on fire during an air raid. As the station began to collapse due to enemy air action, Smith was partially buried under falling debris, but despite the injuries he received he continued to carry out his duties and set a magnificent example to his men.

Section Officer William Norman Tudman of the Greenock AFS was in charge of a fire float when a bomb struck a quay, killing one of the crew and injuring another. The craft was also machine gunned by the Luftwaffe. Nevertheless, with the casualties aboard, the float was taken to its appointed post and was immediately put into action. Tudman displayed considerable courage during operations and was outstanding in the cool manner in which he went about his duties, and continued to encourage his men. He displayed great qualities of leadership under extreme and dangerous conditions, which contributed in no small measure to the success of the Fire Brigade operations carried out in this raid.

Robert McCallum, a Messenger with Greenock Auxiliary Fire Service, showed great gallantry and devotion to duty, carrying messages in the face of considerable difficulties. Time after time McCallum's bicycles were damaged by debris and or bombs, and he had to discard six of them which were rendered unfit for further service. On one occasion he was warned that the wall might collapse. As he jumped clear the wall fell, burying his bicycle. He promptly commandeered another and continued his journey. On another occasion, shortly after leaving his bicycle it was blown to bits; however he continued undaunted and delivered his message on foot despite the air raid being ongoing. Several times he had to carry his bicycle over debris and craters, and on one occasion was blown from his cycle by a bomb blast. McCallum showed outstanding courage and devotion to duty.

Fireman Patrick Reid Meiklejohn of Greenock AFS was entrusted with an important message during an air raid. During the journey he ran into a bomb crater and sustained head injuries. Although dazed and injured and suffering from shock and

The remains of South Shields town centre after a heavy night of air attacks.
Courtesy of Tyne and Wear Fire and Rescue Service.

concussion, he insisted on continuing his journey and delivered his message. After a short rest he resumed his duties and though ordered to a first aid post, remained on duty, displaying great courage and giving valuable service.

One of the Luftwaffe's principal targets on Clydebank was the Admiralty oil storage depot at Dalnottar, where eleven huge tanks had been destroyed and others severely damaged. Countless millions of gallons of fuel were lost and the resulting inferno blazed for two weeks. Once the air attack began, hundreds of incendiary bombs fell on the oil depot, starting a great many fires. The Officer in charge of the Admiralty outstation, Mr William Charles Tew, without hesitation assumed command of the strategic element of the situation, and immediately deployed his firefighting resources to deal with the outbreaks, which were quickly extinguished. However, within minutes of the incendiary attack a second wave of bombers dropped high-explosive bombs, which started a number of extremely serious fires involving the oil tanks. Throughout the four days and nights of this major incident Mr Tew worked without a break, and handled a very grave and difficult situation with great resource and courage, and was assisted in this work by Mr William Cutherbert the depot chargehand who had responsibility for firefighting.

Despite the hellish cacophony of explosions and a growing conflagration, Mr Fred Goodrich, the Admiralty Outstation's Chief Fire Officer, directed the firefighting operations with a cool sense of command, bringing his professional experience and qualities of leadership to bear on the incident. This was to prove of great assistance to the Auxiliary Firemen, many of whom were at their first fire. The Firemaster of the Dunfermline Fire Brigade, Mr William Bell Muir, who was in attendance with his crews, displayed exceptional courage in wading through oil to get to and ascend a vertical steel ladder attached to an oil tank, so that he could reach the top of the tank, and so make a clearer assessment of what was a critical and possibly catastrophic situation. Muir organised firefighting measures, and showed leadership, energy and resolution of a high order throughout the enemy action.

Auxiliary Fireman Harry Kerr demonstrated outstanding bravery: when standing waist deep in oil, he over a long period of time continued playing his jet of water against the burning tanks at close range, repeatedly driving back the flames. Fireman David Tervit of Dunfermline Fire Brigade displayed great coolness and bravery when, over a protracted period he manipulated his jet to keep flaming oil from being driven round a tank, while two other jets were played on him to counteract the intense heat. During this part of the operation the water to the jets which were cooling Tervit failed, but despite the intense heat, and the very obvious danger of continuing his work, he stood firm until the water supply was restored, and waded through the oil and succeeded in extinguishing the flames. The utilisation and maintenance of water supplies, the replenishment of fuel, and the management of relief crews were the responsibility of Section Officer William Fleming Crichton of the West Lothian AFS, whose great initiative and power of organisation contributed in no small measure to the success of the operation. As well as directing the logistics of this critical occurrence, he led his small group in driving back the spread of flames on a number of occasions.

Divisional Officer Graeme Hardie of the Dunbartonshire Auxiliary Fire Service throughout the period of these intensive air raids showed great professionalism and devotion to duty, mobilising units to the various outbreaks of fire, and later going on foot during the height of the raid to the Dalnottar oil storage depot to arrange for reinforcing appliances and equipment. His calmness in the midst of such a potentially disastrous situation set a great example to the men under his command. Hardie, a forty-two year-old Glaswegian company director, and a former officer with the Scottish Rifles (The Cameronians), was one of the first to volunteer to serve in the county's AFS.

Firemaster W. B. Muir, Chief Fire Officer F. Goodrich, and Mr W. C. Tew were awarded MBEs; Auxiliary Fireman Harry Kerr and Fireman David Tervit were awarded the George Medal, and British Empire Medals were awarded to Divisional Officer G. Hardie, Section Officer W. F. Crichton and Charge Hand W. Cuthbert. When the site was finally cleared, ninety-six bomb craters were counted.

Of course as with all air raids, indeed all peacetime incidents of whatever magnitude, firefighters are most certainly not the only people to render assistance or show courage in face of overwhelming danger. During the Clydebank Blitz gallantry awards were also earned by the following individuals, although many others could be mentioned in this tribute:

Firstly James Craig and John Stewart, both foremen with ARP on Clydebank. Craig led his Rescue Party with courage and initiative, and was on duty almost continuously over the seventy-two hours duration of the enemy air attack. At one incident where a tenement property had been partially demolished, a young woman was trapped in the basement. Craig tunnelled through the debris, notwithstanding the fact that fire twice broke out during these operations. He succeeded in jacking up the joists and after working relentlessly for a period of nine hours managed to rescue the woman alive. In view of the dangerous nature of the work, he refused to allow any of his party to enter the tunnel to relieve him.

Stewart displayed great courage when he crawled through a small opening he had created in rubble to gain access to a building which was partially demolished as a result of a direct hit from a bomb, and extricated several persons from under the wreckage, despite being fully aware that the structure was extremely unstable. Shortly after he completed the rescues the walls of the building collapsed.

Police Sergeant John MacLeod of Dunbartonshire Constabulary, and Police Constable Archibald Walker of Glasgow City Police. Sergeant John MacLeod, when on his way to take up duty, witnessed bombs demolishing houses on either side of him in Second Avenue and Albert Road, Clydebank. From the ruins of one of these houses he heard children shouting and he immediately clambered through the wreckage and rescued them. He then entered another wrecked house, and from under the debris assisted in the rescue of three children who were thankfully still alive. MacLeod then took charge and supported further rescue operations while the air raid was at its height, and when all casualties had been removed continued on his way to report for duty. Walker was knocked down and badly shaken by the blast from a bomb which demolished part of a two-storey tenement dwelling, and despite suffering from shock he entered the building and helped people to evacuate. Then, although the masonry and roof were in a very dangerous condition, he set to work lifting furniture, beams of wood, and heavy stones, in order to free those who had been trapped underneath. He refused to rest until all the victims had been found and released, and was in great danger at all times as the walls and the roof were liable to collapse at any moment. By his courageous and unceasing activity Constable Walker was instrumental in saving the lives of two of the persons who had been trapped.

For their gallant actions and devotion to their duties under terrible and dangerous conditions, James Craig and John Stewart of the ARP and Police Officers John MacLeod and Archibald Walker were awarded the George Medal.

In 1955 the *Lennox Herald* looked back on this terrible experience, and here are extracts from their retrospective coverage:

> The great fire of Clydebank … was far bigger than anyone imagined a fire could be. Almost from the start those who had to fight it thought of it not in terms of fires, but areas of fire. The biggest ran from Kilbowie Road to Duntocher Road and from Second Avenue to Hawthorne Street. It included Singer's wood yard and it was a mile square. Another ran from Duntochter Road to Mountblow Road, and from the railway to the Clyde. It covered about two-thirds of a square mile. Finally there were the Admiralty tanks at Dalnottar. By the second night 12,000,000 gallons of oil were blazing there. The fires were fought by the local brigade and by close on 2,000 firemen drawn in from Dumbartonshire, Lanarkshire, Renfrewshire, Stirlingshire, Edinburgh and Glasgow. As there was no central plan to outline the story, the Clydebank fire blitz can only be described through the eyes of these original men. This is how it seemed to two of them, the only professional firemen now alive who were in the Clydebank brigade at the time. The first was Sub Officer William Smillie describing the first two hours of the raid:

> I went to Second Avenue and saw three incendiaries lying on the road. I was 'earthing' them over when I heard some-one shouting: 'For God's sake come and help us'. A shelter had collapsed and there were men in it trying to hold the roof up with their backs. I put my crew in and ran for a rescue squad. A gas main was leaking and when I got back four of my men were unconscious.

I got them to the stage where they were vomiting but on their feet, and then we tackled a burning tenement in Montrose Street, but before we got far with that a 'screamer' came down and blew me over the wall into the church-yard, unconscious. When I came to the pump was dry, the bomb had taken half of Kilbowie Road and the big water main with it, and left the upper part of Clydebank without water. The hydrant was dry so we used the crater. I got the men together and we had another go at the tenement, and then after that a four storey tenement in Kilbowie road and then some villas. We did those jobs and then reported back.

The difficult thing to appreciate about this story is the time element. This fireman had dealt with incendiaries, fetched a rescue squad, revived his gassed crew, been blown up, recovered consciousness, found an emergency water supply, and fought four fires all inside two hours – and still had two and a half days without rest or sleep ahead of him! He is very vague about time after that. He remembers staggering with exhaustion. He remembers just flashing the hose from one room to another trying to keep the flames down. He remembers thousands of incendiaries raining into the sea of fire, and the screamers that sent him flat on his face in the mud. When buildings collapsed the gas mains nearly always caught fire. He remembers digging in the rubble to find them and then jamming a potato into the broken pipe. The thing he cannot get out of his mind are the people who pled (pleaded) with him to come to their homes. He had one pump in a street that was blazing from end to end with a square mile of fire behind it, and could not be everywhere at once. He had to pick the place where he could do most good, and then stick to it, however many people wanted him to save their homes, their wives or their children. He did what was best, but does not like to think about it.

'It was the same with all of us', said William McGregor, the other surviving professional. Folk were coming all the time pulling at your sleeve. 'Everything I've got's going up'. 'My wife's trapped, you've got to come.' All the time there were folk like that and we could only do one thing at a time. When one man was pleading with me I felt the ground move below my feet. It was someone alive in the rubble. I didn't go with the man, I started digging. What else could I do?'

McGregor's engine was completely buried when a wall was blown down, but he and his crew managed to dig it out, lever the smashed mudguards off the wheels with crowbars, and jockey it over the rubble to the next fire. Like Smillie his memory is confused after the first few hours. He remembers inching his machine over the small craters left by unexploded bombs; he remembers rows of dead lying on the Kilbowie road; churches blazing 'like huge bird cages, and the shower of incendiaries falling everywhere as if they'd been shovelled out of a truck. He was so thirsty that he drank canal water and liked it. He does not remember eating. Day came and night again, and the next raid, and another day and night, and then it was Sunday. At midnight he and his crew were still fighting fires, out on their feet, when a message came calling them in to rest.

These two experiences covered only one small corner of one fire. Multiply them a thousand times, and one begins to have a faint conception of what the Clydebank blitz was like, and what the men were like. A dozen fires started and went roaring to meet each other while the next load of incendiaries came whistling down. One of them landed on the Clydebank Burgh engine and destroyed it as its crew were driven back by the flames. Soon the whole yard burned. Though it lay in a sea of fire a mile square it dwarfed all around it, an enormous pillar of fire whirling upwards in a shower of sparks, and so hot that no one could approach it. The firemen saw it was hopeless and turned elsewhere. It burned like a torch throughout the raids. By this time there were two separate and distinct battles going on, one of them to save Clydebank and the other to save the Admiralty oil. The situation in Clydebank was almost beyond belief. Even early on the first night, with high explosives and incendiaries still raining down, over 3,000 houses were alight and the fires were behaving much as the stacks of timber in the yard had done. They were running together.

The firemen fought their losing battle from the Thursday to the Sunday, through two raids without sleep or rest. Said one of them: 'After the first night we were working by instinct. We didn't think. We couldn't think. It was our training that told us what to do, not our brains'.

Said another: 'They pulled us out at midday on Sunday and put us on a bus and drove us up to Whiteinch baths. We were so dead beat that we didn't know what we were doing. When we'd cleaned up … some went to hospital and most of the rest of us should have gone. We'd never had our rubber boots off, and we were raw flesh from ankle to thigh'.

They had done what they could but it had not been enough. The weight of the attack had been so overwhelming that most of the Burgh simply burned itself out. Even so, for two and a half days they had fought without respite against impossible odds, and for that no praise can be too great, 230 of these firemen were killed and seriously injured.

These are the main facts about the great fire of Clydebank, ... the greatest Scotland has ever seen, and God willing will ever see.

THE AWARD OF THE GEORGE MEDAL TO DIVISIONAL OFFICER GEOFFREY VAUGHAN BLACKSTONE AND ACTING SUB-OFFICER SYDNEY HERBERT BOULTER, 19TH MARCH 1941

Geoffrey Vaughan Blackstone was born on 9th May 1910 in Easton on the Hill, Northamptonshire, the son of Harold and Jesse Blackstone and raised in Stamford, Lincolnshire. He was educated at Uppingham School, Rutland, leaving that establishment in 1927 to be apprenticed to the family firm which manufactured pumps, diesel engines, generating plant and agricultural equipment. He attended the Paris World Fair in 1928, where the company was an exhibitor, and after qualifying as an engineer worked as a salesman of the company in Glasgow, Birmingham and Bristol. Concurrently he was in the Territorial Army and ended as a Captain of the Somerset Yeomanry.

In 1938 Blackstone made application to join the London Fire Brigade as a principal officer having answered an advertisement in the *Times* which read: 'Young man who has served as an officer in the Army or Navy or is a trained engineer to join the London Fire Brigade as a Principal Officer'. There were only eight Principal Officers in the whole of the LFB at that time, including the Chief Officer and his Deputy. After rigorous training he was appointed a Divisional Officer, and by 1940 was responsible for London south of the river.

The worst bombing, of course, was of the docks and there were many days and nights from September 1940 to March 1941 when Blackstone had little sleep. On the one occasion in November he took leave to visit his family in Stamford, Lincolnshire, and during this break he was ordered to Coventry after the raid on 14th November. The whole of the medieval centre of the city was burned out. The Fire Service response was so chaotic that it was, largely as a consequence of Blackstone's report, that the Home Office decided to nationalise the Fire Service, and according to Blackstone the Fire Service had never since been so efficient.

On the night of 19th–20th April 1941 at approximately three o'clock in the morning a high-explosive bomb, in the region of 2,000 lbs, the largest that had fallen on the Woolwich area since the commencement of hostilities, struck a one-storey annexe of the cookery centre of the Mulgrave Place school, Woolwich, in which was situated a sub-fire station. The whole of this building was demolished, except for one wall which was left in a dangerous condition, and five members of the fire service were trapped under the rubble. Willing helpers commenced the removal of the debris in an attempt to reach those trapped, but it was not until the arrival of further fire service personnel that their location could be established.

Blackstone, who was directing operations at several fires, immediately proceeded to Mulgrave Place school. On his arrival he ascertained that three of the beds on which personnel were resting at the time of the explosion were near to the unstable wall, which continued to sway dangerously due to the effects of currents of air from the blasts of German bombs which unrelentingly rained down on the area. The debris was supported by iron girders which were inclined against the wall, and its condition was such that any weight thereon might have caused the wreckage to subside. It was therefore, only possible for one person to work. Blackstone in his assessment of this critical situation must have fully realised the probability of the wall falling, and the consequent extreme danger, and that it would only be possible for one person to attempt a rescue. He decided that that person should be himself, and he commenced to burrow from the centre passing the debris back to a chain of helpers. After a few minutes of this strenuous work, voices were heard, and this helped Blackstone to better locate the casualties. However, this now meant that he would have to recommence his tunnelling operations from a different direction.

After much intense labour a bed was found, and the first casualty located and dragged through the tunnel created by Blackstone, but was found to be dead. Having heard voices again, Blackstone wriggled through the hole onto the bed and discovered Mrs M. F. Hermitage, an auxiliary; she was alive but pinned by a larger steel girder. To exacerbate an already extreme situation there was an escape of gas, and dust from the debris threatened to suffocate the casualty. Blackstone, while working strenuously from the first bed to remove debris from below and above the girder, continuously fanned Mrs Hermitage so that she could breathe, and eventually after a great deal of hard work managed to extricate her. A third trapped person, Station Officer Burden, had been talking to Mrs Hermitage earlier in the operation and it was believed that he was still alive. This information spurred Blackstone to redouble his efforts; unfortunately on extrication Burden was found to be dead.

Blackstone had worked continuously with his bare hands for some four hours in darkness and a foul atmosphere to affect these rescues. He had on occasions, in order to free the bodies, to take the weight of a girder on his shoulders while passing debris back through his legs. Throughout this rescue operation bombs were falling in the area, and Blackstone would most certainly be aware that one incautious move would almost certainly bring a serious fall of debris or cause the wall to collapse on the victims and himself. By the end of this incident Blackstone was physically exhausted and suffering from the effects of the gas and bad atmosphere in which he had been working. The wall collapsed soon after the rescues were completed.

Geoffrey Vaughan Blackstone George Medal in fire kit.
Courtesy of Baroness Blackstone.

An oil painting of Blackstone GM.
Courtesy of Baroness Blackstone.

Chief Superintendent T. F. Watkins of the London Fire Brigade wrote in his report of this incident:

> In the early hours of the 20th April, 1941, I was informed that No. 42 'W' Station, Mulgrave Place School, had received a direct hit and personnel were buried under the debris.
>
> On arrival at the station, I found that Mr Blackstone was in charge of the operations and was personally endeavouring to extricate the five persons buried. This task was made more dangerous by … the tottering wall. Mr Blackstone, however, continued his untiring efforts to reach the victims and, by tunnelling, he succeeded in locating beds on which three persons were lying. A superficial examination under very difficult and dangerous circumstances revealed that two of the occupants of the beds were dead and Auxiliary Hermitage (Women's Auxiliary Fire Service) was alive and pinned by a large steel girder. This woman was in imminent danger of suffocation by dust and debris falling from above, but, thanks to Mr Blackstone, who had wriggled into position on a bed occupied by a dead woman, this was averted, for he, in addition to working hard to secure her release from beneath the girder (which he accomplished by burrowing over and under it), was engaged almost continuously in keeping her face clear in order that she might breathe.
>
> After some hours, during the whole of which time many bombs were dropped in the vicinity, all the victims were extricated, two Auxiliaries – Mrs M. F. Hermitage and Despatch Rider J. R. A. Cable – being slightly injured and the remainder dead. Mr Blackstone showed an utter disregard to his personal safety by undertaking risks with the full knowledge of the dangers involved, especially in regard to a wall which fell soon after the rescues were effected. I have no hesitation in stating that Mrs Hermitage owes her life entirely to the efforts of this officer.

Auxiliary Mrs M. F. Hermitage in her report of the incident wrote:

> At about 0315 hours on the 20th April 1941, I was resting in the temporary Control Room at 42 'W' station … when the whole building was demolished by an enemy explosive bomb which buried four other members of the Fire Service and myself in the debris. After a time I heard voices and digging operations taking place above me, and I heard the voice of Mr Handley (the District Officer from Woolwich fire station) who spoke encouraging words to me and told me to be of good cheer, and that I would soon be extricated. I was able to give him a brief outline of how I was pinned down by the debris.

After digging had been in progress for some time, Mr Blackstone located me and cleared my face of debris giving me a drink which I sorely needed, and spoke such encouraging words to me that greatly helped me to keep my spirit in this terrible ordeal. By superhuman efforts, Mr Blackstone was able to clear the debris which was pinning me down and eventually he extricated me.

I cannot speak too highly of the wonderful work carried out by Mr Blackstone in extricating me from a most perilous position.

In a letter to the Deputy Chief Fire Officer in command of London Fire Brigade, dated 19th May 1941, Mr C. Walker the Squad Leader of the Rescue and Demolition Team based at Powis School, Macbean Street, Woolwich wrote:

On 20th April 1941, I was in charge of a squad engaged in rescue operations at the Auxiliary Fire Station, Mulgrave Place School … which had been severely damaged by an enemy high explosive bomb, burying several members of the London Fire Service in the debris.

In the rescue operations we were greatly assisted by members of the fire service, and it was most outstanding that a superior officer of the Brigade, who I afterwards ascertained was a Mr Blackstone, at great personal risk, tunnelled under dangerous debris to locate the missing persons. Although he was repeatedly warned of the danger of a large collapse as the enemy was still bombing, he took no notice and his coolness and courage was an inspiration to all parties present, and his untiring efforts were … responsible for the rescue of one woman and one man …

On this same night Acting Sub-Officer Sydney Herbert Boulter, serving at Woolwich fire station, although on leave, displayed such a level of commitment and bravery at the above incident that he was awarded the George Medal.

Boulter, a Kentish-man from Gravesend, had joined London Fire Brigade in 1937 after having served as an Officer Cadet in the Merchant Navy for three years until his ship, the MV Pacific Trader, took fire, leaving him in the early days of the great depression without a berth. Being of an adventurous disposition and having no ties, he took himself to North America, where he worked as a sailor on the Great Lakes, on log-runs in lumber camps, and as an off-shore fisherman on the southern Californian coast. Having enjoyed his experience of working in the United States of America and Canada, Boulter returned to England and resumed his career in the Merchant Marine, but eventually became disillusioned with the almost stagnant promotion prospects which prevailed; many of his comrades holding Master's tickets, but unable to secure a ship. Consequently Boulter made application to join the ranks of the LFB, and after recruit training served at Deptford, Greenwich and Woolwich fire stations.

On the night of 19th March 1941, Sub-Officer Boulter was off-duty, but in view of the severity of the air raid then in progress, he decided to return to his fire station at Mulgrave Place school, Woolwich in order to assist his comrades. On his arrival at 2345 hours Boulter found that all appliances were attending incidents, and that a number of incendiaries had dropped on and around the station. He therefore took charge of the fire patrol and dealt with several small fires in the vicinity. At about five minutes to one that morning a parachute mine demolished a large part of the school, starting a serious fire in the western end of the building. The mine caused tremendous damage in the adjoining street, spreading a great deal of debris, much of it timber, and so potentially combustible, between that part of the school which was on fire, and houses in Rectory Grove in which persons were known to be trapped.

The force of the explosion flung Boulter across the office in which he was working and buried him under falling rubble, causing severe lacerations to his hands and face. Boulter managed to extricate himself, and began to work to free a women telephonist who was trapped by debris. After arranging for first aid to be administered to the telephonist, and sending an assistance message to the next nearest fire station by messenger, he made an assessment of the damage to the area of the school, and could see that the western end, of what remained of the building was well alight, and the fire was spreading quickly through the timber wreckage towards the house in which he knew persons were trapped. Although dazed by the explosion and bleeding profusely he managed with the assistance of an auxiliary from the fire patrol, to get line of hose to work directly from a hydrant in an attempt to hold the spread of the fire. While working the jet of water a nearby wall collapsed, and falling bricks struck his head and shoulders, knocking him over and partially stunning him. He narrowly escaped being buried by this collapse, and with great difficulty he forced himself to his feet by sheer willpower and determinedly carried on with the task holding the branch and directing the jet of water. When his senior officer arrived, Boulter, although bruised and shaken, was holding the fire in check. When further help arrived, he was sent for first-aid treatment, but returned immediately afterwards and assisted in getting another hydrant to work on the top floor of the damaged school.

Exactly one month later, in the early hours of 20th April, a high-explosive bomb fell on a single-storey annex of the school's cookery centre, completely destroying the building and burying five members of the Fire Service. Boulter, although still attached to that station, was attending a fire when the incident occurred. He returned to the station, and although completely wet through after seven hours of strenuous firefighting, he assisted with rescue work. Two of the trapped personnel were on the side of the ground floor away from a dangerous wall. The body of one woman auxiliary was soon found, and it was established that Dispatch Rider Cable was under that portion of the debris. Boulter commenced to tunnel downwards, being held by his feet so that he could wriggle vertically through the debris. Eventually he managed to locate the man who was pinned down by a steel girder and covered in masonry. It was only after three hours of work in darkness, and in a dusty and gas-laden atmosphere that the man was released and brought out alive. After this rescue Boulter assisted another rescue party until the last body had been recovered.

In his recommendation for the award of the George Medal to Sub Officer Boulter, Major F W Jackson the Deputy Chief Officer Commanding the London Fire Brigade wrote, 'Boulter suffered from physical exhaustion and the effects of the bad atmosphere in which he had been working, but did not go sick. Boulter displayed endurance and great courage in the face of realised danger. ... Boulter's tenacity, courage and devotion to duty were exceptional and his prompt handling of the fire undoubtedly prevented the development of a very serious fire situation and delayed the fire so that the trapped persons could be rescued.'

District Officer F W Handley who attended the fire at Mulgrave Place school, wrote in his report on the incident, 'I arrived on the scene shortly after the commencement of both incidents ... Sub Officer Boulter's courage, initiative and devotion to duty were undoubtedly instrumental in saving life. His disregard for his own safety has always been an outstanding example to all ranks.'

Divisional Officer Blackstone in his witness statement comments: 'I visited the site next morning of the first incident referred to and it was obvious from the amount of fire damage in the west half of the school and among the scattered debris that this young sub-officer had done an exceptional job in holding the fire until the arrival of help from the local station. I was present at the second incident ... Boulter's clothes were sodden with a night's firefighting but he never let up for an instant and performed excellent work in the rescue of the dispatch rider and women telephonist, and the early recovery of the bodies of a woman telephonist, boy messenger and Station Officer.'

By the time the National Fire Service was formed in 1941, Sydney Boulter had achieved the rank of Station Officer, and was posted as instructor to the Fire Service College at the Ocean Hotel at Saltdean, near Brighton, lecturing mainly on ship fires. He was then appointed Column Officer at Newport Docks and Monmouthshire, and relocated, accompanied by his wife Vera, a former Auxiliary Firewoman, who was herself on the receiving end of number of explosions during the London Blitz. Mr Boulter later volunteered to join the Overseas Column of the NFS, which had been formed to protect supplies after the 'D' Day landings. Attached to General George Patton's Third Army he finished his war in Frankfurt. After the war he served as Sub-Commander at Cardiff, and then as Deputy Chief Officer of Worcestershire and Worcester Fire Brigade, where he was awarded the Queen's Fire Service Medal in Her Majesty's Birthday Honours List of 1961. On 1st January 1962 he took up the appointment of Chief Fire Officer of the City of Oxford City Fire Brigade, retiring on the amalgamation of that Fire Brigade with Oxfordshire Fire Brigade in 1974. On his retirement CFO Boulter was honoured by the award of the Dutch Fire Brigades' Medal of Honour, presented by the Burgomaster of Leiden. Mr Boulter passed away on 5th November 2008.

It is important to point out the Blackstone and Boulter were not the only rescuers to be honoured for their work at that incident that night. Also heavily involved in the operations to extricate the AFS personnel trapped at Mulgrave Place School were the men of the MacBean Street Rescue Squad Depot, Woolwich, under the direction of Squad Leader Cephas Percy Walker, a thirty-seven year-old bricklayer; who at great personal risk worked steadily and determinedly for six and a half hours throughout the night to effect the release of firefighter Cable. Walker's cool, courageous work was an inspiration to the other rescuers, and his untiring efforts and great initiative resulted in two of the buried persons being released alive. District Officer F.W. Handley of the London Fire Brigade wrote in a recommendation to have Walker recognised:

> I cannot speak too highly of the initiative and courage displayed by Squad Leader Walker who was in charge. At great personal risk he tunnelled under the debris, administered restoratives to Cable, and by speaking encouraging words to him, kept up his courage until he was fully extricated. The work was very difficult, as Cable was pinned down by iron beams on which were resting several slabs of concrete. To release Cable, Walker had to cut these slabs with a hammer and chisel, which necessitated several hours of continual labour. During this time he was working under the most difficult and dangerous conditions, as there was a possibility of large steel girders falling on him, also the danger of a large wall which was left standing without support collapsing on him, as the enemy was still bombing.
>
> Although he was repeatedly warned of the danger, he took no notice and continued working until Cable was eventually released. Although suffering from exhaustion, he continued to direct operations until all persons were accounted for.

In support of this recommendation, Doctor Laurence Holmes, the Woolwich Medical Officer of First Post number 1 wrote:

> At 3.30 am on April 20th 1941 I was called to attend a trapped fireman at Mulgrave School, Wellington Street, Woolwich. On arrival I found that a man was pinned down in a prone position beneath large quantities of debris. Access to him was difficult and in fact had only been made possible by the sterling work of the rescue squad. Considerable quantities of debris had already been

removed by tunnelling and it was obvious to me that the squad must have done an immense amount of hard work, and been most ably led and directed.

Owing to the fact that I was on duty at First Aid Post No. 1, I was unable to stay after administering the necessary treatment. I understand, however, that the fireman was removed alive an hour or so later. The rescue squad and their leader, in my opinion, should be highly commended for the excellent work done.

Also on 19th March 1941, thirty-three year-old Station Officer George Edward Switzer, attached to fire station 28 Whitechapel, was in charge of operations to deal with a number of fires which were raging in St. Katherine's Dock. At around fifteen minutes past midnight he was informed by Mr Arthur Clarke, a Horse Keeper employed by Messrs Henry Viles & Co, Cartage contractors of East Smithfield, that his premises had been struck by a shower of incendiary bombs, was on fire, and that horses were stabled within this building. Switzer immediately proceeded to this location, with two of his fire appliances. On arrival he found a two-storey brick built structure, with the roof and upper floor well alight, and some thirty-nine horses stabled within a dark and very smoke-logged area; and that incendiaries were burning amongst the horses. The greater part of this stable had a corrugated iron and wooden roof, and the remainder was situated beneath the forage store; which contained hay, straw, chaff and oats; this great accumulation of highly combustible feed was ablaze. Station Officer Switzer without delay set his crews of firefighters to work extinguishing the incendiaries and fighting the fire in the forage store. As this was proceeding, he sought the assistance of Horse Keeper Clarke, two fire watchers who were employed on the premises, two Port of London Authority police constables and two Auxiliary firefighters, and led them into the choking darkness of the stable area, where they commenced to release and remove the unfortunate animals from the burning building, taking them to the relative safety of St. Katherine's Dock some eighty yards away. Several journeys had to be made, and this was rendered all the more difficult because of the restive state of the horses and the fact that bombs were continuing to fall in and round the district.

Thanks to Station Officer Switzer's promptitude, inspiring courage and leadership all horses were rescued, with only one injured, and the building was saved from complete destruction. George Edward Switzer was awarded the British Empire Medal.

Section Officer Thomas David Young, from Kentish Town, who had served with the London Auxiliary Fire Service for three years, although on leave on 19th March 1941 was in Chester Road fire station, and as a response to the seriousness of the ongoing air attack he volunteered to join the crew of a heavy unit being ordered onto an incident in East Ham. On arrival this crew got to work dealing with a serious fire in a rubber warehouse at King George V Dock, and after extinguishing this blaze their attention was directed to a number of half-submerged barges moored to a ship lying alongside the quay but lying off the vessel by some thirty feet, which were well alight. In order to effectively attack the fire it was necessary for the barges to be boarded, and a jet of water got to work from this position. The only direct method of reaching the barges was to slide down the mooring line from the ship's deck, a very dangerous feat indeed. This Thomas Young did, and once on the barge hauled a line of hose from the quay onto this vessel, getting it to work on the barges, so preventing the fire from spreading to an adjoining large transport ship.

Subsequently Chief Fire Officer W. E. Greenhalgh of Tottenham Fire Brigade was lowered onto the barges by a derrick to direct and assist Young in his strenuous and hazardous work. Young remained in this precarious position for some hours, despite the very real danger of them sinking due to instability caused by the application of firefighting water. During this time no other person would venture to slide down the mooring rope, and it was not until a tug was obtained and the barges pushed ashore that help could be given. In recognition of his courage and commitment to his duties, and as a result of the report by CFO W. E. Greenhalgh of Tottenham he was awarded the George Medal. That report reads as follows:

Dear Sir,

May I respectfully bring before your notice the very commendable actions of a Leading Auxiliary Fireman named Young of, I believe, 75 U, London Fire Brigade. On the night of Wednesday the 19th instant, I was directing operations at King George V Dock and it was necessary for my purpose to board some half-submerged barges which were well alight.

The only way to reach this objective was from the decks of a ship moored to the quayside. From the deck of this ship to the barges was some 30 feet and this fireman slid down the mooring rope to the barge, a very dangerous feat. Having reached his objective a line of hose was enabled to play on the other burning barges which made the safety of the large transport certain. It is also worthy of note that for a number of hours this man kept his precarious position even though the barges were in a dangerous sinking condition and I thought his actions very creditable. Officers in the vicinity tried unsuccessfully to get relief to Young but none dared the feat of sliding down the mooring rope and it was not until a tug in the vicinity pushed the barges ashore that much needed help could be given.

On that same night thirty-one year-old Auxiliary Fireman Albert William Clarke stationed at the fire station annex in Waller Road School, New Cross, South London was off-duty at his home in Moremead Road, Catford, when a bomb struck a block of two-storey dwellings near to his home, causing three houses to collapse and trapping one woman under the stairs of her house. Clarke displayed great courage and initiative in entering one of the damaged properties to search for the women, despite knowing that the upper floor of the building was in imminent danger of collapse. After locating the woman both Clarke and the casualty were trapped by a serious fall of debris.

When the rescue party from the London County Council Rescue Service arrived, the Team Leader, Mr C. H. J. Smith found that there was no possible means of getting access to the casualty without lifting the debris, and cutting a passage through the wreckage from the back of the house. This operation was immediately commenced, but halted as soon as Clarke communicated with the team, explaining where he and the injured women were, and how they were trapped. The Rescue Team then attempted to reach both casualties from the front of the house, but this was also abandoned. Finally the LCC Rescue Squad entered the adjoining house, cut through a party wall and eventually reached the casualty.

At Clarke's request a doctor was sent for to administer an injection of morphine to the woman, who was now in great pain, which would have been exacerbated by the cutting away of the stairs because of the severely cramped and confined conditions; the roof and ceilings being less than twelve inches from the ground where the women was trapped. Because the rescuers could not manoeuvre past Clarke to extricate the woman, the team's carpenter Mr Richard Jenkins passed a saw to him through a hole that he had made in the debris. Clarke then cut away parts of the staircase and a human chain was formed to drag the woman out of the wreckage, with each man lying on his back easing the casualty out inch by painful inch, until she was passed through the hole, and put on a stretcher, by which time the effects of the morphine had worn off.

Throughout this two-hour-long operation, Clarke, the unfortunate woman and the rescue party were subjected to a heavy concentration of coal gas, and the danger of the whole building collapsing and crushing everyone of them, quite apart from further enemy damage as the raid continued in its intensity. In a report on this incident, Rescue Team Leader C. H. J. Smith commended Auxiliary Fireman Clarke's courage (although he did not use his correct name, erroneously naming him as Cooke) in the following terms:

> …a high explosive bomb hit a block of two-storey cottages, causing three houses to collapse, trapping one woman under the stairs of her house. When the rescue party arrived, the leader found there were no possible means of getting at the casualty without lifting the debris and cutting … into the wreckage from the back. This was immediately started and on contacting a man already under the wreckage, the work was stopped while the unknown man explained just where he and the casualty were and how placed. An attempt was then made from the front of the building, but this also had to be

abandoned. Finally the Rescue Party entered the adjoining house and cut through the party wall to get at the casualty. This was successful.

At the unknown man's request, a doctor was sent for to give the casualty an injection of morphia as she was in pain and the cutting away of the stairs to release her would cause more pain. The doctor gave the injection and came out. The upper part of the building was carried on the first floor, wedged up and a saw passed through the hole to the man as it was impossible for anyone to pass him. The [walls, roof, ceilings, etc] were less than 12 inches off the ground floor, at the point where the woman was trapped. He then cut away parts of the staircase and a human chain was formed to drag the woman out, each man lying on his back easing the casualty out inch by inch until she was passed through the hole and put on a stretcher, by which time the effects of the morphia had worn off.

The entire job took … over two hours to complete and during that time there was a heavy concentration of coal gas and a continual danger of the entire premises collapsing and crushing everybody, the attack being at its height. Fireman Cooke … wormed his way to the casualty while the building was still falling, … and it was entirely due to Cooke's action that the woman's life was saved, as she would undoubtedly have died of shock had she been alone. Also if the Rescue Party had carried on as they had started, the debris would have collapsed further and crushed her. Only by fireman Cooke directing operations from inside was this prevented.

Fireman Cooke was in a state of collapse when he got out, incidentally he was the last man out, and after a little reviver had been given to him, the Rescue Party men all shook hands with him and he quietly walked home. We would very much like this man to receive some recognition of his wonderful services.

After investigation it was found that the Fireman in question was indeed Clarke.

Also on 19th March 1941, a crew of five firefighters from Beckenham Fire Brigade – Wesley Drew, Stanley Short, Frederick Moore, Dennis Fitzgerald and Leslie Palmer – whilst proceeding to a major conflagration at Silvertown were killed when a parachute mine floated silently into Plaistow Road and annihilated all five of them.

During the air raid of the 9th–10th April 1941, Auxiliary Firemen William Wilford Bennett and James Henry Meers were on duty at the AFS Sub-Station on the premises of L. H. Newton & Co, Thimblemill, Nechells, Birmingham. They had already dealt with a number of incendiary bombs, some of which had penetrated the upper floor of the four-storey block of Newton's premises when a high-explosive bomb pierced all four floors, and exploded on the ground floor making a large crater which exposed part of the basement. The upper floors were severely damaged and parts were well alight, with a large amount of heavy machinery becoming unstable, and falling through to the ground floor. Two men who were on the second floor at the time of the explosion were killed, and a third who had been operating a machine was blown by the blast through that floor, and was lodged across an exposed girder, where he received extensive burns to the face, arms and body, and was in grave danger of being burnt to death.

Both firefighters, although badly shaken by the explosion, heard the man's cries for help and entered the burning part of the works in an endeavour to effect a rescue. Meers attempted an ascent of what remained of the burning staircase, which had collapsed under the weight of falling masonry. Bennett, in the meantime had located the casualty, but in his first attempt to reach him was beaten back by the intensity of the flames. However, they eventually succeeded in reaching him from the staircase, and together succeeded in bringing the injured man to safety.

During this rescue the fire spread rapidly and involved the whole works, necessitating the evacuation of a large basement shelter housing some 400 employees, several of whom had been injured and were receiving first-aid treatment. Despite the intense heat and dense smoke, Meers and Bennett helped to remove those persons and later, hearing cries for help from the basement which had become heavily smoke-logged, made another entry to guide two men who were in extreme difficulties to safety.

Both men then rejoined their AFS colleagues, and became involved in the firefighting operations. There can be no doubt that Meers and Bennett saved this man's life, and throughout the incident they displayed enormous courage and a complete disregard for their personal safety.

The award of the George Medal was made to Bennett, and the British Empire Medal to Meers. In addition the King's Commendation for Brave Conduct was awarded to NCO Phillip Henry Bermingham of 5th Birmingham Battalion the Home Guard for the prominent part he played in the evacuation of the 400 people, and in spite the fact that the building was ablaze and beginning to collapse, he broke his way through into the armoury and recovered and brought to safety all the arms and ammunition of his Home Guard Unit.

During the above air raid, premises at Messrs Postans, Morley Bros & Birthles Paint, Varnish and Oil manufacturers in Trevor Street, Birmingham, were struck by incendiary bombs. The north east block of the factory was soon well alight and the wind rapidly drove the flames towards the main part of the building. Whilst the firefighting operations were commenced a great explosion occurred in the part of the building, which was burning when a bomb was dropped amongst the varnish tanks, igniting some 5,000 gallons of varnish. The man on the first branch (directing a jet of water onto the blaze) had been forced to withdraw because of the intensity of the blaze, but Auxiliary Fireman John Francis Clancey without hesitation went to the edge of the fire and directed the jet, and on his Station Officer's instructions tried to hold the spread of the fire whilst he (the officer) went to arrange for more jets to be brought to bear on the fire. When the Station Officer returned he found that Clancey had not only checked the spread of the flames, but had actually driven the fire back, despite the imminent danger of an explosion occurring in the shop where three tons of nitro-cellulose plastic was stored, the great numbers of high explosive bombs which were being dropped in the area at that time, and of the presence of delayed action bombs near to the premises. Despite this imminent and extreme danger he continued his courageous work and was subsequently awarded the British Empire Medal.

INCIDENTS IN THE VICINITY OF CHARING CROSS HOTEL, NORTHUMBERLAND AVENUE, CHARING CROSS RAILWAY STATION AND HUNGERFORD BRIDGE

At 9.00 pm on the night of 16–17th April 1941, the Luftwaffe commenced perhaps the heaviest raid of the war thus far, when 700 bombers attacked industrial targets on the banks of the Thames, and then spread their seeds of destruction throughout the capital. Some 1,200 Londoners perished that might, and almost twice that number were seriously injured.

Station Officer John Adlam of the London Fire Brigade was the officer in charge of a fire station which covered the area in the vicinity of Northumberland Avenue, Strand and Victoria Embankment. Soon after midnight a shower of incendiaries caused numerous fires in the areas of the Strand, and Buckingham Street, and whilst Adlam was visiting these incidents to ensure they were being adequately attended to, a large bomb set fire to the Royal Empire Society's building in Northumberland Avenue. At about this time a terrific explosion occurred in the Embankment Gardens causing injury to a Sub Officer and two other firefighters, and damaged Adlam's vehicle.

Station Officer Adlam immediately took charge of the firefighting operations at Royal Empire Society building, and assisted a number of people from the premises. During these operations it was discovered that a man was trapped on the roof of the burning building, and although an attempt to reach this man via the internal staircase had been attempted, it had been found to be impractical. Adlam therefore ordered on further fire appliances, and sent an assistance message requesting the attendance of a 100-foot turntable ladder which was already in use at another fire; on its arrival he supervised the successful rescue of this unfortunate casualty.

At 0415 hours it was reported to District Officer Beal who had earlier assumed command of the incident that there was a fire in the Charing Cross Hotel and Charing

Cross railway station, and that there were numerous fires on Hungerford railway bridge. As no additional appliances were available at this time in the London Fire Brigade area, Beal ordered Station Officer Adlam to take one trailer pump to commence firefighting operations at the Charing Cross Hotel, and Station Officer George Watling, a veteran of twenty-one years service in the London Fire Brigade, to proceed with one heavy unit to take charge of the fire on Hungerford Bridge. He later sent Station Officer Arthur French with an escape van to the downstream side of Hungerford Bridge to provide firefighting water supplies.

Watling got his heavy unit to work and ordered two lines of hose to be taken from Victoria Embankment to the upstream side of Hungerford Bridge. He was informed by an air raid warden of the location of a landmine on the bridge, which was lying across the railway lines, close to one of the supporting pillars. At this time Watling could see that there were several fires in progress on the bridge, and at one spot the fire was within feet of the mine. Station Officer Watling got two hand-held water jets to work, one within fifteen yards of the landmine, manned by Auxiliaries Hill, Blanchard, and himself. Later Watling and Blanchard proceeded along the bridge, dealing with numerous small fires, whilst ensuring that the blaze did not approach too close to the land-mine. His prompt action in dealing with these outbreaks materially assisted in preventing the spread of fire.

Earlier in the incident Station Officer French had been sent with an escape van, and an *ad hoc* crew from the London Fire Brigade Headquarters in response to an urgent call for assistance with a rescue in Northumberland Avenue. On arrival they found that the rescue had been completed, and consequently they were ordered to assist in dealing with the fires on Charing Cross Station and Hungerford Bridge. Under French's direction hose was taken from a fireboat which was moored nearby to a point from which he could see clearly that three railway carriages, a signal box and the railway track were well alight. Whilst laying out the hose he was informed of the presence of the landmine by a police constable. Presumably to gain a better vantage from which to assess the situation, Station Officer French climbed to the level of the railway, and was able to see that Watling and his crew were dealing with the fire, and that it was now within only a few feet of the mine.

Although Station Officers Watling and French and the members of their crews fully realised the danger to which they were exposed, they did not hesitate to tackle the fires on the bridge. These officers displayed bold and fearless leadership, and all concerned in the incident showed continued courage and persistence over a period of more than four hours in successfully preventing the flames reaching the land-mine, thus saving the railway station and an important rail and foot bridge over the Thames.

Earlier in the incident the Principal Officers' fire control had dispatched Superintendent H. E. Skillern to assume command of the incident, and he informed Station Officer Adlam of the presence of the land-mine on Hungerford Bridge, before he took charge of firefighting operations which were in progress on the top floor of the Charing Cross Hotel. The hotel being only 250 yards from where the landmine lay, Adlam must have been fully aware that, had it exploded, he and his crew would have been in considerable danger. Notwithstanding this fact he, without hesitation, tackled the fire in the hotel, eventually confining it to the top two floors.

In the early hours of the morning when the mine disposal officer arrived to defuse the mine the fire had not been completely extinguished, and it was only with considerable difficulty that Station Officer Adlam was persuaded to leave the fire whilst the defusing operations were carried out. The Station Master of Charing Cross Railway Station, Mr F. Bassett, in his witness statement relating to this occurrence wrote:

> A number of fires were started to the roof of the Hotel, trains and platforms, etc, and the services of the Fire Brigade were requisitioned. A land-mine came to rest near the Charing Cross signal box but did not explode. It was necessary, however, for warnings to be given of the presence of the mine. The London Fire Service arrived, and notwithstanding the great danger the firemen worked continuously to bring the fire under control, to save the flames reaching the land-mine, signal box and the bridge timbers. Their efforts were met with success when the fire was only about fifteen feet from the land-mine.

> The importance of the Hungerford foot and rail bridges, also the signal box, cannot be over-estimated. I am of the firm opinion that the firemen carried out their duties in a most fearless and courageous manner.

The London Fire Brigade District Officer in charge of the incident, Lieutenant-Commander K. N. Hoare, wrote in his witness statement of 29th May 1941:

> I was in charge of the fires in the area of Northumberland Avenue and Canon Street on the night of 16/17th April. At about 5 o'clock I received a message that the railway track on Hungerford Bridge was alight and that efforts were being made to control the fire before it reached an unexploded land-mine which was lying on the track. When I visited this occurrence at about 0530 hours the position was as stated, Station Officer Watling himself was at that time within about ten yards of the mine ... [and] set a very excellent example to his crew and carried out a hazardous duty with skill and determination and undoubtedly this crew under his leadership, were successful in preventing serious damage to an important London railway bridge.

In a separate report also dated 29th May 1941, referring to the work of Station Officer French, Lieutenant Commander Hoare wrote:

When I visited the occurrence at about 0530 hours the position was as stated
… The fire was by this time under control and the crew under Station Officer
French were working on the Bridge within 20 yards of the mine. This officer
set a very excellent example to his crew and carried out a hazardous duty
with skill and determination. His action and leadership of his crew
undoubtedly contributed in assisting to save from destruction an important
London railway bridge.

The mine-disposal officer who attended this incident, Sub Lieutenant Ernest Oliver
Gidden of the Royal Naval Volunteer Reserve, wrote of the firefighters attending this
fire in a report dated 2nd July 1941:

When I arrived at the incident on Hungerford Bridge I found about half a
dozen firemen working within 15 feet of the UVPM (unexploded mine). This
had already lost its filling plate, exposing the explosive to the naked fire should
it have reached it. Luckily for the bridge and several important Government
offices the firemen were able to prevent this happening. I warned the men of
their imminent peril but they seemed not to care a jot, and I had to order
them away. They left with great reluctance.

I then informed the squad working on the Charing Cross Hotel roof that
whilst I was working on the mine they were in danger of being blown off the
top of the Charing Cross Hotel, but they informed me they thought this was
a legitimate risk and carried on with their work. I again had to order them
off. Even the vibration of the firemen's footfalls around this mine could have
set it off, as we have already learnt to our bitter experience.

On the arrival of Sub-Lieutenant Gidden at this incident shortly after dawn, a
number of trains and a great many of the sleepers were still on fire, and the Charing
Cross Hotel was burning in the background. The underground trains had been stopped,
and many buildings evacuated, including the War Office. Sub-Lieutenant Gidden found
that a parachute-mine was lying over a live electric wire, with the bomb fuse primer
release mechanism facing downwards. Before he could release the fuse he had first to
turn the bomb over; this was accomplished with great care as at any time the clockwork
fuse could have detonated. The metal casing had melted with the heat, and in order to
apply the gag to prevent detonation he first had to remove this obstruction. This he
did calmly and slowly over a period of six hours with a hammer and chisel until finally
the molten metal was removed, and the gag could be applied. Speaking to the
firefighters he remarked: 'You firemen are damned lucky not to have been blown up.
If you'd put a jet of water on this thing, it must have gone up.' The reaction of the fire
crews to this snippet of information is not recorded!

Throughout this time the wooden sleepers on the railway line continued to burn, producing a cracking sound which was less than helpful as Gidden had to move closer to the bomb to listen for it ticking. Eventually having disarmed it, he removed the bomb in a wheelbarrow. For his great gallantry in defusing this mine, Lieutenant Gidden was awarded the George Cross. He was later awarded the George Medal for dealing with a mine which had landed between two houses in Harlesden, and made an OBE for his great bravery and steadfast devotion to duty.

Station Officers French and Watling were awarded the George Medal for their parts in this incident, and Station Officer Adlam and Auxiliary Fireman Alfred Blanchard the British Empire Medal.

During that night the frontage of Burton Court, Franklin Road SW1 was severely damaged by a landmine, and the staircases of the building were destroyed by the blast. Fire broke out and while the fire brigade was fighting the blaze it was learned that a woman was trapped in one of the upper rooms. On the outside of the rear of the building there was a service lift, which could be operated by hand. Sub Officers Alfred George Gibbs and Alfred James Layte got onto the top of the lift and were hoisted up by members of the crew. The lift shaft was about eighteen inches away from the end of the roof, and owing to damage to the shaft the top of the lift could only be brought to within two feet below the roof level. From this position both Layte and Gibbs were able to clamber onto the projecting roof, from which an entry could be made to the room. Layte had been observed in a backroom on the third floor. The room next to that in which the woman was, and the floor above her, were alight, and jets of water were being directed onto the fire from an adjacent roof. Sub Officer Layte first attempted to rescue this woman by ascending to the third floor by means of a hook ladder, but owing to the overhanging coping and debris he was unable to complete this operation. However, undeterred he managed to climb onto the projecting roof, and entered the room, where he located the casualty and brought her out and along the roof; where with the assistance of Gibbs, he managed to get her onto the top of the lift. This was a matter of some difficulty as the woman was struggling violently, and it was necessary for Layte, with the woman on his back, to climb around the framework of the shaft, and then drop down a distance of about two feet to the top of the lift. As an additional safeguard the woman was made fast to Layte's back by means of a line held by Gibbs, who paid out the line as the two were lowered to the ground.

The following letter of recommendation from Major John Ross the Senior ARP Warden for Section B1, Chelsea was received by Major Jackson:

Dear Sir,

I wish to recommend to your favourable attention the excellent and gallant conduct of Sub Officers Layte and Gibbs in rescuing an old lady, Miss Higford, from one of the top flats at Burton Court, SW3, on the morning of Thursday 17th April, 1941. After the fire resulting from the explosion of a land mine about 3:00 am in which the two blocks of flats ... had been burning for some three hours or so, a (fire) watcher on York House at the rear of Burton court, saw Miss Higford in her flat. An attempt to reach her by ladder was made but this was not practicable and Sub Officers Layte and Gibbs were hoisted by the Tradesmans' lift and walking along a ledge, were able to reach Miss Higford. One of the Sub Officers carried her back to the loft and assisted by the other Sub Officer had considerable difficulty in getting onto the lift which was at an awkward angle for approach; the task not being made easier by Miss Higford who struggled a great deal.

An ambulance was called ... when it was discovered that there was a woman in the building, and Miss Higford suffering from shock was taken to hospital.

In a recommendation for both men to be awarded the British Empire Medal Deputy Chief Fire Officer Major Jackson wrote of their exploits: 'It was largely due to the courage displayed by the two officers that the woman was saved.'

Also on the night of 16–17th April 1941, a high-explosive bomb fell in Drysdale Street London N1, severely damaging the basement of the factory of Chippendales' Cabinet Makers, in which a number of persons were sheltering, bursting a large water main which flooded the basement. Some of the people taking shelter were killed outright, and others trapped by the rapidly rising water.

Sergeant Neil Robertson McFarlane of the Metropolitan Police G Division was quickly in attendance, and on reaching the ground floor of the premises commenced clearing wreckage and removing brickwork which had been loosened by the explosion. He then saw an ARP Warden trapped in a cellar about ten feet below, who was in imminent danger of drowning. By lying full length across an edge of a damaged wall he managed, with assistance, to get a rope round the victim and eventually succeeded in dragging him to safety. In the meantime Sergeant James Alexander Sherlaw, also of the Met's G Division, working up to his waist in water, cleared some of the debris and extricated several women whom he removed to safety. While trying to release another woman he was joined by McFarlane and together they succeeded in rescuing her. As cries could still be heard, they again entered the shelter and rescued two men. McFarlane and Sherlaw then searched for persons trapped in a damaged Vicarage, the basement of which was filling with water. During this operation there was a significant risk of the roof collapsing, which is in fact what happened shortly after both police officers vacated the basement. Sergeants McFarlane and Sherlaw displayed great courage and devotion to duty saving a number of lives, and were consequently awarded the George Medal.

When the first fire brigade appliances arrived in Drysdale Street from fire station 38X Laburnham Street, under the charge of Sub-Officer Jack Hurrell, a twenty-nine years old professional fireman of some two and a half years of service, several small fires were in progress, and the water from the burst main was rapidly pouring into and filling the basement shelter. Regardless of the heavy bombing in the vicinity, and with great promptitude Hurrell detailed certain members of his personnel to deal with the fires, and ordered two trailer pumps to be utilised to pump water from the bomb crater in an attempt to arrest the inrush of water into the basement, so that efforts could be made to rescue those still trapped in the basement. A few casualties were removed and transported to hospital by ambulance; by this time, however, the basement had filled with water to within two feet from the ceiling, in which numerous corpses were floating. Notwithstanding the evident and extreme danger of becoming lost, and being aware that any slip would have plunged him into eight or nine feet of water from which, in all probability, he would not have survived, Hurrell entered the basement, which was in total darkness, and crawled from bunk to bunk in an effort to locate and rescue any other persons who may still have been alive.

In a letter of commendation dated 18th April 1941 Chief Fire Officer and Assistant Regional Fire Officer Mr W. E. Greenhalgh of Tottenham Central Fire Station wrote to the Regional Fire Officer of Hurrell's actions in the following terms:

> I attach herewith a copy of a letter I have sent to the Shoreditch Town clerk and I send it for your observations since it was in connection with a duty you assigned to me on this night. I should like to say in further support of this letter that every endeavour was made to recover the entombed people as quickly as possible and once again may I bring to your favourable notice the action in connection with this operation of Sub-Officer J. Hurrell, 38X Sub-Station, Kingsland.

> This officer rendered me great assistance in getting pumps to work at points indicated, but above all, when there was barely 2 feet of air space between the water and the roof of the shelter, I decided to risk an entry into the basement in the hopes that people may even still be alive and without hesitation this Sub-Officer crawled from bunk to bunk in complete darkness and with extreme danger to himself, since a slip meant being plunged into 8 or 9 feet of water, and indeed many people were recovered floating about in this manner but unfortunately they had all expired.

In the short space of time I was with this Sub-Officer I very much admired his composure and his efforts generally.

In another report on this occurrence, this time addressed to the Town Clerk of the Borough of Shoreditch, Chief Fire Officer Greenhalgh gives some idea of the chaotic situation on that terrible night, and wrote prosaically of this incident:

It was decreed by fate that I should be the officer in charge of an incident which occurred in your authority's area on the night of Wednesday, the 16th instant, when a number of people lost their lives whilst sheltering on the premises of Chippingham's Factory, Old Street, in the basement.

I had the unfortunate task of attempting rescue and recovery of the bodies in this shelter and I was horrified and amazed to find that the escape doors, which permitted communications with each part of the shelter, were in every case obstructed by shelter bunks, and not only were the trapped people prevented from escaping through these exits but my own endeavours were severely restricted by the bunks referred to. It was not a pleasant sight to see these women and children as you will agree, but I am sending this letter in the hopes that you will take some action in having these bunks so arranged that means of ingress and egress are not restricted for the sake of the occupiers of any of your other shelters who may be placed in this unfortunate position.

I will long remember this particular assignment which, to say the least, was unfortunate and unpleasant.

In a letter of recommendation for some form of acknowledgement of Hurrell's courage and commitment, Station Officer P. A. T. Farley of Number 7 Sub-District Fire Station, Shoreditch stated:

'At about 0500 hours I was informed of an incident that had occurred at Chippendales, Cabinet Makers, Drysdale Street. An H.E. bomb bursting the water main and blowing away the side of an underground air raid shelter in which people were sheltering, they were trapped and … Sub-Officer J Hurrell, who was in charge of a T.P. (Trailer Pump), immediately set into the flooded crater and was untiring in his efforts to extricate these people. When further assistance arrived in the form of three pumps, with Chief Officer Greenhalgh, of Tottenham Fire Brigade, in charge, I left to attend other fires and incidents on my ground as the supervision of this incident appeared adequate. I later ascertained that thirty-six bodies were recovered from this shelter.'

During the enemy air attack that night a heavy bomb had completely demolished number 75 Ecclestone Square, London, and caused severe structural damage to adjoining properties at numbers 76 and 77, and two females, Veronica More and

Rosemary Horstman who were members of the Women's' Auxiliary Air Force, were trapped on the fifth floor of 76.

Four Auxiliary firemen – John Alfred McDonagh, William De Mont (who were both employed as musicians by the BBC), Harold Stanley Ingram and Dugald McGregor McColl – all from No. 5 W fire station, at Montrose Place SW1, were amongst those attending this incident. Owing to the severity of the structural damage, and the location of the women, high up in the increasingly unstable building, the four firefighters had to make an entry through number 78. From this house they progressed by means of an extremely hazardous crawl over the severely damaged roof of No. 77, which had little structural support owing to the collapse of the framework and interior fabric of the building, in darkness with the air raid still ongoing, and with great difficulty they managed to hack a hole through the roof of No. 76 Ecclestone Square. Once a suitable means of entry had been created, McDonagh and De Mont lowered firefighters Ingram and McColl by means of a line into the building, and Veronica More and Rosemary Horstman were hauled up and out of the building.

Unfortunately their rescue work was not completed, as the women and their rescuers had to return to the relative safety of the street via the treacherously damaged roof, which was shaking with every bomb explosion in the area, and was visibly disintegrating with each move they made, McDonagh and De Mont carried both of these women on their backs via this difficult and dangerous route. One of the rescued women, WAAF Assistant Section Officer Veronica More, later wrote in her statement which resulted in all four firefighters receiving the British Empire Medal:

'I was in bed on the 5th floor … on … 16/17th when a bomb demolished the two houses next door. I was covered in debris, but managed to get clear; my companion Rosemary Horstman, was pinned by the head. I managed to free her. We then tried to go down but found there were no stairs. We shouted for help, but remained there until we were found by the fire brigade, who hauled us up through a hole they made in the roof. They carried us across the neighbouring roofs, and down through another house'.

THE AWARD OF THE GEORGE MEDAL TO FIREMASTER ALEXANDER HODGE NISBET

Alexander Hodge Nisbet, a thirty-four year-old professional firefighter of twelve and a half years' service, was the Chief Fire Officer, or Firemaster, of Coatbridge Fire Brigade near Glasgow, and was temporarily attached to London Fire Service to gain practical experience of firefighting under air raid conditions. On the evening of 19th April, 1941 during heavy and intense bombing, Nisbet was accompanying Chief Superintendent T. P. Watkins of the London Fire Brigade's D Division as he toured a great many fires in and around the Woolwich and Plumstead areas.

The first occasion on which he displayed great initiative and courage was at a fire which occurred at the High Street School, Plumstead, South London. On arrival it was found that the roof of the building was well alight, and although a number of auxiliary firemen were working to hold back the spread of the fire, it was not until Nisbet took command of the crew, and led them into the roof void, which was because of the smoke and extreme heat becoming untenable, that firefighting became effective, and the blaze brought under control. This action took place during very heavy bombing, and his cool professionalism and qualities of command and leadership proved to be inspirational to the members of this crew.

As a number of serious fires had then been reported in the neighbourhood, the vehicle in which Chief Superintendent Watkins and Firemaster Nisbet were riding was ordered onto the premises of Siemens Bros. & Co. Ltd, in Woolwich Church Street, where it was found that several buildings were well alight, and that three auxiliary firemen were trapped on the first floor by a raging inferno which was gradually moving towards them, and they were becoming overcome by the acrid fumes. The intense heat and smoke from burning cables made it almost impossible for anyone to approach the buildings. Here again, Nisbet demonstrated his great initiative and courage. A short ladder was procured with the intention of reaching the trapped men, and rescuing them, but owing to the building being surrounded by barrels and cable reels, it was found that no firm base could be established on which the ladder could safely be pitched. As a last resort Chief Superintendent Watkins and his Staff Officer Station Officer Black with great difficulty held the ladder in some form of balance, whilst Nisbet without the slightest hesitation ascended the vertical and unstable ladder; which unfortunately fell short of the first-floor window. However, by securing a hold on surrounding piping, Nisbet managed to scramble into the window, where he assisted the three trapped men to descend by placing himself in a very precarious position on the ledge, and retreating only when he had assisted the last man to escape. Although cut and bruised and suffering from exhaustion, he applied himself to assisting firefighting operations in the vicinity.

In Major Jackson's recommendation of 12th May 1941 for the award of the George Medal to Nisbet, he describes his actions so:

> If it had not been for the very courageous act of Mr Nisbet, the three men would certainly have lost their lives, as a raging furnace was slowly creeping towards them and they were already being overcome by the acrid fumes. Although cut and bruised and suffering from exhaustion, Mr Nisbet after a very short rest, applied himself to the task of assisting to fight other fires in the neighbourhood.

Throughout the night of 19/20th April, 1941 this officer was an outstanding example of unselfish voluntary service. He never spared himself in the slightest

degree and by his initiative, courage and endurance, rendered valuable
assistance at a time of great danger.

Chief Superintendent T. F. Watkins in his witness report concerning these incidents
wrote of Firemaster Nisbet:

Firemaster A. H. Nisbet is temporarily attached to the London Fire Service
for voluntary practical experience of fires under air raid conditions.

During the night of 19th April, 1941, he attended the many fires which
occurred through enemy action in Woolwich and Plumstead. I was in charge
of operations at the fires which occurred at Plumstead High Street School and
the premises of Siemen's Bros. & Co. Ltd, Woolwich, and witnessed the valiant
work done by Firemaster Nisbet. There is no doubt that had it not been for
the outstanding initiative and courage displayed by Mr Nisbet, who at great
personal risk to himself was responsible for the rescue of the three auxiliary
firemen, the men would have lost their lives.

This officer throughout the night was an outstanding example of unselfish
voluntary service, never sparing himself in the slightest degree and by his
initiative, courage and endurance rendered valuable service in a time of
extreme danger.

In 1941 Nisbet was appointed the Fire Force Commander for the Northern Area
of the NFS, in 1943 Deputy Fire Force Commander for the Western Area (No.1), and
in 1946 Fire Force Commander for the Eastern Area, and awarded an MBE for his
services. On the return of the Fire Service to local authority control in 1948 he was
appointed to the post of Firemaster of Lanarkshire, and was awarded an OBE in the
King's New Year's Honours List of 1950.

The heavy enemy air attacks of that night also caused serious damage and disruption
to the Beckton Gasworks, East Ham, which was the largest site of its kind in Europe,
and dominated the skyline of the Greenwich peninsular. Beckton Gas Works covered
an area of 150 acres, with a river frontage stretching for just over a mile. The raid that
night started fires in the benzole and tar plants, and Mr William Brodie, a member of
the Gas Light and Coke Company Works Fire Brigade, took charge of the firefighting
operations in this area, and assisted by pump man Robert George James fought the
fires throughout the night. Both men worked in extremely dangerous conditions, being
ankle deep in tar pitch and surrounded by exploding tanks. More than once they had
to be hauled out of the tar when they became trapped, but they nonetheless remained
at their post despite the increasingly hazardous situation; eventually bringing the fires
under control, and saving much valuable material. In recognition of their courage,

determination and devotion to duty Brodie and James were both awarded the George Medal. They were given valuable assistance by Works Fireman Alfred Thomas Linney and Electrician Robert Corke, who were both awarded the British Empire Medal for their gallantry.

At the same time in another area of the Beckton Gasworks, high-explosive and incendiary bombs had started a number of serious fires. Steam pipes, water mains and electrical cables were fractured throughout the site, and many barrels of tar were ablaze and exploding. Broken gas mains flared providing further illumination for the Luftwaffe bomb-aimers, and the blaze was fuelled and further exacerbated by benzole dripping from damaged flanges. Works fireman James Coppin was on duty in the valve room when an explosion occurred, which quickly enveloped the premises in steam and flames. Coppin, with no regard for his own safety, got his hose lines to work and after three hours of punishing work managed to extinguish the blaze. Afterwards he continued throughout the night to organise the firefighting operations in the works, being very capably assisted by James Nichols, an assistant engineer, and Peter Eldridge, a dehydration plant attendant. All three men were awarded British Empire Medal for their gallantry.

As a result of gallant actions at the same incident, the George Medal was also awarded to David Craig Bertram, the Deputy Station Engineer, and Draughtsman Robert Edgcombe Robinson. Bertram displayed outstanding courage and leadership in dealing with this critical and perilous situation. He ran through the flames to shut down gas valves, put out fires on the top of a gas holder, and with Mr Robison made gallant efforts to rescue two men who were trapped in a plant house which had been wrecked by a bomb, blowing the walls outwards and so causing a partial roof collapse. Robinson, despite great difficulties in working his way through the wreckage managed to get into the building, and made his way to the basement where he thought the men might be. Here he found great blocks of concrete and wrecked machinery everywhere. He was warned that the rest of the roof was in an extremely unstable condition, and fortunately he managed to get out of the wrecked building just before it collapsed. Despite the danger of being trapped himself, the presence of steam, burning gas and flaring benzole, Robinson displayed outstanding courage and determination in making further attempts to reach the trapped men, but was eventually forced to give up when the basement flooded.

At 2.00 am on 20th April 1941, St. Peter's Hospital, Valance Road, Whitechapel received a direct hit from a high-explosive bomb which penetrated all floors and caused a serious fire in the building. At that time a dual-purpose fire appliance was at work opposite the building relaying water to another fire.

Cries for help were heard coming from a window on the second floor of the hospital, adjacent to that portion of the building which had collapsed, and a man was seen crouching on the window sill. With great difficulty, owing to the roadway being strewn with fallen masonry, the crew of the appliance at once slipped the heavy wheeled-escape ladder from the roof of the fire appliance and pitched it to the window. Auxiliary Fireman Thomas Lancelot Black, who had been injured by the blast from the explosion, without hesitation mounted the escape and brought the man to relative safety. The driver of the fire appliance, Temporary Fireman Patterson, realising that an immediate supply of water was vital to the success of the rescue operations, with great promptitude ran out a length of delivery hose from his pump to attack the fire.

Station Officer Robert Albert Pullinger, a thirty-two year-old officer with some eleven years of service, accompanied by Sub-Officer William Everley Grant Dewdney who had served two and a half years with the London Fire Brigade, then ascended the escape bringing with them a line hose, as by that time the fire had taken hold and was issuing from the window by the head of the ladder. It was obvious to them that no one could enter the building to search for casualties without the fire being held in check. While Pullinger attacked the fire with the jet of water from the head of the ladder, Dewdney entered the room via the window, and rescued a man from a bed which was some five feet from the window. Dewdney then carried the man to the window, and placed him across Pullinger's shoulders, who proceeded to carry him down the ladder while Dewdney took over the task of fighting the fire.

By this time the floor of the room which had already been partly damaged by the explosion was now sloping at a dangerous angle. At the farthest side of the room from the window, two bedridden patients were seen to be on the floor and near to an exposed part of the building. Pullinger, on being appraised of this situation, again mounted the escape, clambering over Dewdney who was still working his water jet against the flames from the head of the ladder, and entered the smoke-filled, burning room. Although the floor by now seemed on the verge of collapse, Pullinger made his way across to the two men, and carried one to the window, and re-crossed the room to effect the rescue of the other casualty. One man was placed on Dewdney's back and carried down the escape ladder, whilst Pullinger took over the branch and continued firefighting.

Meanwhile Temporary Fireman William Albert Cooper ascended the escape with a lowering line (a rope of approximately 120 feet in length with two adjustable loops designed to be placed around the body and legs of a casualty prior to lowering from upper floors) entered the room and took over firefighting from Station Officer Pullinger. Pullinger and Dewdney then lowered the last four patients to the ground. The floor finally collapsed within minutes of the final rescue being effected. While these rescues were being carried out, the building was well alight, and bombs were being dropped nearby. The incident eventually required the attendance and intervention of twenty pumping appliances. In his report as officer-in-charge of this incident, Superintendent H. B. P. Drage is quoted as saying:

Station Officer Pullinger undoubtedly acted with the utmost bravery in the rescue of the persons trapped. It was due to his persistent efforts that the work was successfully carried out, as the building at that time was well alight and the floors in danger of collapse. After the rescue Station Officer Pullinger carried on with the work of extinguishing the fire until he collapsed from exhaustion, but even then refused medical attention. I have no hesitation in recommending him for an award for his gallantry at this incident.

Sub-Officer Dewdney showed great courage and ability in the rescue of persons trapped. Not only was the building well alight, but the floors were in danger of collapse; which they did shortly after rescues had been carried out, and I have no hesitation whatever in recommending this Sub-Officer for an award for the gallantry which he definitely displayed.

District Officer W N Ayres who attended the incident wrote of Dewdney's actions: Sub-Officer Dewdney showed exceptional courage and persistence under very dangerous conditions which made it possible for this rescue to be carried out, and the lives of three patients to be saved'.

Evidence of the outstanding courage displayed by these firefighters at this incident was corroborated by medical personnel at St. Peter's Hospital, and the following letter of commendation, dated 5th May 1941, was sent by the Medical Officer of London County Council's Public Health Department to Major Jackson the Deputy Chief Fire Officer in Command of London Fire Brigade:

I have received from the Medical Superintendent of St. Peter's Hospital a report of the incident on the night of 20th April, 1941, when the hospital unfortunately suffered severely through enemy action. At approximately 2.15 am ... E Block of the hospital was hit by a high explosive bomb which caused an immediate fierce fire. I also wish to draw your attention to the action of certain members of the London Fire Brigade who entered the other side ward E.2 which is on the second floor, through the windows as no other means of entry was possible and rescued four men, three of whom were quite helpless and some of whom were at the edge of a large hole in the floor through which flames were shooting fiercely. It is very unfortunate that three of these patients have since died as a result of their burns. This, however, in no way detracts from the merit of the firemen's action but should I think be regarded as an indication of the dangerous place into which they entered in order to effect these rescues. I should be very grateful if you would be good enough to convey to the Chief Officer ... my very great appreciation and high regard of these men's conduct.

Major Jackson in his report stated: '…Pullinger showed good leadership and he and Dewdney displayed exceptional courage and a total disregard for their own personal safety, in rescuing three patients who would otherwise have lost their lives. Black's endurance, courage and great promptitude enabled him, in spite of his injury, to rescue the first patients from a precarious position. The fact that water was almost immediately available was largely the result of Patterson's quickness of thought and action. The last rescue was achieved largely through the promptitude and foresight of Cooper…'. Station Officer Pullinger and Sub-Officer Grant Dewdney were awarded the George Medal for their part in this rescue, and Auxiliary Fireman Black and Temporary Fireman Cooper awarded the British Empire Medal for bravery.

When the bomb fell on St. Peter's Hospital, twenty year-old probationer nurse Edgar Alexander Turner was at the entrance of the side wards of that block. In this side ward were two young boys and three male adult patients. Although badly shaken by the blast of the bomb, which had passed through the floor at the entrance to the main ward quite close to where he was working, Turner picked up one of the boys, ensured that one of the adult patients, a Mr Jonescu, had the other child, and then led them along a corridor which was already burning, but which was the only possible remaining exit into an adjacent undamaged block. His presence of mind and speedy action undoubtedly saved the lives of these patients, as within a few seconds this side of the ward and the corridor were a mass of flames.

The people of Plymouth had enjoyed a fine, and cloudless evening on Monday 21st April, many hoping and praying that the destruction visited upon them by the Luftwaffe four weeks before, on the very day that Their Majesties King George and Queen Elizabeth had visited the city, would not be equalled. They little realised that the balmy, clear weather they had enjoyed was ideal for accurate bombing, and were unaware that on the airfields of France 120 aircraft and their crews were in the final stages of preparation for the first of a series of highly destructive attacks on Plymouth.

The devastating German air raids of the nights of April 21st, 22nd, 23rd, 28th and 29th have become termed the Plymouth Blitz, and over that period some 590 civilians were killed and 427 serious casualties were detained in hospital. The Luftwaffe dropped over 1,000 high-explosive bombs, seventeen parachute mines, and tens of thousands of incendiaries, which on the first three nights started more than 1,300 fires, while in two nights of the following week over 932 fires were begun, so continuing the mass destruction.

As the incendiaries rained down on the city night after night the local firefighters did their best, but casualties were heavy, and requests were made for support from other parts of the UK. It is against this milieu that Station Officer Cornelius Legg, Acting Sub-Officer Leonard Arthur Burley, and Leading Auxiliary Fireman William Charles Killbourn of the London Fire Force of the National Fire Service were moved to Plymouth as members of a firefighting contingent.

On the night of 23rd–24th April 1941, when it was said that the flames could spread down a street as fast as a man could walk, all three men showed great courage and devotion to duty in fighting fires under heavy bombardment, and their rescue work was carried out with a complete disregard for their own safety. During an air attack bombs fell close to where Killbourn was working, and damaged a public shelter, trapping the occupants. The debris which had fallen nearby had also trapped three auxiliary firemen and a war reserve police officer. Killbourn, in spite of the continual fall of masonry, led his men in clearing away the debris in an endeavour to rescue the victims. He was joined by Legg and Burnley, and with the assistance of other fire service personnel the four men were eventually extricated. Attempts were then made to rescue the people in the damaged shelter, despite the continuing heavy bombing, and the resultant collapse of seriously damaged buildings around them. Because of the danger, Station Officer Legg ordered the men away and, at considerable risk to himself, went into the bomb crater in order to locate the entrance to the shelter. Once in the crater Legg began to remove debris, and began tunnelling. At this point Burnley and Killbourn went into the crater to help Legg who was working in very cramped space, and in extremely arduous conditions. Legg eventually, and after much persistent hard work, created a small opening through which he was able to crawl and enter the shelter. He was then able to release seven of the casualties whom he passed to the men outside.

To recognise their courageous actions, the award of the George Medal was made to Station Officer Cornelius Legg, and the British Empire Medal to Acting Sub-Officer Leonard Arthur Burley, and Leading Auxiliary Fireman William Charles Killbourn of the London Fire Force of the National Fire Service.

Fire crews manhandle jets (presumably in training).
Courtesy of London Fire Brigade.

THE BLITZ AROUND
THE UNITED KINGDOM

THE BLITZ ON LIVERPOOL

The night of 3rd–4th May 1941 was by far the worst of the Liverpool Blitz, with the city centre and the whole eight miles of Liverpool's docks burning furiously; and the Liverpool dock fire HQ destroyed with six of its firefighters missing. Enemy action had caused a serious fire at Huskisson Dock, where the SS Malakand, a freighter of about 4,000 tons loaded with some 1,000 tons of live ammunition, was berthed ready to sail to the Middle-East. It is thought that the blaze was caused by a deflated barrage balloon falling onto the deck of the vessel, and bursting into flames. The ship and large sheds alongside were soon well alight, as bombs continued to fall in the area. With the full knowledge of the tremendous risks involved, an AFS crew, under the leadership of fifty year-old Section Officer Lappin, determined themselves to fight the fires in a gallant but vain effort to reach and save the blazing ship.

As the fire crew made their way to the SS Malakand, through a gauntlet of smoke and flames, the strong wind carried sparks which then began fresh fires right under their noses; more than once that night they were almost surrounded by blazing ships and quayside warehouses. The Malakand was moored alongside a shed which ran the whole length of the dock, and within minutes it was blazing from end to end, throwing great showers of sparks onto the super-structure of the vessel, creating fresh fires which soon gained a firm hold. To add to Lappin's problems, the dock gates had been hit which prevented the fire float from coming alongside and fighting the fire from the dock.

After two and half hours of firefighting with six powerful jets at work, nothing seemed to have been achieved, and the cacophony of the bombers and the anti-aircraft guns, gave way to the hiss of the jets, the roar of the fires, the throaty hum of the pumps, and the rather less than comforting sound of the Malakand's ammunition exploding. The adjacent shed continued to burn fiercely, whilst outside of the dock one of Liverpool's biggest cold stores was well alight, and would end the night totally gutted. On a number of occasions during that night the branches and hose lines had to be tied to secure objects so that the firefighters could evacuate as this critical situation became even more hazardous; after each retreat they returned to their posts. Eventually the Master of the Malakand decided that the ship could not be saved, and the jets were tied down for one last time. Finally the Malakand was destroyed by its precious cargo.

When the ship eventually exploded, Lappin rallied the men under his command, and although on the verge of collapse from the extremes of fatigue, he continued to hold the situation. Lappin displayed a fine example of courage and devotion to duty and led his men without any regard for his own safety. Lappin, who died in July 1947, was awarded the gold medal for rare outstanding services to humanity by the Transport and General Workers' Union. Section Officer Landau aged thirty-four, a building contractor and formerly the Commandant of the Bootle AFS prior to nationalization, showed bravery and unyielding devotion to duty, courageously obeying all commands in the most nerve-testing of circumstances. Although he knew there would be a second explosion, Landau stayed on and attended to the removal of the dead and injured, personally rescuing many of the casualties and organised their removal to hospital in improvised ambulances. Auxiliary Fireman Henry Hodge, who turned out to the fire although he should have been resting, showed great devotion to duty and his courage inspired his colleagues to continue with their dangerous task.

Auxiliary Fireman James Roach was several times thrown to the ground by the blast of the falling bombs, but continued at his post throughout the night, working indefatigably until the vessel exploded and he was injured by the shock waves of the blast and the flying debris. The resulting explosion completely destroyed the dock and parts of the ship were thrown up to two and a half miles away. Despite all attempts to extinguish the fire, eventually the Malakand had to be abandoned. Incredibly, considering the enormity of the explosion, only four people were killed. The Master of the SS Malakand later said of this terrible incident and of the firefighters who fought the fires that night: 'Although the fire brigade officer and his men knew well the extent of their danger, they would not be deterred, the officer stating that such risks were demanded of the Fire Service!'

The George Medal was awarded to Section Officer John Lappin, and British Empire Medals to Section Officer Noel Landau, Auxiliary Fireman Henry Hodge and Auxiliary Fireman James Roach, Liverpool Auxiliary Fire Service. Also awarded the George Medal for his work that night was Section Officer John Miller Bennion of Liverpool Auxiliary Fire Service. When bombs struck the General Post Office in Stanley Street, Liverpool, causing a fire in the armoury which stored hand grenades and ammunition kept as a response to earlier Sinn Fein threats, Bennion entered the burning room and began to remove containers of ammunition nearest to the blaze which were already exploding, and with assistance he removed the remaining boxes thus saving the building from destruction.

The supplement to the *London Gazette* of 5th September 1941 stated: 'Bennion displayed a very high degree of courage, and his coolness and determination were a magnificent example to his men.'

On that same night eight persons were trapped under the wreckage of a house in Great Mersey Street, Everton, which was on fire. James William Coulthard, a member of a street fire party, crawled through an aperture between some fallen rafters and a wall and released a woman who was pinned underneath a gas stove. By this time Coulthard was overcome by exposure to the smoke and fumes, and was severely cramped and had to be pulled out of the wreckage. After a short time he recovered and returned to the rescue work, taking with him water for those people who were still trapped underneath the building. Twenty minutes later he was again affected by the products of the fire, and was compelled to leave the immediate area of rescue operations, but not before he had succeeded in locating the position of those trapped. Coulthard showed great courage and initiative and it was due to his efforts and the information he supplied that the victims were located and eventually extricated. For his great courage Coulthard was awarded the George Medal.

Also on the night of 3rd–4th May 1941 a dwelling in Towson Road, Anfield, Liverpool was wrecked by enemy action. On the arrival of the Fire Service, Auxiliary Fireman Thomas Flood commenced tunnelling under the wreckage of this house, and after working strenuously for more than an hour he heard a baby crying. He continued his efforts and eventually found the child under a pram. Despite the continuing problems brought by the enemy attack Auxiliary Fireman Flood managed to obtain food for the child, and fed her under the rubble of her house. He eventually managed to remove the baby from the wreckage unharmed.

Flood continued his arduous search of the wrecked house, and again heard the cries of a child coming from the remains of the building, and after tunnelling for a further seven feet and with some difficulty sawing through an iron cot, he was successful in rescuing a small boy. Whilst Flood was under the rubble carrying out the rescue of the children, heavy pieces of masonry and timber were continually falling, making his task both arduous and dangerous, and creating a dust-laden atmosphere which made breathing in these cramped conditions extremely difficult. After the rescue of this child was completed Flood was completely exhausted, but refused to be detained in hospital. Although he was too weak to take any physical part in the ongoing rescue work, he was able to assist by directing further operations which resulted in the release of a further two children. Flood displayed great gallantry and determination in effecting these rescues, and was awarded the George Medal.

Throughout the enemy air attacks Patrol Officer Joseph Goldson displayed outstanding leadership and resource. On one occasion during a raid he made rapid arrangements for relaying water from the docks, and by the astute tactical positioning of his appliances and firefighting equipment, he undoubtedly prevented a fire spreading to the adjoining buildings. Unexploded time bombs nearby in no way deterred him, and in order to satisfy himself as to the safety of his men, he constantly exposed himself to considerable danger from falling debris.

During these attacks on Liverpool, Auxiliary Fireman John Edmund Jones was noted as acting with commendable coolness and courage. On one occasion although suffering from an eye injury and the effects of a blast from a nearby explosion, Jones took up a very dangerous position in order to prevent the fire from reaching an air raid shelter. He maintained his position despite the knowledge that an unexploded bomb was only a few feet away from him, and that he was in danger of being trapped by fire. His calm and courageous devotion to duty were an example to all those in the shelter, and gave them much confidence.

When ammunition fell on railway sidings the train carrying this extremely dangerous cargo caught fire and the contents of the railway trucks exploded. On the arrival of Liverpool Fire Brigade, Sergeant Elymer Ankers immediately took charge of the firefighting and rescue work. In attempting to control the fires and remove the ammunition from the area, he showed a complete disregard of his own safety and acted with courage and resource.

Patrol Officer Joseph Goldson, Auxiliary Fireman John Edmund Jones and Sergeant Elymer Ankers were all awarded the British Empire Medal for their courage and devotion to duty at this incident.

The MBE was awarded to Divisional Officer Robert Morland of Liverpool AFS for his leadership and courage during these air raids on Liverpool. The citation in *London Gazette* reads:

> Throughout the enemy air attacks on Liverpool Divisional Officer Morland has been in charge of a Division which has borne the brunt of intensive raids. He has displayed outstanding firefighting abilities with total disregard for his own safety.
>
> On one occasion the region surrounding the Divisional Headquarters was subjected to very heavy bombing and fierce fires broke out in an adjoining building. Morland remained at his post until a wall fell on the station, and partially demolished it, thereby cutting off communications. He at once established a secondary headquarters and by very prompt and carefully thought out action enabled effective control to be maintained over the raid conditions.

Divisional Officer Morland has shown courage and ability, and has set a splendid example to his men.

George Medals were also awarded to Thomas Tolen of the ARP organisation, Sergeant Christopher John Gartland, Constable Herbert Frederick Collier Baker, and Constable John Edward Willington Uren of Liverpool City Police for their courageous work that terrible night.

Enemy action had demolished a building in Cornwallis Street, Liverpool, the exterior wall of which was leaning dangerously inwards, and the interior walls in a state of collapse. Gartland, Baker and Uren, accompanied by Tolen entered the building well aware of the extremely hazardous condition of the structure, and after searching in complete darkness located a fire watcher trapped and almost completely buried under debris on the ground floor. When some of the wreckage had been removed a large wooden beam, which was carrying the weight of the debris of the roof and upper floor and which was directly over the trapped man, appeared about to collapse. Constable Uren immediately got under the beam, supporting it with his shoulder. He remained in this position for a considerable period, during which the other three rescuers worked furiously to free the casualty. The weight of the beam became too much for Uren to support and Baker took up a position beside him. It was clear that the whole building might collapse at any moment, and Sergeant Gartland, a man of not inconsiderable strength, placed his arms around the victim's body and with a powerful and sustained effort pulled him clear of the debris. Constable Baker got away from the beam, but owing to the great weight Uren was unable to move. Sergeant Gartland then took hold of Constable Uren and snatched him from under the beam to relative safety, and as he did so the upper floor collapsed, completely covering the area where the rescuers had been working a moment before. During the whole of this time Tolen had been untiring in his efforts to release the trapped man, having no regard of the imminent danger. Constables Uren and Baker, by supporting the beam for over an hour made the rescue possible. Had they collapsed under the severe strain, the rescuers and rescued would undoubtedly have been killed. Sergeant Garland, who was in command of the operation, displayed initiative and leadership of the highest order with complete disregard of the danger.

By the end of that week, known in Liverpool as the May Blitz, 1,741 people had been killed and 114 people seriously injured.

THE AWARD OF THE GEORGE MEDAL TO FIREMASTER STANLEY PRATTEN MBE, SUB-OFFICER WILLIAM NEILL AND AUXILIARY FIREMAN JAMES BERRY GREENOCK

On the night of 7th–8th May 1941, in the early stages of an air raid, a stick of high-explosive bombs struck the Ardgowan Distillery, Greenock starting a fire of serious proportions in warehouses containing some three million gallons of whiskey. The water mains were so badly damaged by the initial attack as to render them useless for the larger areas of fire, and it was necessary to relay water from the harbours and from aqueducts at the back of the town. From this time on, the area was systematically bombed, and many neighbouring premises were set on fire; consequently the fire service was powerless to control the initial fire, and the situation rapidly deteriorated.

As soon as it was apparent that a heavy raid had developed, assistance was requested of the Area Officer, but because of the damage inflicted to the telephone lines, it took ten minutes for the first call to be made, and during this period it became necessary to increase the number of pumps requested from ten to thirty. Eventually reinforcements totalled ninety-two pumps, plus a further 100 firefighters from Edinburgh. Three special operations Officers were sent on from Glasgow, and the Firemasters of Glasgow, Paisley and Johnstone also attended to offer their services.

Against this hellish backdrop, Firemaster Stanley Pratten, Sub Officer William Neill and Auxiliary Fireman James Berry were in attendance at the Ardgowan Distillery and were faced with a potentially catastrophic fire situation, which called for decisiveness and courage of an almost reckless nature. In an attempt to halt the progress of the blaze, all three men waded into the spirit under the tank and with difficulty managed to extinguish the flames. However, alcohol which was seeping from the seams of a large vat ignited on a number of occasions, and several times during this extremely hazardous operation the three men were cut off from the exit by the flames running back over the spirit. Pratten, Neill and Berry displayed great courage and initiative, and by their endeavours much valuable material was saved, all three men were awarded the George Medal for their work that terrible night.

Firemaster Stanley Pratten in his report on this major incident wrote:

> Having regard to all circumstances, particularly the lack of pumps and manpower at a critical period, the lack of pressure water supplies and the intensity of the raid, the fires were, generally, well handled and some very good 'stops' made.
>
> Unfortunately, some calls were received when there were no pumps to dispatch and it was necessary to await the return of a local pump or the arrival of a reinforcing pump before attention could be given.

When the Municipal Buildings were on fire it was necessary to use half the communication staff, the maintenance staff, sailors and civilians for firefighting operations. However, when the raid was over, progress in controlling the fires was rapid and I was able to report to the District Commissioner, at 10.15, that the fires were well in hand and should be blacked out before the following night. Apart from the spasmodic outbreaks and a small section of the distillery this was possible.

Contrary to first beliefs, no pumps or vehicles were destroyed. At the moment there are eight pumps and three vehicles out of commission, but these are capable of repair. When the pumps and vehicles were withdrawn from the fire operations considerable attention was necessary to put them back into commission. The work was quite beyond the Brigade's resources in a short while and I obtained for a day the assistance of eight civilian mechanics from Paisley and three A. F. S. mechanics from Glasgow, through the co-operation of the respective Firemasters. Tyres suffered severely from broken glass and debris and a number have had to be replaced.

The local Fire Brigade organisation stood up to the Blitz remarkably well. It was overwhelmed by the number and size of the fires which were started in so short a time, but the organisation did not collapse and when reinforcements started to arrive the issue was never in doubt. The control organisation worked smoothly and well and was proved to be capable of dealing with an even greater raid. A marked feature of the whole experience has been the ready co-operation and willingness to assist on the part of other brigades. In particular, the Firemasters of both Glasgow and Paisley, and the Regional Fire Brigades Inspector, have been most helpful and this has had a decided effect upon the problems facing the local service.

THE BLITZ ON KINGSTON-UPON-HULL

Just as the clocks in Kingston-upon-Hull had finished chiming a quarter past eleven on the night of 7th May 1941, the air raid warning sounded, and the first high explosive bomb of the night fell on Cleveland Street. This was the start of two nights of heavy air attacks during which more than 300 high explosive bombs, parachute mines, oil bombs, and almost 20,000 incendiaries were dropped on this major port. The Fire Service was to deal with over 800 fires, and more than 700 persons were rescued by the emergency services. The Quayside was devastated, the Guildhall and City Hall were both seriously damaged, and the greater part of the city centre was well alight, with almost all of the large stores and hotels being completely destroyed; it was said that the blaze could be seen nearly 100 miles away. In every road leading out of the city centre to the suburbs of Hull, buildings of all descriptions and uses were ablaze, and whole streets impassable to fire appliances, ambulances and other emergency vehicles because of the mounds of debris and bomb craters. Some 3,000 homes were destroyed, 9,000 had minor structural damage, and a further 50,000 suffered minor blast or shrapnel damage. A direct hit on the Corporation bus depot destroyed numerous vehicles, the supply of coal-gas failed as 200 mains had been hit, and several railway lines were put out of action.

It is reputed that when the scale of the attack was realised every member of the Civil Defence Services reported for duty, despite the extreme danger and difficulties. Older school children even volunteered to act as messengers, as most of the telephones were out of action.

The first fires were reported in Montrose Street, followed by reports from Chapman Street, Cleveland Street, Spring Bank and Wright Street, and soon the telephonists were overwhelmed with messages from all parts of the city. Those firefighters not working the jets or pumps climbed to the roofs of warehouses near the dockside, and kicked hundreds of incendiaries to the ground. The crew of a fire brigade petrol tanker carried out stirling and extremely hazardous work travelling through the city delivering hundreds of gallons of petrol throughout the night to ensure that the pumps had sufficient fuel to keep them working; not a single pump stopped for the lack of petrol. One of the most significant fires of the attack occurred at the premises of Messrs Cornelius Parish Ltd, Anlaby Road. Here firefighters worked under a torrent of oil bombs, incendiaries and high explosives, and four of their number were killed and several others injured when a wall collapsed on them. A further three firefighters were killed when the Central Fire Station was hit, and twenty-two were attended to medically but permitted to go home. Scores more received attention at their stations or at first aid posts for cuts, abrasions and burns, refusing further treatment so as not to add to the burden of the hospital staffs.

In those two nights more than 40,000 people had to be helped, the homeless brought to reception centres, shocked and frightened children calmed, settled and fed, and a diaspora of relatives reunited. This work was carried out with outstanding efficiency and great humanity by the Women's Voluntary Service. The casualties over those two nights totalled 1,200, 200 being fatal. So many of the dead were unidentifiable that a communal funeral was held.

Amongst many gallant acts that night was one that was to earn Messenger James Alfred Hodgson of Kingston-upon-Hull AFS the British Empire Medal, and Mr Harry Gelder Cardwell, who was a Lighterman, the George Medal. Houses in Lister Street were flattened by a high-explosive bomb, and a girl was known to be trapped under the wreckage of her home which was on fire. Cardwell at great personal risk tunnelled through the tightly packed debris, and after much exertion eventually located the casualty, and remained with her for several hours giving her comfort whilst the rescue work went on around them. Owing to the very cramped nature of the aperture he was unable to give her a drink of water, so he exited the ruined house and Hodgson being of smaller build wormed his way through the darkness of the highly unstable rubble, and reached her. After giving her a drink, he came out and before Cardwell could re-enter, the remains of the house collapsed. Both Cardwell and Messenger Hodgson worked continuously for many hours despite the danger of further collapse. The fate of the unfortunate girl is unknown to the writer.

THE BLITZ ON BELFAST

Throughout the period of the heavy attacks on London and other mainland conurbations during the autumn of 1940 and early 1941, Belfast was relatively unaffected. However, with the establishment of so many Luftwaffe air fields in Northern France, the city came within easy reach of enemy bombers. Although Belfast had a high population, there were only 200 public shelters available, and when the first large scale raid commenced on the night of 7th–8th April, 1941, the city's defences were woefully inadequate. Most searchlight units were not operational, there were no RAF night-fighters, and there was a lamentable shortage of anti-aircraft artillery. Just after midnight the small enemy force began illuminating the city with parachute flares, and dropping incendiary and high explosive bombs. One of the first major fires to develop that night was at the McCue Dick timber Yard in Duncrue Street, where auxiliary firemen Archibald McDonald and Brice Harkness were killed when a parachute mine exploded near to where they were working.

Although steps were taken to progress the air defence systems in and around Belfast after this first raid, insufficient resources were committed by the authorities. To make matters worse little time was available to them to ameliorate the situation, as on the evening of 15th April, no less than 200 enemy aircraft arrived over the city at 2030 hours, bringing with them an inundation of death and destruction. The first wave of bombers dropped parachute flares to illuminate the targets, and the following squadrons delivered an estimated 800 incendiaries, 674 high explosive bombs, and seventy-six landmines, mainly onto the heavily populated areas of north and east Belfast. High explosives were dropped on the city's waterworks, and at first it was thought that the Germans had mistaken this reservoir for the shipyards, where many ships, including HMS Ark Royal were being repaired. However this was not the case; the enemy's rationale had been to ensure that as the fires took hold, water supplies would be inadequate for effective firefighting operations.

Short Brothers' aircraft factory was targeted, killing several fire watchers, and damage was inflicted on the Harland and Wolff shipyard, and Ewart's Mill on Crumlin road was hit by incendiary bombs and was still burning twenty-four hours later. York Street linen mill was hit by high explosive bombs, bringing a large section of its wall, some seventy feet high and 180 feet long, crashing down onto terraced houses killing thirty-five people. One crew of part-time Auxiliary firefighters was mobile to a fire at York Road railway station in a private motor-car towing a trailer pump, when a bomb landed close to them, killing fireman Hugh Castle and messenger George Spence. Despite suffering shock from the bomb blast, and the trauma of losing their comrades, the three remaining crew members, Jack Walsh, Clyde Rainey and Jimmy Lee, determinedly salvaged what they could of their gear and continued onto the fire. All five were awarded the King's Commendation for Brave Conduct.

By the early hours of the 16th, the telephone exchange and the main telephone lines were out of commission, and the local fire and rescue services were completely overwhelmed. With much of the north of the city in flames, water supplies totally inadequate, firefighting equipment damaged, and four conflagrations, nineteen serious fires, and more than 100 smaller incidents to deal with, the situation was unsustainable. As a result, telegrams requesting assistance were sent to the Home Office in London, and to the Mayor of Dublin. Consequently thirty-two pumps and 200 personnel from Glasgow led by Station Officer James Melvin (later to win the George Medal for his part in an audacious rescue after the war), ten pumps and 100 firefighters from Liverpool, and five pumps from Preston were dispatched across the Irish Sea. Thirteen pumping appliances from Dublin, Dundalk, Drogheda and Dun Laoghaire in the Republic of Ireland also responded under the command of Divisional Officer Rodgers, crossing the border at Kileen escorted by the RUC. One of the most haunting sights to greet the firefighters from England and Eire were the number of corpses without apparent injury. Their lifeless eyes were wide open as though in surprise, and mouths gaping although still seeking breath; for when the city's gasworks exploded, it created a vacuum, which not only extinguished all flames, but all life.

By the end of this terrible night there were 900 dead and 1,500 injured, 56,000 houses (more than half of the city's housing stock) damaged, leaving 100,000 people temporarily homeless.

THE ATTACKS OVER THE SOUTH-EAST OF ENGLAND

Because of the intensity of the air attacks on London, it naturally followed that the whole of the South East of England would receive the unwanted attentions of the Luftwaffe. Here is an outline of some of the memorable stories of that region's firefighters who were awarded the British Empire Medal for their gallantry.

A serious fire occurred in a bomb dump in Elvedon, Suffolk, and many tons of ordnance and various types of ammunition were involved. Explosions had already ignited heath land, and the breeze was fanning the flames towards a number of stacks of bombs. The access to the heath for firefighting was along the immediate edge of the sector which was on fire, and in which bombs and ammunition were exploding. Column Officer Walter Sidney Vaughan, and Company Officer Horatio Edward Daniel Turner of Norwich volunteered to try and get two water tenders on to the heath. Vaughan led his appliance along the immediate edge of the involved sector and got through on to the heath. The water tender was hit in a dozen places, including the windscreen which was shattered by shrapnel from exploding anti-personnel mines. When on the heath Vaughan remained in charge of the section allotted him and, after leading his men continuously for two hours, succeeded in his objective of stopping the fire spread.

Turner displayed very high qualities of courage and leadership when explosions of a heavier nature occurred and flying shrapnel set fire to another sector of the bomb dump where stacks of 250-pound bombs were stored. He rallied his small body of men, and disregarding all danger of flying shrapnel and continuous explosions, went in and successfully extinguished the fire. Turner set an extremely fine example of cool, calculated courage and leadership, and he and Vaughan displayed complete imperturbability, under extremely dangerous conditions, and prevented what would have been a catastrophic explosion.

A fire broke out at a returned ammunition dump (this is believed to be the above incident) and following a major explosion the firefighting personnel were withdrawn until a reconnaissance could be made. Mr William Henry James Benton the Chief Regional Fire Officer, Eastern Region, undertook to do this with Assistant Fire Force Commander Reginald Clarence Welch. During this inspection which extended well into the danger area, continuous minor explosions occurred, and there was a possibility that further major explosions might take place at any moment. Chief Officer Benton not only displayed courage and initiative of a high order, but set an admirable example to all personnel by his coolness and disregard of danger. In conditions of considerable complexity and danger Assistant Fire Force Commander Welch demonstrated courage and outstanding devotion to duty while carrying out his responsibilities as officer in charge of the incident. Company Officer Leonard Cyril Crickmore, of Southend Area NFS was in charge of the first of the fire crews in attendance at the incident, and showed great energy and initiative in tackling the initial problems, and commencing the firefighting operations. Shortly after Crickmore's arrival the first major explosion put a number of fire appliances out of action, which necessitated the temporary withdrawal of the fire crews. Although Crickmore was badly shaken, he continued to command and control the situation until the arrival of a more senior officer, when he was able to hand over the management of firefighting operations. He afterwards collapsed and was taken to hospital but as soon as he was released he reported back for duty at the fire. Crickmore showed courage, endurance and commitment to duty.

When a fire developed in a hanger holding twenty-six aircraft in Cambridgeshire, the Works Fire Brigade, with great determination, managed to confine the damage to one aeroplane. It was known at the time that the tanks of the burning aircraft contained highly volatile aviation fuel and it was obvious that if they exploded, the hangar and all the other aircraft would be destroyed, and the firefighters killed or seriously injured. Firefighters Eric Donald Ankin and Stanley John Driver, regardless of the extreme danger to which they were exposing themselves, climbed on the top of the blazing aeroplane, and with extinguishers kept the flames away from the fuel tanks. Simultaneously other personnel fought the flames with foam and water from major pumping appliances, and the fire was eventually put out. Both Ankin and Driver were aware of the great danger they were facing while keeping the flames away from the tanks, and it was mainly due to their courage and determination that a major disaster was averted.

During an air raid over Essex, bombs caused damage to a number of houses, and as a consequence a great many fires were started. Having organised his appliances in the area of these incidents, Company Officer Thomas William Dodd went to a fire where a woman was trapped beneath debris. Without hesitation he crawled into a very limited space and remained amid the wreckage with her until she was released two hours later. During this time there was continual danger of further collapse of debris. Dodd then went to another incident and again rendered invaluable assistance by crawling through a hazardous section of debris to a woman and child who were trapped, and remained there for some hours with the possibility of the floorboards, which were supporting the debris above, collapsing at any moment. Company Officer Dodd showed conspicuous gallantry and devotion to duty whilst engaged in firefighting and rescue work.

Fireman Frederick James Walter Maskell was off-duty when his attention was drawn to an outbreak of fire at a house in Tunbridge Wells, Kent. Having ascertained that there were children in the house, he immediately gave instructions for a call to be made to the Fire Brigade, and entered the building, which was by this time well alight, and made his way to a room on an upper floor. After searching through the smoke and heat he found one child who was already seriously burned, and he brought that casualty to safety. He then re-entered the blazing house and rescued three more children who were on the ground floor. Having done this Maskell was informed that another child was still unaccounted for, and was believed to be still on the ground floor. Without delay he re-entered and located a baby asleep in its pram, and made another rescue. Having assured himself that all persons were accounted for he attacked the fire with a stirrup pump until the arrival of fire appliances, when he continued to assist in firefighting operations. Maskell's prompt and courageous action undoubtedly saved the lives of these children.

During an air raid bombs caused severe damage to tanks of oil and spirit in Thurock, Essex, which ignited. While the fires were being fought the enemy attacked with machine-guns and further bombs were dropped on the site. Acting Chief Fire Officer

Harold William Heptinstall of Thurock Urban District Council Fire Brigade, who was in charge of the firefighting operations, climbed onto a portion of damaged holder which had been blown against a burning spirit tank and directed a foam jet onto the fire. His leadership encouraged the men to take up positions and the fire was eventually extinguished. Heptinstall showed great courage, and worked without regard to his own safety. It was not until the fires were put out and he had seen his men safely away that he disclosed that he had been injured by the blast of an explosion; he was awarded an MBE for work at this incident. Mr Heptinstall had previously been awarded the British Empire Medal in recognition of his bravery and fine leadership at a fire caused by enemy action which had developed alarmingly.

The Supplement to the *London Gazette* of 21st February, 1941 stated: 'Following an enemy air raid a large fire broke out. Deputy Chief Officer Heptinstall handled the incident in a magnificent manner. It was largely owing to his bravery and fine leadership that the fire which at one time assumed alarming proportions, was extinguished.'

A tanker off the Essex coast was damaged by enemy action and the spirit it was carrying ignited and sprayed a considerable distance on shore and over the water, endangering an oil works. Despite the terrific heat, and continued enemy air activity Section Officer Henry John Harvey of Thurock Urban District Council Fire Brigade in charge of two fire floats, endeavoured to close in on the fire. After several attempts he was able to move closer to the tanker, and bring his monitor to work in cooling the ship. Regardless of the danger, Harvey boarded the burning vessel and altered the valves in order to allow any surplus spirit or gases to escape. Later, assisted by Station Officer William Henry Monk he manoeuvred the valves so that the forward hatch could be flooded. Despite the obvious risks, the efforts of these two men were not relaxed until their task was completed. Whilst they were aboard, a violent explosion occurred and it was with difficulty and good luck that they escaped down the fire hose dangling from the ship's side. Monk was in charge of the firefighting operations on shore and in spite of machine gun attacks, the fires which started among the oil tanks were quickly extinguished. Section Officer Harvey and Station Officer Monk were both awarded the British Empire Medal.

THE AWARD OF THE GEORGE MEDAL TO STATION OFFICER LAWRENCE BARCLAY YOUNG, NEWCASTLE-UPON-TYNE

Lawrence Barclay Young was born on 30th April 1914 in South Shields, and after working in the family horse-drawn haulage business in that town, he joined the Newcastle-upon-Tyne Police Fire Brigade in April 1938.

On Saturday 31st May 1941 a crater made by an enemy bomb during an earlier air raid in Tarsett Street, Newcastle-upon-Tyne was practically filled with debris, but a small cavity ten feet deep and two feet wide remained, through which seven year-old

Irene Page fell whilst at play. There was an unsuspected concentration of gas in the hole, and twelve year-old Boy Scout Edward Smith very courageously volunteered to attempt a rescue, and tied a rope around his body and was lowered into the hole. After the courageous Scout had reached the bottom there was no movement from him, and it was thought that he had fainted; he had however succumbed to the fumes. At this point hysterical screams from women who had come to the scene brought a number of people to the spot including two members of the Auxiliary Fire Service who happened to be passing; thirty-five year-old John Tulip and thirty year-old George Wanless. Tulip, who was the uncle of Irene Page, dropped into the hole to help the unconscious children, and he managed to secure a rope to the boy who was then hauled to the top, but he failed to reappear. Wanless then committed himself to the crater, and in what proved a gallant, though futile, rescue effort, he collapsed at the bottom of the hole. Leading fireman George Bruce then made an attempt to effect a rescue, but was badly affected by the gas and was rescued by Fireman Larry Young on his arrival. Young, although aware that previous attempts at rescue had almost certainly proved fatal, and without any protection against the fumes immediately entered the crater, and after removing some debris which had fallen on the casualties, was able to place ropes around them. He made three descents into the gas-filled hole and brought out the victims. Young was badly affected by the gas, but on recovery helped apply artificial resuscitation until all casualties were removed to hospital.

It was believed that sewer gas was to blame for the deaths of the two children and two firefighters, but evidence at the inquest given by the senior gas identification officer for the Newcastle Air Raid Precautions organisation, Dr. Richard Raper of King's College, who had entered the crater to take samples, strongly suggested that carbon monoxide fumes from the high-explosive bombs had remained in the hole because debris from a collapsed wall had sealed the fissure.

On 14th August 1941 the following letter was sent to Larry Young by the Ministry of Home Security:

Dear Sir,

I am directed by the Minister of Home Security to inform you that the Chief Constable of Newcastle-upon-Tyne drew his attention to your gallant conduct on 31st May, 1941 when, although fully aware of the presence of lethal gas, you entered a crater at Tarsett Street, Newcastle-upon-Tyne and brought out three persons who had been overcome by fumes.

Mr. Herbert Morrison felt that your courageous action was deserving of high praise and he took steps to bring the matter to the attention of His Majesty the King who was pleased to award you the George Medal in recognition of the courage which you displayed.

Lawrence Barclay Young George Medal of Newcastle-upon-Tyne Police
Fire Brigade with his family outside Buckingham Palace.
Courtesy of the Young family.

Two views of Tarsett Street, Newcastle, where Larry Young GM
carried out his gallant rescues.
Courtesy of Tyne and Wear Fire and Rescue Service.

On the following day Larry Young was paid the sum of £1.11.6d by the BBC for a radio interview in which he spoke about the rescue. Fireman Young was invested with the George Medal on 2nd December 1941 at Buckingham Palace. Leading Fireman Bruce received the King's Commendation for brave conduct for his part in the rescue attempt and one of the victims, Auxiliary Fireman Wanless, was awarded a posthumous commendation, and Edward Smith awarded the Bronze Cross of the Scout movement for his great courage.

Young went on to join the RAF as a Flight Engineer, serving first of all in air-crew with 463 Bomber Squadron of the Royal Australian Air Force at Waddington, Lincolnshire, flying Lancasters; as part of 5 Group of Bomber Command, and was heavily engaged during the battles of Berlin and the Ruhr. Larry later moved to 83 Squadron of the Pathfinder Force, the unit of Victoria Cross holder Flight Sergeant John Hannah, which took part in many famous raids, including that against the German V weapons experimental station at Peenemunde, and on railway targets in France, Belgium and Western Germany in preparation for 'D' Day. Indeed on the night of 5th–6th June 1944, they bombed gun emplacements at La Pernelle on the Normandy coast, and on 8th–9th June, four of the squadron's Lancaster bombers acted as a target-illuminating force in the highly successful operation in which the famous 617 Dambuster Squadron, used 12,000 lb bombs to block the Saumur tunnel.

After the war Larry Young returned to the National Fire Service, and was appointed to the rank of Station Officer on the formation of the Newcastle and Gateshead Joint Fire Service in 1948, where he was known as a quiet, sober, fair-minded and modest man, who demanded the highest standards. Later in his career he was, with his crew, commended by Chief Fire Officer Patrick Watters for his work in resuscitating a man at a house fire in November, 1967.

Station Officer Lawrence Barclay Young George Medal, heroic flyer and firefighter, retired from the fire service on 18th April, 1968, an extremely well respected hands-on, practical fire officer and leader of men. He died in 2008, and his funeral was attended by an Honour Guard from Tyne and Wear Fire and Rescue Service, many of his brother Freemasons, and three generations of firefighters, including the author.

On 7th August 1941, known as Black Friday by the people of Aberdeen, German bombers scored a direct hit on a tenement building in South Market Street, close to the harbour, leaving the partly demolished structure on fire and in an extremely unstable condition, being almost on the point of collapse.

Senior Fire Guard Mrs Marion Patterson, a small and slightly built woman, without hesitation crawled under the wreckage with a stirrup pump and managed to extinguish the blaze before it could fully develop. A sailor was known to be trapped under the rubble of the building which was in a highly unstable condition. Despite this knowledge Mrs Patterson burrowed under the debris for fifteen feet, and directed rescue operations from underneath, so that a path could be cleared to affect the man's rescue. Once Mrs Patterson had reached the man she found that he was trapped by a heavy piece of timber which lay across his legs, so she continued to work down into the debris so as to create space to move the lumber and bring about his release.

Mrs Patterson showed great courage and initiative, without regard to her own safety. Throughout the operations she was in great danger, which was illustrated clearly when the building collapsed one minute after she emerged from the ruins.

Marion Patterson was born in Aberdeen and emigrated to Canada as a small child with her parents Mr and Mrs Chalmers. In Canada she married Guthrie Patterson, a native of Dundee, who enlisted in the Royal Air Force in 1939 shortly before the outbreak of war. During her husband's period of service Marion returned to her native city, where she ran a hairdressing business. In 1944 she decided to go back to Toronto in order to be reunited with her twelve-year-old son, Douglas. In later years Marion made several return visits to Aberdeen.

Mrs Patterson was also awarded the 1939–45 Star, the Defence Medal, Canadian Volunteer Overseas Medal, and War Medal 1939–45, as well as being elected to honorary membership of the Royal Society of St. George, in recognition of her service and actions as a Civil Defence senior fireguard. During this time she was a mother bringing up young children.

Marion Patterson's George Medal group and associated memorabilia were purchased for the City's collection from a London dealer with the assistance of a generous donation from the Friends of Aberdeen Art Gallery and Museums. The acquisition was reported to Lady Betty Boothroyd, former House of Commons Speaker and patron of the Memorial to Women in World War II Fund, who replied expressing her congratulations.

On 31st August 1941, the SS Anglo-Norse a 7,988 ton former whaler, which had been originally built in Norway in 1914, as the Maricopa, was in the Tyne at Jarrow, and was carrying a cargo of fuel oil. On that morning she took fire, and the blaze was initially confined to the engine room and bunkers. River and shore fire appliances were quickly in attendance including fire floats but when, at one point, there were fears of the fire spreading, it was decided to tow the ship to the harbour mouth. Tugs took her up and she was eventually beached on the Herd Sands, where she lay enveloped in thick smoke. The fire developed quickly and was soon burning furiously, and the vessel's magazine was threatened. It became apparent that, unless the ammunition was immediately thrown overboard, serious damage would result. Knowing full well the risk of the ammunition exploding, Company Officer George Richardson of No 1 Fire Force Area NFS, and Francis James McNulty, a Master Stevedore from South Shields, volunteered to assist in this operation, and boarded the vessel, which was heavily smoke-logged.

As they groped their way along the alley leading to the magazine, the fire was gaining an increasing hold, and as they got near to the magazine a violent major explosion occurred throwing them violently to the deck. A second explosion immediately followed and the men were blown several feet apart. Richardson and McNulty were both badly burned and severely injured, and although still within the danger zone of further explosions, Richardson, disregarding his own injuries gave assistance to another firefighter who had sustained injuries when the explosions took place, and helped him to ascend the ladder to the main deck, and carried him to safety from the ship. Three other firefighters were also seriously injured.

McNulty and Richardson showed great courage and resolution in their attempt to save the ship and its valuable ammunition, and were both awarded the George Medal. Richardson had previously been awarded the King's Police and Fire Service Medal for gallantry when he was Chief Fire Officer of Jarrow Borough Fire Brigade, on the south bank of the river Tyne. At 7.45 am on 19th February 1938, fire broke out at the works of the British Oxygen Company, Jarrow. The fire spread rapidly, and cylinders of liquid oxygen stored in the factory, began exploding with tremendous force, shooting pieces of metal through the air and giving cause for an immediate evacuation of the buildings surrounding the area. Mr Richardson, not being satisfied that all the workers had been cleared from the factory, re-entered to make an inspection of the area, and search for any personnel still in the danger area. Whilst in the factory he went into a highly dangerous compression room and sprayed water onto the cylinders to keep them cool and so reduce the likelihood of further explosions. He ordered his men to keep back while he continued his search, and although he was blown over several times by subsequent explosions, he was fortunate to escape injury.

THE GALLANTRY OF WALES' WARTIME FIREFIGHTERS

From 1941 to the mid-point of the Second World War, British Empire awards were made to the following firefighters in Wales, and I should like to take this opportunity to pay tribute to at least some of them.

The BEM for gallantry was awarded to Fireman Brinley Evans of the Port Talbot Fire Brigade (Supplement to the *London Gazette* of 28th February 1941), who was a member of a crew engaged in firefighting in a factory, when the building in which they were working received a direct hit from a high-explosive bomb. One of the firefighters working with Evans was completely buried in the debris, and because his hose line was still under pressure with no immediate means of closing down the flow of water, there was every probability of the man drowning, quite apart from the already precarious position he was in. Evans immediately commenced rescue operations and was, with great difficulty, able to get through the rubble to reach the firefighter, who was pinned by the wreckage in a crater which was now rapidly filling with water. Fireman Evans battled to keep the man's head above the water, whilst he continued to work to release him, persisting in his efforts without thought to his own safety. After nearly an hour Evans was at last able to bring his comrade out of the wreckage to comparative safety.

The MBE was awarded to Chief Fire Officer Alfred Francis of Tenby Fire Brigade and Horace Lloyd Howarth the Commandant of Milford Haven Fire Brigade. When a large fire, as a result of enemy action, threatened to spread to a nearby town, Commandant Howarth, surmounting great difficulties, successfully organised water relays involving a great many pumping appliances and other equipment to keep the firefighting jets supplied. He was joined by Chief Officer Francis whose great practical experience as a commander of serious fires, combined with the initiative and organisational skills displayed by Howarth greatly assisted in bring the firefighting operations to a successful conclusion despite the best efforts of Reich Marshal Goering's fliers. Both officers led their men with courage and displayed devotion to duty and resource in dealing with a very serious situation.

The award of the MBE was announced as being made to Divisional Officer Charles Richards No 21 (Camarthen) Area of the National Fire Service, and the British Empire Medal to Senior Company Officer John William Edmunds Jones of the NFS Regional HQ Cardiff in the fourth supplement to the *London Gazette* Tuesday of 12th March, 1943. A fire broke out in a ship conveying a cargo which included munitions twelve hours before its arrival in port. All efforts of the Master and crew to check the spread of the fire proved of no avail, and a call for assistance was made to the National Fire Service. However, operational firefighting procedures were not feasible until the ship had arrived in harbour. Divisional Officer Richards displayed great initiative and leadership in commanding operations, and was responsible for the prompt attendance of reinforcing fire appliances and specialist equipment at this potentially very serious incident. At considerable personal risk, he entered the affected hold wearing breathing apparatus in a courageous and persistent effort to locate the seat of the fire. Richards was eventually overcome and had to be rescued from a very dangerous situation, but on his recovery from partial asphyxiation he made repeated attempts to continue his work.

Senior Company Officer Jones was a member of the Breathing Apparatus crew which entered the burning hold of a ship. After a feat of considerable physical effort and skill, fraught with great danger, they eventually located the fire. In the darkness, and in thick smoke and fumes, Jones climbed through very awkward places where any incautious move might have cost him his life, as rescue would not have been possible, there being only room for one person at a time to pass. Jones also discovered a second fire on board which was spreading amongst highly flammable and dangerous explosives, and succeeded in extinguishing it. His skill and daring were responsible for the fire in the hold of the ship being confined and held in check until such time as it could be extinguished.

At another similar incident, a fire broke out in a merchant ship when she was at sea, and soon raged out of control and spread towards the magazine, with the obvious danger of explosion. Consequently the ship's Master ordered that part of the vessel to be battened down. On docking, National Fire Service personnel boarded the ship and Section Leader Walter Stark of No 20 (Cardiff) Area led a team of breathing apparatus wearers into the burning quarters with a jet. There was constant danger of the contents of the magazine exploding, particularly as the compartments were opened up to allow the firefighters to enter the risk, and consequently air was admitted. Despite the extreme danger involved in this operation Stark showed great courage and worked regardless of his safety to ensure that the fire did not spread further and would be extinguished. His courageous leadership and determined work in extreme conditions undoubtedly saved further damage to the ship which, as a result was quickly repaired and made seaworthy. The British Empire Medal was awarded to Section Leader Stark in recognition of his brave and very committed action at this dangerous incident.

In the same supplement to the *London Gazette* of 18th December 1942, page 5519, the following firefighters were named as being awarded the King's Commendation for Brave Conduct for fighting a fire in a ship (presumably for the same incident):

Leading Fireman Francis Alfred Pellow Ingram, Leading Fireman William Voyce and Company Officer Charles Norman Bidgood, all of No 20 (Cardiff) Area NFS. Mr Bidgood later became one of Her Majesty's Inspectors of Fire Service.

The award of an OBE was made to Mr Thomas Arthur Varley, the Chief Regional Fire Officer of No 8 Region (Wales), and to John Farrell, Fire Force Commander No 22 (North Wales) Area; the British Empire Medal was awarded to Company Officers John Richard Allen and Harold Grimbledeston, and to Leading Fireman George Hughes, all of No 22 Area. This was announced in the Supplement to the *London Gazette* of 27th March 1942 in recognition of their outstanding work at the following incident.

A tanker was making for port when she was hit by high-explosive bombs and consequently had to be abandoned. Chief Regional Fire Officer Varley gave preliminary instructions for men and materials to be mobilised, and then left for the port accompanied by Fire Force Commander Farrell and Company Officer Grimbledeston. The party reached the vessel and Varley, who fully appreciated the great risk involved, went on board, quickly assessed the situation, and directed operations until the fire was completely under control. The vessel and its cargo were saved through the cooperative and excellent team work of the firefighting personnel under the competent and courageous leadership of Chief Regional Fire Officer Varley. Farrell assisted in the supervision of operations and remained throughout the incident setting a splendid example to his officers and men. Leading Fireman Hughes worked at a point of great danger and had to contend with intense heat and smoke from a burning tank which was less than ten feet away. The decks were too hot for him to stand upon and an improvised foothold of pieces of rough timber were his only protection. The soles of his boots were actually burnt owing to the intensity of the heat. He remained at his post without seeking relief or help of any kind for a considerable period.

Grimbledeston planned and maintained the supply of foam under most trying conditions, and without any regard for his personal safety, descended below deck to combat the fire. Allen, although of limited experience, mobilised the equipment on hand and volunteered to go out to sea to ascertain the best form of assistance the National Fire Service could render. He showed courage and initiative and in difficult conditions, took the correct preliminary steps to tackle the fire pending the arrival of his superior officers.

During the Second World War the gallantry awards made to members of the British Fire Service, that is, to local authority fire brigades, the Auxiliary Fire Service, and later the National Fire Service were as follows:

George Cross	2
George Medal	91
CBE	1
OBE	5
MBE	27
BEM	209
King's Police & Fire Service Medal.	7
King's Commendations.	421.

THE POST-WAR PERIOD

THE DEATH OF FIREMAN FREDERICK DAVIS GC

On 23rd August 1945 the National Fire Service (London Area) received a call to a fire involving premises which consisted of a shop and a house of five rooms in Craven Park Road, Willsden, which was to lead to the posthumous award of the George Cross to Fireman Frederick Davies.

Davis was recruited into the London Auxiliary Fire Service in February 1941, just before his twenty-sixth birthday, and on the invasion of Poland by German troops he was mobilised as a full-time fireman. Other than a brief posting to North Kensington, Davies spent the war working out of Willsden fire station, where he was a popular member of the team, and a keen sportsman.

Davies reported for duty to Willsden fire station in the early evening of 22nd August 1945, to repay a colleague a shift worked for him the previous week. At a quarter past one on the morning of the 23rd a fire broke out in the kitchen on the first floor of 5 Craven Park Road, Willsden, occupied by the Pike family, and spread rapidly via the staircase to involve the upper floor and the roof space. Two of the family's three children, Jean aged eleven years, and Avril, eight years, became trapped by the flames despite a gallant rescue attempt by their father Alfred. Three minutes after the outbreak the fire bells issued their piercing alarm, propelling the firefighters of Willsden into action.

On the arrival of the first appliances three minutes after the alarm had sounded, they found a serious and well developed fire in progress, and were informed that two children were in the front room on the second floor. An assistance message was passed to control and further appliances were dispatched from Acton and Kilburn. The wheeled escape (a heavy duty, fifty-foot extension ladder) was immediately slipped from the roof of the fire appliance, and pitched to the middle window of that floor. Before the escape was in position Davies ran up the ladder, without the benefit of water to keep the flames from him, to effect a snatch rescue of the children. By this time the second floor of the building was well alight, with flames pouring from the windows, and licking up the face of the building. Upon reaching the building, Davies was momentarily halted by the ferocity of the fire, but undaunted he took hold of the windowsill and turning his back on the inferno managed with great difficulty to climb through the window into the room. Davies was followed up the wheeled-escape by Leading Fireman Norman Wilfred Thorn, who saw him attempting to remove his tunic (presumably to wrap around the child later identified as Avril, to afford her some protection from the flames) but by this time his hands were too badly burned for him to do so. After a period of searching he brought one child to the window to be rescued, and was next seen to fling himself out of the window onto the escape ladder, with the whole of his clothing on fire. Thorn took the weight of Davies across his arms, as he held desperately onto Avril, fighting desperately to keep his place on the ladder secure. Davies was helped to the ground, the flames from the remains of his uniform extinguished, and he was then conveyed to hospital suffering from severe burns. Fireman Frederick Davies later died from the injuries sustained in gallantly attempting to rescue these two children.

A disquieting and quite tragic aspect of this incident was that the firefighter to whom Davis handed the girl, Leading Fireman Thorn, most unfortunately, and perhaps almost inevitably, dropped her from the head of the ladder, presumably due to her slippery condition owing to burns. This firefighter must have suffered enormous emotional anguish believing that he had contributed to the unfortunate girl's death. However, a post mortem established that she was already dead when Davis effected her rescue.

Fireman Frederick Davies was interred at Kensal Green cemetery with full Fire Service ceremonial honours, led by a National Fire Service Band, and the remains of his scorched and blackened steel helmet and webbing belt and axe were placed on his Union Flag draped coffin.

On 30th July 1946 His Majesty The King pinned the George Cross onto the chest of Frederick's son Raymond at a ceremony at Buckingham Palace. In the supplement to the *London Gazette* of 1st February 1946, Leading Fireman Thorn was listed as being awarded the King's Commendation for Brave Conduct, but as a result of injuries received during this rescue attempt Thorn was forced to retire from the Fire Service.

FIRE AT THE GOODS DEPOT, ELDON STREET LONDON

Shortly before a quarter to eight on the evening of Friday 21st December 1951, two pumping appliances from Bishopsgate fire station, and one pump each from Redcross Street and Shoreditch, plus a turntable ladder from Canon Street, responded to a fire-call to the rail goods depot at Eldon Street, at the eastern end of the city of London. Seventy-five minutes later, two firefighters were dead, another dying, and a number of others, including the Deputy Chief Fire Officer, seriously injured. A total of 500 firefighters, with 119 pumping appliances, and eight turntable ladders, used no less than forty-one jets of water to extinguish perhaps the biggest post-war fire dealt with by the London Fire Brigade.

Completed in 1886, Eldon Street goods depot was a rectangular building with a frontage in excess of 100 feet, and was 250 feet deep, consisting of five floors, a basement and sub-basement, and was separated from Broad Street Railway Station by a covered goods yard some 150 feet square. Because of the relative narrowness of the surrounding streets, and a wide covered area on the east side, access for firefighting was severely limited.

On the afternoon of the 21st December the third and fourth floors of the building were vacated at 1700 hours, and a party in the book-room on the second floor finished half an hour later. At about 1900 hours two cleaners entered the book-room and spent twenty minutes working in that area, and later declared that when they left that room there was no suspicion of fire. At 1915 the telephone operator in the building saw a 'doll's-eye' on his switchboard drop, indicating that a phone in the book-room had been actuated. He answered the phone but received no acknowledgement, and assumed that the line was defective. Five minutes later a similar actuation was received, and no action taken. At 1932 hours, three off-duty City of London policemen were in Eldon Street, and saw smoke emerging from windows at the west side of the warehouse. They brought this to the attention of a railway employee, who it is alleged informed them that railway authorities were already aware of this. Shortly before 1940 hours another railway employee saw fire on the second floor, and told a member of the railway fire brigade, and a fire-call was made to London Fire Brigade

When the first appliances arrived under the command of Leading Fireman Wheeler it was seen that the two upper floors were well alight, and it could be seen through windows on the eastern side of the structure that the main body of fire was in the centre of the warehouse on both of these floors. At 1948 hours, pumps were 'made four', and this quickly escalated to twenty pumps and four turntable ladders within five minutes. An indication of the seriousness of the situation, and how rapidly the fire was developing, was that at 1958 hours the Deputy Chief Fire Officer Mr C. P. McDuell assumed command of the incident, and three minutes later handed it over the Chief Fire Officer Mr Frederick Delve. Both of these men were extremely experienced and very well respected fire commanders.

Mr Delve, after serving in the Royal Navy, had joined the Brighton Fire Brigade, where at the age of twenty-seven, he was appointed the Brigade's Second Officer, the youngest in Great Britain. He moved to the Croydon Fire Brigade as Chief Officer in 1933, and under his leadership they became the first in the country to install radio communications between all appliances and HQ. Delve was one of a small group of young, dedicated senior fire officers who had been pressing the Government to take seriously the threat of firebombing in any future war. It was not until after the air attack on civilians in Guernica during the Spanish Civil War that, in 1937, the Home Office set up a committee, on which Delve served, to advise on changes in the fire service in Britain. He went on to serve as Deputy Inspector in Chief of the National Fire Service from 1941 to 1943. After the war, when the NFS was disbanded, Delve remained in London as Chief Officer of the re-formed London Fire Brigade where he had the honour of being the first Chief Officer of the LFB to be knighted in office.

After being briefed by his deputy, Delve decided that DCFO McDuell should take charge of operations at the south and west sides of the fire, organise the deployment of turntable ladders in Eldon Street, and the use of wheeled escapes to effect entry to the building in Eldon Street and Finsbury Avenue so that jets could be brought to bear on the main body of the fire in the central part of the warehouse. This in effect meant the DCFO McDuell would be outside of the warehouse. Entry to the warehouse was only obtainable at the north end of the building, and it was here that CFO Delve decided to effect an entry and attack the fire at close quarters. He appointed Divisional Officer Shawer to take charge of firefighting on the second floor, and Assistant Divisional Officer Varndell on the first floor, with Divisional Officer Leslie Leete co-ordinating these operations. The intense heat and choking smoke severely hampered the progress of all crews in this area, but they managed to keep seven jets working, and materially prevented the fire from reaching the first floor.

At the southern end of the building, branch-men under Sub-Officer Creegan had four jets of water at work on the second floor. When three of the firefighters working for him were taken to hospital suffering the effects of heat and smoke, and two for burns treatment, Creegan reluctantly withdrew his party from the risk. DCFO McDuell now had two turntable ladder monitors working in Eldon Street, and four jets working from wheeled escapes pitched to the second floor windows. Twelve minutes after assuming command CFO Delve made pumps up to thirty, and turntable ladders to four. By 2035 hours there were fifteen powerful jets of water being directed at the heart of the fire on the three upper floors with little effect. Consequently at 2046 hours pumps were made up to forty.

When a portion of the wall at the north-east end of the building collapsed at 2048 hours, Mr McDuell hurried to the scene, only to be advised that there were no casualties. On his return to Eldon Street he was advised at 2053 hours that a bulge had developed in the southern wall, indicating an imminent collapse. The DCFO confirmed that he was aware of this, and had ordered all personnel to vacate the building. The collapse of coping and brickwork came six minutes later and amongst the injured was Mr McDuell, who was found lying under the fore-part of a turntable ladder covered in debris. As a consequence of the injuries sustained he had part of his right leg amputated. Three wheeled-escape ladders were pitched in Eldon Street. On the centre positioned escape were two crews from Whitefriars fire station under the command of Station Officer Handslip. The crew, consisting of Leading-Fireman Dickenson, and Firemen Cluney, Skitt, Aldridge, Harwood, Joy and Lloyd, were gathered around the foot of the ladder whilst the Station Officer ascended the escape to release the line of hose secured at its head. Handslip was half way up the ladder when the wall collapsed, killing Firemen Skitt and Harwood. Station Officer Handslip and a number of his crew were later hospitalised, as were three members of the crew of one of the other escape ladders. Fireman Thomas Joy later died later of his injuries.

Two turntable ladders – one from Canon Street and one from Kingsland Road – were also at work in Eldon Street, and were damaged by the collapse. The first ladder, with fireman Jenden at its head, was being lowered when masonry struck it, causing the motor to cut out. The ladder continued the process of housing itself, when Leading Fireman Goldsmith, by means of the handbrake, held the ladder while Jenden descended unaided. The other turntable ladder with Fireman Walls at its head had been working above roof level, but had been lowered to the fourth floor to enable a jet to be worked through a window frame. The falling masonry hit the head of the ladder and caused it to suddenly descend for about twelve feet, when its maximum extension was then about fifty-five feet. To make his escape, Fireman Walls slid down the strings (the vertical members which hold the rungs or rounds) of the ladder, and was later admitted to hospital with a dislocated shoulder, abrasions and shock. No member of either these crews was seriously injured.

At 2103 hours Chief Officer Delve ordered 'pumps to be made sixty'. At 2115 hours a further structural collapse occurred on the west side of the building, seriously damaging three of the wheeled escapes, but fortunately causing no injuries. Over the next seventeen minutes, coping and brickwork collapsed at the north end of the building involving practically the whole of the upper floor, and at the east side the collapse involved a large portion of wall in the centre, and a large section of girders supporting the roof of the goods yard. Fortunately no further injuries were sustained.

At 2345 hours it was reported to fire control that thirty-six jets were in use, and consequently the scale of the blaze was diminishing to the point where Mr Delve relinquished command of operations in favour of Divisional Officer Botten, and was able to visit his firefighters who had been admitted to hospital.

On his retirement from the Service, Mr McDuell, most unusually, received a letter of good wishes from the Lord Great Chamberlain, the Marquess of Cholmondeley, thanking him for his excellent work during one of the most intense air raids of the War, when the Palace of Westminster was bombed and the roof of Westminster Hall set on fire. His letter expressed the thanks of both Houses of Parliament.

THE GREAT FLOOD OF 1953

On the 31st January 1953, a low pressure system in the North Atlantic west of Ireland passed the north of Scotland and turned its awesome force down into the North Sea, bringing with it a great and terrible storm surge that swept southwards, breaching East Anglia's insubstantial sea defences with ease and heralding the worst natural disaster to befall Great Britain during the twentieth century.

The hurricane force winds gusting from the north, had destroyed more trees in Scotland than would be normally felled in a year, and produced storm waves over six metres in height which, because the North Sea becomes narrow and more shallow in the south, contributed to the exceptionally high water levels along the east coast of England. By the early hours, Felixstowe, Harwich and Maldon had been flooded, and the sea walls on Canvey Island had collapsed, drowning fifty-eight people. From Tilbury to London, docklands, oil refineries, factories, gasworks and electricity generating stations were put out of action. In London's East End, 100 metres of sea wall collapsed, causing more than 1,000 houses to be inundated and the Thames to flow through the streets of West Ham. This great flood caused 307 deaths in Great Britain, and over 30,000 people were evacuated from their homes. Over 20,000 residential properties were flooded, and 100 miles of the road, and 200 miles of the rail network were impassable. A staggering 1,835 people died in the Netherlands.

There was little in the way of a crisis management structure or flood warning system to deal with this major incident, and the first most people knew of the danger was when waves crashed into their homes. Because many telephone lines in Lincolnshire and Norfolk had been brought down, virtually no warning of the storm's severity could be communicated to counties further south. Consequently the response to the situation was spontaneous and community-led; indeed the main search and rescue operations had concluded before central government became involved. Although the emergency services responded very positively and with alacrity, there can be little doubt that the decisive factor in mitigating this crisis was the availability of armed forces personnel based in East Anglia. Amongst the first units to respond was the United States Air Force based at Scunthorpe, who mobilised to the lower Hunstanton area of Norfolk, and rescued a number of families. When attempts to reach people trapped in their homes using a motor boat and other craft failed, Airman 3rd Class Reice Leming, a non-swimmer, took a rubber launch and waded on his own into the flood waters.

He made three long and perilous trips to isolated homes, and rescued twenty-seven people that night. He was in the water for four hours, and suffering greatly from the effects of cold and exhaustion. With his protective clothing damaged he was often in danger of being submerged and carried away by the flood waters. After his third rescue trip he collapsed, succumbing to the effects of exposure; he became one of very few non-British recipients of the George Medal.

The disaster area extended from Spurn Head in the Humber estuary to the coast of Kent. Unseen, the mountainous water moved ominously along the coast reaching a maximum height at King's Lynn at 1920 hours. Sea walls were damaged beyond repair, and in Suffolk and Essex, the sea surged up estuaries breaching river banks, deluging coastal towns and villages, forcing its way into beach cottages, chalets and the ubiquitous and flimsy prefabs which simply disintegrated as the water struck, drowning the occupants. As the water continued to rise, people climbed onto roofs, where they sat shivering in the freezing wind and darkness; whilst below, the overwhelming deluge and the debris it carried had the potential to destabilise those very houses, and throw them into the deep and swirling waters.

Amongst many heroic rescue attempts undertaken were those by Leading Fireman Frederick William Sadd of Great Yarmouth Fire Brigade who was awarded the George Medal, and Sub-Officer Sidney William Lancaster of Stalham Fire Brigade, and Leading Fireman John Edward Barlow of Ipswich Fire Brigade, both of whom received the British Empire Medal.

Leading Fireman Sadd was in charge of a fire appliance which attended an emergency call to Gorleston where a small estate comprising sixteen prefabricated bungalows, and some thirty two-storey houses was completely flooded to a depth of more than five feet. Sadd, seeing there were several people trapped in their homes, and hearing their cries for help, instructed fishermen to collect a boat and report back to him with it. Meanwhile, as something approaching panic was reigning in most of the flooded buildings, Leading Fireman Sadd, accompanied by two members of his crew, began to wade towards the bungalows. However, the water soon proved too deep to continue with any degree of safety, and consequently Sadd ordered his crew members back, and continued on his own, well aware that his chances of surviving this rescue attempt were negligible. As he moved forward in the pitch darkness, the water level continued to rise and become more turbulent, and a severe gale was blowing. At times Sadd was completely submerged, but he alternately waded and swam his way from house to house, reassuring the occupants and promising them that he would return with a boat and rescue them. He then made his way back to high ground where the fisherman had by now arrived with the boat, but unfortunately without oars. Nonetheless Sadd with great determination refused to abandon the rescue attempt, and by wading and at times swimming through the exceedingly cold water, he guided the boat to each of the bungalows, and overcoming great difficulties rescued the occupants. In almost every case it was impossible to take the boat close up to the bungalows, and Sadd had therefore to carry each person in turn from home to boat. After rescuing five adults and five children in this manner, Sadd collapsed. After receiving first aid he was ordered to return to his station, where he responded to a similar incident, personally rescuing six adults and nine children. Throughout these incidents Sadd showed courage of the highest order, with little or no regard for his personal safety.

Leading Fireman John Barlow of Ipswich Fire Brigade answered a call for assistance in dealing with flooded premises in South Lowestoft. The situation was serious owing to the depth of water and his first efforts were directed towards allaying the fears of the residents. Whilst passing from house to house, Barlow saw the floating body of a man, and without thought for himself he immediately waded out into the fast flowing and swirling waters until he was immersed up to his neck. He reached the body, but had great difficulty in maintaining his foothold whilst supporting the unconscious casualty owing to the turbulence of the water and the weight of his sodden fire kit and boots, which seriously hampered his movements and made swimming impossible. However he managed, with great difficulty, to cling to a nearby lamp–post and eventually with the assistance of local residents the man was taken into a house where Barlow applied artificial respiration, and the man eventually regained consciousness. Although soaked to the skin, exhausted and suffering badly from the bitter cold Barlow insisted upon continuing with the rescue for a further four hours.

Sub-Officer Lancaster of the Stalham Fire Brigade in Norfolk responded to a call to Sea Palling where the water was running at a terrific pace and far too deep for the use of a pumping appliance. A large number of persons had been cut off when the sea broke through the sand dunes, and were signalling for assistance. Lancaster obtained a boat and immediately began rescue operations. Throughout the night and completely immersed in water, he worked on, until he was finally overcome by exhaustion and the extreme cold. The conditions were deplorable, with the tide running strongly, high winds and the whole area littered with all types of floating debris. Sub–Officer Lancaster's leadership and initiative were responsible in the main for the initiation of rescue efforts and his courage and resourcefulness were outstanding.

George Medals were also awarded to Constable Leonard Charles Deptford and Inspector Charles Lewis of Lincolnshire Constabulary.

During that night the sea defences on the Lincolnshire coast had been breached in several places, and serious flooding occurred. PC Deptford made his way to some flooded bungalows in the village of Chapeland St. Leonards near to Skegness, and searched one which had collapsed into the sea. He then made a most hazardous journey across the remains of the sea-bank and sand hills to a two-storey house where seven persons, mostly elderly, were sheltering in an upstairs room. Part of the house had disintegrated and the foundations were in a precarious state. Deptford took control of the situation and organised an immediate evacuation. He roped the party together and urged them forward whilst mountainous waves broke through the gap. He inspired the party by his cheerful determination and competent handling of this desperate situation and eventually all reached safety.

Deptford then made another attempt to cross the broken sea bank but was forced back by the strong tide. He then returned to the police station and set out to rescue an aged and bedridden couple and their daughter who were marooned in their bungalow. As no boats were available, Deptford obtained six forty-gallon drums, roped them together and removed the stretcher-bound casualties on this improvised raft. After competing this rescue, PC Deptford, with great difficulty, managed to reach another bungalow in which several elderly people were taking shelter, and guided them to safety over the sea bank, and along the beach to the village. Mud and flood water had to be traversed in the strong gale which was blowing, and at intervals Deptford had to carry two infirm members of this party over the worst parts of the route. He continued with his rescue work throughout the next twenty-four hours. Constable Deptford displayed gallantry of an exceptionally high order in crossing the broken sea wall at the height of a very strong gale, and in the face of mountainous seas, and successfully led a most hazardous enterprise.

When the neighbouring sea bank gave way, the police station at Mablethorpe was soon surrounded by water several feet deep; all services were put out of action, and the road outside became impassable. Hearing cries for help, Inspector Lewis opened a window in the police station and climbed out. The water was by now rushing in a torrent, carrying with it railings, trees, parts of sheds and all manner of debris, with the gale lashing the water into waves which came up to the Inspector's neck, but with great determination he eventually reached the garage drive, where an elderly man and his wife were in danger of drowning. Inspector Lewis managed to get the woman on to his shoulders, and struggling across the street found shelter for the unfortunate couple in the upstairs room of a house. Before re-crossing the street he had to dive under the water to pass lengths of railings which had been washed into the entrance of the house. Lewis then obtained a lorry and set out for Sutton-on-Sea where much of the promenade and the sea defences had been carried away. The main street was covered in sand and water to a depth of from two to eight feet, and some 100 people had taken refuge inside a nearby cinema. The Inspector then organised the evacuation of these people and others. Having achieved this he then went onto the village of Trusthorpe, where some elderly people were in danger of drowning in their bungalows. Despite the approach to these properties being difficult and hazardous Lewis, with the cold waters lapping around his neck and over his head, managed to rescue seven people from the bungalows and cottages. When Lewis was at last able to book off-duty he had been working continuously for fifty-four hours, twenty-six of which he was constantly in and out of ice cold and turbulent water.

THE SMITHFIELD MARKET FIRE

On a cold January night in 1958, two London firefighters, Station Officer Jack Fourt-Wells and Fireman Richard D Stocking, lost their lives during a major underground fire at the City of London's Smithfield meat market, where dense smoke and intense heat in confined spaces produced one of the worst post-war incidents ever tackled by London Fire Brigade.

To give some idea of the problems faced by the Breathing Apparatus crews at this tragic incident it is important to present an outline description of the structure of Smithfield Market, also known as the London Central Markets. Smithfield Market occupied an area of some ten acres and comprised four buildings of equal size, with the building in which the fire occurred, the Poultry Market, being approximately 255 feet by 245 feet, consisting a ground floor, galleries and a basement. The basement was separated into ninety storage compartments, a number of which were internally sub-divided. Some could be entered from underground corridors, whilst others were accessible only through trapdoors in the ground floor of the market, with the basement itself separated into areas of almost equal size by the roof of a disused railway tunnel which passed diagonally through it. Lifts and trap openings in the pavements surrounding, and also within the market itself, provided limited access to the basement. A tunnel containing refrigeration equipment connected the plant room of the Union cold storage building in Smithfield Street with the basement of the market, and the main corridors which gave access to the basement were fitted with heavy insulated doors to form air locks to maintain the low temperature required in the basement. At the time of the fire it was estimated that approximately 800 tons of poultry, game and meat were in storage.

The first call was received by fire control at 0218 hours on Thursday 23rd January, and the initial attendance of one pump-escape, one pumping appliance, and an emergency tender from Clerkenwell under the command of Station Officer Jack Fourt-Wells, a pumping appliance from Whitefriars, and a turntable ladder from Canon Street were dispatched.

On arrival at 0222 hours, Station Officer Fourt-Wells was met by an employee of the market who led him to the plant room tunnel, where they encountered thick smoke. At 0229 hours an assistance message was transmitted to fire control requesting an additional pumping appliance, and at 0231 hours Station Officer Fourt-Wells, rigged in BA, entered the tunnel with four members of his emergency tender crew to locate the source of the fire. The heavily smoke-logged plant room tunnel was searched in zero visibility by the BA team, but no fire was found. At this juncture information was received that the fire was possibly in the main basement, which was secured by a padlock, and eventually the crew were provided with a key and gained access. By this time all wearers were running low on oxygen, with one wearer having a cylinder pressure of ten atmospheres, another of five, and the remainder reading zero. As three of the team turned to leave the basement they heard the Station Officer say:

'Leave the door open I'm just going to take a look'. Within minutes of the three crew members reaching their original entry point and fresh air, they realised that Station Officer Fourt-Wells and Fireman Stocking were not with them, and enquired of Acting Station Officer John Bishop of Clerkenwell Station if he had seen their missing colleagues. It was then evident that neither Fourt-Wells nor Stocking had exited the risk, and given that all members of the BA team were low on oxygen prior to making an egress from the area of the fire it was obvious to all that a serious and potentially fatal situation faced the firefighters, and emergency measures were at once implemented.

By this time the fire was developing rapidly, and it was feared that it would break through into the market above. Breathing apparatus crews reported that the fire was coming down the tunnel like a train, and although they couldn't see the flames whooshing over their heads, they most certainly could hear and feel it as they pressed their bodies as low as possible to try and find some relief from the searing heat. The deadly black acrid smoke from the burning cork walls, which were soaked through years of accumulated meat fat, was issuing so thick and forcefully from the pavement lights that when a firefighter climbed onto the ladder leading through a street flap, he disappeared from view even before he made a descent into that deadly labyrinth. The first emergency crew under the direction of Station Officer John Bishop was committed to searching for the missing men, but due to the complex configuration of the basement it was almost an hour before their bodies were found. Station Officer Fourt-Wells' body was located first, and then Fireman Stocking's body was found buried under a collapse of frozen meat and only a matter of yards from an exit and fresh air.

After the bodies of Jack Fourt-Wells and Richard Stocking had been located, the Brigade's first and over-riding priority was still to locate the seat of fire and ascertain its extent. For some twenty-four hours this objective was sought, but dense smoke and intense heat made worse by a severe lack of ventilation and the burning cork and bituminous insulation materials, the congested nature and complex construction of the premises, greatly restricted the progress of the crews to no more than a yard in two hours. These extreme conditions would not permit firefighters wearing breathing apparatus to be in the basement for more than fifteen minutes at a time, and in some cases the duration was considerably less. Throughout the day the conditions gradually worsened, with some men suffering the effects of heat exhaustion having to be rescued; ultimately all crews were withdrawn. Indeed fifty members of London Fire Brigade required hospital treatment.

Mr Bishop commented on the incident: 'There was no sign of flames, just lots of smoke, but conditions were getting worse. It was a maze and we used clapping signals.

I was going down the centre and I'd send men down a passageway here and there. You would walk along one step at a time, with the back of your hand in front of you in case you walked into something red-hot, making sure you were not going to fall down a hole. All we could find was passageways with meat packed either side from floor to ceiling. The smoke got thicker – you could eat it; black oily smoke. It was very cold down there and you were cold, even though you were sweating. That was fear!'

In his written statement, Acting Station Officer John W Bishop said of this incident:

At 0200 hours on Thursday 23rd January, 1958 the pump [the appliance Bishop was riding that night at Whitefriars fire station] was ordered to a fire at Smithfield Street on B20's ground. On arrival I found that B20's crew had run a hose-reel into the basement engine room of the cold storage premises on Smithfield Street. I reported to Station Officer Fort-Wells who was at the door of the first chamber from where smoke was issuing. He instructed me to send back a message 'Make pumps four' and said that he had sent back for a breathing apparatus set. I returned to the surface and gave instructions to fireman Ford of B20 Clerkenwell to send the assistance message back, which he did by radio-telephony. I then returned to the basement engine room and went back to Station Officer Fort-Wells. He was not wearing breathing apparatus at that time. Divisional Officer Shawyer arrived and ordered all men not wearing breathing apparatus to return to the street, and all men who were qualified, to rig in breathing apparatus. I thereupon returned to the street and donned my breathing apparatus set.

I was then ordered ... to Charterhouse Street and from there down into the basement to assist the emergency tender crew from B61 Lambeth ... After doing this we returned to West Smithfield where a civilian was opening the cover of a lift shaft. We went down this opening via a first floor ladder and there met Leading Fireman Martin and Fireman Knott, who asked if I had seen Station Officer Fourt-Wells and Fireman Stocking. I told them I had not and ascended the ladder and informed Divisional Officer Shawyer that it appeared that Station Officer Fourt-Wells and Fireman Stocking were missing. He ordered me to search and I went into the basement again with the crew and joined Leading Fireman Martin and Fireman Knott. We commenced to search in the direction of what we thought to be the seat of the fire, i.e., the bridge over the railway. We crossed the bridge and arrived at the Charterhouse entrance and then retraced our steps through the basement passage, back to West Smithfield. Here I reported to Divisional Officer Shawyer and he ordered us to search again from the basement engine room at Smithfield Street as that was the last place where Station Officer Fourt-Wells and Fireman Stocking had been seen. [We] entered the basement and after a considerable amount of searching, I heard somebody shout and proceeded in the direction from whence it came and I found several firemen carrying Station Officer Fourt-Wells. I asked about Fireman Stocking and was told that Station Officer Fourt-Wells had been found in the direction from whence they had come. I proceeded to search the area and found Fireman Stocking lying face downwards against a blank wall. He was wearing breathing apparatus and his mouthpiece was in his mouth. I called for assistance and other personnel came along. I felt Fireman Stocking's pulse and his heart but there was no response and he was very cold.

Assisted by Fireman Knott and another man whom I believe was Fireman Simpson, Fireman Stocking was carried towards the West Smithfield entrance, Fireman Brown leading the way. We were unable to give Fireman Stocking any oxygen at that time as our cylinders were almost empty. We arrived at the West Smithfield left shaft, and commenced to apply artificial respiration. A line was then made fast around Fireman Stocking and he was hauled to the surface. We were then ordered to the surface where a roll call was taken.

In an attempt to fight the fire without further endangering the crews, it was decided to flood the basement. However, this did not achieve the anticipated outcome, and nearby underground rail lines were put out of commission because of electrical faults caused by the water from the firefighting jets.

At about 0300 hours on Friday 24th January, the fire broke through the ground floor of the market, which in some places was two feet thick. Intense heat, flammable gases and billowing smoke were thus liberated, and quickly filled the whole of the Poultry Market. This brought with it potentially very serious structural problems as the roof of the market was supported by unprotected cast-iron columns. Fortunately the course of the fire had been fully anticipated and all firefighters had been withdrawn in time from the interior of the ground floor of the market. Ground monitors producing jets of water without the need for firefighters to hold and direct them were placed in position to prevent the spread of the fire to adjoining markets and surrounding premises from becoming affected by the radiation and convection of the intense heat. During this critical period the flames at times reached a height of 100 feet.

The Brigade's plan to confine the fire to the area of the Poultry market was successful, and there was no spread to adjoining markets or surrounding premises, and the 'Stop' message was sent at 1645 hours on January 24th when twenty-five jets were in use. Up to Friday 7th February a total of 2,000 firefighters had worked at the fire in relays.

As a result of this incident there were calls from the Chief Fire Officer of London, and the Fire Brigades Union for safer procedures to be adopted. Consequently the Home Office set up a committee of inquiry into the operational use of breathing apparatus, and the recommendations that were made and accepted have now become the basis of the breathing apparatus control procedures which are still followed by Fire Brigades today.

THE CHEAPSIDE STREET FIRE, GLASGOW

On Monday 28th March 1960 one of the worst disasters in the history of the city of Glasgow occurred at the Bonded warehouses occupied by Messrs Arbuckle, Smith & Co, at 76/118 Cheapside Street, Anderston, Glasgow. The premises were opened as usual at 0800 hours that day jointly by the foreman and an officer from HM Customs and Excise. Twelve men were employed in the warehouse sections of the premises, which were of brick construction comprising a basement and six floors. On that day none had occasion to be on the upper floors of the two principal sections of the warehouse, with the exception of the cooper whose task was to pass through all levels and examine and repair the casks.

On most days the warehouse would have closed for business at 1700 hrs, but due to additional work it remained open into the evening. At 1915 hours the initial 999 call to this dreadful and tragic incident was made by an employee of a nearby business because of the presence of a strong smell of burning wood, and smoke issuing from the second floor of the number one Bond. As a result two pumping appliances, a turntable ladder, a fire-boat, and a Glasgow Salvage Corps Tender were mobilised by fire control. The caller immediately brought the urgency of the situation to the attention of the foreman and the Customs officer, who alerted the employees who were inside the premises, where over a million gallons of whisky and rum were stored.

By the time the first fire appliances were in attendance (three minutes after the call had been received by the fire service) the smoke had become much heavier, and was now billowing from almost every level of the premises. The officer-in-charge ordered breathing apparatus (referred to as BA) crews to enter the building to locate and extinguish the fire, and at 1921 hours radioed an assistance message to the effect of 'Make pumps five', that is requesting another three pumping appliances, in this instance, presumably, to task the pump crews as supporting BA teams. On the arrival of these reinforcements an emergency tender – an appliance not carrying water and hose, but equipped with various special rescue apparatus and tackle, and staffed by firefighters trained to organise and implement the command and control functions of a major incident – crew established a BA control point to coordinate the activities and search patterns of the crews, and organise relief teams and emergency measures.

Because of the internal construction of the premises, the intensity of the smoke-logging due to a lack of ventilation, and a most unusual absence of radiated or convective heat, the BA crews, despite their most determined efforts, were unable to locate the seat of the fire; although at one stage a glow of purplish-blue flame, characteristic of alcohol, was reported at the ground floor ceiling, and attacked from outside with a jet of water. Because of the serious situation, and its potential for being a protracted incident the Assistant Firemaster who was now in attendance dispatched a 'Make pumps eight' assistance message at 1948/49 hours. As this officer gave instructions for his message to be sent he was approaching the scene of the fire from the south end of Cheapside Street when a sudden and unforeseen explosion occurred inside the warehouse, and the front and rear walls of the building were blown outwards simultaneously into both Cheapside Street and Warroch Street.

The personal observation of Firemaster Martin Chadwick CBE, the Chief of the Glasgow Fire Service, published in a special supplement of *Fire* magazine in September 1960, gives the following description of the scene of the explosion taken from the evidence of various witnesses:

> Due to the extensive dimensions of the premises with frontages in Cheapside Street and Worrach Street, it was not at first realised that the explosive forces had a 'through-and-through' effect causing collapse in both streets simultaneously. There was no prior warning whatsoever of an impending explosion, and all witnesses suggest that the type of explosion was unique in so far as the sound was not violent as with detonation, but was more like an echoed 'whoosh' followed by the thud of falling debris. The impression was one of the sudden release of high pressure.

As soon as the explosion occurred an assistance message making pumps ten, and requesting the attendance of the Ambulance Service was sent. Cries of distress were heard coming from the debris at both sides of building, where firefighters were unaware at that time of the extent of the destruction, or the scale of casualties. A turntable ladder positioned in Cheapside Street, and the firefighters standing by the appliance at that location, were all completely buried by falling masonry following the explosion and collapse. The driver was extricated from debris with extensive leg injuries; the fate of the remainder of that team was unknown at that time. A salvage man was similarly rescued in Warroch Street by fire service personnel who had only just escaped the effects of the explosion. Also in Warroch Street, a second turntable ladder had been sited to inspect the upper levels of the premises to provide an early indication of fire spread, and consequently a firefighter was positioned at the head of the ladder when the explosion occurred. The force of the explosion made the ladder sway erratically, causing the firefighter to lose his footing, but fortunately his safety harness saved him falling from the head of the ladder. Despite this ladder being seriously damaged by the falling debris, and for a time enveloped by flame owing to the rapid spread of fire, the driver displayed great presence of mind, and calmly brought the head of the ladder, and with it his colleague, to the relative safety of ground level.

A perilous and urgent search of the two devastated areas was made particularly hazardous by further structural collapse, and the severity of the rapidly spreading fire. So dangerous were the conditions that the search was, with great reluctance, abandoned, as it was felt certain that no one trapped in such conditions could possibly have survived.

By 2012 hours Firemaster Chadwick had assumed command of the incident and ordered a 'Make pumps fifteen message' to be sent, and eight minutes later upgraded the incident to twenty pumps. As these reinforcements began arriving, an Incident Command point was established on a safe site on Anderston Quay to the south of the fire area. The duties of this unit were to co-ordinate the logistics of this now disastrous fire, collate intelligence on the occurrence that may be of use to the Incident Commander, and organise a full roll-call of personnel; from which it was ultimately possible to ascertain that nineteen men were unaccounted for, that is five Salvage men and fourteen firefighters.

The fire situation had by now developed into one of alarming proportions, being made considerably worse by the further collapse of walls, floors and other structural elements, which posed a serious and continual danger to those engaged in fighting this fire. This grave state of affairs was exacerbated by the congested nature of the entire area, and the critical exposure threat to surrounding buildings from a rapidly deteriorating fire situation. On the opposite side of Cheapside Street was another bonded whisky warehouse of six floors and an attic, the roof of which had taken fire on a number of occasions during the incident. It was from these premises that a number of firefighting jets were brought to bear on the fire. Of even more concern was the large engineering works of ship-builders Harland and Wolff in Warroch Street, which held liquid air and oxygen, and so required immediate and robust measures to be put in place to prevent the fire spreading to that location. An additional threat arose when casks continued to explode, resulting in burning whisky flowing on the surface of the firefighting water which was by now pouring from the area of the affected premises, and flowing freely along the street. Water curtains were deployed over a wide area in order to retard the exposure effects of the radiated heat, and the fire boat carried out invaluable work throughout this protracted incident by keeping the pumping appliances supplied with water from the river.

At about 0100 hours an attempt was made to reach the bodies of the personnel in the Cheapside Street area of the incident, as it was known that their position was near to the turntable ladder on which part of the building had collapsed. This was only possible by making an entry through the bonded warehouse building and grounds on the opposite side of Cheapside Street because of the continual falling of masonry in the fire area. After some considerable time three of the bodies were located, and eventually extricated. The condition of the bodies was such as to suggest that their deaths had been instantaneous following the explosion and collapse of the building.

The recovery of the bodies at the other side of the fire-ground was, however, a considerably more problematical operation because of the numbers of casualties believed to be trapped, the quantity and compactness of the debris, and the very restricted area of operations offered by the dimensions of Wardoch Street. These difficult conditions dictated the use of mechanical appliances, but because of the dangers posed by the vibrations from such work, a number of potentially very dangerous structures had to be brought down before the recovery operation could be commenced.

Thus the battle against what was an overwhelming and catastrophic fire situation, the like of which would only have been experienced by those firefighters who fought the fires of the Blitz, continued throughout the night and early hours of the morning. The salvage men and firefighters of Glasgow, many of whom attended the incident although off-duty, worked under the most acute and testing of circumstances, accompanied by the demoralising knowledge of the terrible fate which had befallen so many of their colleagues. Only by the most resolute and resourceful response by all ranks in the performance of their duty in checking the spread of the fire, and step by laborious step penetrating the heart of the blaze, was the conflagration brought under control by 0618 hours the following morning. The recovery of the bodies of the salvage men and firefighters in Wardoch Street was not completed until 1020 hours on 31st March.

At its peak, 450 men were engaged in fighting the blaze, which sent fierce blue flames leaping into the night sky, and some thirty pumping appliances, five turntable ladders, and four other special appliances attended this incident.

The intense sense of communal grief, not just in Glasgow but throughout the country, was expressed in many ways, and not least by the gesture of Her Royal Highness Princess Margaret, visiting the scene of the disaster on Wednesday 30th March while in Glasgow fulfilling other engagements. The Princess had many associations with Glasgow, and her personal attendance to express the sympathy of Her Majesty the Queen was very much appreciated by all associated with the Glasgow Fire Service.

The public funeral of the victims of the disaster took place on Tuesday 5th April, when the general headline in the press, 'A City Mourns', conveyed succinctly and movingly the feeling of the day. The poignant funeral processions to Glasgow Cathedral and St. Andrew's Roman Catholic Cathedral took place against a background of dignified and subdued solemnity with full Fire Service Honours. Contingents from almost every Local Authority Fire Brigade in the United Kingdom took part in the Parade, along with mourners from every aspect of the civic and business life of Glasgow, led by the Lord Provost and Magistrates, together with representatives of the Secretary of State, Scottish Home Department officials, Chief Officers of many Fire Services. The accommodation in both Cathedrals was taxed to the limit, and the attendance of invited members of other organisations being so great as to preclude admittance of the general public. The interments took place at the Glasgow Necropolis Burial Grounds where common vaults were placed at the disposal of Glasgow Corporation through the generosity of the Merchants House of Glasgow, with the graveside Services being conducted with solemn dignity by the clergy of the various denominations concerned. The entire funeral arrangements were carried out in a manner which epitomised the various extremes of grief, from the personal sorrow of the relatives to the quiet mourning of the subdued citizens of Glasgow who thronged the cortege routes. The hundreds of floral tributes received and laid out in the Necropolis were a further expression of the grief felt in all parts of the United Kingdom.

Firemaster Martin Chadwick inserted the following letter in the public press as it was impossible to acknowledge all expressions of sympathy individually:

> I have never addressed a communication before to the Editor of a Newspaper, but I would be extremely grateful if I could be afforded an opportunity through the channels of your Newspaper to express not only on my own behalf, but on behalf of the Officers and Men of the City of Glasgow Fire Service, our most grateful thanks and sincere appreciation of the magnificent kindness, sympathy, co-operation and understanding we have received from the members of the public of this great City in the disaster which befell us.
>
> Such kindness is a source of great inspiration to the Staff of the Fire Service and I can assure you that the Officers and Men on the operational establishment will continue to give of their best in dealing with outbreaks of fire in this City, especially when they know that their services are so sincerely appreciated by the members of the public.

Typical of the kindly interest shown by various people was the hand-sewing of a beautiful Pulpit Fall by the Ladies of the Guild of Work of Govan Old Parish Church. The Fall was presented by Firemaster Chadwick to St. Paul's (Outer High) and St. David's (Ramshorn) Church, Ingram Street – often referred to as the Fireman's Kirk because of its proximity to the Central Fire Station – and dedicated by the Minister, The Rev. Matthew Liddell, B.D., on Sunday 22nd May to the memory of those who had given their lives on the tragic night of 28th March 1960. A memorial plaque subscribed to by the personnel of the Central Fire Station was unveiled in the Appliance Room of the Central Fire Station on Sunday 7th August 1960 by Bailie Philip Stinton, J.P. and dedicated by the Rev. Matthew Liddell, B.D.

The George Medal was awarded to Fireman James McMurray Dunlop, who at the time of the incident had served only two years one month as a firefighter and this was the first fire at which he had to operate the turntable ladder. The outer wall of the warehouse blew out into Warroch Street, with a consequent out-rush of burning spirit which enveloped the base of the turntable ladder. The shockwave from the explosion and collapse of the wall seriously affected the stability of the turntable ladder on which Dunlop was working, and cut the hydraulic power by which Dunlop controlled the ladder. Despite the extremely hazardous situation he found himself in, Fireman Dunlop remained at the controls and worked the starter until it eventually responded, and he was able to lower the ladder to the housed position. He then assisted Fireman Watters to safety and thereafter took part in firefighting operations for several hours.

Also awarded the George Medal, was Station Officer Peter Johnstone McGill who had led a party of three or four firefighters wearing breathing apparatus into the whisky bond from Cheapside Street to try to locate the seat of the fire. During the time McGill and his team were in the building the explosion occurred, but with great presence of mind and command of an extremely hazardous situation McGill led his men to safety. Once returned to Cheapside Street, at serious risk to his life, he made gallant but unavailing attempts to reach three men buried under masonry. He operated throughout the night under the most harsh and exacting conditions, giving leadership and searching for the trapped firefighters.

The British Empire Medal for gallantry was awarded to Fireman John Nicholson of Springburn Fire Station, who after the explosion occurred took his place at the head of a 100-foot turntable ladder. Despite further explosions, tremendous heat and rolling sheets of flame which almost completely surrounded him for long periods, he remained at his post for three hours.

Forty-six year-old Charles Neeson, a Sub Officer working out of Knightswood Fire Station, and his men were working in the area of the D.C.L. bond, and so partitioned from the blaze by forty feet. Neeson, an experienced operational officer with twenty-one years' service, was aware that the igniting of the bond behind him would almost certainly result in the death of him and his men. Despite the constant danger from the flow of burning whisky from the main fire, and exposure to and danger from further explosions, Sub Officer Neeson encouraged his men to continue firefighting operations and by maintaining this dangerous position for about three hours, prevented the spread of serious fire to the D.C.L. bond.

Constable James Gribben, a twenty-four year-old former Scots Guardsman with two years' service in Glasgow City Police, was on duty in Cheapside Street when the explosion occurred. Gribben immediately climbed over the debris and though unable to see because of dust and smoke, reached a firefighter trapped by the fallen masonry.

Constable Gribben and Fireman George Buchanan Alexander attached to the West Fire Station, with the help latterly of other members of the Fire Service freed the trapped man. Shortly after the rescue there was a further tremendous explosion and the area became a raging inferno. Both men must have been well aware of the tremendous risk they were taking in exposing themselves to the danger of burning whisky, further explosions and falls of masonry, as they worked to save the life of the trapped man.

Fireman William Watters, who was at the head of the turntable ladder when the explosion occurred, was awarded the Queen's Commendation for Brave Conduct. Although in a severely shocked condition, he tried to reach the area in which he knew his colleagues had been trapped or killed. Fireman Watters had been previously awarded the Corporation Medal for Bravery in 1958, when he took part in rescue work after an explosion aboard H.M.S. Blake in Govan dry-dock. Later he collapsed from shock and exhaustion.

The then Secretary of State for Scotland, Mr John Maclay, sent letters of appreciation to the following for their gallantry and devotion to duty:

Divisional Officer Robert Herbert (Central Fire Station); Leading Fireman Robert Clark (South Fire Station); Fireman Charles Biggerstaff (Central Fire Station); Fireman Joseph McGhee (West Fire Station); Salvageman Joseph Smith and Leading Firewoman Mary Nichol (Central Fire Brigade Headquarters) who had been with the Fire Service for nearly 18 years and controlled the mobilising operations during the fire.

Firemaster John Swanson observed in his annual report after succeeding Mr Chadwick as Chief of the Glasgow Fire Service: 'The name of Cheapside Street will forever bear a hallowed place in Fire Service records and in the history of the City of Glasgow, on the one hand recording the supreme sacrifice of so many fine and courageous firefighters in the course of duty and, on the other, reflecting the selfless courage and devotion to duty of their comrades who toiled bravely throughout the long night of adversity and danger until the battle against flame and burning spirit had been won.'

From the *Glasgow Herald* Weekender supplement of 23rd March 1985 by Jack Webster:

> Against the hideous glow of an inferno, Willie Watters was silhouetted as a
> helpless rag doll cast about at the top of a fireman's ladder, rather in the
> farcical manner of a Harold Lloyd movie. But this was far from slap-stick.
> Right in the heart of Glasgow they were acting the greatest peace-time
> tragedy in the entire history of British firefighting service. Before the final

curtain that night, nineteen courageous men from the city's fire brigade and salvage corps had gone to their deaths in what became known as the Cheapside disaster. What started out as smoke emitting from a three storey bonded warehouse containing whisky and tobacco, just off Broomielaw, suddenly became a … nightmare when a double explosion blew out the walls at both ends of the building, one into Cheapside Street and the other into Warroch Street, which lay parallel. Though Cheapside gave its name to the disaster, it was actually in Warroch Street that sixteen of the men perished as hundreds of tons of falling masonry enveloped them and their fire engines as they stood.

From that moment onwards, half an hour after the firemen had arrived on the scene that early evening, large vats of whisky now exposed and free to tumble, came dancing down, bursting and catching fire before they reached the ground. As word spread and crowds gathered, the leaping flames lit up the evening sky, creating that daylight effect of a wartime air-raid. Indeed not since the Clydebank Blitz when twenty-five firemen died, had anyone seen anything like this. It seemed as if some madmen were putting on a crazy pyrotechnic show, with clouds of whisky vapour detaching themselves and drifting independently up, up and away from the main scene of the fire.

Back at the scene, as hundreds of firemen struggled to contain the blaze, there were anxious officers trying to conduct a roll call which would tell the full extent of the horror. Personal stories abound. One of the luckiest men alive is forty-seven year old Jack Muir from Fairford Drive, Cumbernauld, who was actually inside the building and out again before the explosion. On duty at the West Station in Cranston Street he was engaged in drill on the backcourt when the call came at 7.15 that Monday evening.

'As we arrived at Cheapside Street and saw the smoke, I remember a civilian crossing the street and saying it was only tobacco curing. Another fireman and myself took a hose and managed to enter the building. Wearing breathing apparatus, we went up two wooden stairs. I still remember how my face and hands were stinging from vaporising alcohol. It was like a nip of after-shave. Station Officer McGill, who later got a George Medal for his service that night, came up the stair and we could not find the seat of any fire so we came back down to see if we could enter by Warrock Street.'

Then a Customs Officer appeared to help them gain further entry into Cheapside Street. Just as they were about to enter, Jack Muir realised that he

did not have enough oxygen and turned away to get another cylinder. It was
at that moment the walls exploded in both directions. Meanwhile, round in
Warrock Street, Fireman James Dunlop was having his first ever night as the
driver-cum-turntable operator, in the way that firemen switch roles to gain
experience. He had changed places with Willie Watters, who was now on a
ladder and making the very first report that he could see that blue-mauve
flame associated with whisky. That was all there was time to report.
Meanwhile Dunlop had wound the turntable ladder to take twenty-eight year
old Willie Watters high into the sky. But at the point of explosion, he joined
everyone else and ran for his life. Still serving as a Divisional Officer based at
Johnstone, he remembers it like this:

'I then looked back and saw Watters stranded at the top of the ladder,
swinging about like a puppet, his feet off the steps and his body hanging only
by the safety belt. I knew I was responsible for putting him there so I had to
go back there and get him down.'

Watters' ladder, in fact, had been struck by the falling masonry and was
dipping and rising and swaying, as you see in the old slapstick films. Amid the
chaos Dunlop ran back and operated the mechanism which would bring
Watters as near to the ground as he could jump. For his bravery, Dunlop was
awarded the George Medal.

Now fifty-three, Willie Watters has just retired from Polock fire station and,
when I tracked him down this week, he spoke very quietly and calmly about
his experience. What was it like to dangling in the jaws of an inferno, at the
mercy of a swaying ladder and fierce flames which could engulf you at any
minute?

'Ach, it wasnae so much fear as confusion,' he says. 'It was actually my first
time at the top of a ladder during a fire, but my number wasnae up.' David
Lavery, now an Assistant Firemaster at Strathclyde Headquarters, was off duty
from the Partick (fire) station that night, but like every other available man,
rushed to join his colleagues. Odd memories linger. A non-whisky drinker,
Lavery remembers his lungs were so full of the vapour that he belched whisky
for a long time afterwards.

From the *Scottish Daily Express* Tuesday 29th March 1960 by Reporter Stanley Stewart:

> 'I almost died with the gallant firemen in the Cheapside Street horror last night. I went there with photographer Ian Elder on what seemed to be a routine story, a small fire. Firemen were checking smoke coming from a burning building, so often a false alarm or some burning waste. It looked like just another fire investigation. But this was a whisky bond. And last night it all started so quietly. When we arrived in Cheapside Street there was only smoke billowing from the building. Firemen wearing breathing apparatus were dashing in and out trying to trace the sources of the smoke.
>
> With another press colleague I approached a small man wearing dungarees who seemed to work in the bond. At this time there was still no sign of the flames although the smoke seemed to be coming more forcibly from the windows of the four-storey building. Little did we know within seconds many firemen were to die in one of Glasgow's worst fires for many years. This is how it happened: We were just about to speak to the little man in dungarees when the smoke began to rush from the building. Then I saw the walls of the building bulge before my eyes. In the split second it took me to take to my heels and race for my life I saw, I think, several fire men standing further down the street from me, where the wall was bulging. There was also a fire engine or salvage tender. I could not be sure. As I dashed up the street the building exploded outwards and upwards with a deafening roar. I could hear the screams of people being trapped by the hundreds of tons of masonry.
>
> When I stopped and looked back, fifty yards from the scene of the explosion, dust was billowing from the massive heap of rubble. And around me firemen were shouting: 'Get first aid. Get ambulances. Switch on all car lights. Bring up spotlights'. Moans could be heard coming from the rubble. By this time only seconds had passed since the building exploded and collapsed. There were still no sign of flame, and firemen were dashing to search the rubble for their mates. There was nothing I could do. But I thought photographer Elder was under the rubble. I made my way cautiously back down the street to search for him. Firemen and police had no time to speak to me as I asked for Elder. It was ten minutes later before I found him, safe and sound, and taking pictures. Elder, too, had raced for his life but had turned back before I did. He was hidden from my view by a fire engine as he risked his life to take pictures of the terrible blaze.

I must say this: 'Thank God for the calibre of the men in our fire service'. Last night I was trembling with fear after having narrowly escaped death. But their first thought, in fact without giving any thought, was the rescue of their mates although it was obvious that other parts of the building might collapse at any second. And we watched them standing close up to the inferno, pumping thousands of gallons of water on to it, while other firemen sat on the roof of another whisky bond just opposite, damping the building. As far as they knew there was every danger of that bond exploding also.

It was a terrifying and horrible experience last night. But it proved to me again the almost impossible courage of firemen. Thousands of Glasgow people watched them fighting the blaze last night. I know their feeling must be the same as mine.

THE DUDGEON'S WHARF TRAGEDY

Dudgeon's Wharf on the Isle of Dogs consisted of a tank farm of more than 100 containers of various capacities up to 200,000 gallons, used for the storage of various oils and spirits on a plot which measured 350 ft by 300 ft. Tank 97 on this site was of a welded construction measuring twenty-seven feet in diameter, and was thirty-five feet high, with a capacity of 125,000 gallons. Two manhole covers, one on the roof and one at ground level, were held shut with steel plates secured by three nuts and bolts. Although this tank had been empty for two years it had previously held Myrcene (a member of the turpentine family), and this chemical would have left a thick, gummy deposit on the inside of the tank, which if heated would give off a highly flammable vapour which, if mixed with air, would be potentially explosive.

At 11.21 am on Friday 17th July 1969 a call was received by London Fire Brigade to a fire on the North bank of the River Thames at Millwall. Less than two weeks before this incident a fire had occurred on the same site where forty firemen with eight pumping appliances used six jets and two foam-making branches to tackle a fire involving waste oil in a derelict oil tank. The brigade had also attended numerous other small fires on the site, caused by sparks from hot cutting gear used in demolishing the tanks. On receipt of the call a pump escape and pump were ordered from Millwall Fire Station, and one pump from Brunswick Road. The foam tender from East Ham was also ordered on, followed later by the fireboat Massey Shaw from Greenwich.

The fire brigade's first attendance arrived very quickly with Station Officer Innard in command. In assessing the state of affairs at the site, Innard enquired about the fire situation but was given misleading information. Consequently he, not unreasonably, thought that the fire was most probably out, but decided to make sure by putting a spray branch into the top of the manhole which had been removed from the top of

Tank 97. Sub Officer Gamble with firefighters Appleby, Breen, Carvosso and Smee joined him on top of the tank alongside Mr Adams, one of the on-site staff. It is thought that using the spray branch caused air to be drawn in and mixed with the flammable vapours given off by the burning or hot Myrcene deposits, and this greatly increased the risk of an explosion.

Station Officer Innard along with Station Officer Snelling decided to look into the tank from the bottom manhole to see if any fire remained and, if so, direct the positioning of the spray branch accordingly. To facilitate this tactic the bottom manhole cover would need to be removed.

Station Officer Snelling sent a firefighter to fetch a spanner to remove the bottom manhole cover, but as it was impossible to undo the nuts, an unidentified person suggested that the nuts be burned off. As Station Officer Innard descended from the top of the tank to see what was going on, an employee working on the demolition of the tank farm applied a cutting torch to one of the nuts. As soon as the cutting flame was applied to the first nut, the vapours inside the tank ignited almost instantaneously, blowing off the roof of the tank together with the five firefighters, and a workman. This was believed to be due to flames or sparks from the cutting torch entering the tank and igniting the highly explosive mixture within.

Divisional Officer Abbitt who was in the area, upon being informed that appliances were in attendance at the riverside wharf, proceeded to the incident, arriving at 1150 hours, just two minutes before the explosion occurred. Immediately after the explosion occurred a further three pumping appliances from Bethnal Green and Bow were ordered on at 1154 hours. The most unenviable job of these oncoming fire crews was to recover the bodies of their comrades who had been killed; those firefighters were Temporary Sub Officer Michael Gamble aged twenty-eight; Fireman John Victor Appleby aged twenty-three; Fireman Terrance Breen aged thirty-seven; Fireman Paul Carvosso aged twenty-three and Fireman Alfred Charles Smee aged forty-seven.

At the time of the explosion Station Officer Harold John Snelling and Fireman Ian Malcolm Richards were standing on a pathway close to the base of the tank. The force of the blast blew Snelling into an adjacent dyke containing a mixture of oil and water and he was completely submerged, whilst Richards was also thrown off the pathway but was able to cling to the dyke wall and was partially immersed in the oily mixture. Fireman Richards called for assistance and a workman threw him a length of hose and he was able to pull himself out. He then passed the hose to the Station Officer, holding onto the end, whilst Richards climbed back onto the pathway. At this point in Snelling was informed that a man had fallen into the tank, and although suffering from shock and covered in oil which was seriously affecting their eyes, Snelling and Richards reacted immediately to this information, and climbed the external ladder to the top of the thirty-five foot high tank. This ladder had broken away from the side of the tank and was in an extremely unsafe condition. On reaching the head of the ladder they found that the top of the tank had been completely blown off, and that the body of a firefighter was lying at the bottom of the tank. Station Officer Snelling instructed Richards to fetch lines and breathing apparatus, but without waiting for this equipment to arrive, Snelling climbed down an internal steel ladder into the tank. When Fireman Richards returned with the breathing apparatus the Station Officer was already in the tank and Richards abandoned the equipment as quickly as he could, and joined Snelling inside the tank. The base of the tank was covered by an oily sludge which was two or three feet deep in places, the atmosphere was hot and very humid, and dangerous fumes were present. The injured firefighter was partially submerged in the toxic sludge, and Snelling and Richards with difficulty managed to free the body from some piping and then carried it to a dry area from which they hoped he could be raised by lines. Unfortunately the man was found to be dead. By now both men were suffering greatly from shock, exhaustion and the effects of the fumes. Divisional Officer Abbitt who was now in attendance, realising that they might be overcome in this extremely hazardous location, ordered them out of the tank. On reaching the outside both men collapsed and were taken to hospital. Although both Station Officer Snelling and Fireman Richards were suffering from shock and the effects of the explosion they did not hesitate to climb unsafe ladders and descend into a fume-laden tank to assist their comrade and throughout the operation they acted without regard for their own safety.

Both Station Officer Harold John Snelling and Fireman Ian Malcolm Richards of London Fire Brigade were awarded the British Empire Medal for their part in this tragic incident.

London Fire Brigade's in-house *London Fireman* magazine of September 1969 carried the following account of the funeral these firefighters:

> On a sunny morning in July Londoners said farewell to five men. Officially it was the funeral of John Appleby, Alfred Smee, Michael Gamble, Paul Carvosso and Terrence Breen, but it became something more as crowds lined the pavements of East London.
>
> The loss of these five men in a sudden explosion at Dudgeon's Wharf was a personal matter to every man and woman, uniformed and non-uniformed, in the Brigade, but the people of East London, to most of whom these men were only names in a newspaper, demonstrated the regard in which they hold the men who daily go about the job of protecting them from fire.
>
> The sombre day began with a requiem mass for firemen Breen at St. Mary's Church, Hornchurch. Then the five men who had shared the proud title, London Fireman, came to start their journey through the streets of West Ham Parish Church. The gleaming scarlet of the turntable ladders bearing the flag-draped coffins and the blaze of flowers which each one carried struck a

The firefighters of Dudgeon's Wharf are taken to their final rest
aboard the turntable Ladders of London Fire Brigade.
Courtesy of London Fire Brigade.

contrast with the silent crowds at the pavement's edge., as here and there a handkerchief fluttered as a woman wiped away tears and men stared impassively straight ahead, with an occasional twitch of an eye-lid betraying their emotions.

Inside the church the mass of dark blue uniforms, the splashes of silver rank markings picked out by the sunlight, and the sombre suits of the VIP's mingled with the summer dresses of ladies with shopping bags who had quietly joined us to say farewell to five men they knew only as anonymous faces under black helmets as they sped on their way to a job.

The service, conducted by the Reverend Thomas Griffin, was simple but appropriate, Monsignor Shanahan reading the lesson and Brigade Missionary Jack Woodgate giving the address which captured the feelings of everyone present. Then the sharp and haunting notes of the Last Post, played by Brigade trumpeters, signalled the next phase of the solemn progress as the coffins were once again placed on the five shining appliances.

Onwards through the busy streets of Stratford the cortege moved, watched by mothers with young children and others who had decided that their brief lunch break could wait while they stood at the kerbside under the hot sun and perhaps offer a silent prayer. A brief pause as the procession passed Eastern Command Headquarters, and TLs moved slowly forward to lay fireman Breen to rest at Eastbrook End cemetery, Dagenham, while his four comrades were carried to the City of London Cemetery and Crematorium, Manor Park. There the cortege moved with solemn gravity through the quiet cemetery, along the narrow pathway to the small grey stone chapel, where the last words were to be spoken for the four comrades in death.

And still the sun shone in an almost fiery splendour, while five hundred firemen stood lining the route of the cortege, at attention, unmoving, bound together in a moment of disciplined respect, unified in their common tribute, but each thinking his own thoughts.

From the great turntable ladders, with their clean, efficient contours softened by some 250 wreathes draped on them, the pall bearers gently carried the coffins into the chapel. One by one the dark limousines brought the mourners.

A brief sermon, heard outside on loudspeakers by the many people who could not get into the packed chapel, was especially poignant for a moment when the muted sobs of a woman broke through over the voice and music … then it was over … and the mourners, as if unbelieving, slowly almost reluctantly, left the cemetery.

More than 1,000 firemen formed the guards of honour at the different ceremonies, and over 300 floral tributes were received. In the midst of the awesome ceremonies we joined Londoners at the kerbside and watched and listened. Sometimes firemen have told us that they think the people of London take them for granted. From what we heard and saw we doubt if this thought would ever be voiced again by anyone who had stood with us on the pavements of East London on a sunny morning in July.

Thinking back to this day two words keep coming to mind. They were used by Mr Woodgate in his address when he described these five men as being good firemen. We cannot think of a simpler or a finer epitaph.

NORTHERN IRELAND

In the summer of 1969 civil unrest in Northern Ireland deteriorated into a period of insurrection, and although it is true to say that the civilian service which suffered the most from the rioting and terrorism was the Royal Ulster Constabulary GC, there were most certainly instances of the Provinces' firefighters coming under attack. In this regrettably brief chapter I should like to pay tribute to the courage and commitment of our comrades in Northern Ireland.

On Thursday 14th August 1969 at least twelve factories had been destroyed by arson attacks, as had over 100 homes in Belfast. Two fire officers, Assistant Chief Officer Whyte accompanied by Assistant Divisional Officer Sefton, were travelling to a fire in the Falls Road, Belfast to give support to the crews attending the incident, when an extremely aggressive crowd surrounded their vehicle. The windscreen was broken and petrol bombs thrown into the car, which engulfed both men in flames, causing them to lose control and crash. Although both Whyte and Sefton were able to escape the flames and indeed the crowd, both were seriously burnt, and required many months of hospitalisation before being able to return to work.

On 10th May 1972 a call was received by Belfast fire control to a report of an explosion at the large Co-operative store in York Street. When the first appliances arrived they found that an explosive device had detonated on the third floor of the vast building, destabilising the external walls and two floors. A serious fire had developed due to oil pouring out of a storage tank on the roof, and the fact that the sprinkler system had been rendered inoperative by the blast. As a number of person were unaccounted for, firefighters and members of the security forces began searching the premises, but owing to the excessive heat and smoke all had to withdraw, with the exception of Divisional Officer Johnston and Sub-Officer Warden who continued their work despite the deteriorating conditions. Eventually both firefighters found themselves trapped by heat and smoke on the roof. Fortunately a turntable ladder was sited below them and it was extended and elevated to their position, but the appliance's automatic cut-out mechanism prevented it reaching them. Consequently they had to leap from the roof and cling to the underside of the ladder whilst it was rotated and they were able to jump onto an adjoining roof.

On Wednesday 7th February 1973 twenty-six year-old firefighter Brian Douglas was shot dead by a gunman whilst on duty in Belfast. That evening Douglas was a member of the crew of the major pump from Chichester Street fire station, Belfast, which responded to a fire call to the Groovy Boutique at the junction of Sandy Row and Bradbury Place. On arrival all street lights had been extinguished, and the three-storey building housing these premises was well alight, with flames issuing from all windows, so creating an ideal scenario for a gunman to have potential targets silhouetted in his sights. Hostile crowds were in the area, and a detachment from the Royal Artillery was in position to protect the fire crews. Some idea of this serious and extremely hostile situation can be gleaned from the following extract taken from one soldier's deposition to Her Majesty's Coroner for the City of Belfast, Mr J. H. S. Elliott:

> On Wednesday 7th February 1973 I was a member of a mobile patrol located at that time in the Donegall Pass area. The patrol was mounted in a Landrover, commanded by 'A' … I was armed with a Self Loading Rifle … which was fitted with a magazine containing ten rounds. 'A' received a radio message from our Battery Op's room to investigate a petrol bomb incident at Bradbury Place … on arrival I saw that house number 63 was engulfed in flames and a hostile crowd was running along Sandy Row. I stopped the Landrover around the corner outside … number 2 Lisburn Road. We debussed and the rest of the patrol deployed within the immediate area, whilst 'A' and I went to clear the flats where the fire was. As I was entering the ground floor door …
> I heard two LV (low velocity) shots and I saw two gun flashes coming from the junction of Donegall Road/Sandy Row. I went out into the street, knelt down and cocked my SLR. I then fired three … rounds at the position where I had seen the flashes. I then went back to the flats. A few seconds later I heard a burst of automatic HV (high velocity) fire, it was only a small burst and I have no idea where it came from. About three minutes later a fire engine came down Bradbury Place … I stopped this vehicle and told the driver to warn all the firemen that there was a sniper in the area. I then moved to a new

position. This was behind a lamp post … a gunman then opened fire from the junction of Blythe Street/Sandy Row with an automatic weapon. I saw the gun flashes and returned two rounds …

The crew of Chichester Street fire station's major pump immediately got a jet to work, using a nearby building as cover, and were advised by the Assistant Chief Fire Officer (ACO) who was in attendance, not to proceed past the corner as a sniper was in Sandy Row. As a second line of hose was being run out, firefighter Douglas went past the corner but was ordered back for his safety. As Douglas and another firefighter were readying a second jet for use, a burst of automatic gun fire was heard, and the crew ran for cover. Douglas was seen to hold his chest as he fell to his knees, and heard to say, 'I've been hit'. Two of his comrades quickly grabbed Douglas and helped him to the relative safety of the side of the pump escape, and brought blankets and a first aid kit. Their hose line had now become charged with water and the branch was lashing about wildly due to the jet reaction to the pressure. Seeing this very dangerous situation the Assistant Chief, with great presence of mind, and not a little courage, crawled along the length of the hose line, secured the branch and directed the jet of water onto the fire. At this point he heard the Leading Fireman shout, 'ACO, Brian has been hit'; the Assistant Chief then closed down the branch, abandoned the jet and ordered on an ambulance. Firefighter Douglas was then removed to the Royal Victoria Hospital, where he was pronounced dead.

Just after eight o'clock on the morning of 16th November 1978, a small grey car holding a number of armed and masked men pulled up at the main gate of Bass Charrington's Brewery in Glen Road, Belfast. As the security guard moved towards the passenger side window, one of the occupants pointed a hand-gun at him and ordered him to open the gate. Having unlocked the gate, the security man walked into his office, followed by one of the gunmen, and told him to lie down saying: 'Do what you're told and you'll be all right.' The gunman then disconnected the telephones on the office desk. Meanwhile the vehicle moved onto the site, and two of the occupants, both masked, one armed with what was described by a witness as, 'Like a machine gun type', and the other carrying a case which resembled a yellow oil can, entered the foyer where the work force were gathered. Whilst the employees were ordered into their locker room, and held by this gunman, the man with the case ran into the Bond store. After two minutes both men ran from the building shouting that they had planted a fire bomb, and consequently the staff immediately evacuated the premises and it was apparent that a fire had already begun. One witness reported hearing a whoosh, and saw smoke coming through the roof and heard the sound of bottles breaking.

The first firefighter to attend this incident was the Assistant Divisional Officer from the Ardoyne fire station in Lisburn Road, who arrived at the Ulster Brewery at 0824 hours, and found the spirit store, a building eighty-three feet by 166 feet, heavily smoke-logged with the roller shutters closed. On the arrival of the appliance from Cadogan fire station, the Assistant Divisional Officer (A D O) ordered that a line of hose be laid out from the pumping appliance with water being fed by a private hydrant in the grounds, in readiness to commence firefighting operations once the security situation permitted. On the arrival of the pump from Lisburn, the ADO briefed the officer-in-charge, fifty-three year-old Sub-Officer Wesley Orr, a well known and respected fire officer, and together they proceeded to the door of the building to obtain a better appreciation of the situation.

In his deposition to Her Majesty's Coroner for the district of South Antrim this officer, whose name is withheld for reasons of security as well as confidentiality, said:

> I ordered a jet to be taken to the door of the building and to use the protection afforded by the outside wall to direct water where bottles could be heard exploding. There was the matter of ventilation to be considered and the thought that the building could become one large bomb, not due to explosives but because of the amount of spirit involved and the lack of ventilation. The longer the fire burned the more spirits burst and spilled over the floor making the situation more dangerous every minute due to the ... alcohol vapour.

> I went into the building and opened a roller shutter to get a better appreciation of the situation and decided to close it again and wait before proceeding further. One fire-man said he could see the fire at ceiling height through the smoke and a jet was directed at the base of the flame. The flames were beaten down and I called Sub-Officer Orr and had the jet knocked off for a while. I told him that the building was a high bay warehouse, and that there were long passageways between the storage racks which were about 40-50 feet high. I said to him that I thought fires were at the lower parts of the racks, and that they would be weak from heat. They were fully stocked. I therefore said that no man should venture into any of the passageways under any circumstances. Sub-Officer Orr kept all personnel out of the passageways throughout the incident.

> I went into the building a few feet and opened the roller shutter again, and let it remain open for a few minutes to ventilate ... and prevent a flashover ... while the men were still in the building. When a few minutes had elapsed I ordered two breathing apparatus wearers to go into the building with a jet. Sub-Officer Orr and myself were only a few feet behind the BA wearers. I donned a BA set to get a better look at the situation for a few minutes. Eventually we could enter the building for about 40-50 feet, and extinguished three large seats of fire. The last seat of fire to be reached was about 45 feet

inside the building and we had it under control. I left the building for a look outside and put a message back [to fire service control room] and entered again, going up to the last seat of fire where Sub-Officer Orr was, with at least three other men. The building was still smoke-logged. Sub-Officer Orr was in what I would call buoyant mood on reaching what was the last seat of fire, and he and myself were on our haunches for air. He said to me 'We could cut off the jet now, a hose-reel will finish this off'. He was pleased at having won the day. I said to him, 'You stay there and keep the men from going into the passages. I'll get a reel'. I went outside and told the pump operator to 'knock-off' the jet. I got hold of a young fireman and had him don a BA set, and brought him and a hose-reel to Sub-Officer Orr.

After giving the Sub-Officer the reel I turned to walk out of the building and was just outside, about forty feet from the Sub-Officer when there was a blast. The time was about 0915 hours. It was just appreciably bigger than the sound of the exploding spirit bottles. I and the ATO (Army Technical Officer) who was just about ten feet from me turned and ran towards the building. We were met by four or five fire-men, including Sub-Officer Orr fleeing from the building holding their faces which were full of small cuts and abrasions. I ordered ambulances, and before their arrival an Army ambulance removed Sub-Officer Orr to hospital. The BA Entry Control Officer ran up to me and said there was a fire-man missing. I grabbed a hose-reel, and ran into the building to where Sub-Officer Orr and his men had been. I went up two passages … and into a recess area shouting for anyone there. The inside of the building was fairly quiet, and there was no reply. I spent no more than two minutes in the building and came out. I questioned the BA Control Officer and some fire-men, and concluded that the fireman was accounted for. I closed the roller shutter gate and ordered on a 'Hi-Ex' (high expansion) foam unit to flood the building from a distance.

The seat of fire which Sub-Officer Orr was dealing with when the blast occurred was not very much bigger when I went into the building to look for the 'missing fireman'. Later an empty tin of petrol was found which had disintegrated in an explosion. There were pieces of tape on the remains which had possibly been used to attach an explosive device.

The Army Technical Officer who attended the fire at the Bass Charrington Brewery wrote in his deposition as follows:

The warehouse was itself now on fire, and the fire brigade were already present tackling the fire. I was also informed of a report of a further device in the office area … nearest the front gate. A search was progressed of this building and all remaining areas … to ascertain if indeed another device could be located. At about 9.15 am I arrived at the bonded warehouse. At approximately 9.18 am I was standing with some of the firemen at the entrance to the bonded store, and could observe the outline of firemen inside … at this time the area was filled with smoke. I heard a low order explosion and the firemen who were tackling the fire inside the warehouse withdrew, after withstanding injuries, two of these firemen collapsed after reaching the outside area. Myself and another … immediately entered the building to establish if any crew members were lying injured within the warehouse, we did not discover any. Inside the warehouse I noticed two fires blazing at the centre of the spirits warehouse, and we both withdrew. Outside I immediately advised the fire officer not to approach the building again until at least 10.30 am. I then, in an armoured suit, approached the building and lowered the steel shutter doors to seal the building, after depositing a fire monitor with the warehouse'.

Sub-Officer Orr, a well respected member of the service, was the most seriously injured of the firefighters, and died later that day in hospital. His funeral was attended by colleagues from throughout Northern Ireland, Great Britain and the Republic of Ireland, and the route of the cortege was lined with thousands of people who just wished to pay their respects to a firefighter who given his life for his community.

GLASGOW'S KILBIRNIE STREET TRAGEDY

On Friday 25th August, 1972 Glasgow Fire Brigade was again visited by grievous loss, when seven of its firefighters were killed during a fire at Sher Brothers cash-and-carry premises at 70/72 Kilbirnie Street, in the Eglinton Toll area of the city. This building, some seventy-two feet long by sixty-two feet wide, comprised a ground floor and two upper levels, with four load-bearing outer walls of brick construction. The ground floor consisted of a loading bay to the south, and this area was bounded by stock rooms to the north and east. An open timber stairway led from the loading area to the two upper floors.

The fire was discovered by a female employee who had visited the first floor to obtain items for a customer, and whilst there heard an unidentified 'popping' sound which seemed to come from above. She was prompted to investigate, and as she approached the attic saw smoke and flames, and whilst two male employees attempted to tackle the blaze with portable fire extinguishers, she returned to the ground floor and reported the outbreak. At 11.21am the first emergency call was received by the Glasgow Fire Brigade's mobilising control.

On arrival Station Officer Carroll, in charge of the first attendance of three fire appliances, although well aware of the inherent dangers which would attend such an incident, did not consider that this fire presented any particular difficulties. The staff of the warehouse had already been safely evacuated by the time the first units arrived, and normal firefighting procedures were initiated. To evaluate the dynamics of the situation Carroll went to the top floor of the building, where he found heat and a pall of smoke, but no flame was visible; consequently he did not anticipate any excessive danger to his firefighters. He ordered two of his firefighters into breathing apparatus to take charge of a line of delivery hose, and while awaiting the arrival of the BA crew the fire was tackled by firefighters Gray and Murray, who aimed the jet of water at the ceiling inside the west store passage, which came back hot, indicating that there had been some cooling effect on the blaze.

Although the stairs were clear of the products of combustion, the west store was heavily smoke-logged, and although having no respiratory protection, the two firefighters penetrated a further ten feet into the passage, and seeing the glow of flame through the choking black clouds of smoke they immediately attacked and extinguished it. Breathing apparatus wearers Rook and Howie arrived having donned one-hour oxygen sets, and taking over the branch moved to the attic level. The latter firefighter discovered that his nose-clip assembly had become detached, and had to return to the Street to obtain a replacement, whereupon Leading Fireman Smith immediately volunteered to take his place. Howie quickly obtained his replacement nose-clip and returned; consequently there were three breathing apparatus wearers who worked the hose-line towards the seat of the fire. They advanced further into the west store to find the fire taking hold at the north-west corner, and having dealt with it, they discovered that the fire had spread across the floor.

It is worth noting that even in the early 1970s breathing apparatus was available for use only in the most severe smoke conditions, which would render respiration impossible. In fact BA was viewed by many of the more experienced firefighters of the time as having the disadvantages of being an encumbrance that deprived the wearer of the perception of knowing that he was approaching the heart of the fire as his discomfort in breathing in a smoke-laden atmosphere may have become easier, the in-drawn air becoming more focal, and the exposed areas of his face indicating the proximity and intensity of the fire.

The firefighting operations to drive the flames towards the north gable wall, contain and extinguish it, were thwarted by a number of factors such as the unusual design of the attic, which was 'U'-shaped, and a very confined space; the volume of the smoke being generated; and the density and stacking of the stock, much of which was in cardboard boxes stored on shelving supported by lightweight metal framing, or simply stacked on the floor with space between giving room for the free-flow of air to feed the fire and the hot gases to move via convection. Storage was of such high density throughout the building that the fire-loading was extremely high.

During this phase of the operations Divisional Officer Andrew Quinn arrived at the incident and proceeded to the top floor, and conferred with Carroll, who was his nephew. It was decided to 'Make pumps four'. This would bring two more appliances with their crews, and extra equipment in case operations had to be extended in the difficult and heavily smoke-laden conditions that prevailed. This message was received at mobilising control at 11.26 am, and one appliance was ordered on from Queen's Park, and one from West Marine Fire Station.

Quinn called for a BA wearer to investigate the situation in the East Store, and Fireman Howie, having returned to the landing at the stair head entered the East Store, and Fireman Murray, who was not wearing breathing apparatus, accompanied him part of the way. They discovered that fire had spread into the north part of the East Store, and Howie returned and made a report to DO Quinn, who called for another hose-line and a further two BA wearers to deal with this development. Station Officer Carroll then left the building to organise this second hose line.

When the West Marine appliance arrived at 11.33 am Carroll ordered the officer-in-charge of the appliance, Sub Officer Stewart, to ventilate the heat and smoke via the top of the building. After gaining access via a forty-five foot extension ladder the crew created ventilation holes in the roof, but found that the volume of heat and smoke rising through the openings, made their position untenable.

At approximately midday there was a substantial fall of debris and three firefighters were brought out by colleagues, two suffering from burns, and one from smoke inhalation and heat exhaustion. Fireman Rook was now unaccounted for.

Station Officer Carroll, after having spoken with DO Quinn, was making his way back to his appliance to send a radio message requesting the attendance of an Emergency Tender for more breathing apparatus sets, when he heard Quinn shout: 'Where's Rook?' Carroll ordered an ambulance onto the incident, and had a resuscitator taken to the top floor. At the scene of operations Quinn ordered that a search be made for Rook and requested 'Two more good BA men'; and firefighters Crofts and Bermingham were immediately dispatched. At this time flames were seen in the area where Rook was believed trapped, and Quinn was heard to say, 'I'm not leaving here until I find Rook. I must find him.' Station Officer Carroll went to the street and ordered a line of hose to the first floor, and made pumps eight. Re-entering the building, he made his way back to the top floor, when the ceiling flashed over, and he shouted: 'Get out', grabbing a firefighter who was crossing in front of the flames and pushed him down the stairs. He later said that because of the sudden and unexpected nature of the flashover, 'Anyone left in the building had no chance of survival.'

Leading Fireman Smith, who had been the officer-in-charge of the crew of which Rook was a member, had advanced a line of hose into the north-west corner of the top floor, and pushed over some bales which were obstructing their way and saw that the whole north-end of the wall was alight. Concentrating on fighting the fire, and in the obvious confusion of the situation, Smith thought that Rook was still behind him. When relieved by another BA wearer he went out to the landing, and was so exhausted that he did not notice that Rook was not with him. After two minutes in fresh air Smith re-entered the building where he learned that Rook was missing. He took a line of hose on to the first floor but found that it was impossible to continue as the whole floor was a mass of thick black smoke, which then erupted in flames.

Leading Fireman Murray of Central Fire Station responded to the Station Officer's call for BA men and was ordered by DO Quinn to enter and search for Rook, but he had to deal with a fresh outbreak of flame first. More BA wearers arrived, including Bermingham, and as they were removing bales and climbing over them to get at the seat of the fire, they heard a BA distress warning signal operate, and tracing the sound found Rook sitting, hunched forward, with his legs trapped by bales; still wearing his breathing apparatus. Murray supported the racking and shone a torch so that Bermingham could see to pick the bales from Rook with both hands, and eventually he was dragged 'by the scruff of his neck' towards the door. Murray held up the racking until he judged that sufficient time had been allowed to get Rook clear, and dropped to his hands and knees and crawled to the stairs. Conditions were becoming increasingly difficult with little or no visibility in a complex structure which was seriously congested with highly combustible material. At one time Murray heard a scream from ahead of him but did not know from whom it came. When he reached the head of the stairs he tumbled down onto the half-landing, dislodging his mouthpiece and nose-clips. Following the hose, which was now his life-line, with flames raging above him, he made his way down to the first floor, and lost the hose at that level where some of the stock had collapsed and buried it; a situation which is a nightmare for all firefighters. Searching the immediate area he fortunately found the hose again, and on exiting the building it was found that his face and hands were burned.

Leading Fireman Walsh, officer-in-charge of the turntable ladder which arrived as part of the first attendance, was involved in fighting the fire at the back of the building when he was told to take a resuscitator to the top floor, and found Liddell being escorted down. He used the resuscitator on him before going back to the top floor, where someone shouted: 'Get out' and he was pushed down the stairs, where he found himself with Smith. There then was a muffled roar, and flames were running across the ceiling and coming down to the sheeted stock. Walsh then heard a distress signal unit sound for a few seconds on the top floor, followed by the sound of moaning. Looking up the stairs, he saw Murray's yellow leggings and helped him down to the ambulance. He then assisted in getting the turntable ladder to work.

At about 12.12 pm Carroll had re-visited the first floor and discovered that the fire had burned from above through the ceiling at the north-west corner. Although this spread was negligible, he was very concerned as it indicated that the fire was burning at the north-west corner of the attic floor where the rescue operation was taking place. He returned to the street and ordered a line of hose to be taken up to deal with it. It was at this point that he informed Quinn that he thought conditions were now seriously deteriorating. Quinn replied that as soon as Rook was extricated they would all evacuate the premises, and told Carroll to deal with the fire which had broken through to the first floor. Unexpectedly the fire then spread with tremendous speed, and both Welsh and Carroll had to run to the stairs to escape the searing blast of heat, only to return within seconds to attack the blaze with a jet.

After the explosion of flame, Deputy Firemaster Peter McGill, who was now in attendance, ordered two officers, DO McKinnon and Station Officer Campbell, to break in through a first floor window to mount a further attack on the fire and allow any gases to vent, to permit an entry; as an all-out attack would have precluded any attempt at rescue. There was also a danger that the top floor would collapse, and consequently he could not position men on the first floor. McGill, a former Scots Guardsman, and a highly respected and experienced firefighter, and certainly the most highly decorated member of Glasgow Fire Brigade, then climbed through the first floor window with McKinnon and Campbell who had a jet with them; however conditions were too severe for them to remain. McGill and Campbell re-deployed and worked a hose line up the internal stairs, and McKinnon took a jet through the window despite the obvious fact that the building was by this time in a very dangerous condition, and ready to collapse. It was McKinnon who found the bodies of Bermingham, Findlay, McMillan and Hooper on the half landing of the stairs between the first and top floors. 'It was obvious from their position', he said, 'that the men had been met by a wave of intense heat which prevented them going forward. It was also obvious that they were moving towards the seat of the fire when they were overcome.' Considerable quantities of debris, mostly stored goods, were moved on the first floor and beneath were found the bodies of Quinn and Crofts in the passageway leading to the second floor stairway. Rook's body was found later on the top floor.

It was conjectured by Deputy Firemaster McGill that Quinn had remained in the building because one of his men had been trapped, and it appeared that he and his rescue team had been overcome while trying to find Rook. Mr McGill believed that Quinn's decision to fight the fire from the inside was certainly the most appropriate course of action.

In the latter stages of the incident the fire was tackled with a considerable volume of water, and aerial jets were applied from two turntable ladders, two hydraulic platforms and a 'Scoosher' monitor (this piece of equipment, unique to Glasgow, was introduced in 1968 and had a hydraulic boom with an infra-red detector, a steel spike and a water monitor, all of which allowed the operator on a platform at the rear of the appliance, to detect the fire, smash open a window and send a jet of water into the building to extinguish it), which were supplemented by hand-held jets surrounding the building. When the fire was brought under control the building was in an extremely dangerous condition, and so the task of recovering the bodies of the victims was in itself a very hazardous one.

The *Scottish Daily Express* of 26th August 1972 wrote of the Kilbirmie Street tragedy:

Six firemen heroically plunged through searing heat and flames in a desperate search for a trapped colleague in the Glasgow warehouse disaster yesterday.

Seconds after the rescue squad vanished into the blazing building there was a 'blow-out of fire' and part of the roof crashed down, burying all seven. This was revealed early today when details of the official police report were released. [The] first hint of the tragedy came when two of the first three firemen to enter the warehouse ... staggered out, gasping that they had been hit by a 'heat blast'. As they were given emergency oxygen the rescue squad pulled on breathing masks and ran towards one of the doors. Then came another flash of flame ...

The disaster happened in the space of 45 minutes at the height of the blaze in Sher Brothers' cash and carry warehouse in Kilburnie Street. Then as the firemen won control of the blaze, searching teams entered and made their grim discoveries. In a dramatic kerbside interview at the scene the city's Deputy Firemaster, Mr Peter McGill, his face black with smoke, read the roll call of the dead. Glasgow's Lord Provost and senior police officers listened closely as Mr McGill said:

'A fire occurred in these premises and the normal attendance for a fire responded. They asked for a further two appliances and after that it was known that men were trapped.'

The horror began at 11.30 in the two-storey clothing warehouse as a staff of ... eight women and four men, heard shouts from two workmen outside that the building was one fire. Smoke was pouring from the top floor which contained blankets and woollen clothes. Minutes later the first firefighters arrived some wearing breathing apparatus, and began to tackle the flames. After half an hour as fire tenders encircled the building, pouring thousands of gallons of water from turntable ladders into the inferno, two firemen, David Liddle and Brian Murray were carried out of the building suffering from the intense heat. Moments later there was a roar and the roof collapsed with a number of the firemen still inside. Eye witness Bill Frazer a labourer ... who was working on a nearby roof said: 'We saw the men going in, but they vanished in the smoke. They never came out again. The roof just seemed to explode and flames leapt nearly 100 feet into the air.'

Anxious firemen's fears grew as they scanned the control board which indicates the oxygen supply. It was only minutes before their fears became a horrible reality. A senior police official said that seven firemen were unaccounted for … and their oxygen supply had run out. Suddenly the whole fire horror was mirrored by two young firemen, leaning exhausted against railings after coming out. As they were ordered to go back in, one of them dropped his head in despair and muttered: 'You're not sending us back in there again, are you?' But seconds later he slipped on his oxygen mask, spoke to the control … officer and went back into the blaze.

At 2:15pm as 100 firemen brought the giant fire under control, police moved everyone back a hundred yards from the main entrance as the first four bodies were carried on the blue shrouded stretchers by grim-faced mates. But the battle to recover their three other colleagues was hampered by the fire. A senior fire official said: 'We have located them but we cannot get near them for the blaze'. Two more bodies were recovered from the ruins at four o'clock.

At the fire station in nearby Centre Street, many of the wives in the thirty fire houses waited in dread for the tragic death toll. But only one family there was to face heart-break, and for Mrs Cathy Hooper it was an extra cruel blow. For her forty-three year old husband Bill who died yesterday had survived the Cheapside fire in 1960. Said eldest son Mathew … one of the five Hooper children left fatherless: 'We hoped he would be one of the lucky ones.' The relieved wives of Centre Street rallied to comfort Mrs Hooper. Meanwhile firemen stood about in solemn groups, discussing the tragedy in whispers.

A sad reminder of the dedication of the men who risk their lives constantly came when the fire engines returning from the blaze parked neatly back in the station awaiting the next call to duty. But the seven who died had answered their last call yesterday. Fireman David Liddle escaped with his life, because he fainted. He had been one of the first men to enter the warehouse, wearing breathing apparatus, but he passed out soon after and was carried to safety. Mr Liddle … his scorched face covered in cream, said at home: 'I went upstairs on to one of the upper floors wearing breathing apparatus to investigate. There was smoke you couldn't see through. Then suddenly there was a terrific burst of heat. I collapsed, overcome by the heat. I completely blacked out. I saw my colleagues walking through the smoke all around me and that's the last thing I remember. When I opened my eyes next I was in an ambulance on my way to the Victoria Infirmary. The ambulance man told me my mates had carried me out after I fainted. If they hadn't done that I would still have been in the building with the men who were trapped a few minutes later. I don't know what caused the fire or how the men died. I just know that I was one of the lucky ones.'

Representatives from every fire brigade in the United Kingdom attended the funerals of the seven 'fallen' firefighters. A Requiem Mass was offered for DO Quinn at Holy Cross Church, Crosshill, by Bishop James Ward, Vicar-General of Glasgow's Archdiocese, and at Glasgow Cathedral the Rev. Dr William Morris conducted the funeral service for the other six men. Some 3,000 mourners, including an estimated 500 firefighters, were in the Cathedral and loudspeakers relayed the service to a further 2,000 outside. Amongst fourteen lorry-loads of wreaths was one from the Frankfurt Fire Brigade, which has close links with Glasgow. Among the mourners was Mr Gordon Campbell, Secretary of State for Scotland. One lesson at Holy Cross Church was read by the Firemaster of Glasgow, Mr George Cooper, and firefighters acted as pall-bearers, with a lone Fire Service piper playing a lament as six of the flag-draped coffins were prepared for interment at Glasgow Necropolis; where a brief service was conducted by Bishop Ward and Dr Morris.

Her Majesty The Queen sent the following message to the Lord Provost of Glasgow: 'I am much distressed to learn of the tragic deaths of seven firemen in the fire in Kilbirnie Street this afternoon. Please convey my deep sympathy to the families of those who have lost their lives.'

Firefighters Iain Bermingham, Alastair Crofts, Allan Finlay, William Hooper, Duncan McMillan and Andrew Quinn were all awarded the Queen's Commendation for Brave Conduct posthumously for their part in attempting to rescue James Rook.

FIRE AT THE WORSLEY HOTEL, CLIFTON GARDENS, MAIDA VALE, LONDON

At 0332 hours on Friday 13th December, 1974, the first 999 call was received by London Fire Brigade's Wembley control room to a fire at the Worsley Hotel, Clifton Gardens, Maida Vale, London, W9, which was a terraced building of eight inter-connecting houses, three of which were five floors high with attic rooms in the roof space. An initial attendance of a pump escape, pump, turntable ladder and emergency tender from Paddington Fire Station under the command of Red Watch Station Officer Neil Wallington, and a pump escape from Manchester Square and pump from Belsize were dispatched. By the end of this night one firefighter, Harry Pettit, would have lost his life and three others would have been seriously injured.

The Worsley Hotel was only half a mile or so from Paddington fire station and even before the appliances had left the appliance room, the sight and strong smell of smoke billowing across the front of the station indicated that a large fire was already in progress. The junior officer in charge of the Emergency Tender, most unusually, gave the order to his crew to don BA sets before the appliance had even moved. On arrival at the Worsley Hotel at 0335 hours, only three minutes after turning out to the first of many 999 fire calls, Station Officer Wallington and his crews were faced with an extremely serious situation. Many people were screaming and hanging out of windows, and clinging to ledges at every level of the five floor building awaiting rescue. In the midst of a chaotic and extremely critical situation, Station Officer Wallington, keeping a calm and measured sense of command, immediately ordered that an assistance message be transmitted to the effect of: 'Make pumps eight, persons reported'.

The first rescue of the night was a relatively simple affair with a man brought down a 'first floor ladder' from the top of a porch by firefighter Pettit and other Paddington crew members; this occurred within minutes of the first appliances arriving. This was the first of five rescues involving Pettit, who was also a member of one of the original crews to enter the building, with a hose line which they worked down a corridor on the ground floor in middle of the building. As oncoming appliances started to arrive, firefighters from Paddington were already pitching a fifty-foot wheeled escape ladder into the third floor as well as bringing hook ladders into use. The reinforcing firefighting crews also took hook ladders to the rear of the building, and began affecting numerous rescues by means of this precarious, but much valued, piece of equipment.

So serious was the escalating fire and rescue situation that further assistance messages requesting two more turntable ladders and seven additional pumping appliances were transmitted. By this time, fifty percent of the second, third, fourth and fifth floors were well alight, and somewhere in the region of thirty people were awaiting rescue on the upper floors.

In the centre of the building, two of Paddington's firefighters were advancing a hose line from the ground floor to the first floor amid thick smoke and intense heat to bridge a partially collapsed stone staircase via a fire brigade ladder, when ordered out of the building by a Station Officer for their own safety. The Station Officer's rationale, based on his operational experience and a study of the elements of building construction, being that jets of water were being brought to bear from the rear of the hotel, and it was likely that any stone stairway above this crew, having been subjected to great heat, might well collapse when hit with a powerful jet of water. Withdrawing across the ladder with the hose line was a far from easy manoeuvre, but spurred on by the obvious danger they were in, they moved swiftly but cautiously, dismounted the ladder and made for the exit and into the cold night air. As they left the burning hotel, a hot blast of air rushed past them: one of the stone staircases had indeed collapsed onto where they had been working. Their good luck and fortuitous escape prompted by that Station Officer's prescient sense of command was, regrettably, not to be shared by other of their colleagues that night.

Divisional Officer Robert Keable wrote of this incident in his report:

> At about 0342 hours on Friday 13 December, I was informed by telephone by Wembley control that a 15 pump fire was in progress at the Worsley Hotel, Clifton Gardens, and I responded immediately. On arrival at that address, which was a row of eight terraced houses of four and five floors and a

basement, about 200 feet by 60 feet, converted for use as a hostel for hotel staff, I saw that a very serious fire involved two or three of these houses on all floor levels and was spreading to the roof and horizontally to the houses on each side. I instructed that my Brigade car and the A Division control unit should be sited clear of the frontage, to enable oncoming appliances to get to work. I saw that three wheeled escape ladders were pitched to the front of the building from the service roadway, as was the turntable ladders from A21 Paddington; also first-floor ladders and hook ladders were pitched at first and second floor levels respectively. Several jets were already at work tackling the fire, and rescues were still being effected down one of the wheeled escapes at the Randolph Road end of the building.

Station Officer Wallington reported to me that multiple rescues had been carried out at all floor levels at the front by ladders of all types, and that a similar situation prevailed at the rear, except that only extension ladders and hook ladders could be used, as the only access was via the garden or through the premises involved or adjacent thereto. He also told me some internal staircases had already collapsed.

The crews in attendance were fully committed, and I remained at the front for a few minutes to direct crews of the reinforcing appliances which were still responding to earlier requests for assistance from both Station Officer Wallington and Assistant Divisional Officer Rowley. ADO Rowley then reported to me and confirmed the information given by Station Officer Wallington, and I asked him to remain in charge at the front of the premises while I surveyed the rear.

On reaching the rear of the premises I saw several extension ladders and hook ladders pitched into various windows, and it was reported to me that all persons known to require rescue had in fact been rescued. Several jets were already at work, and the spread of fire appeared to me to be more extensive than it was at the front. I instructed that more extension ladders and hook ladders should be provided to enable a more rapid search of the back rooms, and that jets should be got to work internally where possible and also from the heads of ladders of the extension ladders where they would be more quickly effective.

As I returned to the front I met ADO Baldwin and asked him to take charge of firefighting and searching at the rear of the premises.

Assistant Divisional Officer Baldwin wrote in his report:

> On arrival at the rear of the premises, I saw that fire had involved most of the
> two upper floors and roof and was spreading laterally and downwards. I was
> informed by members of the crews in attendance at the rear that G 26
> (Belsize) pump's crew had carried out a rescue from one of the upper floors
> using hook ladders, and that one other man had been taken off a drainpipe at
> second floor level. I at once ordered a line of hose and jets to be got to work
> at the rear of the premises, with the idea of preventing further lateral spread of
> fire. Two jets were used to cover the roof and the outside of the premises, and
> three jets were taken into the first and third floor levels via extension ladders.
> During the course of firefighting, two of the three stone staircases, which
> crews were using to gain internal access to the upper floors and roof,
> collapsed. Crews were withdrawn and firefighting at the rear of the building
> was then confined to jets working from the outside, and those that could be
> worked into the upper floors via the windows, using numerous hook ladders
> to gain entry.

At 0406 hours Divisional Officer Keable ordered-on another five pumping
appliances, making the incident a 'twenty-pump' fire. DO Keable continued in his
report:

> I ... detailed A 28's (Kensington's) pump crew and C27's (Clerkenwell's)
> emergency tender crew to tackle the fire internally on all floor levels from the
> nearest intact staircase at the Warwick Avenue end of the premises, while other
> crews did the same from the Randolph Road end. At this stage the three
> wheeled escapes at the front were continually being re-sited from window to
> window, so that the crew could tackle the fire from the ladders by directing
> jets through the windows. Three turntable ladders were now at work...'

Shortly after the 'Make pumps twenty' message had been sent to fire control,
Deputy Assistant Chief Officer Pearce arrived at the incident and was appraised of the
situation by DO Keable; he then assumed command of operations. As water supplies
were seriously overstretched due to the number of jets in use, all crews fully engaged
in firefighting and rescue work, and as the fire was spreading at third and fourth floor
levels and along the roof he decided to request a further ten pumps.

At about this time a crew of four firefighters, including Harry Pettit, were ordered
to take a jet into the second floor of the building via a wheeled escape ladder which
was pitched into the window of Room 213 on the smoke-logged second floor. From
within this room, the crew led by Station Officer Colin Searle of Westminster fire
station started to work towards the corridor. Other crews worked jets up the surviving
internal staircases and all of the 200 firefighters now in attendance were conscious of

the seriousness of their situation and that not all persons had been accounted for at this time.

However, some eighty-five minutes after the first 999 call, the firefighting effort was beginning to have an effect on the inferno when the extent of the punishment being inflicted on the structural roof members by the flames suddenly caused a failure of the fire-weakened beams in the attic. This began a cascading collapse of roof joists, rafters, beams, a staircase and a large water tank down into the fourth floor, then into the third and then finally into the second floor at Room 213, where a four man Paddington crew was at work. Two firefighters were trapped under the burning debris in Room 213 itself (Station Officer Searle and firefighter Stewart), whilst firefighters Martin Walker and Harry Pettit were buried close by in the adjacent corridor. Because of the noise of operations and the fact the collapse had taken place well above the heads of most firefighters, only very few on the fire-ground were aware that a disastrous failure of the hotel's structural integrity had occurred.

One of those who became aware of the sudden drama was Station Officer Wallington, who had just descended a wheeled escape ladder from Room 213 when a mass of falling sparks alerted him to the structural collapse above. Instinctively, he and several others nearby scrambled back up the escape ladder and gingerly climbed into the smoking debris of Room 213 to try to locate those buried and begin the rescue of the entombed firefighters.

Prior to the collapse Sub Officer Ron Morris and firefighter Peter Lidbetter had been working together extinguishing flames in the room next door to the collapse, but were unaware of it because of the background noise and roar of their water jet hitting the walls and ceiling. Lidbetter moved into the passage to straighten the hose line on the landing, and was approached by two firefighters who informed him that someone trapped under the collapsed floor. He immediately went into the room and shone his torch through the smoke and dust to be faced by a picture of total devastation, with a mound of wreckage sloping away from him, and began searching for the trapped man. Guided by the man's cries for help he was able to locate firefighter Martin Walker, whose hand protruded from the wreckage. Lidbetter shouted for assistance, but to no avail, as his voice would not carry over the noise of operations. He was though able to remove some of the surface debris from his colleague, but could make little headway as a large wooden beam had pinned Walker. After a few minutes Morris shut down his branch in the room, and hearing Lidbetter's shouts for assistance, made his way through the darkness to where this lone rescue bid was taking place. By now Walker was complaining that his foot was burning under the rubble. Leading firefighter Jim Griffin then joined them, and seeing that there was not room for a third man to remove debris, brought the hose line from the corridor and applied water to the area of Walker's foot.

Meanwhile, the rescue of Searle and Stewart in Room 213 by the team led by

Station Officer Wallington continued but there was a considerable amount of hot debris including heavy timber beams and impacted masonry to be carefully removed with the constant threat of further collapse upon the rescue scene from above. After an hour and a half of dangerous and very delicate work in difficult and cramped conditions, the team in Room 213 extricated firefighter Stewart and very soon after were also able to free Station Officer Searle, who had suffered particularly severe burns to his lower limbs.

Lidbetter and Morris continued their work in removing the wreckage in the corridor, and eventually managed lift the beam and prop it against the wall. However, it was another one and a half arduous and smoke-filled hours with the ever-present possibility of a further collapse or fire spread before Walker was released by his comrades, also with serious burns to his feet. During his rescue Walker continually asked about Harry Pettit with whom he had been working before the collapse, but sadly, soon after Walker's release and removal to safety, it became evident that Harry had not survived.

In addition to Harry's tragic death, six hotel residents also perished in the Worsley fire but thirty-six persons were, miraculously, rescued from perilous situations that night by Red Watch fire crews from windows and ledges at all levels along the hotel frontage. Thirty-eight fire appliances and almost 200 firefighters of all ranks attended the Worsley Hotel that night, London's largest fire of 1974.

Following the fire, London's Chief Fire Officer, former special forces Chindit, Joe Milner, awarded twenty-two Certificates of either Commendation or Congratulation to various firefighters for their various actions at the fateful fire. Some months on, Roger Stewart, Ron Morris, Peter Lidbetter and David Blair were awarded the Queen's Gallantry Medal, and Neil Wallington, Eric Hall and Ray Chilton the Queen's Commendation for Brave Conduct. Harry Pettit was posthumously awarded the Queen's Gallantry Medal.

These Queen's awards for actions during the Worsley hotel fire were the largest number of gallantry honours given by Her Majesty for a single United Kingdom emergency incident in peacetime.

On 10th July 1975, a kitchen porter, Edward Mansfield, aged forty-one years, was charged at the Old Bailey with three cases of arson (one at the Worsley Hotel on 13th December and two at the Piccadilly Hotel on 19th and 29th December) and the murder of seven people, at the Worsley Hotel. He pleaded not guilty. On 23rd July the jury failed to reach the required majority verdict and were discharged.

The retrial of Mansfield at the Old Bailey on the same charges began on 12th November 1975. John Mathew, QC, was again the prosecuting counsel and this time some twenty-four personnel of all ranks of the London Fire Brigade gave evidence for the prosecution. The second trial ended on 1st December when Mansfield was found guilty of the manslaughter of seven people, including Fireman Harry Pettit, and of three charges of arson. He was jailed for life.

THE WOOLWORTHS' FIRE PICCADILLY GARDENS, MANCHESTER

Just before 1.30 pm on Tuesday 8th May 1979, a taxi driver was parked in a rank opposite the Woolworths' Store in Piccadilly Gardens, Manchester, when he noticed a fire on the second floor of the store and informed his radio controller, who then dialled 999, and was put through to the Greater Manchester Fire Brigade Control. This was the first of twelve emergency calls received for this incident, none of which originated from the store.

This retail outlet consisting of six floors, basement and sub-basement levels was built in 1929, and was believed to be the largest Woolworths' store in Europe. It was of brick construction with load-bearing beams and columns on all floors, and no sprinkler system was installed. It is believed that somewhere in the region of 500 customers and staff were inside the building when the fire broke out.

A predetermined attendance comprising three pumping appliances, a hydraulic platform and a mobile Station Officer were dispatched. As the appliances left the fire station the crews observed smoke billowing forebodingly through the streets of Piccadilly. The fire appliances arrived within two minutes of the first call, and as they were greeted by the sight of flames and heavy smoke issuing from the second floor windows, members of the public directed them to the Oldham Street side of the building. On his arrival the Station Officer immediately sent a message to 'Make pumps ten'. A number of people were trapped on the second, third and fourth floors, and women were seen at barred windows on the second floor, frantically calling for help. Others who had made their way to the roof were also shouting for assistance.

The supervisor in the furniture department, Steve Wood, on being alerted to the developing fire took himself quickly to the restaurant to inform the store manager, and then ran to the switchboard to get the operator to dial 999. Wood then ran up the stairs to alert other employees on the third, fourth and fifth floors, and returned to the restaurant to ask people to evacuate the premises; some of whom, incredibly, declined to leave their meals. The inquest would later hear evidence that seventy year-old Mr Albert McNally, who lost his life in the fire, refused to budge from the restaurant because he had just purchased a bowl of soup! Williams then bravely attempted to tackle the blaze with a hose-reel. Speaking to the *Manchester Evening News* on the thirtieth anniversary of this fire, Mr Wood said: 'I was helping people get out, but the place was filling with thick black smoke that started at the ceiling and was working its way down, eating away at the oxygen. While I was going down the stairs from the second floor, I was on my hands and knees, gasping for air. I was grabbing people and taking them with me.'

Among the victims was sixty-eight year-old Cyril Baldwin, a former wartime firefighter employed by Woolworths', who bravely and with an admirable sense of duty had remained in the building to assist others in making their escape.

Rescues were begun from two 13.5-metre extension ladders which were slipped from the roofs of their fire appliances, and pitched to the second floor windows resulting in the rescue of three persons. The hydraulic platform was elevated from the street to the third floor where a further three persons were assisted into the cage, and brought to safety. Several members of the public were found at ground level and were brought out to safety by firefighters. At 1335 hours an Assistant Divisional Officer arrived and requested the attendance of a turntable ladder to rescue a man seen on the top floor. By this time other appliances were arriving, and further 13.5-metre ladders were pitched to the barred windows, and rigorous and determined efforts were made to prise open the bars using pick axes and crow bars, whilst cutting gear was made ready for use. These attempts were unsuccessful, and an air operated Cengar saw was brought into use from the head of one ladder. This was no easy feat as the reciprocating blade is powered by the compressed air of a breathing apparatus cylinder, which must be held by the operator, who in this instance would also be holding onto the ladder. Firefighters managed to cut two of the bars, then with great effort bend them outward to enable the rescue of six persons; two of whom needed the urgent administration of oxygen when they were removed.

Within twelve minutes of the first appliance arriving, two hose lines had been laid up an internal staircase from Oldham Street to the second floor by breathing apparatus crews, who found the conditions unbearable with intense heat preventing further penetration into the building, even though they had crawled on hands and knees in an attempt to get underneath the layer of super heated gases. Just before a quarter to two a Divisional Officer took command of the incident and sent an assistance message to the effect of 'Make pumps fifteen'. In the meantime, a second hydraulic platform had rescued a woman from a second floor toilet window, and had begun to remove a further twelve persons from the roof. A firefighter had been taken to roof level in the cage of a hydraulic platform, and had remained there whilst the rescues were carried out, comforting those awaiting removal. By 1345 hours all those who had been seen calling for help at the windows, and on the roof had been rescued.

A second line of hose was laid up the Oldham Street staircase to the first floor and was used by breathing apparatus crews to tackle a fire that had now involved the escalator. This team was then tasked with making their way to the second floor which was well alight, whilst another crew also started to tackle the second floor fire, this time entry was by stairs from Piccadilly.

At six minutes to two, the message 'Make pumps twenty' was sent to mobilising control. BA Crews using jets from the head of two 13.5-metre ladders, and protected from the heat and flames by covering jets from pavement level, attacked the fire on the second floor from the frontage of the store. Two other hose lines were now laid into the back of the second floor from Piccadilly, despite the padlocked and chained doors which had made access difficult. By the time the Assistant Chief Officer assumed control of the incident at a quarter past two, a further rescue had been carried out from the top floor by turntable ladder, two emergency tenders ordered on for breathing apparatus requirements, and eight jets were now being worked into the second floor. Conditions inside the store were finally beginning to improve.

Hydraulic platforms being used to fight the fire were constantly having to close down their jets due to their hindering work carried out inside by BA crews. At three o'clock one firefighting team had to be rescued by turntable ladder as they had been cut off after having traversed the third floor and made their way to the roof. Another crew had been cut off by collapsing stock within the store and were rescued from a window by a hydraulic platform. The fire had now died down, but severe smoke-logging continued, and it was decided to use a high-expansion foam generator for smoke extraction purposes. The message 'Fire Surrounded' was sent at nine minutes to four, the fire now being almost out and conditions having improved to allow a thorough search of the building.

Station Officer William Jolley of Greater Manchester County Fire Service was awarded the Queen's Gallantry Medal for his part in these rescues. The supplement to the *London Gazette* of 3rd October 1980 reads:

> On arrival at the scene it was evident that the fire had taken hold in a very short time and flames accompanied by a large volume of smoke were billowing from the second floor windows, while at the rear of the premises smoke was issuing from the windows, many people were caught on various floors and several women could be seen trapped behind the bars at a second floor window.
>
> A ladder was placed at the barred window and Station Officer Jolley climbed up and attempted to remove the iron bars by using a large axe on the masonry. When this proved unsuccessful, he cut through two of the bars with a compressed air saw and levered them upwards sufficiently to gain access. Despite the seriousness and intensity of the fire, Station Officer Jolley entered the building taking with him only a resuscitator set in order to provide some swift temporary relief to the six women he was attempting to rescue.
>
> The smoke-logged room was by now filled by poisonous fumes and the women had great difficulty in breathing. The officer managed to calm and reassure them and was able to assist them onto the ladder and to a hydraulic platform cage which had then been positioned close to the ladder. When the last woman had been removed to safety the Station Officer returned to the room to make sure that there was no-one else remaining. He decided to search further and opened the door of the general office giving

access to the second floor shopping area which was by then burning fiercely. Crawling along the floor, he attempted to penetrate further but this proved impossible because of the heat, flames and smoke in the area. Before withdrawing, the officer waited and called several times in case there were any customers or staff still trapped, but no answer was given and nothing could be seen through the fire and dense blanket of smoke. Finally, when he was satisfied that he could give no further assistance and now severely affected by the effects of the heat and fumes he was forced to use the resuscitator himself before making his way back to the window.

Station Officer Jolley displayed bravery of a high order when, without the support of other personnel and at risk to his own safety he rescued the six trapped women and then, although suffering from the effects of heat and smoke, continued to search for survivors.

It is believed that the fire originated on the second floor between windows facing Piccadilly, by a damaged electrical cable that had furniture stacked in front of it, so obstructing any view of the fire in its incipient stages. Statements from various witnesses indicated that the first sign of fire was the appearance of flames over the tops of wardrobes in this area, which appeared to be originating between this furniture and the external wall. The effects of the fire starting on or spreading to the vertical face of the stacked furniture would result in a much more rapid degree of fire spread than if the piece were in a horizontal position. This rapid development was caused by the flames and hot gases rising vertically and along the face of the furniture and igniting or pre-heating materials above the base of the flames, which would lead to an increased rate of fire spread up the vertical surface of the furniture.

The furniture was constructed of polyurethane foam which, once alight, would have spread rapidly, producing large amounts of dense, toxic smoke which would have soon obscured the exit signs. This would have led to confusion and, together with the irritants in the smoke affecting people's vision and causing breathing difficulties, have severely hindered any attempts at escape. Severe fire damage was caused to ninety percent of the second floor, and there was heat and smoke damage to the third, fourth and fifth floors. Ten people lost their lives, twenty-six were rescued by the fire brigade, six others assisted from the building, forty-seven people removed to hospital, and six firefighters incurred slight injuries.

THE 1980s

FIRE AT THE TOP RANK BINGO HALL, MILL STREET, LUTON

At 0335 hours on 28th December 1982, Bedfordshire Fire Brigade control received a 999 call to a fire at the Top Rank Bingo Hall, Mill Street, Luton, a brick-built, detached building of four floors and a basement, and three appliances from Luton fire station were dispatched. The night was to end with two firefighters being trapped in a structural collapse, a number of others injured, and one, Georgy Gray Celine, earning the Queen's Gallantry Medal; firefighter Celine later wrote of the incident:

> I was riding Luton's Water Tender Ladder, with Sub Officer Puttock in charge of a crew of five. We knew we did not have very far to go before reaching our destination, and as is always the case en-route to a fire, the crew cab was a beehive of activity with every member of the crew getting their fire kit on, whilst at the same time anticipating the braking, swerving action of the appliance on its way to an emergency call, by now of course the adrenalin was in full flow.

> Upon arrival the driver parked his appliance before the entrance to the 'Top Rank' car-park, immediately opposite the Bingo Hall. Sub Officer Puttock leapt from the appliance to survey the situation, and liaised with Sub Officer Kelso whose appliance was first in attendance. Sub Officer Kelso immediately 'made pumps six'. Upon his return Sub Officer Puttock ordered all crew members, bar the pump operator, to get rigged in BA. He turned round and said 'George you come with me'. I did so as quickly as possible; meanwhile Fm Jeffries and Fm Harding had also rigged in BA. I followed the Sub Officer

to the car park entrance, and we made our way up the fire escape and across the flat roof to the first floor level double exit doors. Upon arrival Fm Sexton had already set up BA entry control. A team of BA wearers consisting of Fm Steve Markham and Fm Charlie Ingle had already gone in taking with them a charged length [of hose] to fight the fire.

Prior to entry I realised my tally [a rectangular identity tag giving various pieces of relevant and perhaps critical information, including the BA wearers name, rank, the air pressure of the BA cylinder, and time of entry to the risk] was missing. I informed Sub Officer Puttock of my mishap, he then asked me to go back and find it. I quickly retraced my steps checking along the way for signs of my tally only to find it on the seat in the crew cab. I quickly made my way to BA control only to find that Sub Officer Puttock and Fm Jeffries had already entered. I now had a new BA wearer partner Fm Harding. The orders from the BA control officer were to standby awaiting entry as when needed.

Looking back, that unfortunate mishap meant that I was left outside. Knowing what was to follow that night my only conclusion is that fate and luck must have played a big part in my involvement.

At this juncture appliances arrived from Toddington and Dunstable, and the first and second floors, and the roof were now heavily involved in fire, which was being fought from inside the building by six BA wearers with two lines of hose. By 0406 hours the fire had broken through the roof, and Divisional Officer Whitam who had by now taken command of the incident requested the attendance of a turntable ladder to direct a jet of water from above through the break in the roof to attack the seat of the fire. As the fire developed Senior Divisional Officer Higgins, who had now assumed control of operations, and Divisional Officer Witham had both entered the burning building in order to make a critical risk assessment of the incident as felt and seen by their BA crews, and decided that as the fire situation had deteriorated significantly, and as the condition of the structure was highly unstable, they would order all personnel to withdraw. Consequently, the evacuation signal was sounded.

It was now approximately 0418 hours, and as the officers began to make their way down the stairs to exit the Bingo Hall, the roof suddenly collapsed into the lower floors, bringing down tons of steel work, hot masonry and burning timber. Higgins found himself trapped by the collapse on the staircase, with his head and the right side of body pinned against a wall, and although able to move his left hand did not have sufficient strength or leverage to free himself. Seeing DO Witham further down the stair he shouted to him for help, and despite being hit by an avalanche of masonry and burning timber, Witham returned to Higgins and proceeded to pull him free. Firefighter Celine continued in his statement:

> I noticed Sub Officer Ridgley [from] Toddington about to go in, and prior to making an entry he turned around and shouted 'George watch that building, the fire's broken right through the length of the roof.' Words of wisdom I shall never forget, which had the desired effect of increasing my awareness of the seriousness of the situation. It brought home to me our close proximity in relation to the building, approximately one or two feet away from the outside walls. I was then frequently and nervously checking the eaves where heavy dense smoke was issuing, and generally looking along the length of the building.

Whilst waiting at the BA entry control point with firefighter Ray Harding, Celine looked up to again check the condition of the wall, and to his horror saw it was, as if in slow motion, falling outwards. Shouting a warning to his comrades, Celine and the other firefighters ran for safety. Returning to Georgy Celine's narrative:

> It was then a case of every man looking out for himself. I turned away from the wall and sprinted … Suddenly whilst in full flight I heard the crashing down of bricks and masonry behind me with a tremendous impact and deafening noise. I suddenly realised that I was out of running space as the railings at roof top level loomed up. It suddenly occurred to me to put 'the brakes on' before crashing into the barriers, or going over the top. Trying as hard as I could I was slowing down, and I suddenly began to lose balance and control and ended in a heap crashing against the barrier. Crisis over I turned around and shouted to Fm Harding, who then answered my call. Up to this day I shall never know how either of us made it; but we did by a whisker … I turned round to see the full damage done by the impact. Seconds prior to the collapse Fm Sexton had been checking the safety of the breathing apparatus wearers just inside the building, this action I learned later was due to Martin [Fm Sexton] having heard the evacuation whistle sounding to warn the BA wearers of the immediate danger. As he moved back to safety in the doorway of the double exit doors the collapse occurred. It is said that due to the tons of falling masonry and brickwork, the sheer weight of which cleaved through ten foot x ten foot in sections of reinforced concrete beams, Fm Sexton standing directly in the door way was sucked as a vacuum cleaner … picking up dust, from the 1st floor level to the ground floor and landed amongst tons of masonry and brickwork.

Celine left his place of safety by the barriers and moved quickly to the large gaping hole that opened up the flat roof, and shouted to firefighter Sexton, who acknowledged his comrade. As the smoke and dust momentarily cleared Celine could see a figure lying amongst brick and rubble trying to remove a large piece of brickwork from his chest. The collapse also trapped firefighter Markham who had become wedged between the wreckage of the upper floors and an exterior wall. Fortunately he was able to free himself and crawled through the debris to where Ingle was lying under the wreckage with only his hand protruding, and made a concerted effort to release him. Clearing away part of the debris Markham realised that Ingle was pinned down by a rolled steel joist, which he attempted to move. Realising the futility of his solo efforts, and with the fire situation intensifying, and urged by Ingle, Markham made his way out to alert the others and bring assistance.

All of the firefighters outside responded with the greatest urgency to this call for assistance, and Celine entered the building via a ledge, which was a precarious remnant of the flat roof, and passing firefighter Markham asked the whereabouts of Ingle. After following Markham's directions he located Ingle by the light on the encroaching fire, lying on his side trapped beneath a steel joist with rubble and bricks amassed on top. Whilst Celine worked to remove the debris Ingle informed him that he had broken his right leg. A quick glance towards the lower half of his body confirmed this as his right leg and the toe cap of his fire boot were facing completely the wrong way, and protruding from of the rubble. The steel joist which ran the length of the building had come down during the collapse, with one end of it still lodged against an unsupported wall, and the other end bypassing fireman Ingle, and pinning him down by his left shoulder, whilst the framework of his BA set took the weight. Having gained a better appreciation of Ingle's situation Celine suggested to him that if his BA set could be taken off they might be able to free him. He then proceeded to undo the shoulder straps, but because of the position and weight of the joist he was unable to remove Ingle's BA set. At this point Jeffries joined Celine and they continued to clear the debris from the lower half of Ingle's body, and managed to remove the obstructions from his fractured leg. Despite the pain, and great trauma, Ingle remained cool and calm. After checking Ingle's cylinder pressure, which indicated that he was running out of air, Celine left the scene of the rescue operations to bring jacking equipment. Celine takes up the story once more:

> I started to make my way out of the building, where upon I met Sub Officer
> Puttock who was nursing an injured right shoulder. I informed him that
> fireman Jeffries was with fireman Ingle, and that required 'EPCO' (hydraulic
> jacking equipment). Due to the temperature rising uncomfortably around
> fireman Ingle and fireman Jeffries I asked him if he could hold back the fire
> using what was available, a burst length of hose. He did so, remaining until his
> BA cylinder emptied, then he released his face mask and stayed at his post
> until he was relieved. I carried on making my way out of the building
> whereupon reaching the double exit doors I found a ladder bridged to the

remains of the flat roof. I made my way across the bridged ladder on all fours, meanwhile my face mask started to mist-up. Upon arriving at the other end I reported to Sub Officer Kelso, informing him that fireman Ingle was running out of air, that fresh BA cylinders and 'EPCO' would be needed.

I then made my way back across the bridged ladder to fireman Ingle who was attempting to dislodge his facemask which by now, due to his cylinder emptying, was hitting his face. I quickly removed his face mask and found him to be breathing comfortably, and decided to remove my own facemask and close down my BA set. I told fireman Ingle that help was on its way, at the same time surveying the extent of damage … occasionally roof sections and debris came crashing down around us.

By now the heat inside the ruined building was becoming unbearable for the trapped man, and Celine directed the firefighters working a jet of water near to them so that they could get better access to the blaze and control its spread. Once this was achieved dense clouds of steam enveloped both casualty and rescuers, however the roar from the fires still burning beneath them, and the obvious unsteadiness of the walls gave Celine grave concerns for the welfare of Ingle as they awaited the arrival of the hydraulic rescue equipment.

Suddenly fireman Ingle spoke out and said 'George if we cut through these straps I reckon I'll be out'. So simple but under pressure I never thought of it, I had tried everything else. I quickly asked for a knife, by this time Sub Officer Kelso, fireman Deegan and DO Witham were at the entrance … and Kelso then made his way to me and handed me his knife. I cut through the straps and fireman Ingle was free. I started to drag him inch by inch and had moved him approximately four or five feet when DO Witham came up and assisted me. I had my BA set on but was tiring as fatigue had set in, as is always the case under stressful situations, therefore I decided to remove my [breathing apparatus] set and helmet. We then immobilised fireman Ingle's leg, [with] DO Witham at his feet, myself taking his body weight, we lifted and dragged fireman Ingle to the double exit doors where assistance from Sub Officer Kelso and fireman Deegan helped us get him onto a stretcher on the bridging ladder. Assisting on the ladder was fireman Bellingham to whom fireman Ingle turned and said 'Malcolm I never thought I would say this but I am glad to see you!' The joy, jubilation and cheer of fireman Ingle and the rest of the crew at that particular moment is one I'll always savour. I remember returning to the station absolutely drained and shattered along with the others. The next day the atmosphere … was that of being at a morgue. Those who were not on duty heard the story of what happened at Mill Street. We all realised and knew how lucky we had been as a watch, instead of two injured it could have been nine firemen dead!

The rescue of Martin Sexton was carried out by the Toddington crew who proceeded to the second floor via an external escape to commence rescue operations. Having gained access to the second floor level they found that the conditions required them to don breathing apparatus. Referring again to firefighter Celine's statement:

Before leaving to provide a BA team, and a jet, Sub Officer Ridgley instructed both myself at flat roof level and fireman Witts at second floor level to watch above as the main roof was heavily involved with fire. As he left a collapse occurred and he managed to jump clear onto a fire escape, and as the debris settled he saw at ground level amongst the rubble a yellow fire helmet. A ladder was counter balanced and dropped to the ground floor, he then climbed down the ladder to the ground floor. As he rounded a support pillar he found fireman Leonard who had been at second floor level already there rendering aid to fireman Sexton. Fireman Leonard had on his own initiative worked his way from the second floor to the ground via the building, which was heavily smoke logged, with BA or firefighting equipment. He had located fireman Sexton and was in the process of removing him … After having cleared the debris fireman Leonard then lifted Sexton onto Sub Officer Ridgley's back and between them they carried him through the ground floor out in to Mill Street to an awaiting ambulance.

The supplement to the *London Gazette* of 9th August 1984 which announced the award of the Queen's Gallantry Medal to firefighter Georgy Gray Celine reads:

Celine dug with his bare hands to remove the debris, constantly reassuring the trapped firefighter, who by now was in some pain from his injuries. The rescue work, involving the manual removal of brickwork, masonry and timber, progressed in cramped and difficult conditions directly underneath several tons of unsupported roofing and debris. The remaining structure of the surrounding building was known to be dangerous and further burning debris continued to fall intermittently on the area of the rescue operation. The successful extrication of the trapped firefighters was achieved after some thirty minutes. Celine's readiness to put himself in considerable danger over a prolonged period displayed gallantry of a high order'.

FIRE ON THE MV POINTSMAN

On the 15th June, 1984 an improbable chain of events took place which was to place great demands on the courage, commitment and total professionalism of Dyfed County

Fire Brigade in a combination of two of the operational scenarios most feared by firefighters: a ship fire, and a flash-over.

The whole situation was one that, in theory, should not have occurred, as is so often the case when such disasters happen. The pump room of the MV Pointsman, a coastal tanker of 4,620 tonnes with a crew of thirteen, had been declared gas free by a reputable firm of chemists, and experienced dockyard workers and ships' officers were detailed to commence repair work on what should have been a standard maintenance job. Unfortunately, this routine task resulted in four fatalities, and serious injuries to a further eleven persons, including nine firefighters.

After discharging a large quantity of diesel oil, the Pointsman left Avon Docks so that work on two valves and other ancillary work could be carried out. During the voyage certain tanks were in ballast and others were washed and rendered gas free. Number four centre tank had been designated as the main slop tank, to which all contaminated washings would be pumped; and the tank cleaning was commenced under the supervision of the Chief Officer. Prior to the last cargo, the pump room stripping lines had been drained into a slop tank, which was located beneath the deck plating, and would have contained a mixture of petroleum spirit, diesel oil and water. The contents of this slop tank were reported to have been transferred into starboard wing tank number three, which already contained ballast. This had necessitated the removal of the bolted cover from the manhole of the pump room slop tank, and the lowering of a 'water driven eductor'. This operation was begun at midnight.

Evidence given in statements by the crew indicated that the liquid residue was removed, the tank freed, the gasket replaced, and the hatch cover re-secured. Unfortunately only one stud out of a possible twenty was in place; three other of the studs had nuts seized on to them, and were used as bolts leaving sixteen of the designed fastenings unused. The stud holes in use, did not however, penetrate through to the slop tank. The pump room itself was then washed with hand held hoses and gas freed by means of a fan blowing air into the pump room.

The Captain ascertained from the crew that everywhere was gas free before proceeding to Milford and tying up at 0700 hours at Hakin Wharf. Sometime after midday, water was found in the number two port tank, and work carried out to remove it, and despite gas free certificates being issued, a smell of gas oil was noticed, and a fan brought into use. Shortly after 1.30 pm two dockyard workers prepared to commence work in the pump room taking with them a fire extinguisher and oxyacetylene cutting equipment, which was fed via lines from cylinders left on the quayside. Two members of the crew were also working in the pump room at this time, replacing a seal on the starboard pump. These four persons were later confirmed as the four fatal casualties.

The first explosion occurred at about 2.30 that afternoon. The ship's Chief Officer attempted to rescue the casualties with breathing apparatus and a torch, but succeeded only in an attempt at ventilation by opening the trunking hatch of the fan. He did in fact locate one casualty and later assisted firefighters by indicating the area of search. The Captain of the vessel initiated the call to the fire brigade by radio and Dyfed County Fire Brigade Control who dispatched two pumping appliances from Milford Haven, and the duty Station Officer mobilised.

As the first appliance arrived the smoke increased dramatically and the Master of the vessel turned off the fan as the fire was still burning and the smoke was being driven from the pump room and forcing any would-be rescuers away from the pump room door. The officer-in-charge of the first appliance on being appraised of the situation ordered two breathing apparatus wearers to take a line of hose into the ship, and sent an assistance message requesting another pumping appliance, and the attendance of an emergency tender. A further message from the Station Officer requesting that a further two pumps (making five altogether) and a foam tanker be sent. Meanwhile the first and second BA crews, that is four firefighters all together, with the advice and assistance of the Chief Officer had located a casualty who was found two levels down.

The Deputy Divisional Commander for the area, Divisional Officer Mike George, an experienced and well respected officer of twenty-one years' service, was at Pembroke dock fire station when he was informed by the brigade control room of this fire. Realising that this vessel was an oil tanker, he instructed the mobilising staff to designate the incident as a 'Category 2' call, which was the local procedure for occurrences involving oil tankers and refineries, and provided for a predetermined attendance of five pumps and four special appliances. After a ten-minute drive Divisional Officer George arrived at Milford Docks, where he was briefed on the situation by Station Officer Phillips. He then assumed command of the incident, and boarding the vessel went to the pump room at the main deck level, where he saw a ring of fire below him, which suggested a fire around the manhole lid.

Terry Langdon, leading an unusually large team of BA wearers consisting of one other whole-time firefighter and four retained firefighters – Bellerby, Mayne, Kingston, Ormond and J. Davies – had managed to penetrate the lower compartments, despite the atrocious and potentially deadly conditions which prevailed, and located the Second Engineer who was lying above the pumps, and so difficult to access and rescue. Ignoring the fire which was now developing in the pump room, Langdon and another firefighter managed to carry the casualty to a vertical ladder to be hauled up by firefighters on the upper level; an arduous task when encumbered by BA, restricted by confined spaces, and whilst suffering the effects of heat. Landon and his team had entered well knowing that a flash-over had already occurred, and given the extreme heat, that there was every chance of further flame explosions. The knowledge of the risks involved did not deter them from giving 100% in searching for the unfortunate casualties.

The first crews were at this time struggling with the casualty to get him to main deck level. A third BA team had entered the pump room by this time and the casualty was moved to the pump room door. DO George then lifted the casualty over the combing and ordered the BA crews below to search for further casualties. In his report on the Pointsman incident, Divisional Officer George wrote:

> I went into the pump room at main deck level, and found conditions to be hot with light smoke. I looked over the rail and could see a small fire below my position. I could hear the BA men coming closer. A few minutes later the BA men came into sight. They were carrying a casualty who I could hear moaning. I called to the Station Officer to send in another BA team to assist. I took the casualty from the BA men, and instructed them to go back down
>
> ...

By now further crews had arrived, and an Assistant Divisional Officer who was now in attendance had the presence of mind to ensure that the oxyacetylene cylinders on the quayside were turned off. As the Ship's Engineer was being placed on a stretcher outside the pump room door, an explosion occurred. Again referring to Mike George's statement:

> As I emerged through the door I saw other firemen on deck, fireman Warlow amongst them. From this point I am a little confused as to what happened next. I think that I was bending forward about to place the injured man onto the stretcher, ... when there was an explosion which came from the pump room behind me. I was thrown forward onto the deck. I think that I dropped the casualty. All round me people were down. The BA teams started coming out of the pump room. They were totally disorientated and burnt. Leading fireman Mayne and fireman Kingston were the first I saw emerge. I pulled them all clear because they were exhausted and had become tangled in a rope. At this point I thought I was the last man on board but looking down into the scuppers I saw a naked and burnt person, the original casualty. I picked him up and placed him on the stretcher, and called for assistance to remove him from the ship.

This second of three explosions caused injury not only to those mentioned above, but to Ambulance Service officers who were in the vicinity, and less serious injuries were sustained by other persons who were further away from the door. DO George was thrown some nine or ten feet across the deck, and although badly burnt on his back, remained at the scene and played a major role in bringing other injured personnel from that deck. Despite his injuries George remained in control of what was by now an extremely serious and confused situation, which was made all the more critical by having a number of persons still unaccounted for including one of the BA wearers, firefighter Terrance Langdon, who had been missing for two minutes. Following the second flash-over, and due to his leading position in the rescue team, Langdon found himself alone and with severe burns to his hands and legs. Realising perhaps that assistance was not immediately available, he negotiated two ladders, and all the obstructions of the valve deck to make his way through the blinding smoke out of the pump room unaided. It was considered that his injuries would have made the climb of the first vertical ladder an extremely difficult task. He reached his colleagues before any organised rescue attempt could be implemented. Referring to this in his report Divisional Officer George said:

'I checked the BA entry control board when I left the ship and was informed that … fireman Langdon had failed to withdraw. At this point there were no able bodied men or BA sets to make an immediate entry and search but coming down the jetty were fresh crews from supporting appliances. I instructed ADO Caunt to get BA teams down into the ship to carry out a rescue. It was just then that fireman Langdon made his way onto the deck. He was disorientated, confused and burnt.'

Consequent to this explosion the decision was made to flood the compartment with high-expansion foam, in the hope of mitigating further injuries and preventing an escalation of the situation. The fire-ground commander was aware at this stage that at least one person was still to be brought from the pump room, and as the equipment was being laid out on board to facilitate this strategy, the third explosion took place injuring the two firefighters who were handling this foam-making equipment. Jets that had been laid out as a precautionary measure were used to spray the injured persons and their clothes, before being transported to hospital. Fresh breathing apparatus crew pushed their way through the claustrophobic miasma of high expansion foam, which not only created a dangerously slippery surface for them to move over, but deadened their hearing and completely obliterated their vision, to search for the two persons still unaccounted for, with ever present possibility of further explosions. Due to these conditions and the extremely confined space they were working in, the casualties were not rescued until 17:40 hours. Regular testing of the atmosphere in the pump room gave readings of 100% flammable vapours present, and following the recovery of all casualties personnel were removed to a safe distance and further readings taken periodically. The fire service remained in attendance over the next 48 hours whilst further readings were taken.

Divisional Officer Mike George and Fireman Terry Langdon displayed outstanding devotion to duty, a complete disregard for personal safety, and bravery of a high order throughout the rescue attempt, and were awarded the Queen's Gallantry Medal. Their investiture by the Queen was shown in Her Majesty's Christmas broadcast, to the great pride of all members of the Fire Service.

THE KINGS CROSS STATION FIRE

On the evening of Wednesday 18th November 1987 a total of thirty-one people died and more than sixty received injuries ranging from severe burns to smoke inhalation, at a major underground conflagration at King's Cross underground station, London. Amongst the fatalities was Station Officer Colin James Townsley, who attended the incident as officer-in-charge of the first fire appliance to arrive at the scene.

The terminus for two main rail lines, King's Cross has a labyrinth of tunnels and passageways leading to the five underground lines which converge below its concourse; it was, and presumably still is, London's busiest Tube station.

At approximately 1915 hours a small fire was discovered at the bottom of the Victoria line escalator and extinguished by Leading Railwayman Brickell. Had London Fire Brigade been informed of the outbreak at this time, it is reasonable to suppose that a full and effective firefighting operation would have been commenced some ten or twelve minutes earlier, and that the development of combustion which led to the flashover would have been avoided. Fourteen minutes later a passenger, using one of the escalators, noticed white smoke coming from beneath the wooden escalator on which he was travelling, and reported this to a ticket-clerk within the booking hall, and another passenger seeing smoke, hit the Emergency Stop Button bringing the escalator to a halt, and gave warning to the people behind him. Again had the Fire Brigade been informed even at this juncture the outcome may well have been very different.

Another passenger gave an account of seeing smoke and flames under the escalator and, on reaching the concourse area, informed two Police Officers of his concerns; these Officers had noticed the passenger hit the Stop Button and were in the process of investigating the matter. As the escalator stopped, another passenger at the bottom also noticed smoke, this time grey with flames, underneath the escalator steps. This passenger then made her way to another escalator and upon reaching the top, she informed a member of the London Transport Police. Both of the police officers went to the top of the escalator where the fire had been seen, and could see thicker smoke, but no fire from this point. One of the police officers went up to street level in order to summon assistance on his police radio.

This first call was received by London Fire Brigade's Wembley control room at 1934 hours, and an initial attendance of four pumping appliances and a turntable ladder were dispatched; plus Forward Control, and an Area Control Units. King's Cross is on Euston fire station's ground, but Euston's appliances were already attending an incident, and so Soho having the next nearest available appliances was mobilised.

When Soho's Pump Ladder crew arrived at 1942 hours they positioned their appliance next to the St. Pancras entrance of King's Cross, and Townsley with a crew of three firefighters entered the station concourse to investigate the call, where they should have been met and briefed by a member of London Underground staff. By this time British Transport Police officers took the initiative and commenced an evacuation of the station. Incoming trains were prevented from stopping, and passengers diverted from the Piccadilly Line escalator to that of the Victoria Line; which may have led to the death or injury of some people. However, those police officers could not possibly have foreseen that a flash-over would occur, and that it would engulf that area.

At first the Soho crew could find no signs of a fire, but upon reaching the top of number four escalator, they could see a fire burning some twenty feet down from the top of this escalator. Station Officer Townsley ordered his crew to return to the appliance and rig in breathing apparatus. The next appliance, a pump ladder from Clerkenwell arrived and the officer-in-charge, Sub-Officer Bell, entered the station concourse with his crew, and smelling smoke ordered them to return and rig in breathing apparatus. He then met with Station Officer Townsley, and together the two officers made a rapid assessment of the situation. Standing between escalators five and six at the head of the Piccadilly Line escalators, they could see a fire burning about halfway down escalator four, with flames licking up to the handrail and the fire extended across two treads of the stair; both firefighters ventured further down to make a more detailed reconnaissance. In evidence at the Fennel enquiry Sub-Officer Bell stated that at this time 'It looked like a fire as might be produced by a large cardboard box,' and that there were no signs of the paintwork on the ceiling blistering or catching fire. Townsley then returned to the ticket hall and ordered two breathing apparatus wearers to get a jet to work, and asked for a message to be returned to fire-control advising that this incident was 'Persons reported'.

At 1939 a passenger, Mr Asquith, with his wife went down the subway to the underground station, to find the entrance to the tube lines ticket hall closed. Proceeding to the next entrance they found the atmosphere hazy and hot, and here Mrs Asquith began to experience some difficulty in breathing. Mr Asquith, looking into the tube lines ticket hall through the entrance to the way-out barrier, noted that it was fairly smoky, but there were no signs of panic in either passengers or Underground staff. Turning away after hearing some-one shouting 'get out', he saw a great cloud of black billowing smoke rushing towards him, and immediately felt an enormous blast of hot gases. Asquith and his wife were, fortunately, able to make good their escape, and later was able to state that he had not seen black smoke in the tube tickets hall before turning away; this was immediately before the flash-over.

From 1943 there was rapid worsening of conditions in the tube lines ticket hall, and at 1945 hours, within two minutes of the first crew reaching that area, the flash-over occurred. As a result, the top of the escalators, the tube lines' ticket hall and the surrounding passages were quickly engulfed in flames, and clouds of thick black choking smoke bellowed across the ceiling of the concourse forcing fire crews, police officers, London Underground staff and passengers to retreat rapidly in various directions. Police constable Dixon, who having escaped via the exit to the south side of Euston Road, and after leading a colleague, PC Hanson, to the street, immediately radioed the British Transport Police control room, and informed them of a major incident at King's Cross underground station. Shortly before the flashover PC Hanson was a short distance down escalator nine on the Victoria Line urging people to evacuate the area, when he became aware of dense smoke in the ticket hall, and so went to investigate. When he got about five feet into the hall he saw: '…what I can only describe as a large wall of flame or fire. It was definitely above head high, and immediately following this was like a whoosh … and a large ball of flame, which was about head height, hit the ceiling in the ticket hall itself. This was followed almost instantaneously by dense black smoke … To be more accurate I would say it was a jet of flame that shot up and then collected into a kind of ball. I saw it shoot up across the top of number four, and collect along the roofing…'

Another traveller, Mr Arari Minta, as he neared the top of escalator seven, saw flames shoot from his left and then quickly disappear. He then saw a man at the top, believed to be PC Hanson, who urged them to evacuate, pointing to the way-out barrier. Mr Minta then saw a tremendous flash from his left which hit the man who had been directing them to the exit. The flames then spread across the tube lines ticket hall accompanied by black smoke. Mr Minta dived under the flames, which had not reached the floor level and escaped to the Circle line platform, where he was evacuated by train to Farringdon station, having sustained severe burns.

Very few of the people who were in the tube lines ticket office at this time survived, and most of those who did were seriously injured.

Station Officer Osborne from Manchester Square then ran to the Victoria line escalator and shouted for the passengers coming up the escalator to run back down to escape the fire. At this point he met a badly burned man, and after helping him to the bottom of the escalator, he found a fire extinguisher and used it to cool the unfortunate man's burns. Evidence given at the investigation chaired by Mr Desmond Fennell QC indicated that a firefighter in a white helmet was seen moving across the concourse with a torch encouraging passengers and staff to evacuate, which pointed to the fact that instead of making good his escape, Station Officer Townsley had purposely remained in an extremely dangerous area. Whilst there, he saw a woman who had succumbed to the heat and smoke, and went to her assistance; however, Townsley also collapsed due to the intense heat and overwhelming smoke. In only seconds, a mass of heat, smoke and flames had erupted from the head of number four escalator, completely engulfing the station concourse. The fire crew from Clerkenwell did not even have time to start up their BA sets, they had no option but to run for their lives, dragging passengers to safety at the same time. During this time they could hear the screams of those caught in the flames of the concourse.

Station Officer Townsley's body was found at the foot of the steps leading up to the St. Pancras Road entrance, his fit kit almost untouched by the heat; lying beside him was the badly burnt body of Miss Elizabeth Byers, the passenger he given his life trying to save. Part of the citation for the award of the George Medal to Station Officer Townsley in the supplement to the *London Gazette* reads as follows:

'To safeguard the public Station Officer Townsley remained near the top of the escalators. At approximately 7.45 pm, there was a sudden and dramatic increase in temperature, a build-up of dense acrid smoke, and fire flashed over the concourse ceiling. Within seconds the concourse was plunged into total darkness. Panic ensued as passengers rushed for the exit points, Station Officer Townsley remained in the booking hall area to assist as best he could those seeking to escape until he was overcome by toxic fumes. He was found lying on the floor close to a badly burned woman. Station Officer Townsley with total disregard for his own safety, had remained within the concourse without breathing apparatus to assist passengers to escape until he was overcome by intense smoke and heat. He displayed selfless devotion to duty and gallantry of a high order when faced with conditions of extreme danger.'

When Sub-Officer Bell reached the bottom of the Piccadilly Line escalators, he began clearing people from the area and tried to prevent them using the moving staircase; he also told the passengers to get back onto the train. At this stage the fire was burning from the steps and side of the escalator, up round the ceiling and back down onto the stair, and flames were curling up the escalator shaft. Bell attacked the fire with a jet of water from a hose positioned in the area, which would, very likely, not have had the pressure that fire brigade hose would have. He was not aware that his colleagues on the surface believed him dead by this time.

When the flash-over occurred Station Officer Osborne was in the Tube Lines ticket hall at the head of Victoria Line escalator shaft, when he saw what looked like a flame-thrower, which by good fortune did not strike, as it burst through. He shouted at passengers to get clear, and saw a badly burnt man come out from the cloud of smoke. Osborne took the man to a place of comparative safety, and used a portable fire extinguisher to put out the man's burning clothes, and give some relief to his pain. Police constables Martland and Kukielka then evacuated the man.

On the surface, fire crews found themselves in an unusual position in an escalating and extremely serious situation, as the officers in charge of three of the pumping appliances were missing, and so the direction of the firefighting operations had fallen upon their shoulders. Firefighters Moulton, Button and Flanagan showed great initiative, and made determined efforts to get into the tube lines' ticket hall in breathing apparatus, but the heat was so intense they were driven back, until Moulton again entered with firefighters Edgar and Button, using their hose to spray his back, so keeping the temperature to a bearable level for brief periods. An extract from the citation for the award of the Queen's Gallantry Medal to Fireman Richard Edward Moulton reads as follows:

> Whilst he was engaged in running out several hose lines and rigging in breathing apparatus, dense, acrid smoke began to pour from the subway entrance. On entering the subway, Fireman Moulton and his two colleagues were confronted by a surge of intense heat and smoke. They were forced to penetrate the subway crawling on their stomachs under cover of jet's spray. They managed to recover a badly burned woman and carry her back to street level where they tried to revive her without success. Fireman Moulton and his colleagues then re-entered the subway. Again, they were forced to crawl on the stomachs because of the heat. Moving past his colleagues Fireman Moulton crawled ahead, disappearing into the intense heat and smoke. At this point he found Station Officer Townsley on the floor. He crawled back past his colleagues to seek the assistance of two other firemen and, with them, carried Station Officer Townsley to street level. Fireman Moulton and another fireman sought to revive Station Officer Townsley until an ambulance crew and a doctor took over. Although at this point physically and mentally exhausted, fireman Moulton once more entered the station and became involved in search and rescue activities until he was withdrawn.
>
> Fireman Moulton working to the limits of his endurance, displayed devotion to duty and gallantry of a high order by repeatedly penetrating the intense heat and smoke, by locating, rescuing and attempting to resuscitate two victims of the fire, and by returning to help with yet further search and rescue work until ordered to withdraw'.

Leading Fireman Stewart Button and Fireman John Edgar were awarded the Queen's Commendation for Brave Conduct, as were Sub Officer Vernon Ronald Trefry, and Fireman Paul Henry Hale.

A number of British transport Police officers had been drafted into the King's Cross area that evening. Two such officers were Terry Alan Bebbington and John Leonard Kerbey. The former officer was in a staff security room in the booking hall area when the fire was first observed, and he summoned the fire brigade via his radio, and after conferring with three other police officers, he left the other to meet the first fire appliances and two to help with the evacuation, whilst he made his way down to the Piccadilly Line platforms to assist with the redirection of passengers. He then assisted a firefighter (who had been prevented by the flash-over from returning to the surface to equip himself with a hose and breathing equipment) to fight the fire, which had by this time enveloped the whole of the shaft, with a line of hose from the platform. As the two men moved through the smoke and up the escalator with the jet, fluorescent light tubes were bursting with the heat, burning fabric was dropping from the ceiling and at one point a large metal handrail shot down on them with some force. Although Bebbington was neither trained nor equipped for such severe conditions, he showed gallantry and great commitment to his duty by remaining with the firefighter, as they made three attempts to ascend the burning stairway, until beaten back by the intolerable conditions which prevailed.

In the meantime PC Stephen Hanson together with PC Kenneth Kerbey were attempting to direct a constant and heavy flow of passengers, who were ascending the Victoria Line escalator, out of the station; as the rising temperature and acrid smoke gradually made their situation untenable. When the flash-over came it knocked Hanson to the floor, and despite the flames swirling down almost to floor level, he crawled under the intense heat and smoke to the head of that stairway and shouted to passengers to keep low and get out by the nearest exit. As the heat intensified, he made good his escape by vaulting over a closed barrier and crawled to where he estimated the exit to be, where he located a casualty on the floor whom he attempted to rescue, but because of his burnt hands he was unable to take hold of the casualty. Before emerging from the Euston Road south exit he collided with a glass panel, causing further damage to his right hand. He was then taken to hospital where he was treated for extensive burns to his hands and face, as well smoke inhalation. Both Bebbington and Hanson were awarded the Queen's Gallantry Medal, and Kerbey, Dixon, Kukielka and Martland the Queen's Commendation for Brave Conduct.

At 1949 hours, four minutes after the flash-over, Assistant Divisional Officer Shore of Euston fire station arrived, and was confronted by an unusual and confused situation as there were no officers in charge of crews to brief him, as Townsley, Osborne and Bell were missing, and there was no London Underground staff to guide him. Assuming command of what was by now a potentially major and disastrous incident he relayed a message to fire-control to 'Make pumps twelve'. On arriving at King's Cross, fire crews were faced with the sight of thick smoke punching from the exits of the underground station, and as they entered with their charged hose lines they were met by a wall of heat so extreme and overpowering as to be impassable. This situation was exacerbated by the tube trains which were still running below ground, as each time a train entered the station it propelled great volumes of air upwards, and into the concourse and then leaving drew air from the surface, so acting as giant and hellish bellows feeding the inferno. Amazingly many passengers were still escaping the fire, although many of them were severely burned, and all having to be given assistance by the emergency services.

By 2015 Deputy Assistant Chief Officer Wilson arrived and took command, and was informed that some brigade personnel were unaccounted for, that three had been removed to hospital (including Station Officer Townsley), and that a roll call was being carried out. Wilson then sent a further assistance message at 2019 hours to the effect of 'Make pumps twenty', and coordinated the work of various control units, made efforts to obtain plans of the underground area, which were delivered at around 2053 hours. Prior to this the fire brigade had to rely on the assistance of a British Rail manager who was able to draw a plan of the area for them. DACO Wilson held command for twenty-six minutes until Assistant Chief Officer Kennedy arrived and took charge at 2041 hours. As there were at least fifty persons still involved, numerous breathing apparatus wearers working in extremely arduous conditions, many suffering from the effects of heat, and smoke inhalation, ACO Kennedy ordered on another ten pumping appliances.

The fire crews worked in nightmare conditions with heat so intense that it would melt a firefighter's leggings, and brought dreadful and traumatising sights as body after burnt body was located in that subterranean furnace. Soon fire crews from outlying stations were arriving, alongside further police and ambulance vehicles. The Leading firefighter managing the BA entry control board outside was overwhelmed by the number of BA tallies he had to deal with; that is, one for each wearer giving the firefighter's name, rank, cylinder pressure, and the time of handing the tally to the Entry Control Officer prior to entering the risk. Normally a BA control board could hold a maximum of twelve tallies, and he had over forty to look after!

The report into this disaster, chaired by Mr Desmond Fennell QC, concluded that the fire was initiated by smokers' material, probably a carelessly discarded lighted match, which fell through the clearance between the steps and the skirting board on the right hand side of escalator four, and fell onto the running track where there was an excessive accumulation of readily ignitable grease and detritus.

On Friday 27th November the capital's streets came to a standstill as Londoners said goodbye to one of London Fire Brigade's finest, and Soho fire station said goodbye to their 'Guv'. The mortal remains of Station Officer Colin James Townsley were carried upon a turntable ladder to his final resting place, saluted by all organisations involved in the incident.

In his report of the disaster Mr Desmond Fennell QC said: 'There are two individuals whom I should like to mention. Station Officer Townsley died a hero's death, giving his life in an attempt to save another. Police Constable Hanson's presence of mind and courage must have enabled many people to escape with their lives. The Court salutes not only those two but all members of the public, the emergency services, and London Underground staff who helped others in any way. It is clear that a large number of members of the London Fire Brigade behaved with conspicuous courage and devotion to duty during the disaster in which they lost a very brave officer, Station Officer Townsley.'

THE 1990s TO
THE PRESENT DAY

THE AWARD OF THE GEORGE MEDAL TO FIREFIGHTER RODERICK MCKENZIE NICOLSON OF TAYSIDE FIRE BRIGADE

On Monday 4th December, 1995 Tayside Fire Brigade was called to the Daltrade warehousing facility located at Perth Harbour, after two men, Alistair Lockhart and Paul Martin, had become trapped in a forty-foot-high soda ash silo which they were in the process of cleaning, even though it had not been fully emptied of its contents. The two men had been drawn downwards and had sunk deeply into the remaining soda ash, which had stabilised as soon as the valve had been re-closed.

On the arrival of the first fire brigade attendance forty-three year-old firefighter Nic Nicolson was tasked with entering the silo via a narrow hatchway located at the top of the structure, and finding he was unable to gain access in his breathing apparatus, removed it on approval from the OIC. He then entered the silo and descended to the foot of the internal ladder, and once in position his BA set was then lowered to him, although he did not put it on as he needed to speak with those trapped. After firefighter Nicolson had reported the situation to the officer in charge safety lines were lowered into the silo, and placed around the two trapped men to secure them and prevent their sinking further and a further line was passed to Nic, for his own safety.

After discussion between firefighter Nicolson and the officer-in-charge, it was decided that it would be too dangerous to re-open the silo's bottom valve, for fear that the suction and additional movement of soda ash would further endanger the trapped men, and the decision was taken that a hole should be cut in the side of the silo to facilitate a rescue. Nic remained inside the silo with the trapped men, and as the cutting proceeded there was a non-consequential fall of loose soda ash from the sides of the silo, and one of the casualties was immediately buried.

Firefighter Nicolson, without any thought for his personal safety, made an instantaneous decision to immediately move from the foot of the vertical ladder and traverse across the surface of the soda ash to start digging it away from the face of the trapped individual. This required a tremendous amount of effort and courage and without doubt saved the life of the individual who was consumed by the soda ash. After making sure that the individual could breathe freely, Nicolson placed his body in a curved position around the man's head to prevent any further fall from burying the trapped man to any greater extent. At that moment, the soda ash below Nic started to move, and he immediately disappeared below the surface and himself became buried. Despite frantic rescue attempts by colleagues involving the use of air-lines, Nic lost his life. Ironically the two cleaners were both rescued alive: one of them, undoubtedly, as a result of firefighter Nicholson's immediate, courageous and selfless action.

Tayside Firemaster Derek Marr, speaking of the horrendous conditions in which his firefighters had worked said: 'I can only commend his courage in going to help members of the public. The circumstances require to be fully examined, but he became trapped and it took some time to extricate him. He lost his life through his brave actions.'

Firefighter Nicolson's wife spoke of her husband with the following quote:

> 'Nic' was a very quiet man with a dry sense of humour, and an accomplished artist having sold around 200 paintings by the time he died. Painting was his passion, his love of everything wild in nature came through in many of his seascapes and mountain paintings. His other love was music and was self taught on guitar, which he would take in on a night shift and have a little jam session with some of the boys. Eric Clapton was his idol but he wasn't quite as good as him! His great love was our daughter Amy, who was never away from his side. This, of course, was devastating for her when we lost him.
>
> What I would add about the fatal day was that Nic always thought everything through, he would add the pros and cons about all questions or problems. So on that day he had weighed up the situation, and unfortunately he got it wrong that time, it was probably the only time.

Firefighter Nicolson had served for twenty-one years with Tayside Fire Brigade. His wife Yvonne, accompanied by their daughter Amy, and family members were received in private by Her Majesty at Buckingham Palace on 24th February 1998, and presented with the George Medal which had been posthumously bestowed upon her husband Nic – a gallant and selfless firefighter; truly a Warrior in Fire Boots.

THE DEATH OF FIREFIGHTER FLEUR LOMBARD QGM

At 1246 hours on Sunday 4th February 1996, an emergency call was received by Avon Fire Brigade control reporting a fire at Leo's Supermarket, Broad Street, Staple Hill, Bristol. These premises were an amalgam of former buildings which had been extensively converted, inter-connected, extended and re-roofed, and occupied an 'L' shaped site. A total of twenty-four repeat fire calls were received for this incident, and within an hour ten pumping appliances were either in attendance or dispatched. Although a large, relatively difficult fire, and one that would be attributed to arson, it would not have claimed any place in Fire Service history, except for the fact it cost the life of a firefighter, Fleur Lombard.

Leo's Supermarket opened at 10:00 am that day with three members of staff at work including the duty manager Andrew Ellis, plus Martin James Cody, a security guard whose first day it was at that site. That morning was little different from any other Sunday, and a steady trickle of customers passed through the shop during the morning and lunchtime period. Sometime after twenty minutes to one Cody was standing near to the cigarette and newspaper kiosk where Mr Ellis was working, when two customers advised the manager that there was a fire near to the door leading to the warehouse. Ellis left the kiosk and went to investigate, whilst Cody went to the staff room and told a member of staff, Miss Claire Mountain, to call the fire brigade, and began shouting in 'a panicky voice' for a fire extinguisher. Having armed himself with a water extinguisher he made an attempt to tackle the blaze, before being ordered to leave the premises. One of the staff, Miss Louise Mains, left her checkout on hearing Mr Ellis shouting for everyone to leave, and later said that at that time she could see smoke at ceiling level. Fearing that some customers might still be in the shop she ran towards the rear of the premises to search, and found that flames were now visible, and noticing that the smoke was getting thicker, realised that the situation was more serious than she had anticipated. Running back to the checkout area she found a man pushing a shopping trolley, oblivious to the blaze now developing. Miss Mains brought him out of the shop.

Meanwhile, in the staff room, Miss Mountain was having difficulty passing the exact address of the supermarket to the fire brigade. When Mr Ellis entered the staff room he took over the telephone call and ordered her to leave; which she did making her way through the now choking black smoke to reach the exit. Whilst passing information to the fire brigade control Ellis became aware of the worsening situation because smoke was by this time drifting into the office. Ellis attempted to make good his escape, but found himself trapped by the smoke in the shop, and retreated to the kitchen, where he tried unsuccessfully to open a wire reinforced window, and had to resort to breaking it with a microwave oven, and climbing through the broken glass, aided by Cody and another man.

Firefighter Fleur Lombard Queen's Gallantry Medal.
Courtesy of Avon Fire Brigade.

During the seven minutes following the first call to the fire brigade at 1236 hours, a further ten messages were received from members of the public; the recordings of these communications later gave a strong indication to investigators of the rapid development of the fire. As the first appliance was arriving, a caller (the sixth) living in the vicinity of Leo's informed fire control that flames were showing from the roof of the supermarket; this was confirmed by Sub-Officer Haydon the officer-in-charge of that pump, and a message was immediately transmitted requesting a further two pumps. The crew immediately commenced firefighting operations from the car park at the rear of the premises with two jets being worked from ground level towards the roof and into the hole from which smoke was issuing. A minute later the second appliance arrived, and its crew commander Sub-Officer Davies took command of the incident as it was within his station area. After making an assessment of the wider situation with Haydon, Davies ordered two of his crew to rig in breathing apparatus, and instructed them to force an entry to the building through the fire exit door adjacent to the kitchen; which they did with a large axe. As the fire had reached the inside of the exit door the BA crew were ordered to make an entry with a jet. On entering the short corridor leading to the warehouse the team were aware of fire on both sides of the corridor, which they extinguished, and once they reached the entrance of the warehouse they could see that the fire had engulfed everything, and noticed the distinctive sound of popping asbestos.

When the third pumping appliance arrived at 1257 hours, it stopped in Broad Street initially to allow Station Officer Rodliff who was in charge to proceed on foot to assess the situation. As he did so he indicated to his driver to proceed into Byron Place and to park near to the customer entrance. He then made his way to the rear car park to confer with Sub-Officers Davies and Haydon, and he was followed by his breathing apparatus wearers, firefighters Rob Seaman and Fleur Lombard, who were rigged in BA, but had not started-up their sets. At this juncture Rodliff assumed command of the incident and decided that a new entry point be established through the main entrance on Byron Place, committing four BA wearers, two with a high pressure hose-reel, and two to lay a 200 foot guide-line, which would enable subsequent crews to search the premises methodically and eventually to retrace their steps to exit the risk. As firefighter Lombard was wearing the only BA set fitted with Sonic radio communications, she was designated team leader, and the bag holding the guide line was attached to her breathing apparatus harness. Her team partner, firefighter Seaman, attached the free end of the guide-line to a steel post next to the entry control officer's board, as the fourth appliance arrived at the scene.

At 1306 hours both teams made their initial entry into the heavily smoke-logged premises, and adopted the search technique of reaching out with the back of the hand in an a circular manner, and making arcs with the feet after each shuffling step, whilst keeping contact with the wall on their left hand side. Proceeding further into the store, some four minutes after the initial entry, the heat intensified alarmingly, to the extent that they had to crouch down to get under the layer of heated gases, and with the roar of the fire becoming louder, Rob Seaman expressed the view that they could not stay in the heat much longer, adding that whenever he and Fleur were teamed up as BA wearers they always got a job!

As firefighters Pat Foley and John Hurford advanced further into the store, they were aware from the direction both of the sound of the blaze and the radiated heat that a substantial fire was in front of them and to the right. However, they could see nothing, as visibility was now non-existent. The conditions were now becoming extremely hot as they encountered an obstruction in front of them (this was the newspaper and magazines fixture). Here they opened up the hose-reel and sprayed high-pressure water onto the ceiling above and in front of them to both cool the super-heated gases which would layer at that level, and deflect the water onto the blaze. As the water hit the gases it turned immediately to steam, and the temperature rose to an unbearable level, which burnt any exposed parts of the firefighters' bodies. At this point the hose-reel crew withdrew, taking about three minutes to reach the open air, during which time firefighters Lombard and Seaman had continued laying out the guide-line, and had progressed down one aisle to its fullest extent. The time was now 1308 hours, and an informative message was sent to fire control by Assistant Divisional Officer Whitham who was now in charge of the incident to the effect of: 'A building of one and two storeys, eighty metres by forty metres, well alight, eight breathing apparatus, three jets, one high-pressure hose-reel, and one breathing apparatus guide-line in use.'

Once the hose-reel team had reported to the entry control officer, firefighter Foley described the deteriorating conditions inside the store, and when he established that their colleagues were still inside urged that they should be ordered to evacuate. It was agreed that the evacuation signal, that is repeated blasts on an 'Acme Thunderer' whistle and a radio message to firefighter Lombard, be given. The BA entry control officer received no response to his radio message, although it might be presumed that she received this signal, as Fleur shouted to her partner: 'Evacuate, evacuate'. At this point a massive flash-over occurred, causing firefighters Seaman and Lombard to become separated. The sudden impact of the flashover threw Rob away from Fleur and onto the floor some three to four metres away, and at the same time causing him to momentarily black out.

Seaman, unaware of the time lapse or of the circumstances, immediately sought to establish if his colleague had come out. On hearing that she had not, he instinctively grabbed a hose-reel, made his way back into the building, and joined by another firefighter, began searching for Fleur. Foley, who was directing his hose-reel jet into the shop from the inner lobby, became aware of someone clambering over parked shopping trolleys and heard someone clearly say, 'She's there, get a jet on her'. Firefighter Foley immediately directed his jet to the area which was alight, whilst

Seaman and another colleague quickly located Fleur just inside, and to the left of the main entrance from where they both brought her out. At this point Rob Seaman collapsed by the entrance door and he was given treatment by the Ambulance Service. Firefighter Foley speaking of this dreadful incident said: 'Also after making our way back to the entry point I changed hose from hose reel to jet before being joined in the area by the emergency team from Temple fire station. It did seem a long time before we found Fleur, Rob vaulted the hand-rail and went straight to her, whereby I moved across with the jet before picking Fleur up under the arms.'

The Assistant Divisional Officer in charge had heard shouts that Fleur was missing, and consequently transmitted an assistance message to the effect of: 'Make pumps six, hydraulic platform required'. Four minutes later he sent an informative message, that was the thing of fire brigade nightmares, stating: 'Breathing apparatus emergency, one firefighter missing in fire.' Rob Seaman in his statement after the incident said:

> I was briefed to lay a guide line and take hose-reel. At first I thought we were expected to take in both the guideline and the hose-reel, and wondered how we were supposed to do that but soon realised that a second BA team were joining us. Up until we realised this, I was quite happy to go in with the guideline and the hose-reel because at that time, having been around the back (of the premises), I thought that the main fire in that area was in hand, and from our entrance we were just dealing with a normal smoke-logged building of typical grey coloured smoke.
>
> I still had in mind that it was persons reported from the observations of the PC at the rear earlier. We both heard this report and were never told any different. When starting to lay the guide-line, the thought was that we were expected to search as we proceeded, and other BA teams would be following us in.
>
> The noise and blackness was frightening, we turned to come out, she had hold of my waist strap and I held her waist strap in my right hand, and the guide-line was in my left. I could see the brightness lighting up the dense smoke ahead in the direction from which we had come. We were crouched down but on our feet and moving between a fast walk and a jog. We were frightened of the explosions and the heat. At some point, something happened which I can't explain and I don't know how far we had got out but Fleur had started to move slightly faster, and had moved level with me then slightly in front. We were still holding each other by the waist harness and I had hold of the guide-line.

At that precise moment, something happened and my mind went completely blank, the next thing I was on the floor thinking I must have fallen over. I was thinking 'Where am I', and then I began to recall what I was doing before and when I realised, I thought 'Where's Fleur'. The back of my neck and ears were hot and probably burning and the conditions seemed to have been a little clearer if anything, but the heat was still intense. My hands felt hot where my tunic had risen up my arms. As I tried to regain my orientation, I could make out the outline of a checkout.

In the process of scrambling around to find the checkout, I was wondering what had happened to Fleur and recall hoping that she had got out. When I felt the checkout, I turned around and could make the outline of other firefighters in the entrance lobby. I can't remember anyone helping me out but when I got into the lobby I asked if Fleur had come out and when I was told no, adrenalin just took over and I grabbed a hose-reel off someone else and scrambled over the trolleys towards the aisle we had retreated from. I remember seeing something on the other side of the trolleys which resembled a human and I think I knew it was Fleur. I remember jumping over the trolleys and saw her slumped forwards and in a crouching position against the wall. I pulled her back and the BA cylinder fell off which I brushed aside. Someone picked her up under the arms, and I picked up her legs and we carried her out to open air and laid her down. After this I can't remember anything until I was sitting in the ambulance.

The incident was finally closed at 1804 hours on Thursday 8th February, after extensive investigative procedures, turning-over and damping-down operations. As a result of the severe damage and the dangerous condition of the remaining structure, the premises were completely demolished shortly after the fire.

Fleur, who was twenty-one years of age had served as a retained firefighter in Derbyshire, and had carried out voluntary work before being accepted as recruit with Avon Fire Brigade in November 1993. Fleur was one of the first four women to join Avon Brigade, and completed her recruits' training course as the winner of the coveted Silver Axe for top recruit. As well as being a fit, committed and determined young firefighter, she was not without a sense of humour. At one particular incident, a man who had attempted suicide by gassing himself, repeatedly asked Fleur whether he was in Heaven. Fleur asked him why he was asking this, and he replied, 'Because I can see the wonderful stars, and the most beautiful golden-haired angel'.

Fleur replied, 'No you're not dead, you've just blown the roof off your house, and I'm a firefighter!' At another incident where an Aged Persons' home had to be evacuated, Fleur played the piano for the residents, leading them in a cheering sing song whilst they were being warmed up with cups of tea.

The cause of fire at the incident which led to Fleur's tragic death was arson committed by twenty year-old Martin Cody, the security guard on duty at the supermarket that day.

Rob Seaman was awarded the George Medal, Fleur Lombard posthumously awarded the Queen's Gallantry Medal, and Pat Foley the Queen's Commendation for Brave Conduct.

Fleur's funeral with full Fire Service Honours was held at Derby Cathedral on Tuesday 13th February 1996, with her coffin being carried on a turntable ladder. Derby was chosen partly because it was close to her family, and most of her non-fire service friends, but also in part in recognition of her prior service with Derbyshire Fire and Rescue Service as a retained firefighter at Whaley Bridge. Avon Fire Brigade subsequently held a memorial service for Fleur at Bristol Cathedral, which was attended by her family. The final word on this incident to Pat Foley:

'Fleur and myself joined on the same day and were trained together, I now work in a training centre where her silver axe is displayed in the reception area. I am responsible for Compartment firefighting training and am currently running a course for new trainees. It will always be a dangerous job, and recent years have shown that we are still losing firefighters regularly. The events of that day continue to motivate me to do everything possible to make firefighters safe.'

THE DEATHS OF FIREFIGHTERS MICHAEL MILLER AND JEFFREY WORNHAM

In the early hours of Wednesday 2nd February 2005, an elderly resident on the sixteenth floor of Harrow Court, Stevenage woke to smell smoke coming from a flat below, and made an emergency call to Hertfordshire Fire and Rescue Service. This was the first of several calls from this eighteen-storey residential block in Silam Road, which indicated that there was a fire on one of the upper floors, and that persons may be trapped.

Earlier, on the evening before, the occupants of flat number 85 on the fourteenth floor of Harrow Court had run out of electricity, and having no meter cards or credit available to them, they approached a neighbour, Mrs Quinlan, who gave them a quantity of tealight-style candles to help illuminate the flat. The occupants, Nicholas Savage and Natalie Close, then spent the evening in their flat drinking with a friend, and around eleven o'clock that night the third person left and they went to bed; leaving the candles, which were on a portable television set, placed on a chair, near to an open wardrobe, alight. Mr Savage said in an interview carried out after the incident that he had woken some-time before three o'clock in the morning to see a flame approximately one foot high coming from one of the tea light candles, and got out of his bed without waking his partner, and went to bring a wet tea-towel to extinguish the fire. The post fire investigation found it likely that the tea candle had burnt in an abnormal manner producing a temperature that was sufficient to start the decomposition of the plastic casing of the television, which in turn ignited the combustible internal components of the set. After a short period of time Savage attempted to return to the bedroom to deal with the outbreak, but was unable to do so due to the heat and the smoke discharging from the room. At this point he shouted a warning to Ms Close but received no response. He then made his way back to the lounge where he remained until he heard someone hammering on the door. In response he shouted, 'I can't get to the door – you will have to kick it in.' Mr Savage then recalled seeing a firefighter enter the room.

On receipt of the first emergency call two fire appliances from Stevenage Fire Station were mobilised to this incident, and were in attendance at Harrow Court within three minutes; firefighters Michael Miller and Jeffrey Wornham were part of this initial attendance. Upon arrival it was very apparent to the fire crews that a serious fire was developing, as one of the crew members, firefighter Dudley, later reported seeing 'Dirty dark grey smoke pumping out of the window'. Firefighters Wornham and Miller together with Temporary Leading firefighter Helen Antrobus entered the building, where they were met by two residents who had made calls to the Fire Service, and were given a more exact location of the fire. Within one minute of arriving, all three firefighters had entered a lift to proceed to the upper floor, with Jeff Wornham carrying breaking-in tools, whilst on the ground floor the remainder of the Stevenage crews worked quickly to provide the necessary equipment required to make a forced entry to the flat, and water to fight and extinguish the fire. Leading firefighter Scotchford, also part of the first attendance, shouted to Antrobus, Miller and Wornham not to proceed, but once they had commenced their ascent in the lift he contacted them via his personal radio requesting that he be kept informed of the situation. Firefighter Dudley said in his statement to Hertfordshire Police that he had been unhappy with the departure of this crew from the lift lobby at that time. As the lift took them to the fourteenth floor Wornham and Miller began to don their breathing apparatus masks. By this time a second crew of firefighters comprising Dudley, Dredge and Boswell were putting various items of equipment into the lift lobby ready for transportation to the floor of the fire.

Arriving at flat eighty-five on the fourteenth floor, the first crew saw a small layer of dark grey wispy smoke coming from the top of the door, which they recognised as a characteristic indication of a fire being starved of oxygen, and consequently, once an entry was affected to the flat, a back-draft, that is the explosive re-commencement of combustion, was likely to occur as oxygen was rapidly drawn in to the fire. Antrobus instructed to Miller and Wornham to prepare for an entry, and she began running out the line of hose that they had brought with them from the fire appliance from the outlet of the rising main designed to deliver water to the fire from the fire appliance pump. Fatefully the riser outlet was chained and padlocked, and so completely inaccessible until a bolt-cropper could be brought into use. By this time firefighter Boswell, who was the designated entry control officer, arrived on the fourteenth floor with Dudley and Dredge, who were rigged in breathing apparatus, with their face masks in place.

However, before any firefighting equipment was ready to hand Michael and Jeff heard cries for help coming from the flat, and they made their gallant, split-second decision to enter the flat and attempt a rescue, ignoring their own safety.

Mr Savage was located quickly by firefighters Miller and Wornham, and he was brought out. At this point he indicated that his girlfriend, Ms Natalie Close, was still in the flat. Both firefighters immediately re-entered to search for her; well aware that the conditions were deteriorating rapidly with intense heat and near zero visibility, and that their chances of surviving a second rescue, having no water to hand, were diminishing by the second. Jeff and Michael in making this decision, knew they had to seriously compromise their own safety in an attempt to do what they were trained to do: save life. Unfortunately, and tragically, as they attempted to rescue the remaining missing person, the whole flat became engulfed in flames; temperatures were estimated to be as high as 800°C. Both firefighters, as well as Ms Natalie Close, died as a consequence of the fire. It is highly likely that Michael and Jeffrey were in the process of rescuing the missing person when the fire intensified killing all three.

Roy Wilsher, then Deputy Chief Fire Officer for Hertfordshire Fire and Rescue Service, paid tribute to Michael Millar and Jeff Wornham in the following terms: 'As you can imagine, it has sent deep shockwaves through the fire service. We are doing our utmost to support the family and friends of the firefighters who lost their lives. It is the worst day for Hertfordshire Fire and Rescue Service for thirty years.'

Mike Miller's mother, Cyndy, was a guest of the Sunderland Remembrance Parade in November 2009, parading with 100 serving and retired firefighters and, proudly wearing her son's George Medal, she laid a wreath in memory of both of those gallant Warriors in Fire Boots.

I very much hope this book will provide the reader with some appreciation of the ultimate price to be paid for the honour of serving as a firefighter, and the extremes of danger to which the men and women of the Fire Service must be, and always have been, prepared to take themselves whenever 'the bells go down'. If the reader were to doubt that firefighters might again have to endure situations as catastrophic, and as overwhelmingly dangerous as the carnage of Tooley Street, or the Blitz, then I would respectfully refer them to the events of 26th April 1986 in Chernobyl, and of 11th September 2001 in Lower Manhattan, and the extraordinary heroism and dedication to duty displayed by our brother firefighters of New York City and the Ukraine.

It is my hope that these stories of courage and of loss will engender in the men and women of today's Fire and Rescue Service an appreciation of a proud, inspirational and valiant history which is, I believe, second to none in the annals of gallantry, and well worthy of our respect. Perhaps in the future I may be able to pay tribute to some of those Fire Service gallantry medallists who have not featured in this book.

The drama and tragedy outlined on these pages does, I hope, clearly illustrate the coming together of the many attributes that firefighting can suddenly, and uncompromisingly demand: fortitude, endurance, humanity, composure in command, teamwork, clarity of thought in the midst of pandemonium, discipline, selflessness and the capacity to balance the contradictory ideals of decisiveness and prudence. All of which, coalescing under critical pressure, may bring forth that most admired of all human qualities, courage. Not fearlessness; but rather a conscious decision, to defy the terrors of that moment, and push forward beyond your personal testing point.

So when next you see fire appliances with beacons flashing, and the crew pulling on their fire-kit to a cacophony of two-tone horns, or indeed as you pay your respects on Remembrance Sunday, perhaps you might, just for a moment, pause to remember the loss of firefighters, from James Braidwood to Fleur Lombard, and the gallantry of Harry Errington, Larry Young and Peter McGill, and all our Warriors in Fire Boots.

Arthur Lockyear